Lecture Notes
in Business Information Processing 493

Series Editors

Wil van der Aalst, *RWTH Aachen University, Aachen, Germany*
Sudha Ram, *University of Arizona, Tucson, AZ, USA*
Michael Rosemann, *Queensland University of Technology, Brisbane, QLD, Australia*
Clemens Szyperski, *Microsoft Research, Redmond, WA, USA*
Giancarlo Guizzardi, *University of Twente, Enschede, The Netherlands*

LNBIP reports state-of-the-art results in areas related to business information systems and industrial application software development – timely, at a high level, and in both printed and electronic form.

The type of material published includes

- Proceedings (published in time for the respective event)
- Postproceedings (consisting of thoroughly revised and/or extended final papers)
- Other edited monographs (such as, for example, project reports or invited volumes)
- Tutorials (coherently integrated collections of lectures given at advanced courses, seminars, schools, etc.)
- Award-winning or exceptional theses

LNBIP is abstracted/indexed in DBLP, EI and Scopus. LNBIP volumes are also submitted for the inclusion in ISI Proceedings.

Knut Hinkelmann · Francisco J. López-Pellicer ·
Andrea Polini

Editors

Perspectives in Business Informatics Research

22nd International Conference
on Business Informatics Research, BIR 2023
Ascoli Piceno, Italy, September 13–15, 2023
Proceedings

 Springer

Editors
Knut Hinkelmann ⓘD
FHNW
Olten, Switzerland

Francisco J. López-Pellicer ⓘD
University of Zaragoza
Zaragoza, Spain

Andrea Polini ⓘD
University of Camerino
Camerino, Italy

ISSN 1865-1348   ISSN 1865-1356 (electronic)
Lecture Notes in Business Information Processing
ISBN 978-3-031-43125-8   ISBN 978-3-031-43126-5 (eBook)
https://doi.org/10.1007/978-3-031-43126-5

This Springer imprint is published by the registered company Springer Nature Switzerland AG
The registered company address is: Gewerbestrasse 11, 6330 Cham, Switzerland

Paper in this product is recyclable.

Preface

Business Informatics has to do with the usage of digital solutions and technologies to help and improve the efficiency and efficacy of complex organizations. In a way, business informatics stands at the conjunction of many different disciplines, ranging from computer science, social sciences, data science, business economics, and many more. Over the years, the International Conference on Perspectives in Business Informatics Research (BIR) has become established as a prominent venue in which researchers from the different disciplines meet.

The 22nd edition of the conference (BIR 2023) was organized by the University of Camerino and held during September 13–15, 2023, in the city of Ascoli Piceno (Marche Region — Italy). This was the first edition held in a Mediterranean country, which testifies to the intention of enlarging the community and increasing the visibility of the conference. In this respect, the 2023 Program Committee saw the participation of 64 reviewers coming from 19 different countries. The increase in areas of interest for the conference is also testified by the submissions that were received. In particular, the 2023 edition received 57 submissions from 21 different countries across 4 different continents (16 EU, 2 Americas, 2 Asia, 1 Africa).

As usual for any BIR edition, a rigorous single-blind reviewing process was adopted. Each paper was reviewed by at least three reviewers. Out of the 57 papers, the Program Committee decided to accept 20 papers as full papers and 4 as short papers. All the accepted papers were then presented at the conference. The acceptance rate of 33% is in line with all the previous editions. The papers included in these proceedings cover different aspects of the discipline, focusing particularly on subdomains such as governance of data and ICT systems, the adoption and impact of AI in business informatics, and finally lessons learned and the impact of solutions concretely applied to specific domains. The conference participants could attend two relevant keynotes. The first one was delivered by Bastiaan van Loenen from the Technical University of Delft. The speech, titled "Open Data: Everything Everywhere All at Once" focused on the "third-wave" of open data and its relevance for our society, outlining the main characteristics that an innovative open data ecosystem should support. The second keynote speech was delivered by Steven Alter, Professor Emeritus of the University of San Francisco. The speech, titled "Roles and Risks of AI in the Pursuit of Sustainable Innovation", proposed an approach for moving the discussion of AI and sustainable innovation forward within business informatics. The result is a view of AI, sustainable innovation, and related opportunities and risks that is directly applicable for determining system requirements, describing operational systems, and evaluating operational results.

In the tradition of the conference, a number of satellite events were hosted on the last day of the conference. In particular, this year five workshops were hosted: the 3rd International Workshop on Blockchain for Trusted Data Sharing (B4TDS 2023), the 13th Workshop on Business and IT Alignment (BITA 2023), the 8th Workshop on Managed Complexity (ManComp 2023), the 1st Workshop on Scaled Agile Development of Complex Software Projects, and the 1st Workshop on Domain-specific Modeling Methods and Tools — OMiLAB Nodes experience & knowledge exchange (OMiLAB-KNOW). Finally, a Doctoral Symposium organized by Barbara Re from the University of Camerino and Björn Johansson from Linköping University permitted young researchers to discuss their ideas with the BIR community.

We express our gratitude to Marite Kirikova and to the BIR Steering Committee members who agreed to have BIR 2023 managed by our team.

In particular, we thank Andrea Morichetta and Robert Andrei Buchmann for acting as this year's workshop chairs and Emanuele Laurenzi for managing the publicity of the event.

We greatly thank all the authors who submitted their work and the Program Committee members who contributed timely reviews to the paper selection process. While numerous strong papers were submitted, the selection process, aiming to preserve the traditional acceptance threshold of BIR, unfortunately couldn't accommodate some valuable contributions in the proceedings.

The Springer team again provided prompt support regarding the proceedings' production. We are thankful to them for the continuous partnership with BIR, which is a major factor for the conference longevity and the prestige of its proceedings.

Last but not least, the University of Camerino team, led by Francesco Casoni, Melania Fattorini, and Federico Valeri, deserves sincere gratitude for managing the organization of the event, and for supporting all the conference attendees.

August 2023

Knut Hinkelmann
Francisco J. Lopez-Pellicer
Andrea Polini

Organization

General Chair

Andrea Polini   University of Camerino, Italy

Program Committee Chairs

Knut Hinkelmann   University of Applied Sciences and Arts
                                 Northwestern Switzerland, Switzerland
Francisco J. Lopez-Pellicer   Universidad Zaragoza, Spain

Steering Committee

Marite Kirikova (Chair)   Riga Technical University, Latvia
Björn Johansson (Vice Chair)   Linköping University, Sweden
Eduard Babkin   National Research University Higher School of
                                 Economics, Russia
Robert Andrei Buchmann   Babeş-Bolyai University of Cluj Napoca,
                                 Romania
Rimantas Butleris   Kaunas University of Technology, Lithuania
Sven Carlsson   Lund University, Sweden
Peter Forbrig   University of Rostock, Germany
Dimitris Karagiannis   University of Vienna, Austria
Andrzej Kobyliński   Warsaw School of Economics, Poland
Raimundas Matulevicius   University of Tartu, Estonia
Erika Nazaruka   Riga Technical University, Latvia
Lina Nemuraite   Kaunas Technical University, Lithuania
Jyrki Nummenmaa   University of Tampere, Finland
Małgorzata Pańkowska   University of Economics in Katowice, Poland
Andrea Polini   University of Camerino, Italy
Václav Řepa   Prague University of Economics, Czech Republic
Kurt Sandkuhl   University of Rostock, Germany
Ulf Seigerroth   Jönköping University, Sweden
Benkt Wangler   University of Skövde, Sweden

Program Committee

Charalampos Alexopoulos	University of the Aegean, Greece
Gundars Alksnis	Riga Technical University, Latvia
Luis Alvarez Sabucedo	Universidade de Vigo, Spain
Saïd Assar	Institut Mines-Télécom Business School, France
Eduard Babkin	National Research University Higher School of Economics, Russia
Per Backlund	University of Skövde, Sweden
Amelia Badica	University of Craiova, Romania
Peter Bellström	Karlstad University, Sweden
Catalin Boja	Bucharest Academy of Economic Studies, Romania
Dominik Bork	TU Wien, Austria
Tomáš Bruckner	Prague University of Economics and Business, Czech Republic
Robert Andrei Buchmann	Babeş-Bolyai University of Cluj Napoca, Romania
Retha de la Harpe	Cape Peninsula University of Technology, South Africa
Massimiliano de Leoni	University of Padua, Italy
Chiara Di Francescomarino	University of Trento, Italy
Antinisca Di Marco	University of L'Aquila, Italy
Hans-Georg Fill	University of Fribourg, Switzerland
Peter Forbrig	University of Rostock, Germany
Aurona Gerber	University of the Western Cape, South Africa
Ana-Maria Ghiran	Babeş-Bolyai University of Cluj Napoca, Romania
Jānis Grabis	Riga Technical University, Latvia
Nicklas Holmberg	Lunds Universitet, Sweden
Amin Jalali	Stockholm University, Sweden
Björn Johansson	Linköping University, Sweden
Miranda Kajtazi	Lund University, Sweden
Dimitris Karagiannis	University of Vienna, Austria
Michael Alexander Kaufmann	Lucerne University of Applied Sciences and Arts, Switzerland
Christina Keller	Jönköping University, Sweden
Marite Kirikova	Riga Technical University, Latvia
Markus Lahtinen	Lund University, Sweden
Emanuele Laurenzi	University of Applied Sciences and Arts Northwestern Switzerland, Switzerland
Michael Le Duc	Mälardalen University, Sweden
Moonkun Lee	Chonbuk National University, South Korea
Ginta Majore	Vidzeme University of Applied Sciences, Latvia

Andreas Martin   University of Applied Sciences and Arts
                                Northwestern Switzerland, Switzerland
Raimundas Matulevicius   University of Tartu, Estonia
Andrea Morichetta   University of Camerino, Italy
Jyrki Nummenmaa   Tampere University, Finland
Jacob Nørbjerg   Copenhagen Business School, Denmark
Victoria Paulsson   Linköping University, Sweden
Jens Myrup Pedersen   Aalborg University, Denmark
Dana Petcu   West University of Timişoara, Romania
Pierluigi Plebani   Politecnico di Milano, Italy
Paul Pocatilu   Bucarest University of Economic Studies,
                                Romania
Barbara Re   University of Camerino, Italy
Václav Řepa   Prague University of Economics, Czech Republic
Ben Roelens   Ghent University, The Netherlands
Christian Sacarea   Babeş-Bolyai University, Romania
Kurt Sandkuhl   University of Rostock, Germany
Hanlie Smuts   University of Pretoria, South Africa
Ann Svensson   University West, Sweden
Torben Tambo   Aarhus University, Denmark
Victoria Torres   Universitat Politècnica de València, Spain
Pedro Valderas   Universitat Politècnica de València, Spain
Alta Van der Merwe   University of Pretoria, South Africa
Filip Vencovsky   Prague University of Economics, Czech Republic
Gianluigi Viscusi   Linköping University, Sweden
Anna Wingkvist   Linnaeus University, Sweden
Hans Friedrich Witschel   University of Applied Sciences and Arts
                                Northwestern Switzerland, Switzerland
Wiesław Wolny   University of Economics in Katowice, Poland
Endri Xhina   University of Tirana, Albania
F. Javier Zarazaga-Soria   Universidad Zaragoza, Spain
Jelena Zdravkovic   Stockholm University, Sweden
Alfred Zimmermann   Reutlingen University, Germany

Additional Reviewers

Abasi-Amefon Obot Affia   Amirhossein Gharaie
Mohsan Ali   Mubashar Iqbal
Syed Juned Ali   Maria Ioanna Maratsi
Mariia Bakhtina   Alessandro Marcelletti
Riccardo Galanti   Alessandro Padella
Aleksandar Gavric   Georgios Papageiorgiou

Lorenzo Rossi   Sergio Martin-Segura
Mari Seeba

Contents

New Trends in Data Governance

Applied Business Informatics

User Interaction Mining: Discovering the Gap Between the Conceptual Model of a Geospatial Search Engine and Its Corresponding User Mental Model

Dagoberto José Herrera-Murillo[1]([✉]) [iD], Javier Nogueras-Iso[1] [iD],
Paloma Abad-Power[2], and Francisco J. Lopez-Pellicer[1] [iD]

[1] Aragon Institute of Engineering Research (I3A), Universidad de Zaragoza,
Zaragoza, Spain
{dherrera,jnog,fjlopez}@unizar.es
[2] Centro Nacional de Información Geográfica, Madrid, Spain
paloma.abad@cnig.es
https://www.iaaa.es, https://www.cnig.es

Abstract. Designers often project into their creations usage models that attempt to idealise and anticipate how users will interact with the future system. However, these conceptual models do not always match the actual mental models of users. This mismatch may result in sub-optimal functioning that negatively impacts user experience. Discovering these deviations, especially in early design stages, could serve to align the system to the existing mental models or to train users appropriately for new paradigms. This paper reports on work in progress addressing the challenge of discovering models of user behaviour from usability tests on user interfaces. We present a case study performed at the Spanish National Geographic Institute, where a new geospatial search engine has been developed. Twenty-one participants, including novice and expert users, were recruited to perform a search task with the new geospatial search engine. The interactions mined were recorded as event logs and analysed with process mining techniques, descriptive and inferential statistics. The results indicate that the mental model of users is biased toward the archetype of a regular search engine, rather than taking advantage of the geographic functions provided by the platform, as intended by the designers. This case study illustrates the potential that interaction mining can add to the design and evaluation of new user interfaces.

Keywords: Geospatial portal · User interface · Mental model · Interaction mining · Process mining

1 Introduction

The use of geographic information has increased exponentially in the last decades. To manage this explosion of data, spatial data infrastructure initiatives

K. Hinkelmann et al. (Eds.): BIR 2023, LNBIP 493, pp. 3–15, 2023.
https://doi.org/10.1007/978-3-031-43126-5_1

were launched to facilitate the availability and access to spatial data. Geospatial search engines are crucial for searching and discovering geographic information resources in spatial data infrastructures [10]. Designing these search interfaces is a challenge. Information search is a complex user-centred process where the functionalities of the information system and the mental models of the user must interact in alignment to produce satisfying experiences. It is difficult for developers to know in advance, during the design and development stages, what will be the most effective information architecture or how the system will be used in reality.

The objective of this paper is to propose a methodology to identify the gap between the design of a geospatial search engine, and the mental models gained by users during the interaction with these search engines. It is known that user mental models help to design or refine the design of user interfaces.

In particular, we have proposed this methodology to evaluate and improve the design of the new geospatial search engine of the National Geographic Institute of Spain (IGN). The institute is the coordinator of the Spanish spatial data infrastructure and the main producer of geographic information in Spain, either through its own legal mandate or as a co-producer. The ecosystem of portals associated directly with the institute consists of the IGN Download Centre, the IGN Map Library and the Online Shop of the National Centre for Geographic Information. Integrating all these sources of information was the main motivation behind the design of a new geospatial search engine.

The remains of this paper are structured as follows. Section 2 describes the state of the art on mental models for user interaction. Next, Sect. 3 describes the proposed methodology to compare the conceptual model of the search engine and the extraction of the user mental model after the corresponding user experiments. Section 4 provides the results obtained after applying the methodology for the new geospatial search engine of IGN. Finally, Sect. 5 provides some conclusions and future lines of research.

2   State of the Art on User Mental Models of User Interaction

"Mental models are the mechanisms whereby humans are able to generate descriptions of system purpose and form, explanations of system functioning and observed system states, and predictions of future system states" [17]. The notion of a mental model has been a widely accepted concept in the human interaction literature since the 1980s [18]. However, the challenge of measuring, representing and using mental models remains with the development of increasingly sophisticated software applications.

In the computer systems design process, it is worth distinguishing between the mental model of designers, also known as the conceptual model, and the mental model of users [3]. In the first case, the system designer has a representation of the target system and translates those ideas into a concrete implementation. While the second recognises what users actually know about the system from their cognitive abilities, previous experiences, problem-solving strategies and individual differences.

According to Nielsen [12], designers often have complex mental models of their own creations, leading them to believe that every feature is easy to understand. In contrast, mental models of the user are likely to be more limited, so they are more likely to make mistakes and find the system much more difficult to use. The common gap between the mental models of designers and the mental model of the user gives rise to a concept called the execution gulf. It is the difference between the intentions of the users and what the system allows them to do or how well the system supports those actions [13].

There are multiple conceptualisations of the types of mental models and how to represent them. De Kleer and Brown distinguish between component and causal models [4]. Component models focus on structure, while causal models explain the functioning of the system in terms of cause-effect relationships. Carroll and Olson compile four types of models: surrogates, metaphors, crystal boxes and networks [3]. Surrogate models mimic the input/output behaviour of systems. Metaphorical models directly compare the target system and some other system known to the user. Crystal box models are a hybrid between metaphors and surrogates. Finally, network models contain the states of a system and the actions that the user can take to move the system to another state.

Knowing the mental model of users has two main areas of application in the context of human-computer interaction, designing interfaces and user training [3]. The interface could be designed to reflect the predominant mental model of the users, allowing them to learn it with less guidance and perform it with fewer errors. On the other hand, a deficient mental model can be a barrier to users taking full advantage of the potential of the system. In this scenario, users can be trained and guided to learn appropriate conceptual models.

The Jakob's law is a proposition fully aligned with the idea of mental models [11]. The law states that users tend to develop expectations of design conventions based on their accumulated experience with other websites. This means that users will likely expect a website to conform to the design patterns and conventions they have encountered elsewhere and may struggle to adapt to new or unfamiliar designs.

Three methods are commonly used for representing or describing the mental models of users [21]. The first one involves eliciting verbal accounts from participants [14], which can be done by asking them to describe a system or its mechanism, provide analogies or metaphors, or think aloud while performing search tasks. Transcripts of these accounts are then analysed to develop representations and assessments of mental models of the system being studied. The second method is drawing, where participants are asked to create a picture or diagram to represent their mental image of a system [7]. The third method involves observing errors during searches to identify gaps in their mental models of the system. When the goal is to represent mental models, the observation method is often used in combination with think-aloud protocols [16].

Over the decades of the existence of the web, numerous researchers have undertaken the difficult challenge of eliciting, measuring, and representing the behaviour of users of digital systems [1,6]. In the context of user interfaces, the concept of interaction mining stands out for its orientation to the design of applications driven by user behaviour data. Interaction mining can be defined as the capture and analysis of both static (UI layouts, visual details) and dynamic components (user flows, motion details) of the design of an application [5].

3 Methodology

The methodology applied to mine user interactions and discover their mental model consists of three phases. Firstly, the target system is dissected to identify its conceptual model and the activities to be mined. Secondly, a search task is designed and executed with representative users, while their interactions are appropriately recorded. Finally, the mined interactions are analysed to discover patterns that can be used to infer the mental model of the user.

3.1 Overview of the Geospatial Search Engine and Its Conceptual Model

The new geospatial search engine of the Linked Cartography project gives access to two million geographic resources that were earlier dispersed across multiple platforms at the institute [2]. Figure 1 displays the user interface for the three navigation levels of the search engine: a) *Quick search*, b) *Advanced search & results*, and c) *Metadata pages*.

We mapped the activities that the user can perform within each level. A text search bar is the central element of the *Quick search page*. In addition, there is a button that allows users to access advanced geographic search options. These options accept a variety of inputs, points, polygons, geometry files, coordinates and cadastral references. Thematic category filters are also available. After conducting a search on the quick search page, users are directed to the *Advanced search & results page*, which is the heart of the platform. The search options available on the quick search page remain at the top of the page. The centre of the page displays a list of search results, each of which can be interacted with in various ways, such as viewing, downloading, purchasing, or locating the corresponding geographical resource. A list of faceted filters is located on the left side of the page, which allows users to refine their search results. On the right side of the page, a map is displayed, which can be used to locate and visualise the results. When a result is selected, the perimeter of the corresponding resource is highlighted on the map. Users can adjust the zoom level of the map, pan around, and add a wide range of additional geographic information layers. Upon selecting a specific resource from the list of results, the user is redirected to a *Metadata page* that provides more detailed information about the resource. This page also allows users to perform actions such as downloading, purchasing, or locating the corresponding resource.

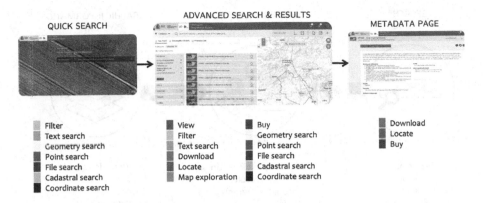

Fig. 1. Semantic search engine interface.

The conceptual model of this geospatial search engine can be understood as a mixed model that integrates a search engine and a geographic information system (see Fig. 2), building upon the metaphorical notion of mental models that compare the system to archetypal systems. On the one hand, the left part is influenced by the typical search engine interface characterised by two attributes: a type-keywords-in-entry-form and view-results-in-a-vertical-list [8]. On the other hand, the right part is influenced by the typical geographic information system where the map is the dominant element—it occupies more than 90% of the area in pure GIS interfaces—[15]. However, designing such a system requires more than simply adding features from each archetype. It is crucial to enable users to explore search results with the flexibility of a search engine while also providing a comprehensive understanding of the geographic context. Therefore, integrating the two systems must be seamless and intuitive for users to have a meaningful and efficient search experience.

3.2 Experimental Setup

Twenty-one participants were recruited for this study and were divided equally into three categories: I. Novice users, II. Expert unfamiliar users, and III. Expert familiar users. This division has been proposed based on the hypothesis that domain experience and familiarity with particular conventions, such as those embedded in the platforms of a specific data publisher, can have an impact on behaviour and mental models. Table 1 displays the sample distribution of each group based on their gender, age, and education. Prior to the session, all participants signed an informed consent form and completed a pre-test questionnaire to confirm their assigned category. The informed consent included aspects such as research objectives and procedures, withdrawal procedure, confidentiality of data and information from the research team.

To comply with security restrictions, external users were unable to directly access the browser version used for testing. Therefore, the sessions were structured in a screen-sharing setting that requires participants to verbally commu-

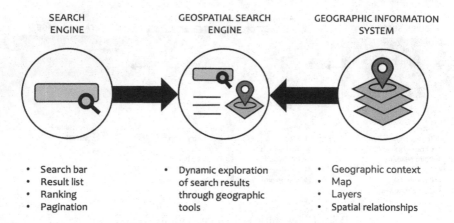

SEARCH ENGINE	**GEOSPATIAL SEARCH ENGINE**	**GEOGRAPHIC INFORMATION SYSTEM**
• Search bar • Result list • Ranking • Pagination	• Dynamic exploration of search results through geographic tools	• Geographic context • Map • Layers • Spatial relationships

Fig. 2. Conceptual model of the geospatial search engine.

Table 1. Participant demographics, n (%).

	Novice users	Expert unfamiliar users	Expert familiar users	All
Gender				
Male	4 (57%)	3 (43%)	4 (57%)	11 (48%)
Female	3 (43%)	4 (57%)	3 (43%)	10 (52%)
Age				
18–24	1 (14%)	– (0%)	– (0%)	1 (5%)
25–34	1 (14%)	2 (29%)	2 (29%)	5 (24%)
35–44	– (0%)	1 (14%)	2 (29%)	3 (14%)
45–54	3 (43%)	4 (57%)	3 (43%)	10 (48%)
54–65	2 (29%)	– (0%)	– (0%)	2 (10%)
Education				
High School	1 (14%)	– (0%)	– (0%)	1 (5%)
Undergraduate	5 (71%)	3 (43%)	7 (100%)	15 (71%)
Graduate	1 (14%)	4 (57%)	– (0%)	5 (24%)
Total	7	7	7	21

nicate their actions to the moderator. Participants were instructed to provide detailed instructions at the lowest possible level, specifying the interface elements they wanted to interact with and how to do it. All sessions started from the quick search page.

The search task selected for the sessions represents the intended use of the geospatial search engine given the importance of tourism in the volume of queries coming into the National Geographic Institute: planning a trip to a National Park in Spain. The task was stated as follows:

"This Christmas you are planning to visit the Sierra Nevada National Park and you would like to have some information about the area. You should use the search engine to look for resources that will help you get to know the area better. Identify information about the park, download files or add to the cart products that you consider most useful for the trip."

The video of the sessions was recorded and, at the same time, a web extension called Record/Replay[1] recorded the clicks made with a time stamp.

3.3   Data Preprocessing and Analysis

This research was designed following the principles of interaction mining [5]. Once the interactions are mined, they can be analysed using a wide variety of quantitative and qualitative methods. In this study, we opted to use a combination of exploratory visual process mining tools along with descriptive and inferential statistics to analyse the data.

Once the sessions were completed, a researcher reviewed the videos to identify the occurrence of the activities of interest. Note that it was not possible to take advantage of the click log generated during the sessions for automatic activity mapping because it was too noisy. The final result of the annotation was an event log consisting of three attributes: case (session identifier), activity, and timestamp. The event log was captured in a comma-separated value file and processed with PM4PY,[2] a process mining library in Python.

For the visual inspection of interactions, dotted and variant explorer charts were used. Dotted and variant explorer charts are popular visual analytic tools that provides a helicopter view of the process [20]. In dotted charts, each event is depicted as a dot in a two-dimensional plane where the horizontal and vertical axes represent respectively the time and class of the event. Whereas a variant explorer shows all the different paths taken by a specific process in the observed cases. These visualisations were made using PMTK[3] (a front-end solution built on top of PM4Py) and Excel (for a customised adaptation of the dotted chart).

In addition, a Kruskal-Wallis test was used to compare the behaviour of different groups of users across variables such as event duration or frequency. This non-parametric method determines whether two or more samples come from the same distribution. If the result of the Kruskal-Wallis test is statistically significant, then a Dunn's post hoc test is used for pairwise comparisons between each group to identify which groups are different. The test statistic, which is a variable calculated from sample data used to determine whether the null hypothesis can be rejected, and the *p-value* are reported. The statistical significance level was set at .05, meaning that *p-values* below this threshold indicate a signifi-

---

[1]   https://github.com/tomgallagher/RecordReplay.
[2]   https://pm4py.fit.fraunhofer.de.
[3]   https://pmtk.fit.fraunhofer.de.

cant difference. These calculations were performed using Python libraries such as *pandas, scipy.stats*[4] and *scikit_posthocs.*[5]

4   Results

Figure 3 shows a dotted chart where each line represents the events corresponding to a session. The horizontal axis has the duration of the session in minutes elapsed. Finally, the colour of each dot is given by the type of activity executed by the participant. To analyse the data, we first grouped the traces by participant type and then sorted them in descending order based on total session duration. We found that the sessions varied widely in both duration (*median* = 44.1, *max* = 20.7, *min* = 7.7) and number and sequence of activities performed (*median* = 16, *max* = 30, *min* = 6). Our analysis also revealed significant differences between user groups. Novice users had shorter session durations and performed fewer activities than the other two categories, as indicated by the graph. These differences were confirmed by the Kruskal Wallis tests ($k = 6.60$, $p = 0.037$ for session duration and $k = 6.05$, $p = 0.049$ for number of activities). A post-hoc test further showed that the novice group was the main source of the observed differences.

Figure 4 illustrates the median number of interactions for each activity type, sorted in descending order by the median of the total. The left section of the figure shows the values broken down by activity type and participant group, with the p-values of the Kruskal-Wallis test for differences between groups displayed in the last column. The right section presents dot plots of the total number of interactions for each activity in three parallel lanes representing the three participant groups: Novice users in pink, expert unfamiliar users in light blue, and

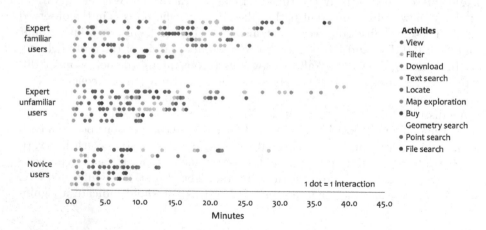

Fig. 3. Dotted chart distribution of the events over absolute time.

[4] https://docs.scipy.org/doc/scipy/reference/generated/scipy.stats.kruskal.html.
[5] https://scikit-posthocs.readthedocs.io/en/stable/generated/scikit_posthocs.posthoc_dunn.

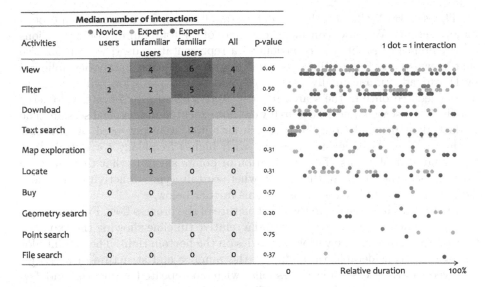

Activities	Median number of interactions				p-value	
	Novice users	Expert unfamiliar users	Expert familiar users	All		
View	2	4	6	4	0.06	
Filter	2	2	5	4	0.50	
Download	2	3	2	2	0.55	
Text search	1	2	2	1	0.09	
Map exploration	0	1	1	1	0.31	
Locate	0	2	0	0	0.31	
Buy	0	0	1	0	0.57	
Geometry search	0	0	1	0	0.20	
Point search	0	0	0	0	0.75	
File search	0	0	0	0	0.37	

Fig. 4. Dotted chart distribution of the events over relative time.

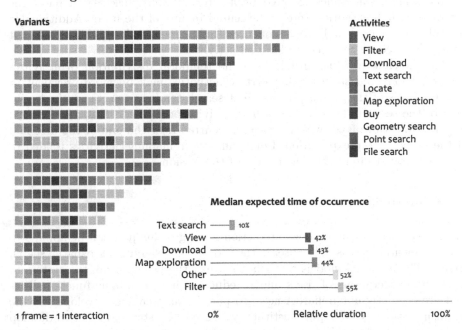

Fig. 5. Variants explorer sequence of events.

expert familiar users in dark blue. The horizontal axis in this section represents duration as a percentage of progress in the session.

The Kruskal-Wallis test did not detect significant differences between groups for any activity. When we consider the median of the total number of interactions as a reference to profile the behaviour of a representative user, we can observe that View (4) and Filter (4) are the most frequently executed activities, followed by Download (2), and finally Text search and Map exploration, which are typically executed once in the search process. Activities such as Locate, Geometry search, Point search, and File search were not executed in a typical session. The Cadastral search and Coordinate search activities were not used by any user in this sample. As expected, activities with higher frequency correspond to a higher number of points. The distribution of points suggests that there may be differences in the timing of the session where certain types of activities are more likely to be executed. We will discuss this further below.

In order to show the diversity and structure of the process flow, Fig. 5 displays a variant explorer graph on the left and a relative timeline showing the expected time of occurrence for the various activities on the bottom right. The variant plot displays the considerable variability in the number and structure of activities observed across the sample of sessions, with no repeated sequences and few generalisable patterns. However, we did note that most sessions began with a textual search, sometimes followed by a filter. In the quick search page, the advanced search activities were not executed by any of the users. Additionally, several traces ended with filter sequences (light green frames), which were not always followed by resource exploration activities.

The timeline provides insight into the temporal distribution of activities across sessions and suggests that certain activities may be more prevalent at certain stages of the search process. Text search tended to occur at the beginning of the session and was the earliest activity performed. This was followed by View and Download, which typically occurred near the end of the first half of the session. Map exploration, Filter, and the remaining activities tended to occur somewhat later, after the middle of the session.

5   Conclusions

In this paper, we explored how interaction mining techniques can be applied to discover mental models of the user in the process of designing a geospatial search engine. These mental models can help to adjust the behaviour of the system to meet the expectations of users and to educate the user about functionalities that are currently unfamiliar. A new geospatial search engine, developed by the Spanish National Geographic Institute, was used as a starting point to develop a case study. During this case study, representative users were recruited to conduct usability tests of the new portal. The sessions were recorded, processed, transformed into event logs, and analysed using process mining techniques along with descriptive and inferential statistics. The results suggest that the observed mental model prioritises the features of an archetypal search engine over those of a geographic information system. This behaviour deviates from the mixed model of the creators of the system.

The analysis yielded several insights for the platform development team. The first relevant finding was the clear distinction between the frequently used functions and the infrequently used ones in an ordinary search. A Pareto dynamic [19], where a limited number of functions are responsible for most interactions, has implications for UX design. Identifying hot spots can help the team narrow their focus, optimise scarce resources, and increase impact. This does not mean that the features that are used less frequently should be discarded, but rather carefully studied for their contribution to the user experience. This is the case for all geographic features that had a marginal interaction frequency with respect to simpler search and explore activities or were relegated to a late phase of the session after trying the simpler search strategies. For example, despite being a tool that can significantly contribute to the exploration of geographic resources and cover a considerable area of the interface, the map received less attention than expected by the product team. This has led designers to rethink the role and presentation that the map should play in the overall search experience. The same applies to other underused functions such as file, cadastral or coordinate search that could be dropped from the initial design.

Modelling user behaviour during usability tests also proved to be a mechanism for detecting quality problems in the system. By observing users when interacting with filters, the design team was able to identify functional problems in the portal. Reviewing session videos revealed that the filtering threads were a user response to malfunctions in the filtering mechanism.

The experiment had several limitations that need to be considered. While the number of participants was appropriate for usability testing, where the aim is to capture an overall understanding of user behaviour, it may be limited for drawing quantitatively sound conclusions. This limitation is particularly relevant for detecting differences between novice and expert groups, which may require a larger sample size to achieve reliable results. Additionally, the use of a think-aloud design mediated by a moderator could be viewed as a potential contaminating factor. The presence of a moderator may have influenced the behaviour of participants, resulting in longer execution times and more complex operations than they would normally perform—particularly for specialised users—. The interference of the moderator may also have prevented the observation of errors that the participants would have made in a hands-free exercise. Despite these potential drawbacks, the think-aloud method proved useful for the researcher in understanding the reasoning behind the behaviour of participants. This information would later be used for modelling and interpreting the observed behaviour. By concentrating on observing the interface and verbalising what they want, users reveal the imprint of what they see or do not see of the system. Finally, it is crucial to consider the impact of the chosen search task. While it may align with the intended use of the platform, it can also significantly influence the results right from the start. For instance, the selection of a holiday tourism scenario inherently lacks a strong organic connection to cadastral references. Therefore, it is not surprising that the frequency of observed searches of this nature is marginal.

This study has identified several lines of future work. Firstly, although the current implementation of an automatic event logging tool did not achieve the intended support for event log annotation, there is still significant potential to automatically model the behaviour of web systems operating under considerable traffic. A major challenge is to accurately map user clicks and keystrokes to activities that are meaningful from a process and business perspective. Secondly, the intervention of a moderator prevented executing a fine-grained analysis of performance, but such an analysis would be valuable in the case of task mining traffic from a portal in operation. Thirdly, other typologies, such as network models (graphs), can also be explored for describing the mental model. Process mining techniques related to flow control can greatly contribute to this purpose. Fourthly, this work only addressed the gap between the conceptual model and the mental model of the user from a process discovery perspective, but there is also an opportunity to deepen this understanding from a conformance verification perspective. This branch of process mining diagnoses the differences between a prescriptive model and the behaviour captured in the event log. Finally, personalised and real-time support mechanisms can be developed to enhance the experience of users with deficient mental models based on their usage patterns of the platform, as proposed by Jansen under the concept of adaptive UIs for users of geoportals [9].

Acknowledgements. This paper is partially supported by the Aragon Regional Government through the project T59_23R. The work of Dagoberto José Herrera-Murillo is supported by the ODECO project. This project has received funding from the European Union's Horizon 2020 research and innovation programme under the Marie Skłodowska-Curie grant agreement No. 955569.

This research was conducted in strict adherence to the ODECO Ethical Principles Guide, encompassing the following key components: a) procedures to identify and recruit suitable research participants. b) an informed consent procedure where all human subjects are fully informed about their participation and the handling of their data. c) Comprehensive model consent forms, designed to be easily understood by participants through the use of accessible language and clear terms.

References

1. Anitha, V., Devi, I.A.: A survey on predicting user behavior based on web server log files in a web usage mining. In: 2016 International Conference on Computing Technologies and Intelligent Data Engineering (ICCTIDE'16), pp. 1–4 (2016)
2. Bucher, B.: Spatial linked data in Europe: report from spatial linked data sessions at knowledge graph in action. Official Publication - EuroSDR (2021)
3. Carroll, J.M., Olson, J.R.: Mental models in human-computer interaction: research issues about what the user of software knows. In: Handbook of Human-Computer Interaction, pp. 45–65. North-Holland (1988)
4. De Kleer, J., Brown, J.S.: Assumptions and ambiguities in mechanistic mental models. In: Mental Models, pp. 155–190. Psychology Press (1983)
5. Deka, B., Huang, Z., Kumar, R.: ERICA: interaction mining mobile apps. In: Proceedings of the 29th Annual Symposium on User Interface Software and Technology, pp. 767–776. ACM (2016)

6. Dhandi, M., Chakrawarti, R.K.: A comprehensive study of web usage mining. In: 2016 Symposium on Colossal Data Analysis and Networking (CDAN), pp. 1–5 (2016)
7. Efthimiadis, E.N., Hendry, D.G.: Search engines and how students think they work. In: Proceedings of the 28th Annual International ACM SIGIR Conference on Research and Development in Information Retrieval, pp. 595–596 (2005)
8. Hearst, M.: Search User Interfaces. Cambridge University Press, Cambridge (2009)
9. Jansen, C.: A change of view: usable interface design propositions for geoportals. Master's thesis, Delft University of Technology, the Netherlands (2020)
10. Lacasta, J., Lopez-Pellicer, F.J., Zarazaga-Soria, J., Bejar, R., Nogueras-Iso, J.: Approaches for the clustering of geographic metadata and the automatic detection of quasi-spatial dataset series. ISPRS Int. J. Geo-Inf. **11**(2), 87 (2022)
11. Nielsen, J.: End of web design. UX & usability articles from Nielsen Norman group, 22 July 2000. https://www.nngroup.com/articles/end-of-web-design/
12. Nielsen, J.: Mental Models. UX & usability articles from Nielsen Norman group, 17 October 2017. https://www.nngroup.com/articles/mental-models/
13. Norman, D.A.: The Design of Everyday Things. Basic Books, New York City (2002)
14. Papastergiou, M.: Students' mental models of the internet and their didactical exploitation in informatics education. Educ. Inf. Technol. **10**, 341–360 (2005)
15. Ren, J., Wang, H., Shao, J.: Experimental study on dynamic map information layout based on eye tracking. In: Ahram, T., Karwowski, W., Vergnano, A., Leali, F., Taiar, R. (eds.) IHSI 2020. AISC, vol. 1131, pp. 1238–1243. Springer, Cham (2020). https://doi.org/10.1007/978-3-030-39512-4_189
16. Roth, S.P., Schmutz, P., Pauwels, S.L., Bargas-Avila, J.A., Opwis, K.: Mental models for web objects: where do users expect to find the most frequent objects in online shops, news portals, and company web pages? Interact. Comput. **22**(2), 140–152 (2010)
17. Rouse, W.B., Morris, N.M.: On looking into the black box: prospects and limits in the search for mental models. Psychol. Bull. **100**(3), 349–363 (1984)
18. Staggers, N., Norcio, A.F.: Mental models: concepts for human-computer interaction research. Int. J. Man-Mach. Stud. **38**(4), 587–605 (1993)
19. Evan, S.: Prioritize quantitative data with the pareto principle. UX & usability articles from Nielsen Norman group, 17 October 2021. https://www.nngroup.com/articles/pareto-principle/
20. van der Aalst, W.: Process Mining: Data Science in Action. Springer Publishing Company, Cham (2016)
21. Zhang, Y.: Undergraduate students' mental models of the web as an information retrieval system. J. Am. Soc. Inform. Sci. Technol. **59**(13), 2087–2098 (2008)

Towards Agile Requirements Engineering in Maritime Freight Transportation

Irbe Apine and Marite Kirikova(✉) (iD)

Department of Artificial Intelligence and Systems Engineering, Riga Technical University,
Ķīpsalas iela 6A, Riga LV-1048, Latvia
irbe.apine@edu.rtu.lv, marite.kirikova@rtu.lv

Abstract. Software developed for organizations operating in maritime freight transportation tends to be very complex, as it needs to handle documentation and the planning of a wide range of cargo and equipment, always complying with the different international regulations, sanctions, and local requirements of software integration with different port systems. At the same time, it must be flexible so as to be able to react in a timely manner to the changes in the turbulent business environment. The goal of this research is to provide a new Agile approach for requirements engineering for organizations operating in the maritime freight transportation industry, that is tailored to specific needs of these enterprises and introduces as many benefits from Agile as possible, to achieve needed flexibility. The proposed approach has its roots in related work on agile approaches and a case study in a maritime freight transportation company.

Keywords: Maritime Informatics · Agile · Requirements Engineering

1 Introduction

According to the World Bank and the International Association of Ports and Harbors (IAPH), an improved digital collaboration between private and public organizations across the maritime freight supply chain will result in significant efficiency improvements, safer and more reliable supply chains, and lower global emissions [1]. Maritime transport carries over 90% of the global merchandise trade, totaling just over 11 billion tons of cargo per year. Digitalizing this sector would bring wide-ranging economic benefits and contribute to a stronger and more sustainable future for the industry [1].

Currently, organizations operating in this industry are struggling regarding flexibility – each local port system in every country is different, customs systems are different, and maritime organizations are facing difficulties in creating software that fits all countries' local requirements and could also be integrated with their systems. In addition, industry standards are always changing – new sanctions are applied, new commodities are restricted, new types of cargoes that need special equipment are being transported, and many more. To fulfill rapidly changing and rigorous customer requirements, one of the most important aspects of the organization is its flexibility. The key to increasing this flexibility is in the software used by the organization. Consequently, in the maritime freight transportation industry, agility is needed in requirements engineering (RE), when the organization is defining, documenting, and maintaining the requirements for its software systems. RE is supposed to provide the appropriate mechanisms to understand customer needs and wants, analyzing them, assessing the feasibility of the requirements and the required solutions, validating specifications, managing, and maintaining them as they are transferred into the finished product – the desired software [2].

The problem addressed by this paper is that *companies operating in the maritime freight transportation industry often are unable to adapt and realize the Agile RE approach for information systems development.* This is caused by the complexity of using Agile RE for this specific industry. Therefore, the *goal of this paper is to develop recommendations for using Agile RE for software development for organizations operating in maritime freight transportation.* The research goal is fulfilled using the following method: (i) the benefits and challenges of agile approaches and agile requirements engineering are amalgamated from the related work; (ii) the current process of requirements engineering in a company operating in the maritime freight transportation industry is analyzed; (c) based on the results in (i) and (ii), the method for changes in the RE of the company is proposed; (d) the possibilities of generalizing the method are discussed.

The paper is organized as follows. The findings from the analysis of the related work are amalgamated in Sect. 2. Section 3 describes the context of the requirements engineering in the maritime freight transportation company (the description is tailored so as not to include sensitive information). In Sect. 4, the method for combining approaches for Agile RE in the company is proposed and applied. The possibilities for generalizing the method and directions of further research are briefly discussed in Sect. 5.

2 Related Work on Agile RE

Requirements are the base for all software products; therefore, RE plays an important role in the respective systems development. Agile methodologies such as Scrum, Kanban, or Extreme Programming provide the process model to develop these products. Comparing the traditional RE approaches to Agile, the main difference is that the general RE activities – requirement elicitation, documentation, validation, negotiations, and management are not separate activities in the Agile RE approach, rather they are replicated in each iteration and only the required information is then detailed before the beginning of the next iteration [3].

Since implementation of Agile approaches in RE, software development tends to move from plan-driven to value-driven models. This means moving from negotiations about pricing models, project plans, and feature quantities to discussing visions, experiences, and human values [3]. Implementing Agile approaches means that RE will be carried out throughout the entire development process, rather than only in the initial phases. The Just-In-Time (JIT) model may be used to refine top-level requirements into low-level developers' tasks. This is achieved by team, user, and developer collaboration. An RE process may begin by creating the requirements through epics – large user stories [4]. These are refined in story maps – user stories, and then split into tasks. The workflow can be managed by the Kanban board, where design, development, and delivery are planned [5]. With Agile, only short-term estimates are made, which the team reviews and updates regularly. Sprint length is fixed and therefore eliminates the issue of shifting deadlines. Agile breaks the project down into manageable sections, so the teams involved can focus on higher quality development and more thorough testing. Additionally, customer involvement is required at all development stages, improving the predictability and control over the product [6]. N. Kama [7] states that Agile RE can be summarized as a set of frequent activities that will ensure the team is building the right project. In software engineering, it is applied throughout the entire project. L. Cao [8] states that Agile RE responds to rapid changes in competitive threats, stakeholder preferences, development technology, and time-to-market pressures. Agile methods are designed to combat rapidly changing requirements.

Based on the reviewed literature sources and available terminology of Agile, it can be concluded that *Agile RE can be defined as an iterative set of activities to facilitate the delivery of right requirements quickly.* This understanding is used throughout the paper when referring to Agile RE.

Based on Agile RE core values, existing Agile RE approaches could be tailored specifically for the maritime freight transportation industry. Different terminology is used in different sources to describe activities related to Agile RE and suggested Agile RE approaches. Based on the literature review, 4 different sources listed in Table 1 were identified as most closely related to the challenges of the maritime freight transportation industry. From these sources, six different Agile RE approaches (listed in the columns of Table 1) were derived from different contexts. As, can be seen in this table, Scrum, Kanban, and XP are mentioned more often than other approaches.

Table 1. Suggested Agile approaches.

Source	Context	Author	Year of Publishing	Scrum	Kanban	XP	Lean	DSDM	FDD
			Agile RE approaches suggested						
[9]	Privacy requirements elicitation due to new law implementation.	Canedo, E. et al.	2022	x		x		x	x
[10]	What are the practices adopted by Agile teams in different organizations.	Coutinho, J. et al.	2022	x	x	x			
[11]	How to manage changes in Agile methods for RE.	Shim, W.	2019	x			x		
[12]	How user stories are transformed into requirements with Agile approaches.	Dalpiaz, F. et al.	2021	x	x				

All approaches listed in Table 1 may be used for the Agile approach to RE, however, the industry context has to be kept in mind. The maritime freight industry is extremely complex and requires complex software development in all its sub-domains. A further description of the industry will be given in Sect. 3. The transfer to the Agile way of working brings many functional and organizational changes to an organization. Therefore, it is important to understand what can be gained from such changes and also what are the potential challenges and threats.

Top Agile development *benefits* [6] include continuous improvement through the retrospects held at the end of sprints so as to reflect on the performance and possible improvements, boosting the teams motivation, and offering the platform to learn. Agile principles support teamwork, ensuring active collaboration between members. Teams become self-organized and cross functional. Developers and business-side employees work together to achieve the best results, enhancing communication. Additionally, working in short cycles sets clear and achievable goals and clearly defines the tasks that need to be done. Agile approaches have made a significant contribution to software development processes. Moving on from the implementation of small teams to large scale complex processes, agile approaches bring in many benefits, but challenges as well. In [13], the challenges were considered, based on the research conducted on requirements engineering approaches implementation for large scale Agile software development. The main issues found by this comprehensive study were grouped into the following *four areas of challenges* [13]:

1. *Build and Maintain Shared Understanding of Customer Value* – it deals with bridging the gap between implementor and customer and building a long-lasting customer knowledge base.
2. *Support Change and Evolution* – managing experimental requirements, synchronizing development, encouraging re-use, avoiding re-specifying, and updating the requirements.
3. *Build and Maintain Shared Understanding about the System* – documentation of the tests and stories, system vs. component thinking, backward compatibility, creation, and maintenance of traces, and studying of long-term knowledge.
4. *Representation for Requirements Knowledge* – manage levels and decomposition, not fitting tools, quality requirements, representation, and consistency.

For each of these defined challenges, a treatment has been proposed in [13] (further used in Sect. 5), however, it is important to define whether organizations operating in the maritime freight transportation industry face the same challenges, and thus determine if the suggested treatment will be feasible.

Regarding the benefits, the three most often listed approaches (Table 1) have been reviewed, to find the common benefits of other organizations that have adopted these approaches. Benefits of Scrum, XP, and Kanban, to a large extent, cover also the benefits of other approaches. Table 2 shows 3 sources where Scrum benefits were listed and six benefits that can be derived from these sources. Similarly, the benefits from XP are amalgamated in Table 3 and Kanban benefits are shown in Table 4.

According to [15], adopting Agile approaches in an organization is not limited to only identifying the benefits. An important aspect is the correct management of these benefits. The authors of [15] propose a process model for benefits management, consisting of the following phases: (i) identifying and structuring benefits – identification of the benefits and establishing the measurements of their success; (ii) planning benefits realization – all activities needed to realize each benefit, including potential process and organizational developments; (iii) executing the benefits realization plan – actual implementation of the benefits plan, which is an integral part of the project management plan; (iv) evaluation and review of the results – evaluation of actual benefits delivered, identification of actions to recover missed benefits; and (v) potential for further benefits – further capitalization on the investments that have already been made. In this paper, the first two phases of this process model [15] will be used to propose changes to the existing RE process of a maritime freight transportation company.

Table 2. Scrum benefits.

Source	Improved control	Backlog management	Team involvement in planning	Precise estimates	Knowledge sharing (transparency)	Improved productivity
[14]	x	x	x	x	x	
[15]	x		x		x	
[16]			x	x	x	x

Table 3. XP benefits.

Source	Cost and time saving	Simplicity	Feedback and transparency	Speed and satisfaction
[17]	x		x	
[18]		x		x
[19]	x	x	x	

Table 4. Kanban benefits.

Source	Visibility and transparency	Flexibility and responsiveness	Increased output	Resource allocation
[20]	x			x
[21]	x	x		
[22]	x		x	

3   The Maritime Freight Transportation Context

In 2022, about 2 billion metric tons of cargo were shipped globally, up from around 0.1 billion metric tons back in 1980. Between 1980 and 2022 [23], the growth of volumes is considerable, and the software supporting this growth has also developed considerably. Nowadays, all the documentation regarding any type of container ship is handled electronically. Huge volumes of documents are involved with international trades and shipping and the software applications used in the industry are very complex.

In this paper, the context for the maritime freight transportation industry software applications is considered in terms of the operations, which are being performed with the company's software. The software systems that maritime freight transportation companies are using are not publicly available, and there is no related literature that would describe how these systems are built, what sub-domains they consist of, what are the requirements for these systems, and what are the approaches for the requirements engineering. However, it is possible to look at the global maritime freight process from the operations side, to then derive the possible requirements approaches that would be needed for the software that supports these processes. Based on the Trade Finance Global, the simplified operational flow of the container shipping process for maritime freight can be described as follows [24]: (i) Order is placed – client places an order with the Shipping organization directly (or through a Freight Forwarder) – rates and timing are agreed upon, based on vessel schedules; (ii) Truck loaded – a client places his goods in a shipping container – the full container is then transported to the nearest (or agreed upon) port terminal; (iii) Ship loaded – if all necessary documents have been provided, the container is loaded onto the vessel and begins a journey towards a destination or a transshipment port: (iv) Discharge – once the containers arrives at the destination port, they are discharged at the terminal and await the customs clearance; (v) Customs clearance – all necessary documentation is checked, and several containers, in case of discrepancies, can be chosen for further inspection; (vi) Pickup – once the container is cleared by customs, it is picked up by the client or freight forwarder and transported to the final destination (this can also be done by train).

Due to the fact that no literature is available for the detailed context of software applications for the maritime freight transportation industry, based on the above-mentioned standard process, and the commonalities imposed by strict directive regulations in the industry, it can be supposed, that the software decomposition into sub-domains for one maritime freight industry company (specifically, Company X, where the case study was conducted), can be applicable to other organizations in the industry in the same or a very similar way. Thus, the context provided for Company X can be assumed as the generic context for the organizations operating in the industry.

What makes the software for this industry so specific and complex are the maritime freight standards, and the need to be integrated with local systems in each country, and also the needed ability to comply with the local rules and legislations. At the same time, the generalization of one software application to the whole industry is limited. General software solutions, such as Marine-digital, Logi-sys, and others, may not always fit all companies, due to other system integration limitations, the volume of bookings that must be processed, the number of users using the system, etc. In addition, the goal of the company is to always strive to offer the best product possible, and such standard software implementations often limit RE for the "delighters" [25].

Considering these risks, if an organization still wishes to implement one of the standard solutions, then the Agile RE approach proposed could be used to generate the additional requirements for the standard solution selected. To find the most suitable approach for Agile RE in the maritime freight transportation industry, the scope which the requirements will be engineered for, must be defined. As described above, the context model developed for one company can be, to a large extent, considered a general context for organizations operating in the industry. Due to the complexity of the rules and regulations organizations must follow, the general context for which the software is developed (to handle the operations and the documentation), in this paper, is broken down into different sub-domains. Each of these sub-domains is responsible for the development of the necessary system functionalities related to their field. The context model for the maritime freight transportation company, shown in Fig. 1, was obtained following the advice in [26] and using interviews and workshops as knowledge acquisition methods in Company X. In Fig. 1, the lines in bold depict direct domain connections, whereas dotted lines show inter-domain information flows. Each component represents the functionality that software must support and perform.

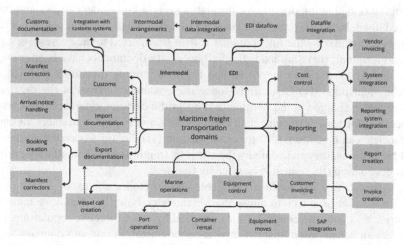

Fig. 1. The model of operational/software components of the maritime freight transportation company

When conducting research within Company X, it was discovered that the organization was not following any frameworks or methodologies in RE. This has resulted in many issues being faced by the organization, including an insufficient RE process:

1. RE being split into separate domains (i.e., customs, EDI, Export Documentation) creates many issues regarding team communication. Each domain specialist tends to work individually and only rarely discusses cross-domain topics. Communication issues result in longer lead times for the deliverables and client dissatisfaction when they are being referred to different domain specialists.
2. Software operating in this industry is required to be integrated with the local customs systems – this integration is in the form of a direct electronic data interchange (EDI), the ability to generate necessary reports in the necessary format, direct documentation interchange, the ability to upload documents directly from the organization into the customs system and many more. These customs requirements are often changing, forthing organizations to be Agile and to adapt to the new requirements as quickly as possible.

3. As the maritime freight industry is constantly evolving, there are new local requirements, and new client requirements that need to be filled; also, Company X is facing
an issue with the lack of continuous improvement opportunities. There is no process
of examining the current workflow, and no room for the employees to reflect and
identify the opportunities to boost the efficiency and quality of the delivered product
and services.
4. There are no defined KPIs for employees to measure their performance. It is difficult
to measure the progress and efficiency of the IT product and the team.
5. The equipment and cargo information handling in the system that has been developed
and implemented is extremely diverse, starting from clothing and edible goods, all the
way to dangerous chemicals and military grade equipment. This diversity leads to the
complexity of the system, as each cargo type, each equipment type, each customer,
etc., needs to be registered and monitored closely to fit all rules and legislation. It
leads to extremely huge databases, which need constant maintenance, and the system
needs to be able to handle such diverse items and workflows.
6. Lack of control and predictability. As in any project, software development carried
out for maritime freight organizations also requires strict deadlines and defined deliverables. However, due to the lack of structure in the teams, this aspect needs improvement. Deadlines for IT project phases are defined; however, they are almost always
extended to fit the actual progress of the project rollout, resulting in late development
and an extended project period.

No single Agile approach would help to solve such diverse challenges, therefore the
aspects from different approaches must be combined [27], to achieve as many benefits as
possible and overcome or avoid as many challenges as possible. The proposed method
for combining the approaches is discussed in the next section.

4   The Method for Combining the Approaches for Agile RE

Based on the complex industry context, to realize as many of the various benefits of different Agile approaches as possible and to avoid the threats of challenges, the following
method was developed and applied:

1. Crosscheck the issues Company X is facing with the groups of challenges and corresponding treatments of the agile frameworks LeSS and SAFe [28], as proposed in
[13]. Select the treatments applicable for Company X (see Table 5).
2. Crosscheck the issues with the benefits from Agile approaches shown in Tables 2, 3
and 4 of this paper. Select the Agile approaches best addressing the issues of Company
X (see the head of Table 5).
3. Develop and analyze the model for the current requirements engineering process.
4. Create a new RE process model including chosen treatments and instruments.

In Table 5, the first, the third and the fourth column are taken from [13], which
provides a very comprehensive overview of the challenges of Agile approaches. The table
demonstrates only one challenge, namely, "Build and maintain a shared understanding
of the system". However, to perform the first step of the method, all four groups of
challenges [13] listed in Sect. 2 should be examined.

When the groups of challenges are examined and relevant treatments for the issues that apply to the company (the second column of Table 5) are selected, the *second step* of the method suggests seeing which of the most popular Agile approaches would work the best for each group of challenges. In the case of Company X, these were *Scrum* for the challenges "Build and maintain a shared understanding of customer value" and "Build and maintain shared understanding about the system" (see the head of Table 5); and Extreme Programming for the challenges "Support change and evolution" and "Representation of requirements knowledge". Additionally, following the suggestions from LeSS and SAFe, the use of the Kanban board was also included so as to be incorporated into the Agile RE of Company X.

The third and fourth steps of the method were performed phase-wise by organizing the Agile RE process into the following *four phases* [29]: (i) *Elicitation* – gathering business needs; (ii) *Analysis* – organizing domain needs and capabilities (the elicited requirements) so that inconsistency, incompleteness, inaccuracy, and ambiguity are minimized; (iii) *Validation* – checking if the requirements defined for development are really defining the system that the client has requested, checking if the right product is being built, based on the requirements elicited; and (iv) *Requirements management* – ensuring that the most important elements are delivered first in accordance with the scope (carried out through the entire RE process). Further in this paper, for the third and the fourth steps of the method, we will illustrate only the first two phases of the RE process.

For the first phase – Elicitation. [30], an additional literature review was performed due to the variety of information sources to be considered in Company X. The results of the review are amalgamated in Table 6.

Requirements gathering techniques were grouped under 3 main categories – questioning, observation, and artifact-based. Under each category, the approaches described in each reviewed article were mentioned (e.g., questioning: interviews + surveys).

Company X currently focuses on the questioning requirements gathering technique, by conducting workshops/training sessions together with users. However, based on the literature review, it was recommended to supplement these workshops with additional interviews and artifact-based techniques, such as requirement reuse, system archaeology, and field reports. Interviews would give further insight into why these requirements are needed and give a better overview of the users' current processes. Artifact-based gathering techniques would make better use of stakeholders' time, by partially limiting the involved parties and working with the gathered data only, therefore possibly eliciting some "delighters" that the users did not even know about [25].

When performing the *third step* of the method for creating the Agile approach, the processes were obtained separately for the first two RE phases (only these are discussed in detail in this paper) and the second two RE phases.

The current process for the first two RE phases in Company X– elicitation and analysis, is referred to as the "Scoping phase". The process is simple and straightforward, flowing in one direction, not providing any opportunities for re-work, improvements, or team collaboration. The process starts with the announcement of the beginning of the new software rollout to all involved stakeholders. A project manager is combining the list of systems key users and end-users and assigns their roles accordingly. An introductory meeting is organized for all involved stakeholders to introduce the roles, the project,

Table 5. Example of applying steps 1 and 2 of the method for combining Agile approaches.

Build and maintain a shared understanding about the system: *The best fit: SCRUM*

Challenge	Is it applicable in Company X?	Proposed practice from LeSS	Proposed practice from SAFe
Documentation to complement tests and stories	*YES – user stories and test cases are sometimes insufficient, and it is difficult for domain specialists or developers to complement these requirements with other artifacts*	–	*Use models to analyze requirements. Propose additional test cases*
System vs component thinking	NO – teams are able to break down systems from components to functionalities	Principle: Whole product focus; Multi-team product backlog refinement; PO engages the team to own the product	Clear breakdown from enterprise level to the team; Feature and component teams; Systems thinking; Tribal unity
Creating and maintaining traces	NO – traces are created in a timely manner and tied to each requirement, there are no issues with current trace maintenance	Link to wiki pages; Backlog items to ancestors, max. 3 levels	Describe the solution (Documentation)
Learning and long-term knowledge	*YES – due to the prolonged lifetime of the requirements, it is difficult for the team to build up and maintain the knowledge. There is no "organization" towards knowledge maintenance*	*Reflection + improvement experiments; Experts teach each other, informal networks; Specification by example*	*ART focus on value, not project; Enabler stories.(Exploration); Feature and Component teams; Community of practice, chapters, guilds*
...			

goals, and timelines. Key users together with the local coordinator fill out the scoping questionnaire (technical questionnaire of expected system functionalities) which is shared with domain specialists. Scoping questionnaires are then reviewed together with domain specialists and the agency's mentor – responsible for consulting the agency. The reviewed questionnaires are transformed into reports, which are shared with involved stakeholders, and the key users may begin the initial training for the usage of the new

Table 6. Requirement gathering techniques (the review of the recent literature).

Ref.	Technique		
	Questioning	Observation	Artifact-based
[31]	Interview + Questionnaire + Workshop	–	Reuse of requirements + System archaeology
[32]	Interviews + Focus discussion groups	Storyboards + User env. Visualization + Remote collaboration	Crowd based RE + System archaeology
[33]	Interviews + Surveys + Customer specifications	Observation	Warranty data + Field reports
[34]	Interviews + Workshop	–	Perspective-based reading + System archaeology
[35]	Workshop	–	Field reports + Perspective-based reading + Crowd based RE

software. Functional and technical reviews of the scoping reports are done by the development team and project manager and, in case any adjustments are needed, they are then incorporated in the report or the questionnaire. In parallel, the development coordinator is preparing the pre-production environment. This is the standard environment that is offered to all clients. The first pre-production environment refers to the industry standards that cannot be changed, therefore the basis of the software for all clients remains the same. Once no more updates need to be done and the pre-production environment is set up, a sanity test can be performed by the separate sanity test team, following a standard functionality testing plan. When the sanity test is finished and all the bugs found have been reported, the pre-production environment is signed-off, and the next phase (in Company X called Gap identification phase) may begin, with the kickoff meeting and end-to-end workshops.

When performing the *fourth step* of the method presented at the beginning of this section, the processes were also obtained separately for the first two RE phases (only these phases are discussed in detail in this paper) and the second two RE phases. The new improved RE process suggested for Company X is represented in Fig. 2.

In the newly suggested process, the base of the flow remains the same – the process is initiated, and an introductory meeting is held. For requirements elicitation, additional requirements gathering techniques were included: interviews and practice workshops. In addition, perspective reading and system archaeology were added as points to be performed by the domain specialist, to define "delighters" and elicit additional requirements, without the involvement of other stakeholders. Moreover, because the international maritime freight industry is so strictly regulated and standardized, Company X can take advantage of already existing industry standards research and apply these requirements to the system as well. Here, the initial requirements gathered through interviews, scoping questionnaires, and practical workshops were also included as domain specialists may work on these without the involvement of the clients. After requirements have been gathered, they are grouped, based on the Kano model, to prioritize the most important requirements. They must also be grouped correctly for the upcoming sprints. This will overcome the current issue of important items staying too long in the backlog, and not-so crucial items being developed quickly, providing incorrect resource management. Next, the information-model is applied to break down the requirements into epic – capability – feature and story, helping with trace-creation and requirement re-usability [36]. An important aspect that the improved flow provides is the possibility to return to requirements elicitation if, by the scoping questionnaire review, the issues were found. This step will improve the overall quality of the requirements. Then handover is communicated, and the functional and technical review is held. The next steps in the flow are the performance of the sanity test, as well as making sure the system is well integrated with all the local customs and port systems, ensuring business continuity and resulting in a smoother subsequent transition to the production environment.

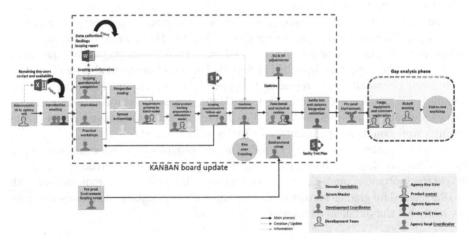

Fig. 2. Proposed requirement elicitation and analysis phase for Company X. Includes (i) *Additional elicitation techniques*: interviews and workshops, and artifact-based gathering technique; (ii) *the Kano model*; (iii) *the Information model (also referred to as the Requirement model)*; and (iv) *the Kanban board*.

The initial product backlog can already be identified, to be used in further steps in the project rollout. In addition, this process is documented on a Kanban board, to have an overview of the user stories that were gathered and what is the progress of transforming them into requirements, and to already start grouping them for future sprints. The last steps of the process move the project to the next "GAP phase", as it is called internally in Company X, or the validation phase. An important aspect added here is the registration of new cargo entities, equipment entities, and new customers into the new system. This registration is one of the main reasons why agility is such an important aspect in the rollout flow, as these lists are rapidly changing and need to comply with different standards; flow leading up to this must be agile, to comply with these requirements. In addition, the roles that are involved have been adjusted. The Scrum master is now overseeing the process, helping with communication, team support, and agile coaching. The product owner is communicating the vision and oversees the kanban board to start managing the backlog, and prioritizes the team's needs.

All additions used in the model are listed in the caption of Fig. 2. The other changes introduced for the other RE phases are briefly listed in the next section.

5   Discussion and Conclusion

In the case of Company X, altogether 12 new components were suggested for Agile RE. Besides the ones for the first two phases of RE represented in Fig. 2, the following improvements for the other phases of the RE were incorporated in the process models: Product and sprint backlog definition, Development split into separate domains (see Fig. 1), Daily Scrum, Sprint review, Retrospective, Small release, Sprint, and User acceptance test. The company saw the transfer to the new Agile RE process as doable, but only in small well-planned steps.

The suggestions given to Company X might be relevant also to other companies operating in the maritime freight transportation domain. However, to respect the individual features of each company, the proposed method for combining agile approaches for RE should be applied as described in Sect. 4. The use of the method is facilitated by the following contributions provided by the paper: (i) the description of the method and example of its application given in Sect. 4; (ii) the suggested approach of using Agile challenge-treatment tables rooted in [13] as in Table 5; the results of surveys of recent research works on Agile amalgamated in Tables 1, 2, 3, 4, and 6.

Further research directions are: (i) following the progress of transformation to Agile RE in Company X, (ii) analyzing the possibility to generalize the approach to maritime freight transportation companies in other countries, which might be complemented with (iii) the method for gradual transformation to Agile RE for companies operating in highly law restricted and turbulent environments in general.

References

1. Digitalizing the Maritime Sector Set to Boost the Competitiveness and Resilience of Global Trade. The World Bank (2021). https://www.worldbank.org/en/news/press-release/2021/01/21/digitalizing-the-maritime-sector-set-to-boost-the-competitiveness-and-resilience-of-global-trade. Accessed 06 Apr 2023
2. Java T Point, Requirement Engineering. https://www.javatpoint.com/software-engineering-requirement-engineering. Accessed 02 Mar 2023
3. Schön, E.-M., Thomaschewski, J., Escalona, M.J.: Agile requirements engineering: a systematic literature review. Comput. Stand. Interfaces **49**, 79–91 (2017)
4. Cohn, M.: User Stories Applied: For Agile Software Development. Addison-Wesley Professional, Boston (2004)
5. Schön, E.-M., Winter, D., Uhlenbrok, J., Escalona, M.J.: Enterprise experience into the integration of human-centered design and Kanban. In: Proceedings of the 11th International Joint Conference on Software Technologies (ICSOFT 2016), pp. 133–140, Lisbon, Portugal (2016)
6. Chapell, E.: 9 Key Benefits of Agile Software Development (2023 Guide). ClickUp. https://clickup.com/blog/benefits-of-agile/. Accessed 13 Apr 2023

7. Elghariani, K., Kama, N.: Review on Agile requirements engineering challenges. In: 2016 3rd International Conference on Computer and Information Sciences (ICCOINS), pp. 507–512, Kuala Lumpur, Malaysia (2016)
8. Cao, L., Ramesh, B.: Agile requirements engineering practices: an empirical study. IEEE Softw. **25**(1), 60–67 (2008)
9. Canedo, E.D., Calazans, A.T.S., Bandeira, I.N., et al.: Guidelines adopted by agile teams in privacy requirements elicitation after the Brazilian general data protection law (LGPD) implementation. Requir. Eng. **27**(4), 545–567 (2022)
10. Coutinho, J., Andrade, W., Machado, P.: A survey of requirements engineering and software testing practices in agile teams. In: Proceedings of the 7th Brazilian Symposium on Systematic and Automated Software Testing (SAST'22), pp. 9–18. Association for Computing Machinery, New York, NY, USA (2022)
11. Shim, W.: An agile method of representing, organizing, and (Re) prioritizing requirements in a large enterprise. In: 2019 IEEE 27th International Requirements Engineering Conference (RE), Jeju, Korea (South), pp. 464–469 (2019)
12. Dalpiaz, F., Brinkkemper, S.: Agile requirements engineering: from user stories to software architectures. In: 2021 IEEE 29th International Requirements Engineering Conference (RE), pp. 504–505, Notre Dame, IN, USA (2021)
13. Kasauli, R., Knauss, E., Horkoff, J., Liebel, G., de Oliveira Neto, F. G.: Requirements engineering challenges and practices in large-scale agile system development. J. Syst. Softw. **172** (2021)
14. Weichbroth, P.: A case study on implementing agile techniques and practices: rationale, benefits, barriers and business implications for hardware development. Appl. Sci. **12**(17), 8457 (2022)
15. Holgeid, K.K., Jørgensen, M.: Benefits management and agile practices in software projects: how perceived benefits are impacted. In: 2020 IEEE 22nd Conference on Business Informatics (CBI), pp. 48–56, Antwerp, Belgium (2020)
16. Marnewick, C., Marnewick, A.L.: Benefits realisation in an agile environment. Int. J. Project Manag. **40**(4), 454–465 (2022)
17. Wibisono, Y., Wardhana, M.A., Pamungkas, W.H.: Design of Google Apps-based helpdesk ticketing system at University using extreme programming approach. In: AIP Conference Proceedings, vol. 2658, no. 1, article id.070005 (2022)
18. Shrivastava, A., Jaggi, I., Katoch, N., Gupta, D., Gupta, S.: A systematic review on extreme programming. J. Phys. Conf. Ser. **1969**(1), article id. 012046 (2021)
19. Merzouk, S., Cherkaoui, A., Marzak, A., Sael, N., Guerss, F.-Z.: The proposition of process flow model for scrum and eXtreme programming. In: Proceedings of the 4th International Conference on Networking, Information Systems & Security (NISS2021). Association for Computing Machinery, New York, NY, USA, article 52, pp. 1–6 (2021)
20. Strickroth, S., Kreidenweis, M., Wurm, Z.: Learning from agile methods: using a kanban board for classroom orchestration. In: Auer, M.E., Pachatz, W., Rüütmann, T. (eds.) Learning in the Age of Digital and Green Transition. ICL 2022. LNNS, vol. 633, pp. 68–79. Springer, Cham (2023). https://doi.org/10.1007/978-3-031-26876-2_7
21. Yadav, A., Jha, G.: Developing an integrated hybrid app to reduce overproduction and waiting time using Kanban board. In: Skala, V., Singh, T.P., Choudhury, T., Tomar, R., Abul Bashar, M. (eds.) Machine Intelligence and Data Science Applications. LNDECT, vol. 132, pp. 239–264. Springer, Singapore (2022). https://doi.org/10.1007/978-981-19-2347-0_19
22. Pereira, C., Santos, A., MacHado, L., Zaina, L.: How developers feel about tools: an investigation on software startup professionals experience with virtual Kanban boards. In: Proceedings of the 15th International Conference on Cooperative and Human Aspects of Software Engineering (CHASE'22). Association for Computing Machinery, NY, USA, pp. 1–10 (2022)

23. Placek, M.: Container Shipping – statistics & facts. Statista (2022). https://www.statista.com/topics/1367/container-shipping/#topicOverview. Accessed 13 Apr 2023
24. Container Shipping – How It Works. Trade Finance Global (2023). https://www.tradefinanceglobal.com/freight-forwarding/container-shipping/. Accessed 02 Mar 2023
25. Frühauf, K., Fuchs, E., et al.: Handbook for the CPRE Certified Professional for Requirements Engineering Foundation Level – Version 1.0.0, p. 74 (2017)
26. Schilit, B., Adams, N., Want, R.: Context-aware computing applications. In: First Workshop on Mobile Computing Systems and Applications, Santa Cruz, CA, 1994, pp. 85–90 (1994)
27. O'Reilly. Agile Practice Guide. 2017, Project Management institute. https://www.oreilly.com/library/view/agile-practice-guide/9781628253993/. Accessed 28 Apr 2023
28. Gendel, G.: SAFe vs LeSS: Understanding the Difference. ScrumAlliance. https://resources.scrumalliance.org/Article/safe-vs-less-understanding-difference-2,l.a. Accessed 01 June 2023
29. DataArt. An Introduction to Agile Requirements Engineering (2016). https://www.dataart.com/blog/an-introduction-to-agile-requirements-engineering. Accessed 02 Mar 2023
30. Häußer, D., Lauenroth, K., et al.: Handbook IREB Certified Professional for Requirements Engineering Advanced Level Elicitation – Version 1.0.3, p. 55 (2018)
31. Gokhool, O., Nagowah, S. D.: A requirement gathering framework for electronic document management systems. In: 2022 IEEE Bombay Section Signature Conference (IBSSC), Mumbai, India, pp. 1–6 (2022)
32. Gómez, V., Peñaranda, K., Figueroa, P.: Lessons learned from requirements gathering for virtual reality simulators. Virtual Real. Intell. Hardw. 3(5), 407–422 (2021)
33. Simonova, S.: Requirements gathering for specialized information systems in public administration. In: 2021 International Conference on Information and Digital Technologies (IDT), Zilina, Slovakia, pp. 100–105 (2021)
34. Jepsen, S.C., Worm, T., Christensen, H.B., Hviid, J., Sandig, L.M.: Experience report: a systematic process for gathering quality attribute requirements for industry 4.0 middleware. In: 2021 IEEE 25th International Enterprise Distributed Object Computing Workshop (EDOCW), Gold Coast, Australia, pp. 166–175 (2021)
35. Dümmel, N., Westfechtel, B., Ehmann, M.: Work in progress: gathering requirements and developing an educational programming language. In: 2019 IEEE Global Engineering Education Conference (EDUCON), Dubai, United Arab Emirates, pp. 1–4 (2019)
36. What are the stories, features, capabilities, and epics in SAFe? Agility in Mind. https://agility.im/frequent-agile-question/what-are-the-stories-features-capabilities-and-epics-in-safe/. Accessed 19 Mar 2023

Managing Variability of Large Public Administration Event Log Collections: Dealing with Concept Drift

Flavio Corradini⬡, Caterina Luciani⬡, Andrea Morichetta⬡, and Marco Piangerelli(✉)⬡

University of Camerino, 62030 Camerino, MC, Italy
{flavio.corradini,caterina.luciani,andrea.morichetta,
marco.piangerelli}@unicam.it

Abstract. The analysis of large event log collections aimed at variability management requires an intensive pre-processing phase. It is intuitive that obsolete behaviour that could be present in the logs must be removed in order to gain insight into the collection. Changes in the information system may indeed generate obsolete behaviour, more specifically, in the case of public administration, changes in the law may imply a change in the process, which must be updated in the information system. The logs containing the updated behaviour can then be used in variability management practices, such as the creation of configurable models. This type of analysis has numerous criticalities, one of which is the difficulty of obtaining an effective representation of the process, without running into excessive complexity of the model produced. Obsolete behavior results in an unnecessary increase in complexity and should therefore be removed. This paper introduces an event log analysis and visualisation technique based on the notion of complexity introduced by Lempel Ziv. The visualization enables process analysts to identify concept drift in the logs, thereby facilitating the removal of outdated behavior. Furthermore, when equilibrium is achieved, it indicates that the behavior is representative of the entire log. Consequently, during variability analysis, it becomes possible to prune the log, reducing computational complexity.

Keywords: Process Aware Information Systems · Event Logs · Complexity

1 Introduction

The large availability of data generated by the use of information systems allows the evolution of new analysis techniques for the management of business process collections. The broad availability of *process aware information systems* made it possible to collect event logs, a type of data set that clearly expresses the behavior of a process by describing it in terms of groups of chronologically ordered

The original version of this chapter was revised: The acknowledgement section has been updated. The correction to this chapter is available at
https://doi.org/10.1007/978-3-031-43126-5_25

activities. This opens the door to many possibilities, such as those provided by process mining techniques, which make it possible to extract value from data, in the form of *process models*. It's not uncommon to stumble upon distinct implementations, in different facilities, of a process. This is the typical scenario for *variability* to occur, which is the manifestation of behavioral differences between distinct process installations. In the context of public administration, this phenomenon is particularly evident: the same service, made available to citizens, may be implemented differently in distinct municipalities, in order to cope with differences between national laws — which all municipalities must comply with — and local laws — which are relative to the region or even to the municipality itself. One of the ways of managing extensive collections of event logs that present the phenomenon of variability consists in using *configurable models*, a kind of meta-models used to synthesize the behavior of distinct installations of a process. From a configurable model, it is possible, through individualization, to derive individual models. The advantage of using these meta-models lies in the greater simplicity in which the process family is represented. The creation of a configurable model is known to be computationally expensive, not to mention that, despite the required effort, the result may be of difficult interpretation for a non-practitioner. Therefore, the production of a truly expressive configurable model requires, at least, an active engagement in upstream reduction of *redundant* and *obsolete behavior*[1]. The very possibility that certain parts of a process may eventually fall into disuse, or be entirely replaced by others, made entire research domains focus on the problem of *concept drift* which definition includes and describes both the previously described scenarios. In a similar direction, the moment of the drift and the successive equilibrium prove that the traces analysed until that moment are representative of the entire log and so there is the possibility to prune the log reducing the complexity in further analysis without losing the accuracy of the results.

In this paper, we present an unsupervised methodology for the inspection, visualization and reduction of the log through the *Lempel Ziv Complexity (LZC)* measure. This measure permits, first of all, the concept drifts to be identified; then, from the observation of the complexity trend, we are able to highlight the minimum meaningful representative behaviour, i.e. identified by the equilibrium condition, of a log. The attainment of the equilibrium allows the pruning of the log reducing the complexity of the problem without loss of information. This enables the application of process mining techniques on large log datasets that would be not manageable otherwise. In addition, the methodology is currently implemented in Python and is extremely easy to reproduce and integrate into any pipeline of analysis of large event log collections, particularly in variability analysis.

In this paper we use the LZC to analyze a set of logs containing information relative to public services provided by different Italian municipalities. The presence of drift, non-drift and equilibrium can be further analysed using process

---

[1] when talking about obsolete behavior, we mean behavioral patterns that were once part of the process under analysis but that can no longer be found in more recent event logs, describing that same process.

mining techniques to discover the causes of such phenomena. In particular, the identification of the equilibrium condition results in a simplification and in a decrease in the computational complexity to be managed for further analysis such as the creation of configurable models with the currently available techniques as shown in Sect. 5.

The paper is organized as follows: in Sect. 2, we provide fundamental concepts that form the theoretical basis of our work. In Sect. 3 we present the related works. In Sect. 4, the usage of *Lempel Ziv Complexity (LZC)* as a complexity measure is presented, equipped with a simple visual representation that allows identification of the concept drift. In Sect. 5, a description of experimental applications of the proposed methodology over a data set provided by a European enterprise operating in the E-Government sector.

2   Background

2.1   Pais and Event Logs

Businesses shifted, over time, from a data-centric perspective to a process-aware one. In order to keep up to this kind of change, information systems evolved to take into account processes' details. The product of this evolution is now generally referred to as *Process Aware Information System* (PAIS) [1]. This type of information system is now capable of managing and executing operational processes involving people, applications, and/or information sources on the basis of process models [13]. PAIS are capable of producing process-aware logs [16] which typically satisfy two minimum requirements. The first one is about logging activities with a unique identifier which makes it possible to identify them as part of a specific process execution (*Case ID*). The second one concerns activities' time framing that should always be clearly stated through *timestamps* [26].

Since the standardization of the *XES format*, approved by the IEEE on November 11, 2016, transferring knowledge about processes has become increasingly simple. In fact, the XES format satisfies both the previously stated requirements, making it possible to analyze processes through information-based models, instead of idealized ones [12,17].

Being the XES logs a standard, they are really useful and widely used in process mining techniques. The main purposes of process mining are threefold: (i) to discover processes currently in use, (ii) to observe the differences between real-world scenarios and (iii) modeled process behavior. These techniques permit to increase the reliability of existing process models by making them consistent with the behavior described by the available event logs [25].

2.2   Variability and Drift

Processes, whether in the same branch or in different branches of the same company, may show a degree of *heterogeneity*. This phenomenon is the result of the influence of contextual, environmental, and organizational factors. Heterogeneity is what lies behind the concepts of *process families* and *variability*. These two notions have been widely discussed in [24], where the focus was on comparing the *understandability* of a set of methodologies used to shape the variability in business process models. Representing variability, therefore, involves the identification of parts of a process model that are subject to change given a context (*variation points*), the detection of all the possible changes for each of these parts (*alternatives*), and the fixation of a context for the identified variations. The variability of a process may also depend on its evolution: the execution of a process may, in fact, vary over time; a common example, especially related to public administrations, consists in the entry into force of a law. Within the literature, this kind of behavioral change is now known as *concept drift* [29].

Creating a process model from real-world data, without taking into account the possibility of obsolete behavior to exist within the data collection which typically happens when concept drift goes by unnoticed, diminishes the representative effectiveness of the produced maps [2]. In order to avoid this, it may be useful to know the main branches of concept drift.

The *analysis* branch describes the possibility to deal with concept drift in a real-time environment, through *event streams*, or in a retrospective way, through *event logs* [8,14]. The *perspective* branch describes aspects of a process that can be influenced by change and is probably one of the most interesting as most of the research work is focused around the *control-flow* perspective, even though not every change in a system is granted visibility through business process models created with this particular perspective in mind [5,6]. Let's move away from business process models for a bit to get a clear vision of what a concept drift perspective exactly is. Imagine an online shop that allows payments through a credit card after the completion of a validation procedure. Furthermore, let's assume that the company operating the online shop owns a fleet of delivery trucks and that customers can ask for delivery within 24 h.

- The company wants the online shop to accept payments through a completely new payment system which is completely detached from the credit card system. The system will now start to record differentiated information about payments which can be interpreted as a concept drift from the *control-flow* perspective.
- The company use to achieve credit card validation through the manual work of a human operator. The complete automation of this process could reduce this activity's execution time, which may eventually result in a concept drift from the *time* perspective.
- It's a busy month for the company and the entire truck fleet is constantly committed to deliveries. Tons of orders requiring delivery within 24 h have been logged by the system, but no business vehicle can be used to satisfy the customers. This situation can be portrayed as a concept drift from the *resource* perspective.

- Let's now imagine that the credit card validation is done by attaching an image of the physical card to the order. Changing this operation in a way that makes the validation possible without the picture attachment changes the information required to perform this activity which could be seen as a concept drift from a *data* perspective.

The *dynamic of change* branch describes how a process can be affected by a change in terms of time granularity most real-life systems apply macro changes through incremental steps; it's up to the analyst to choose whether micro changes should be considered relevant or not (this usually involves a time window which size can be fixed or adaptive). The *type* branch is about how changes occurring in a process shape changes in generated data and business process models describing the process itself. Researchers in [18] identified four types of concept drift depicted in Fig. 1: sudden, recurring, incremental and gradual:

- *Sudden drift* is the situation when a process is completely replaced by another one after a specific period. The new process handles all the ongoing cases, even the incomplete ones. It commonly occurs in emergencies or after a change in regulations.
- *Recurring drift* is the situation where a process or a set of processes disappear and reappear over time (e.g. seasonal influences).
- *Incremental drift* occurs when a process is replaced over time through minor incremental changes.
- *Gradual drift* commonly occurs when, for a certain period, two distinct processes coexist and they both handle ongoing cases. During this period, the new process will start handling more and more cases, leading to the complete deprecation of the first one.

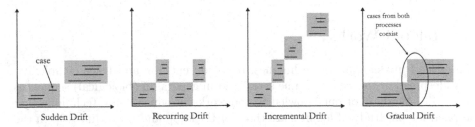

Fig. 1. Different types of drifts, adapted from [6]. The abscissa represents *time*, while the ordinate represents distinct processes. A line inside the grey box represents a case.

2.3 Lempel-Ziv

The LZ methodology allows for an exploratory analysis of a dataset containing processes with different scopes and their respective variants.

The Lempel-Ziv algorithm counts the minimum number of unique "productions" needed to generate a given sequence. The algorithm examines a sequence and determines whether it can be generated. [15]

Lempel-Ziv Complexity (LZC) makes it possible to identify and count distinct traces in a substring. The algorithm is based on the use of two indices: one index (i) indicates the position of the first element of the identified substring, the second index (j) indicates how many elements it has moved relative to element i. Initially, both indices are zero, then the first index locates the first substring, which is initially of size 1. Since it is a string that has never been encountered before, it is added to the set of identified strings. Index i is increased by 1 while index j remains at zero. Iterating the procedure, if a substring that has already been managed is encountered, index j is increased by 1 and, if the substring (of order 2) has never been encountered, it is added to the set. Index i will then be incremented by the value of index j, and index j will be reset to 0. Thus until the end of the string. Consider for example the string:

$$ABCAABCDDABCABCABC \tag{1}$$

LZC identifies distinct traces, i.e. those it has never encountered before in travelling the string. The result of the given string in the example will be:

$$A|B|C|AA|BC|D|DA|BCA|BCAB \tag{2}$$

with a complexity of 9.

3 Related Works

The use of model-agnostic techniques, based on entropy and trace complexity, is widespread in the study of time series and in general of (biological) sequences [4,23]. To the best of our knowledge, the works in which these techniques are applied for the study of log files are those of Back [3], and Corradini [10]. In the first case, we have a methodology based on Entropy and LZC techniques designed for the study of log variability. In the second case, LZC is used for extracting numerical features from trace sets within log files from public administration.

Public administration has always proved to be an exemplary case study for understanding the phenomenon of variability. Processes in municipalities can vary as a result of demographic conditions, problems, and specific territorial laws. In particular, CoSeLoG is a project that was set up with the aim of realising a cloud infrastructure for Dutch municipalities, to manage processes such as the granting of permits, payment of fees, licences, etc. [19–22,27,28]. In the case of municipalities, the use of configurable models offers great advantages. The collection of processes is in fact summarised in a single configurable model, and in the case of a law change, it will be possible to update a single process instead of an entire collection, which saves time, resources and also the likelihood of avoiding errors that may be made when changing individual processes. In [6] the authors observe the phenomenon of process drift in the logs of CoSeLoG Project, using the framework proposed in [5]. In the article is demonstrated that they can reveal concept drift even with a limited number of cases.

Recently, the phenomenon of variability in public administration processes has been explored by two works [9,11] who propose a log clustering methodology aimed at identifying the variants present in the collection, as a pro-processing step to derive configurable models that can describe the collection.

4   Methodology

In this section we present the VLZ methodology for applying the LZ technique to a event-log dataset. With log traces, the LZ algorithm must be slightly modified in order to concatenate the results in a unique set of substrings. Indeed the algorithm will detect new strings if and only if they belong to the same trace. The first step is to merge all traces into a single string, with limiters between each trace. The strings that can be acquired are only those without a delimiter, and in the case of a delimiter in the string, the index i is taken to the first element of the next trace, i.e. the first element after the delimiter. This is necessary to prevent the LZC from revealing behavior that does not actually exist in the log. Furthermore, without the delimiter, the complexity would not be convergent, because longer and longer strings would be identified from the union of more and more traces.

Let the log consisting of the traces be given as an example:

$$Log_1 = \{ABC, ABC, ABC, CDE, CDE, CDE, CDE, CDE\} \qquad (3)$$

They will be merged into a string of the type:

$$ABC*ABC*ABC*ABC*ABC*ABC*CDE*CDE*CDE*CDE*CDE \quad (4)$$

and the strings identified by the LZ will be:

$$A, B, C, AB, ABC, CD, E, CDE \qquad (5)$$

where, for example, the string CA, which would be present without the use of the delimiter, is not included.

Once generated the set of strings, the results can be summarized using a line chart where on the x-axis we consider the progressive number of traces and in the y-axis we plot the cumulative LZC (cLZC).

Table 1. Log1 Complexity

Traces	Strings	Complexity	
ABC	A, B, C	1+1+1	3
ABC	AB	1	1
ABC	ABC	1	1
CDE	CD, E	1+1	2
CDE	CDE	1	1
CDE	–	0	0
CDE	–	0	0
CDE	–	0	0
TOTAL			8

Considering the example of Log1. We can calculate the complexity as reported in Table 1.

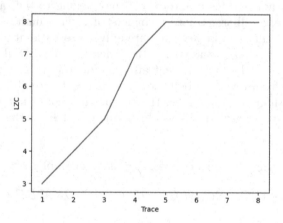

Fig. 2. Example of a LZ Visualization (drift)

Three new strings are detected (A,B,C) analyzing the first trace, in the second trace one (AB), in the third trace one (ABC), in the fourth two strings (CD, E) and one in the fifth (CDE). From the sixth trace on, zero new strings are detected and the log shows a stable condition. The increase of LZC in the number of revealed substrings is visualized in Fig. 2.

Given the nature of the cLZC as a *weakly increasing monotonic function*, i.e. $cLZC(x) \leq cLZC(x+1)$, three potential pattern can be detected in the data; in particular, we named them respectively, *equilibrium*, *non-equilibrium*, and *drift*. The *equilibrium* trend verifies whenever the LZC value, for an event log, reaches its peak after any dynamics (i.e. an initial inertial phase) and remains stable for the rest of the event log as depicted in Fig. 3(a). The *non-equilibrium* scenario, shown in Fig. 3(b), is the one in which the LZC value keeps growing until the end of the event log, thus never reaching a steady value. Finally, Fig. 3(c) shows the *drift* trend where, after an initial equilibrium is reached, new substrings are identified, therefore increasing the complexity value, until eventually, a new equilibrium occurs.

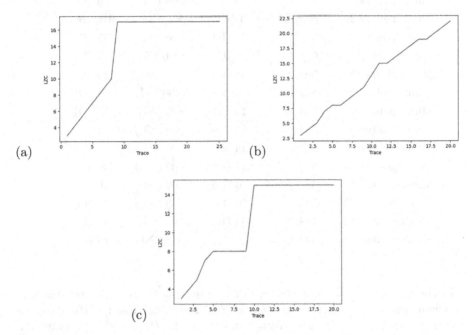

Fig. 3. Visualisation with the VLZ methodology of the *equilibrium, non-equilibrium* and *drift* trend

5   Results

We used the proposed methodology to analyze a data set provided by an European company responsible for distributing information system software for municipal administration offices. In particular, we analyzed the log of 14 municipalities considering 4 different processes *stato_ civile, cambio_ aire, apr_ ini, sin-golo_ acc*. For each municipality and process we highlight the cLZC of the process and the respective trends. We indicate with (E) the *equilibrium*, with (NE) *non-equilibrium* and (D) for the *drift*.

As can be seen from the Table 2, in the *stato_ civile* process can be observed that all municipalities are at equilibrium with a Lempel-Ziv complexity value of 5. The only exception is Municipality#6, which presents a drift and a total complexity of 8.

Table 2. Results on 14 Municipalities and 4 Processes. The numerical values given in the table indicate the Lempel Ziv complexity value of the entire log. (E), (D) and (NE) represent, respectively, the *equilibrium, non-equilibrium* and *drift* conditions.

	stato_civile	cambio_aire	apr_ini	singolo_acc
Municipality#1	5 (E)	14 (E)	500 (NE)	12 (D)
Municipality#2	5 (E)	14 (NE)	250 (NE)	10 (NE)
Municipality#3	5 (E)	14 (E)	600 (NE)	12 (D)
Municipality#4	5 (E)	16 (D)	1200 (NE)	12 (D)
Municipality#5	5 (E)	16 (D)	2500 (NE)	14 (D)
Municipality#6	8 (D)	14 (E)	2500 (NE)	14 (D)
Municipality#7	5 (E)	14 (E)	800 (NE)	12 (D)
Municipality#8	5 (E)	16 (D)	800 (NE)	12 (D)
Municipality#9	5 (E)	14 (E)	500 (NE)	12 (D)
Municipality#10	5 (E)	14 (E)	600 (NE)	8 (E)
Municipality#11	5 (E)	16 (D)	800 (NE)	10 (D)
Municipality#12	5 (E)	16 (D)	250 (NE)	12 (D)
Municipality#13	5 (E)	14 (E)	100 (NE)	12 (D)
Municipality#14	5 (E)	16 (D)	1000 (NE)	12 (D)

In the case of *singolo_accertamento* and referring to Table 2, we identified municipalities that reach the *equilibrium (E)* like Municipality#10, the *non-equilibrium (NE)* as in Municipality#2 and the *drift (D)* as in Municipality#1, 3, 4 etc. Moreover, the proposed methodology was successfully used to detect a concept drift in the control-flow perspective that occurred in the majority of the municipalities around the same period of time. Analysing the acquisition time and the time at which the drift is recorded (shown in Table 3), it can be seen that in all municipalities the drift is recorded in the period of July 2019.

In the process *apr_ini* the logs are very complex, and the complexity LZC vary in a range between 100 and 2500 and the behaviour never reaches the equilibrium.

The methodology offers particular utility in the context of event log filtering. Specifically, when dealing with the creation of configurable models using large event log collections, using unfiltered data can lead to two adverse effects that hinder the attainment of high-quality configurable models. Firstly, techniques for deriving configurable models from event logs are often not easily scalable, necessitating the minimization of the number of traces used to construct the model. Moreover, modeling logs with outdated behavior can increase the complexity of the resulting configurable model, thereby diminishing the benefits of adopting such a representation. In the case of *singolo_acc* of Municipality#1 and Municipality#10 as shown in Fig. 4, the underlying log corresponds to a simple model

Table 3. Timestamp table of the 'singolo_accertamento' process

Municipality	Traces	Start Time	End Time	Drift Time
Municipality#1	267	23/02/2016	20/07/2020	14/06/2019
Municipality#2	12	10/10/2017	05/05/2020	No Drift
Municipality#3	545	21/04/2015	15/07/2020	06/06/2019
Municipality#4	1621	16/11/2010	20/07/2020	15/06/2019
Municipality#5	7969	09/10/2013	20/07/2020	05/06/2019
Municipality#6	13560	07/12/2015	21/07/2020	12/06/2019
Municipality#7	2124	28/07/2015	20/07/2020	06/06/2019
Municipality#8	1747	20/07/2010	20/07/2020	07/06/2019
Municipality#9	670	07/12/2017	15/07/2020	04/06/2019
Municipality#10	1460	03/11/2015	27/12/2018	No Drift
Municipality#11	69	11/09/2013	15/01/2019	Other Drift
Municipality#12	261	28/02/2011	13/07/2020	08/07/2019
Municipality#13	432	31/01/2017	20/07/2020	17/06/2019
Municipality#14	2441	28/10/2013	20/07/2020	04/06/2019

with a maximum of 6 distinct activities. Thus, it is possible to exclude traces that are not essential for model construction. As a proof of concept, using only the previously mentioned logs, we run an experiment with the ETMc, a genetic algorithm that facilitates the derivation of configurable models represented as process trees [7]. The results is shown in Fig. 5. ETMc is a poorly scalable algorithm, but in this case it was possible to reconstruct the configurable models since only two logs of a few tasks each were used. The experiment revealed the presence of an unnecessary configurable point (*Da mandare* and *choose_ acc.*) resulting from modeling behavior prior to 2019, thus removing this unnecessary configuration point simplifies the interpretation (human and automatic) of the produced model.

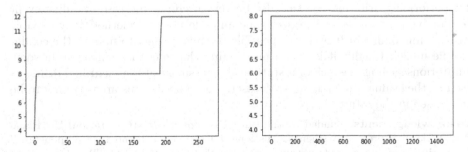

Fig. 4. Visualization with the VLZ Methodology of the Municipality#1 (on the left) and Municipality#10 (on the right).

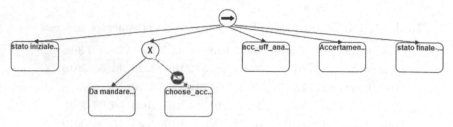

Fig. 5. *singolo_ acc* Configurable Model

6   Conclusion and Future Work

In this paper, the VLZ methodology was presented. It enables us to gain valuable insights into the dataset by incrementally plotting the number of unique substrings revealed through the LZC. First of all, it allows the visualisation of the presence of drift in large collections of event logs. The analyst can identify drift logs and decide, through consultation with domain experts, whether or not to eliminate the redundant/obsolete behaviour or concentrate the subsequent analysis on a restrict amount of logs. The presence of drift may prompt process mining to discover the causes of the drift phenomena. In a specific case, such as public administration, it could be a trace of a different law that has been further regulated, and any event log considered in subsequent analysis could compromise the specified objectives for a process mining analysis. Then, it can be useful in identifying processes at equilibrium, which can be inserted without further evaluation into a dataset to be analyzed by process mining for different purposes, such as those of creating configurable models. Instead, logs that are not at equilibrium could call attention and their inclusion in the analysis requires an ad-hoc reasoning: in fact, in the case of a number of traces too low, the non-equilibrium condition is an indicator that the log can be an outlier; while in the case of a consistent number of traces, a non-equilibrium state can identify a log with a very rich behavior. The identification of such an equilibrium condition results in a simplification and in a decrease in the computational complexity to be managed for further analysis such as the creation of configurable models with the currently available techniques. Moreover, the implementation of LZC as a way for performing drift analysis can also be very useful in the case of online event log analysis. Processes evolve over time and the use of a methodology capable of revealing online drift makes it possible to choose when to update the configurable model. Finally, it is worth mentioning that our VLZ suffers from some limitations such as the lack of a statistical assessment of the identified drifts, as well as the evaluation on a bigger dataset. Those limitations are certainly to be addressed in the future.

Acknowledgements. Funded by the European Union - NextGenerationEU - Piano Nazionale di Ripresa e Resilienza, Missione 4 Istruzione e Ricerca - Componente 2 Dalla ricerca all'impresa - Investimento 1.5, ECS_00000041 VITALITY - Innovation, digitalisation and sustainability for the diffused economy in Central Italy.
Caterina Luciani's work has been funded by Maggioli Spa.

References

1. Aalst, W.M.P.: Process-aware information systems: lessons to be learned from process mining. In: Jensen, K., van der Aalst, W.M.P. (eds.) Transactions on Petri Nets and Other Models of Concurrency II. LNCS, vol. 5460, pp. 1–26. Springer, Heidelberg (2009). https://doi.org/10.1007/978-3-642-00899-3_1
2. Aalst, W.M.P.: Using process mining to generate accurate and interactive business process maps. In: Abramowicz, W., Flejter, D. (eds.) BIS 2009. LNBIP, vol. 37, pp. 1–14. Springer, Heidelberg (2009). https://doi.org/10.1007/978-3-642-03424-4_1
3. Back, C.O., Debois, S., Slaats, T.: Entropy as a measure of log variability. J. Data Semant. **8**, 129–156 (2019)
4. Bai, Y., Liang, Z., Li, X.: A permutation Lempel-Ziv complexity measure for EEG analysis. Biomed. Signal Process. Control **19**, 102–114 (2015)
5. Bose, R.P.J.C., van der Aalst, W.M.P., Žliobaitė, I., Pechenizkiy, M.: Handling concept drift in process mining. In: Mouratidis, H., Rolland, C. (eds.) CAiSE 2011. LNCS, vol. 6741, pp. 391–405. Springer, Heidelberg (2011). https://doi.org/10.1007/978-3-642-21640-4_30
6. Bose, R.J.C., Van Der Aalst, W.M.P., Žliobaitė, I., Pechenizkiy, M.: Dealing with concept drifts in process mining. IEEE Trans. Neural Netw. Learn. Syst. **25**(1), 154–171 (2013)
7. Buijs, J.C.A.M., van Dongen, B.F., van der Aalst, W.M.P.: Mining configurable process models from collections of event logs. In: Daniel, F., Wang, J., Weber, B. (eds.) BPM 2013. LNCS, vol. 8094, pp. 33–48. Springer, Heidelberg (2013). https://doi.org/10.1007/978-3-642-40176-3_5
8. Ceravolo, P., Tavares, G.M., Junior, S.B., Damiani, E.: Evaluation goals for online process mining: a concept drift perspective. IEEE Trans. Serv. Comput. **15**(4), 2473–2489 (2020)
9. Corradini, F., Luciani, C., Morichetta, A., Piangerelli, M., Polini, A.: *TLV-diss$_\gamma$*: a dissimilarity measure for public administration process logs. In: Scholl, H.J., Gil-Garcia, J.R., Janssen, M., Kalampokis, E., Lindgren, I., Rodríguez Bolívar, M.P. (eds.) EGOV 2021. LNCS, vol. 12850, pp. 301–314. Springer, Cham (2021). https://doi.org/10.1007/978-3-030-84789-0_22
10. Corradini, F., Luciani, C., Morichetta, A., Piangerelli, M., Polini, A.: Label-independent feature engineering-based clustering in public administration event logs. EGOV-CeDEM-ePart **2022**, 222 (2022)
11. Corradini, F., Luciani, C., Morichetta, A., Polini, A.: Process variance analysis and configuration in the public administration sector **2872**, 103–112 (2021)
12. Corradini, F., Morichetta, A., Re, B., Tiezzi, F.: Walking through the semantics of exclusive and event-based gateways in BPMN choreographies. In: Alvim, M.S., Chatzikokolakis, K., Olarte, C., Valencia, F. (eds.) The Art of Modelling Computational Systems: A Journey from Logic and Concurrency to Security and Privacy. LNCS, vol. 11760, pp. 163–181. Springer, Cham (2019). https://doi.org/10.1007/978-3-030-31175-9_10
13. Dumas, M., Van der Aalst, W.M., Ter Hofstede, A.H.: Process-Aware Information Systems: Bridging People and Software Through Process Technology. John Wiley & Sons, Hoboken (2005)
14. Ostovar, A., Maaradji, A., La Rosa, M., ter Hofstede, A.H.M.: Characterizing drift from event streams of business processes. In: Dubois, E., Pohl, K. (eds.) CAiSE 2017. LNCS, vol. 10253, pp. 210–228. Springer, Cham (2017). https://doi.org/10.1007/978-3-319-59536-8_14

15. Pentland, B.T.: Sequential variety in work processes. Organ. Sci. **14**(5), 528–540 (2003)
16. Perez-Castillo, R., Weber, B., Pinggera, J., Zugal, S., de Guzmán, I.G.R., Piattini, M.: Generating event logs from non-process-aware systems enabling business process mining. Enterp. Inf. Syst. **5**(3), 301–335 (2011)
17. dos Santos Garcia, C., et al.: Process mining techniques and applications - a systematic mapping study. Expert Syst. Appl. **133**, 260–295 (2019)
18. Sato, D.M.V., De Freitas, S.C., Barddal, J.P., Scalabrin, E.E.: A survey on concept drift in process mining. ACM Comput. Surv. (CSUR) **54**(9), 1–38 (2021). https://arxiv.org/pdf/2112.02000.pdf
19. Schunselaar, D.M., van der Avoort, T., Verbeek, H., van der Aalst, W.M.: Yawl in the cloud. In: YAWL Symposium, pp. 41–48 (2013)
20. Schunselaar, D.M.M., Verbeek, E., van der Aalst, W.M.P., Raijers, H.A.: Creating sound and reversible configurable process models using CoSeNets. In: Abramowicz, W., Kriksciuniene, D., Sakalauskas, V. (eds.) BIS 2012. LNBIP, vol. 117, pp. 24–35. Springer, Heidelberg (2012). https://doi.org/10.1007/978-3-642-30359-3_3
21. Schunselaar, D.M., Verbeek, E., Van Der Aalst, W.M., Reijers, H.A.: Petra: a tool for analysing a process family. In: PNSE@ Petri Nets, pp. 269–288 (2014)
22. Schunselaar, D.M.M., Verbeek, H.M.W., Reijers, H.A., van der Aalst, W.M.P.: YAWL in the cloud: supporting process sharing and variability. In: Fournier, F., Mendling, J. (eds.) BPM 2014. LNBIP, vol. 202, pp. 367–379. Springer, Cham (2015). https://doi.org/10.1007/978-3-319-15895-2_31
23. Szczepański, J., Amigó, J.M., Wajnryb, E., Sanchez-Vives, M.: Application of Lempel-Ziv complexity to the analysis of neural discharges. Netw.: Comput. Neural Syst. **14**(2), 335 (2003)
24. Torres, V., Zugal, S., Weber, B., Reichert, M., Ayora, C., Pelechano, V.: A qualitative comparison of approaches supporting business process variability. In: La Rosa, M., Soffer, P. (eds.) BPM 2012. LNBIP, vol. 132, pp. 560–572. Springer, Heidelberg (2013). https://doi.org/10.1007/978-3-642-36285-9_57
25. Van Der Aalst, W.: Process mining: overview and opportunities. ACM Trans. Manag. Inf. Syst. (TMIS) **3**(2), 1–17 (2012)
26. Aalst, W.: Data science in action. In: Process Mining, pp. 3–23. Springer, Heidelberg (2016). https://doi.org/10.1007/978-3-662-49851-4_1
27. Aalst, W.M.P.: Configurable services in the cloud: supporting variability while enabling cross-organizational process mining. In: Meersman, R., Dillon, T., Herrero, P. (eds.) OTM 2010. LNCS, vol. 6426, pp. 8–25. Springer, Heidelberg (2010). https://doi.org/10.1007/978-3-642-16934-2_5
28. Vogelaar, J.J.C.L., Verbeek, H.M.W., Luka, B., van der Aalst, W.M.P.: Comparing business processes to determine the feasibility of configurable models: a case study. In: Daniel, F., Barkaoui, K., Dustdar, S. (eds.) BPM 2011. LNBIP, vol. 100, pp. 50–61. Springer, Heidelberg (2012). https://doi.org/10.1007/978-3-642-28115-0_6
29. Yeshchenko, A., Di Ciccio, C., Mendling, J., Polyvyanyy, A.: Comprehensive process drift detection with visual analytics. In: Laender, A.H.F., Pernici, B., Lim, E.-P., de Oliveira, J.P.M. (eds.) ER 2019. LNCS, vol. 11788, pp. 119–135. Springer, Cham (2019). https://doi.org/10.1007/978-3-030-33223-5_11

Towards Healthcare Digital Twin Architecture

Mubashar Iqbal[1][(✉)], Sabah Suhail[2], Raimundas Matulevičius[1], and Rasheed Hussain[3]

[1] Institute of Computer Science, University of Tartu, Tartu, Estonia
{mubashar.iqbal,rma}@ut.ee
[2] Institute for Distributed Ledgers and Token Economy, Vienna University of Economics and Business, Vienna, Austria
sabah.suhail@wu.ac.at
[3] Department of Electrical and Electronic Engineering, University of Bristol, Bristol, UK
rasheed.hussain@bristol.ac.uk

Abstract. Digital Twins (DTs) have the potential to revolutionize the healthcare industry by offering effective and efficient healthcare services. However, there is a lack of clarity regarding the challenges pertaining to the creation of healthcare DTs from the components, design, and operational requirements perspective. In this paper, we address these gaps by examining the healthcare challenges and presenting the groundbreaking applications of DTs in healthcare to identify how they can address the healthcare challenges. We then discuss healthcare DTs' design and operational requirements, focusing on considerations that ensure their effective implementation and adoption. In accordance with the requirements, we propose an architecture for implementing healthcare DTs, covering the steps of building DTs from data collection and integration to DT model creation and deployment. Moreover, we present the proof of concept as a prototypical implementation of healthcare DT. Finally, we discuss the open challenges of healthcare DTs and future research directions.

Keywords: Digital twin (DT) · Healthcare · Personalized healthcare · Artificial Intelligence (AI) · Industry 5.0 · Metaverse

1 Introduction

The healthcare industry is facing long-standing challenges, including optimal management of resources such as medical staff, hospital beds, medical equipment, medicines, and vaccines, especially during pandemics or natural disasters. During the outbreaks, disease surveillance demands continuous monitoring and analysis of the disease data to infer information for timely medical and risk assessment. Similarly, disease prediction, diagnosis, and treatment with high accuracy require services such as continuous mapping of data and reproducible visualizations without interfering with the routine activities of patients. Another

K. Hinkelmann et al. (Eds.): BIR 2023, LNBIP 493, pp. 45–60, 2023.
https://doi.org/10.1007/978-3-031-43126-5_4

critical challenge is a scarcity of qualified and skilled medical professionals, which mainly stems from hesitation towards adopting state-of-the-art technologies and following legacy learning and training systems [1].

To address these aforementioned challenges, Digital Twin (DT) technology has been leveraged as a potential solution. DT refers to a virtual replica of a physical object, process, or service [2]. DT gathers data from multiple sources (such as sensor-based or historical data), performs simulation and analyses, and provides optimized and data-driven decisions to its physical counterpart [3]. The continuous exchange and synchronization of data between DT and its physical counterpart for the entire lifecycle make DT a living, intelligent, evolvable, and reproducible model [2] that can support performance and prediction analysis [4]. Under Industry 5.0, DTs are widely adopted in manufacturing, smart cities, healthcare, intelligent transportation, and other domains [2,4]. In the same way, the healthcare domain has seen a surge in using DTs with incredible potential [5]. In addition to DTs, digitalization in the healthcare domain is made possible due to various supporting technologies. For instance, Fig. 1 illustrates various healthcare applications and associated requirements, enabling technologies, their roles, and key components.

However, there is a lack of clarity regarding the specific DTs components, design, and operation requirements needed to construct a successful healthcare DT and the challenges of healthcare DTs that must be considered during their design, implementation, and operation phases. Therefore, in this work, we consider how DTs are applied in healthcare, what their design and operational requirements are, and how healthcare DTs should be implemented and managed to effectively address: (*i*) personalized healthcare and digitalization, (*ii*) healthcare facility management, (*iii*) medical equipment design and development, (*iiv*) testing, training and diagnosing platforms. Our main contributions are five-fold:

- Investigation of potential applications of DTs in the healthcare domain
- Design and operational requirements of healthcare DTs
- Architectural framework for building healthcare DTs
- Prototypical implementation of healthcare DT using a proposed architecture
- Discussion on open challenges and future research directions

The remainder of this paper is organized as follows: Sect. 2 examines the significance of DTs in healthcare and Sect. 3 presents the applications of DTs in the healthcare domain. Section 4 describes the design and operational requirements of healthcare DTs, whereas Sect. 5 discusses the architectural framework for designing, modeling, and implementing healthcare DTs. Section 6 confers open challenges, and Sect. 7 concludes the paper.

2   Significance of DTs in Healthcare: Literature Review

Digitalizing the healthcare domain can help in reducing errors and improve communication among healthcare providers, ultimately leading to better patient treatment. DT is one of the emerging enabling technology to digitalize the healthcare domain. To date, a number of studies exist that leverage DT technology in the healthcare domain (Table 1).

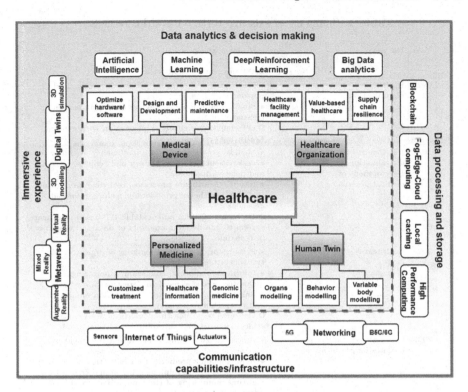

Fig. 1. Healthcare applications and associated requirements along with enabling technologies, their roles, and key components.

For example, Erol et al. [6] discuss the challenges faced by the healthcare industry, such as misdiagnosis, increasing patient demands (e.g., during COVID-19), and the need for personalized care. The notion of DTs in healthcare is investigated to comprehend how DTs can address these challenges, including digital patient, simulation of medical devices, modeling of patient-specific conditions, and optimization of treatment plans. Similarly, tin [7], the authors introduced the DT-based virtual replica of physical systems to monitor, analyze, and optimize the healthcare system to better understand the patient's needs, monitor their condition remotely, and develop personalized treatment plans. The authors proposed a framework that includes sensors and smart devices to collect patient data and simulate different scenarios (such as changes in the patient's environment) using DTs to help healthcare providers in making informed decisions.

Hassani et al. [8] reviewed the applications of DTs in healthcare and proposed a paradigm of "digital twinning everything" as a healthcare service and upgrading healthcare using DTs by considering five dimensions (i.e., physical entity, virtual model, connections, DTs data, and services). Similarly, Sun et al. [9] presented the DTs of a human heart and other organs to simulate the spread of infectious diseases and optimize the design of medical devices. Moreover, the

Table 1. Summary of existing works on healthcare DTs.

Ref.	Year	Use case	★ Problem area ● Role of DT O DT integration challenges
[6]	2020	Healthcare digitalization	★ Misdiagnosis, increasing patient demands, need for personalized care ● Simulation of medical devices and optimization of treatment plans O DTs require an effective integration with existing healthcare systems
[7]	2021	Healthcare digitalization, Development of medical devices	★ Medical errors due to data inefficiency, inability to access patients' medical history and reports, missed and delayed diagnoses ● Improve healthcare processes, real-time monitoring, and help healthcare providers in making informed decisions O Designing efficient and scalable DT-based healthcare system to handle large amounts of data and operations in real-time
[8]	2022	Healthcare facility management	★ Preconception care and logistics of organ transportation ● Information sharing, education, monitoring, diagnosis, precision medicine/treatment, medical resource management, facility operation management, and research advancement O Concerns regarding the equality of access, privacy, ethics, security, and suitability for diverse needs
[9]	2022	Personalized healthcare, Diagnosing platform	★ Precise diagnosis and personalized treatment of disease ● Help clinicians predict various situations in a virtual environment before implementing actual changes, real-time monitoring of the human body, and crisis warning of complex diseases O Difficulties in data collection, data fusion, and accurate simulation
[10]	2022	Personalized Healthcare	★ Inability to distinguish individual persons for personalized healthcare, data-driven-based chronic disease diagnosis ● Personalized DT to support individualized/personalized healthcare O Integration of technologies such as blockchain and AI/ML into a DT-based system to empower personalized healthcare
[3]	2019	Personalized Healthcare	★ Guaranteeing an effective and accurate exchange of real-time information among different healthcare providing systems ● Precision healthcare and real-time healthcare data aggregation O To support precision medicine in the context of continuous monitoring and personalized data-driven medical treatments

authors used DTs to personalize treatment and improve patient outcomes while reducing costs and increasing efficiency in healthcare. However, they note that further research is needed to fully realize the potential of healthcare DTs.

The authors of [10] utilize a personal DT (PDT) to support individualized healthcare by integrating data from multiple sources. PDT includes artificial intelligence and machine learning (AL/ML) techniques to analyze healthcare data. Rivera et al. [3] developed a DT-driven reference model that integrates

DTs, the Internet of Things (IoT), and AL/ML for health monitoring and analysis of patient data, thus, facilitating personalized care and treatments.

In addition to complementing the above-mentioned works, in this work, *(i)* we describe the applications of DTs in healthcare (Sect. 3), and *(ii)* shed light on the design and operational requirements (Sect. 4), then *(iii)* we introduce the architecture that enables a systematic approach highlighting the setup, required components, and implementation procedure for building healthcare DTs (Sect. 5). These are the essential elements to consider in designing and implementing healthcare DTs. Furthermore, although some studies have discussed the challenges of implementing healthcare DTs [7,9,11], many have not thoroughly explored those challenges. Therefore, *(iv)* we identify those challenges, as well as categorize them based on technical and non-technical aspects (Sect. 6). The classification of challenges can provide a more precise understanding to practitioners when implementing healthcare DTs.

3   Applications of Digital Twins in Healthcare

This section explores the applications of DTs in healthcare based on their importance observed during the research and literature review.

Personalized Healthcare and Digitalization: Healthcare providers can use DTs to simulate patient health and track changes in real-time by creating a virtual replica of a patient's physiological system [5]. This can enable healthcare providers to monitor symptoms, detect potential issues early, and intervene before conditions worsen. In this context, IoT (e.g., sensors and actuators), autonomous medical devices (e.g., temperature and blood pressure monitoring devices), and wearable devices (e.g., smartwatches and fitness trackers) can track various parameters such as room temperature, heart rate, blood pressure, respiratory rate, activity levels and feed them into the DT. Such data allows healthcare providers to optimize the patient's treatment plans. Thus, using DT leads healthcare service providers to personalize treatment plans for individual patients based on their unique physiological profiles, ultimately improving healthcare outcomes and reducing healthcare costs. Moreover, telehealth platforms can also benefit from DTs. For instance, healthcare service providers can remotely monitor patients and provide consultations, reducing the need for in-person visits. This can be useful for patients with chronic conditions who require ongoing monitoring and care or during the pandemic (e.g., COVID-19).

Healthcare Facility Management: Due to the lack of digital transformation in the current healthcare infrastructures, healthcare facility management systems are constrained by preventive and well-timed solutions to overcome unforeseen challenges during pandemics or natural disasters. For instance, the COVID-19 pandemic has brought attention to several challenges, such as a shortage of resources, including medical experts and staff, combination products (e.g., surgical and first-aid kits), medical equipment, overcrowded hospital beds, and delays in the treatment of non-COVID-19 related patients [1]. Healthcare DTs can mirror the physical state, and data on physical medical assets can proactively provide measures to prepare for such a crisis. For instance, DT instances of resources can help healthcare staff to monitor and manage the available resources and optimize their usage. It can analyze the operational behavior of the medical assets against malfunctioning and human errors and enables predictive maintenance of medical equipment. With these benefits, healthcare DTs can help reduce medical equipment downtime, increase availability, and create value in the medical service. Furthermore, healthcare DTs can provide an additional feature to assess the security of the assets by analyzing abnormal deviations.

Design and Development of Medical Equipment: The design process of medical equipment must follow the regulations and specifications driven by the Food and Drug Administration (FDA) in the US, Notified Body (NB) in the EU, and National Medical Products Administration (NMPA) in China [12]. The manufacturing of medical devices becomes complicated if the medical devices comprise nanomaterial or biodegradable biomaterials [12]. Furthermore, the design and development of implantable medical devices depend on other processes, such as evaluating the effects and impacts on the human body and/or organs. Therefore, it is necessary to thoroughly follow a systematic design and verification process before manufacturing the medical equipment. In this regard, DT of medical equipment can provide a design and development platform to medical engineers and professionals. Within the twinned environment, the design and engineering teams can analyze, evaluate and optimize the design artifacts of the medical equipment while rigorously verifying and validating each process before their real-world implementation. Such measures at the early design phase can lower the likelihood of defects, failures, and recalls, supporting sustainability and a circular economy. Another pressing issue is to enforce an agile, collaborative simulated environment where healthcare professionals, pharmaceutical companies, insurance companies, and authorities participate in value co-creation. To this end, the blockchain-based DT platform can enable a co-creation environment to facilitate multiple stakeholders [13].

Testing, Training, and Diagnosing Platform: The DT of medical equipment can provide a controlled and supportive simulation environment for testing the medical equipment, including monitoring and investigating equipment failures or recalls, ensuring equipment maintenance and safety requirements, and understanding the potential risks to the medical staff. The DT-based testing platform can enable in silico clinical trials that reduce the need for unethical animal and high-risk human trials [14]. Similarly, DT of medical equipment can facilitate the medical staff by providing a training platform, especially for the trainee operating the equipment. The training environment can be equipped with learning materials such as tutorials, videos, and textual and pictorial descriptions. Furthermore, the trainee's learning assessment can include a set of challenges or exercises. The training phase can extend to other healthcare applications, where health practitioners and researchers can use organs/human DTs to learn and practice critical procedures without endangering patients. Another interesting area is to educate and train healthcare professionals about cybersecurity in healthcare. Cyberattacks in healthcare organizations hold more worth, ranging from monetary value to nationwide threat-to-life [15]. Such culturally adapted educational programs can be specifically designed to provide hands-on training through a DT-based simulated environment to healthcare stakeholders on how to protect ubiquitous digital data from unauthorized access.

Leveraging healthcare DTs for remote diagnosing can overcome challenges, including increasing healthcare demands, unavailability of medical staff, implications of new drugs, triaging and screening of new diseases, and risk of cross-infection. A metaverse-supported diagnosing platform can be integrated with telehealth to provide virtual consultation and remote rehabilitation. To do so, personalized human DT models can be generated to provide personalized decisions promoting decentralized healthcare services. Similarly, integrating testing, training, and diagnosing platforms with enabling technologies, including AI/ML and augmented reality/virtual reality (AR/VR), can enhance their functionalities. For instance, AI/ML can provide predictive capabilities, and AR/VR can provide an immersive 3D experience.

4   Requirements for Healthcare Digital Twins

Healthcare DTs comprise various interconnected components that interact with each other to collect and process data for providing promised services. Interaction in the DTs environment consists of three domains, namely physical, digital, and cyber domains (as Fig. 2 shows). The physical domain refers to the physical objects, people, devices, systems, or healthcare systems of systems (HSoS - defined as a collection of independent, large-scale complex, and distributed systems [16]) that are connected to the DT. The digital domain is responsible for creating, storing, and analyzing the digital data and models used to generate the DT. The digital domain provides real-time monitoring and simulation of the physical domain and passes the captured data and simulation results to the cyber domain. The cyber domain plays a crucial role in managing and processing the collected data. The cyber domain involves various technologies such as AI/ML, which help discover insights and patterns from the data and creates a feedback loop to optimize the physical domain and their operations [17].

The implementation of DTs in healthcare can be diverse and varied, utilizing different forms and approaches. For example, EDITH creates digital replicas of patients' bodies, including internal organs and digital copies of hospital layouts [18]. DTs are also used for drug testing [6] and simulating treatment on a digital representation of a patient [10]. These healthcare DTs can provide real-time reporting to support informed and risk-based assessments and data-driven decision-making to improve health diagnosis and treatment.

The studies (e.g., discussed in Sect. 2) do not differentiate between the design and operational requirements when designing and building DTs in healthcare. These requirements can reduce rework and mitigate potential risks like technical risks such as data security and privacy issues. Moreover, design and operational requirements explain what needs to be achieved and how to achieve it. Also,

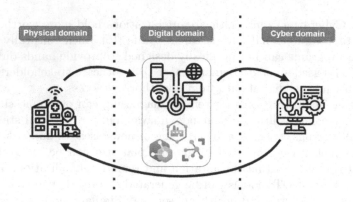

Fig. 2. Schematic overview of interaction within DT environment.

stakeholders can ensure that DTs in healthcare meet their intended purpose, function as intended, and can be maintained and improved over time.

Design Requirements: On the one hand, the design requirements (also refer as design components) involve the integration of the building blocks of DTs, including assets, data sources, services, and interfaces. Therefore, design requirements are essential for ensuring that healthcare DTs can handle the complex and diverse data typically involved in modeling real-world systems or processes. Moreover, identifying and incorporating the necessary components and interfaces leads to the more accurate implementation of healthcare DTs. The design requirements of healthcare DTs are as follows:

- *Data sources:* Data sources comprise multi-modal and multi-source data from heterogeneous sources such as sensors (wearables, implantable), medical devices, medical staff, patients' historical data, knowledge bases, etc.
- *Process knowledge:* Process knowledge defines a set of rules based on the asset (object, process, service) configuration settings, design specifications, domain knowledge, contextual information, historical data, sensory data, and behavioral and state data.
- *Reference DT:* A generic model that describes the basic structure of the underlying healthcare DT in terms of models and ontologies, called a blueprint or reference DT. Such a reference DT can provide a basis to (re)generate similar replicas with distinct functional and behavioral characteristics.
- *Services:* Incorporating simulation, replication, 3D visualization, analysis, and intelligence services enable DTs to analyze patient data, interpret the performance of hospital equipment, and so on. Furthermore, DTs must be able to monitor and analyze patient data in real time, providing insights and alerts to healthcare professionals when necessary.
- *User interface and user experience:* DTs must have an intuitive and user-friendly interface for healthcare professionals and non-informatics staff.

Operational Requirements: On the other hand, operational requirements lay the foundation for the proper functioning of healthcare DTs by specifying the necessary components and resources required to operate and maintain the system. For instance, the operational requirements are utmost to define the components necessary for the effective and efficient functioning of healthcare DTs. The operational requirements of healthcare DTs are as follows:

- *Instantiation and reprogramming:* With the reference DTs, DT instance(s) can be created and reprogrammed to generate customized replicas of the original entity, e.g., generating customized instances from generic human organ DTs.
- *Fidelity:* Fidelity corresponds to the degree of similarity between the virtual and physical entities. The fidelity in healthcare DTs varies based on context and use case.
- *Synchronization:* State and data synchronization between physical and digital entities need to be performed to obtain to-date actionable insights.
- *Integration and interoperability:* The DTs must be able to integrate with different healthcare systems, devices, and technologies to provide a holistic view of a patient's health status or healthcare facility.
- *Scalability:* The DTs should be designed to handle large amounts of data and accommodate the growing number of patients, particularly in the midst of pandemics or calamities caused by natural occurrences.
- *Versioning and maintenance:* Maintaining versions of DTs can provide thorough and useful information during public health surveillance, e.g., they can provide insights into COVID-19 variants over the period. Also, DTs require periodic maintenance and support to ensure that it functions optimally.
- *Security and privacy:* As healthcare data is sensitive and confidential, it is important to ensure the security of DTs and protect patients' medical data against unauthorized access and use.

Mainly, this work objectifies the significance of healthcare DTs and does not discuss the limitations of the proposed design and operational requirements of healthcare DTs. So, unforeseen challenges or obstacles may arise during the design and implementation process, thus, requiring adjustments and additions to the aforementioned design and operational requirements.

5   Architecture of Healthcare Digital Twins

The architecture comprises three layers, healthcare cyber-physical systems (H-CPS), infrastructure, and DT, that highlight the various components to help build healthcare DTs.

The architecture (as Fig. 3 shows) describes the H-CPS layer as a representation of physical objects (e.g., hospital, HSoS, and people), providing the structure, design, and details to create a DT of a physical object. This layer presents the integration of various software and hardware components, the functional roles of each component, and the communication and control mechanisms

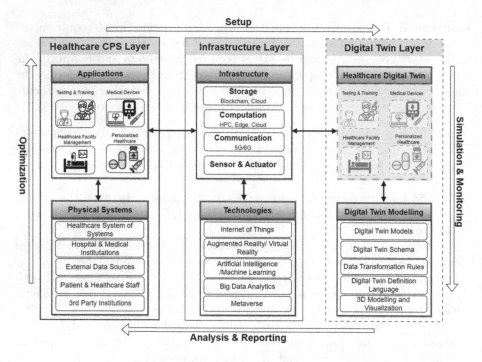

Fig. 3. Architecture of healthcare DTs.

between physical and digital space. Thus, it offers a structured design and modeling of H-CPS, which is crucial in defining the architecture of healthcare DTs.

The infrastructure layer provides the necessary hardware and software components to support the implementation of healthcare DTs. This layer includes storage solutions (e.g., blockchain and cloud), computational tools (e.g., edge and high-performance computing), communication mechanisms (e.g., secure communication protocols and 5G/6G-based communications), and sensors (e.g., room temperature, humidity, and air pressure), actuators (e.g., ventilators) and other smart devices (e.g., autonomous temperature and blood pressure monitoring devices) for generating real-time data about the physical objects being twinned. The infrastructure layer can be improved by integrating advanced technologies such as the IoT, AR/VR, AI/ML, big data analytics (BDA), and the metaverse. Such enabling technological advancements can transform healthcare to make more accurate and efficient diagnoses, personalized healthcare, and better treatment decisions.

The DT layer is responsible for creating digital models of physical objects compatible with the DT environment. This involves defining the parameters of the physical objects and developing DTs schema to generate a DT of the physical object. The key function of this layer is the data collection from the physical objects and allows real-time updates to the corresponding DT. This feature enables healthcare practitioners and other stakeholders to monitor the physical object in real time, allowing them to make informed decisions regarding optimizing the healthcare processes. For example, the real-time updates of a patient's DT can provide doctors with crucial insights into their health, allowing them to adjust treatment plans accordingly. Overall, this layer's ability to collect real-time data and provide constant updates to the corresponding DT is crucial in optimizing healthcare processes and improving patient outcomes.

The proposed architecture (Fig. 3) provides intuitive guidelines to healthcare organizations to implement DTs in their healthcare operations. For instance, it explains the physical domain in conjunction with the required infrastructure for the digital twinning of healthcare applications. Also, it entails the components to provide the preliminary analysis for practitioners and other stakeholders when building healthcare DTs. Additionally, the proposed architecture meets various design and operational requirements for building effective healthcare DTs. However, empirical analysis is required to evaluate how well the architecture addresses these requirements to make a more convincing case.

Prototypical Implementation: Here, we demonstrate the healthcare DT setup and implementation using the proposed architecture and Microsoft Azure Digital Twins (ADT) platform (Fig. 4). For example, when creating a DT for a hospital or an HSoS, we consider these entities as physical objects. They can be equipped with sensors, actuators, and other smart devices that will serve as a basis for building the DT. Next, to create a DT environment of a physical object, Microsoft Azure offers the necessary technological infrastructure, including the ADT platform-as-a-service based on the IoT that renders a DT environment of a physical representation. The ADT allows data collection from IoT devices via the Azure IoT Hub, which acts as a cloud gateway and utilizes the Azure function for data processing and transformation. This process enables the creation of an up-to-date digital replica of an in-operation physical object in real time.

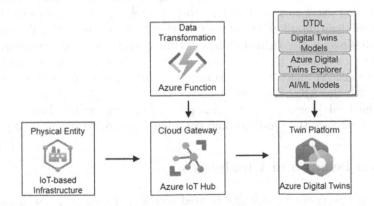

Fig. 4. Implementation of healthcare DT in Microsoft ADT.

We use Digital Twin Definition Language (DTDL)[1] to create the healthcare DT model and schema that is readable within the ADT platform. This DTDL-based model and schema within the ADT platform facilitate the communication and interaction between the physical and digital representations. The healthcare DT model contains sensor models (e.g., room temperature sensor model, temperature and blood pressure monitoring devices models, insulin monitoring device model, etc.) based on DTDL connected with Azure IoT Hub and receives the generated data from these sensors within the ADT platform.

In addition, the DT environment encapsulates the AI/ML models and establishes a feedback loop with a physical object. The feedback loop dependent on AI/ML models helps in the continual monitoring and evaluation of the healthcare system, resulting in better decision-making. For example, in the simulation mode, the healthcare DT continuously receives data through sensors relayed to AI models to comprehend the decision made for better healthcare and healthcare system optimizations. Combining such enabling technologies with DTs makes it possible to create predictive models to anticipate future health outcomes and identify patients at risk of certain conditions. For example, AI/ML algorithms trained on historical data can help healthcare providers take preventive measures and reduce the likelihood of health issues [10].

The ADT platform incorporates the ADT explorer, which enables users to interact with the DT and its associated data. The explorer provides a means to view, modify and understand the healthcare DT model and its real-time data. The explorer provides a query language that allows users to retrieve DTs according to specific criteria. These criteria include each DTs' defined attributes, models, and relationships. Users may quickly search and filter the DTs using the query language to retrieve the required information. This is especially important when a significant number of DTs are present, and it is necessary to discover and evaluate specific data subsets swiftly.

Additionally, the ADT platform offers a 3D visualization of the DT environment, allowing users to navigate, monitor, and respond to changes intuitively. The 3D visualization offers an interactive way to understand the DT environment, including all the twined things within a real-world environment. As a result, users can easily visualize, interpret, and rehearse complex procedures, improving decision-making and optimizing healthcare processes. For instance, together with the AR/VR devices (such as headsets or glasses), physicians can perform medical interventions to practice complex surgeries virtually [19] to potentially enhance their abilities and confidence before treating a real patient.

6   Open Issues and Challenges

This section covers open challenges related to the adoption of DT technology in healthcare and discusses potential solutions to address them. Figure 5 summarizes *technical* and *non-technical* challenges in the healthcare DTs.

---

[1] https://azure.github.io/opendigitaltwins-dtdl/DTDL/v3/DTDL.v3.html.

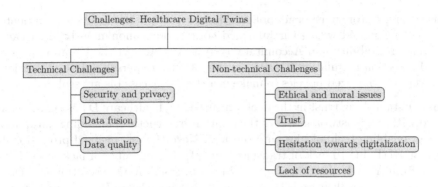

Fig. 5. Challenges in healthcare digital twins.

Security and Privacy: If compromised, healthcare DTs can become the worst scenario of information leakage. Healthcare DTs mirror the physical entities (mainly data and processes). Thus, an attacker can exploit them to gain knowledge about the underlying entity or process. The attackers may also gain access to users' private data. Furthermore, if compromised DT instances are not identified, they may disseminate inaccurate decisions in the long run. Healthcare DTs can be secured by restricting access to the data and services with the support of blockchain-based solutions [13]. Moreover, media sanitization policies must be adopted to discard data that is no longer required. Data privacy of medical data is another critical aspect. To utilize data without disclosing sensitive or private information, one option is to use de-identified data. For AI/ML model training, federated learning can be leveraged to reduce data leakage risks [19].

Data Fusion and Quality: Multimodal and multi-source data fusion make healthcare DT a living data model. To ensure the quality and accuracy of DTs, it is essential to ensure the trustworthiness of data [20]. More specifically, a healthcare analysis based on incorrect patient data could lead to incorrect diagnoses or treatments, putting the patient's health at risk. Similarly, if a study on a new medical device or treatment is based on incomplete or incorrect data, it could lead to false conclusions about the safety and efficacy of the device or treatment, putting patients at risk. Another critical aspect involves the integration and interoperability of heterogeneous data, structured and unstructured, such as sensors, images, videos, signals, speech, text, categorical, numerical, etc., each having its format and structure. Therefore, it is necessary to scale and transform the data in a way such that the quality of the data is not affected. Similarly, integrating healthcare DT with other enabling technologies or concepts, such as metaverse, will bring new data complexities.

Ethical and Moral Issues: Data quality and quantity are crucial to effectively construct and train healthcare DT models that provide actionable insights and decision support. The data sources include public datasets, clinical trial data, claims data, clinical research datasets, or data from other stakeholders. Health datasets are prone to theft, misuse, or privacy concerns. To address privacy concerns, regulators must enact policies that protect patient rights, i.e., patients' data will be shared with their informed consent and anonymously [2]. Health Insurance Portability and Accountability Act (HIPAA) in the US and General Data Protection Regulation (GDPR) in the EU ensure personal data protection. However, standardized policies to make health data accessible are still underway.

Trust: Establishing trust in the decisions made by healthcare DT is tightly connected with the trustworthiness of the entire infrastructure, including data, data sources, enabling technologies, and services. Nevertheless, medical professionals mistrust HDT due to lack of transparency [21]. For example, a lack of explainability from AI/ML algorithms results in dissatisfaction. One solution to ensure user trust in the healthcare DTs is to verify that healthcare DTs are performing as expected by incorporating explainable AI.

Hesitation Towards Digitalization and Lack of Resources: In under-resourced countries, several reasons may act as main barriers to the wide adoption of digital health, including lack of qualified and skilled healthcare professionals due to uneven distribution or concentration in urban areas, lack of user-friendly healthcare applications, adoption of legacy learning and training systems that discourse digital literacy and knowledge transfer in the clinical settings [1], to name a few. To address these issues, potential solutions include free training resources and intelligible interactive interfaces that allow all involved stakeholders (experts or non-expert) to interact with healthcare DTs conveniently.

7   Conclusion and Future Work

DTs can transform the healthcare industry by delivering tailored and proactive solutions. DTs can be used in different settings, including healthcare facility management, medical equipment design, testing and training platforms, and personalized healthcare. To achieve effective implementation and adoption, designing and operating healthcare DTs necessitates broad considerations such as data collection, integration, and digital model generation and deployment. This paper describes the healthcare DTs architecture with the mandatory hardware and software components to support healthcare DTs implementation. We discussed the new challenges that emerge with the use of healthcare DTs, including technical and non-technical aspects when implementing healthcare DTs. In general, incorporating DTs into the healthcare industry has the potential to transform how healthcare services are delivered and monitored, resulting in more efficient healthcare.

Looking toward the future, there are several potential avenues for further research in the field of healthcare DTs. One promising direction would be to develop a comprehensive DTs ontology, which can help standardize the representation and analysis of healthcare DTs. Additionally, there is open research to combine AI/ML models and metaverse to make informed and predictive decisions based on real-time data from DTs, enabling more efficient and effective healthcare delivery. Another direction is to explore the use of DTs as an offensive security mechanism for healthcare applications security, allowing for the identification and mitigation of potential security threats. Finally, there is a need to update the architecture of healthcare DTs to make it more granular, introducing concrete concepts related to DTs, such as DT modeling, DT models, DT building blocks, and DT evaluation. Through continued research and development in these areas, the benefits of healthcare DTs can be realized, leading to a more personalized, proactive, and effective healthcare system.

References

1. Curioso, W.H., Ting, D.S.W., van Ginneken, B., Were, M.C.: Challenges in digital medicine applications in under-resourced settings. Nat. Commun. **13** (2022)
2. Barricelli, B.R., Casiraghi, E., Fogli, D.: A survey on digital twin: definitions, characteristics, applications, and design implications. IEEE Access **7**, 167653–167671 (2019)
3. Rivera, L.F., Villegas, N.M., Jiménez, M., Tamura, G., Angara, P., Müller, H.A.: Towards continuous monitoring in personalized healthcare through digital twins. In: CASCON 2019 Proceedings - Conference of the Centre for Advanced Studies on Collaborative Research, pp. 329–335 (2019)
4. Fuller, A., Fan, Z., Day, C., Barlow, C.: Digital twin: enabling technologies, challenges and open research. IEEE Access **8**, 108952–108971 (2020)
5. Lin, Y., et al.: Human digital twin: a survey. arXiv preprint arXiv:2212.05937 (2022)
6. Erol, T., Mendi, A.F., Dogan, D.: The digital twin revolution in healthcare. In: 2020 4th ISMSIT, pp. 1–7 (2020)
7. Elayan, H., Aloqaily, M., Guizani, M.: Digital twin for intelligent context-aware IoT healthcare systems. IEEE Internet Things J. **8**(23), 16749–16757 (2021)
8. Hassani, H., Huang, X., MacFeely, S.: Impactful digital twin in the healthcare revolution. Big Data Cogn. Comput. **6**(3), 1–17 (2022)
9. Sun, T., He, X., Song, X., Shu, L., Li, Z.: The digital twin in medicine: a key to the future of healthcare? Front. Med. **9**, 1–8 (2022)
10. Sahal, R., Alsamhi, S.H., Brown, K.N.: Personal digital twin: a close look into the present and a step towards the future of personalised healthcare industry. Sensors **22**(15), 1–35 (2022)
11. Attaran, M., Celik, B.G.: Digital Twin: benefits, use cases, challenges, and opportunities. Decis. Anal. J. **6**, 100165 (2023)
12. Wang, L., et al.: Key considerations on the development of biodegradable biomaterials for clinical translation of medical devices: with cartilage repair products as an example. Bioact. Mater. **9**, 332–342 (2022)
13. Suhail, S., et al.: Blockchain-based digital twins: research trends, issues, and future challenges. ACM Comput. Surv. **54**(11s) (2022)
14. Popa, E.O., van Hilten, M., Oosterkamp, E., Bogaardt, M.J.: The use of digital twins in healthcare: socio-ethical benefits and socio-ethical risks. Life Sci. Soc. Policy **17**(1), 1–25 (2021)
15. Porter, S.: Cyberattack on Czech hospital forces tech shutdown during coronavirus outbreak (2020). https://healthcareitnews.com/news/emea/cyberattack-czech-hospital-forces-tech-shutdown-during-coronavirus-outbreak

16. Wickramasinghe, N., Chalasani, S., Boppana, R.V., Madni, A.M.: Healthcare system of systems. In: 2007 IEEE International Conference on System of Systems Engineering, pp. 1–6 (2007)
17. Suhail, S., Iqbal, M., Hussain, R., Jurdak, R.: ENIGMA: an explainable digital twin security solution for cyber-physical systems. Comput. Ind. **151**, 103961 (2023)
18. DigitalEurope: Ecosystem Digital Twins in Healthcare (2022). https://digitaleurope.org/ecosystem-digital-twins-in-healthcare-edith
19. Wang, G., et al.: Development of metaverse for intelligent healthcare. Nat. Mach. Intell., 1–8 (2022)
20. Suhail, S., Malik, S.U.R., Jurdak, R., Hussain, R., Matulevicius, R., Svetinovic, D.: Towards situational aware cyber-physical systems: a security-enhancing use case of blockchain-based digital twins. Comput. Ind. **141**, 103699 (2022)
21. Armeni, P., Polat, I., De Rossi, L.M., Diaferia, L., Meregalli, S., Gatti, A.: Digital twins in healthcare: is it the beginning of a new era of evidence-based medicine? A critical review. J. Pers. Med. **12**(8), 1255 (2022)

Digital Store Window: A Promising Approach for Stationary Retailer in Germany?

Sören Aguirre Reid[(✉)] and Richard Lackes

Technische Universität Dortmund, Dortmund, Germany
{soeren.aguirrereid,richard.lackes}@tu-dortmund.de

Abstract. From the most prominent fashion conglomerate to the independent market stall trader, stationary retailers face a competitive and increasingly digitalized environment. Especially the rising service competition between pure online and stationary retailers has led to a dramatic change. In line with this development, a decline in inner-city attractiveness can be observed. In the European Regional Development Fund (EFRE)-funded "City Lab Südwestfalen" project, we counteract this development by improving the situation of stationary retail through developed digitization tools. One of these digitization tools consisted of making a digital store window available to every stationary retailer so that passers-by could perceive offers from the store even if the store itself was closed. The developed digital store window helps local retailers to get more competitive by offering new services that are principal advantages of online retailers. To further improve our artefact, we evaluated the customers' intention to use the digital store window.

Keywords: Digital Store Window · Window Display · Store Window Design · Interactive Storefront Technology

1 Introduction

Yesterday, today, and still tomorrow? The splendor of the large shopping boulevards, with their brightness, lights, and attractive store windows, invite customers to stroll through the city center for many decades. However, the increasing digitization is putting pressure on the local retail and the city center as a place for the social encounter [1]. This development increases the high vacancy rate in cities and results in customers avoiding the city center even more for shopping. In this case, the store window as an aesthetical element would loss its effect and not help retailers in the same degree to influence customer's willingness to enter a store [2–5] or increases their likelihood of sales [6, 7]. Therefore, the store window must remain "powerful" as an essential advertising medium for retailers because it represents the first contact between customers and retailers [4, 6] - But it is also vital to further develop the store windows of retailers to better address the changing customer shopping behavior. For instance, customers can visit and purchase products independently from store closing hours. Significantly, restricted store opening hours are among the most vital drivers for customers to buy products online [8]. But also, the customer device is a vital driver for online shopping

K. Hinkelmann et al. (Eds.): BIR 2023, LNBIP 493, pp. 61–68, 2023.
https://doi.org/10.1007/978-3-031-43126-5_5

because customers are increasingly mobile-oriented, and mobile devices are an essential resource for in-store shoppers [1, 9]. Not surprisingly, customers need to convince to shop locally with customer benefits (e.g., personal advice) [1] and a shopping "adventure" beginning at the front of the store [1, 4].

However, the majority of studies in the window store field still primarily focussed on the aesthetical elements. 16 out of 21 studies investigated the window store design impact on the customer store entry decision and the customer purchase intention. For the customer store entry decision, studies investigated the design complexity [2], crowded vs. less crowded design [10], merchandise-focused vs. artistic design [5], image [7, 11], presence of mannequins [12–14], the color (e.g., warm vs. cold colors), the lighting, the graphic (e.g., small sized graphic) and props [15] of the store window. For the purchase intention, studies considered similar aspects like the style and originality [16], aesthetics and attractiveness [17, 18], social aspects, informative aspects [19], image, hedonic and further display-related factors [6, 20–22] of the store window.

Only five studies started to investigate interactive storefront technology. Pantano (2016) conducted group interviews to investigate how interactive storefront technologies influence customers. The results showed that most participants were unaware of storefront windows enriched with interactive technology [4]. Reitberger et al. (2009) and Meschtscherjakov et al. (2009) investigated a persuasive interactive mannequin (PIM) in the store window. Both studies positioned the PIM in the store window and observed the interaction between the customer and the PIM. Both studies also conducted interviews to gain insights into customers' opinions regarding user design (e.g., interaction and attitude). Moreover, both studies revealed that customers spent more time in front of the store window [23] and considered the PIM helpful and enjoyable [24]. The study by Campos et al. (2012) designed an interactive window (screen) with the shoe brand's logo. The artefact features a touchpad with sound speakers for marketing messages and multimedia content. The results showed that the interactive window logo grabs customers' attention and influences customers to enter the store [25]. Lecointre-Erickson et al. (2018) investigated the role of interactive technology in window displays and its influence on consumers' affective responses (e.g., purchase intentions). By doing so, they conducted a field experiment. The results indicated that hedonic and utilitarian shopping values are decisive for the patronage intention of customers [3].

Our study contributes to the field in the following ways: First, the current study investigates the interaction between the customers' device as a touch point and the store window for the first time. Second, former studies asked consumers about their feelings towards interactive storefront technology, persuasion [3, 23–25], atmosphere or shopping values [3]. None of them examined the functional aspects of an interactive storefront technology from the customer perspective (e.g., reservation function), but this aspect is important because customers determine the success or failure of new technologies. As part of the "City Lab Südwestfalen" project, this question was investigated, and an artefact, a digital store window, was developed. In a pilot phase, the artefact was tested (14.02.2021–03.03.2022 with 701 customer visits). After the pilot phase, we run a customer evaluation to answer the following research question:

RQ: What drives the customers' intention to use the digital store window?

2 Digital Store Window

The objective of the digital store window is to provide a tool that supports retailer digital transformation and help them to regain competitive power. By following the objective, the digital store window generates a digital twin of the storefront that passers can access by scanning a QR code placed in the store window. Therefore, the photo of the traditional storefront forms the basis for the digital store window.

In view of the objective of the study, only the customer functions are presented. The interested customer can scan the printed QR code banner on the storefront window. The customer scans the printed QR code banner on the storefront window, and it will be automatically forwarded to the mobile responsive digital store window. The front end of the digital store window shows the uploaded storefront photo by the retailers as a landing page. The customer can now interact with the created dots by the retailers. For instance, customers can click on the retailers' contact information dots to see the opening hours or detailed contact information. When the customer clicks on the specific product dots, he will see the information the retailer stores in the product catalog (e.g., different variants, sizes or prices). However, a customer must be registered before he can reserve a product. To do so, the customer must enter his full name, E-Mail address, and password. Registered customers can reserve the product and cancel the product reservation anytime. In this case, the related retailer will receive a reservation notification. Moreover, the logged-in customer has an overview of all customer-related reservations, the status of all reservations, and the remaining time of each reservation. Furthermore, the digital store window has an embedded GoogleMaps function to guide the customer directly to the retailer's location.

3 Theoretical Framework and Hypotheses Development

The customer evaluation will be based on Davis (1989) Technology Acceptance Model (TAM) and the Affinity for Technology Interaction (ATI) [26, 27]. Former IS studies result that applied the TAM identified perceived usefulness and ease of use as significant drivers for customer technology adaption in the retail context e.g., [28, 29]. Therefore, we integrate both constructs into our research model. For the perceived usefulness, we asked for the following aspects of the digital store window: provides a quick overview about the retailers' product in the store window; makes it easier to access product information; increase the productivity of the purchase process; is useful to get product information outside opening hours; helps to save time (e.g., does not have to ask); an immediate overview of the existing product variants; helps to get information about the retailers opening hours and contact details. In line with the findings for interactive storefront technology [4, 7, 24, 30, 31], we hypothesize:

H_1: *Perceived usefulness of the digital store window positively influences customers' intention to use.*

New technologies must be free of effort or easy to use [26, 32, 33]. Otherwise, customers will stop using it because it requires too much effort, and effort is a finite resource that a user may allocate to the various activities for which he or she is responsible [34]. Transferred to our digital store window, we asked "I find it easy": to scan the QR code; to use the digital storefront; to select products using the bullet points; to make a reservation; to manage my reservations (e.g. view status, delete). Overall, I think the digital store window would be easy to use. In line with former studies [26, 33, 34], we hypothesize:

H₂: Ease of use of the digital store window positively influences customers' intention to use.

Customers' personal resources for coping with new technologies are twofold: 1. skills and knowledge regarding the interaction with new technologies and, 2. the way customers approach new technologies (e.g., active or avoid) [27]. Therefore, a sole focus on the system benefits are insufficient because customer adoption is a function of personal resources and system resources (e.g., ease of use) [35, 36]. Moreover, the ATI results helps to identify groups with a lower ATI to develop suitable supporting measures (e.g., tutoring videos) [27]. Transferred to our store window, we adopted the developed questions by Franke et al. [27] except for questions 3, 6 and 8. Hence, we hypothesize that customers with a higher level of coping with new digital applications positively perceive the underlying usefulness and ease of use [37]. This also supports the relationship between affinity for technology and the intention to use.

H₃: Affinity for Technology Interaction positively influence customers' intention to use.

H₄ₐ/b: Affinity for Technology Interaction positively influence customers' perceived usefulness (a) and ease of use (b) of the digital store window.

4 Analysis

The first part of the survey collected data on digital store window adoption. All construct-related questions were measured using a five-point Likert scale ("strongly disagree" to "strongly agree") and were adapted from extant literature to improve content validity [38]. The second part focused on demographic variables (e.g., gender or age) and customer shopping behavior. To understand the customer shopping behavior, we asked the customers to indicate, "How often they shop at local retailers" and "How often have you shopped online?" The data was gathered in August 2022 for one month with the online tool "LimeSurvey". We collected 502 responses in total. 86% of the respondents completed the survey to the end, so 434 responses could be used. The demographics of the respondents show that 148 responses are female, 272 responses are male, four responses consider themselves as divers, and 11 responses did not provide any information regarding their gender; 113 responses are 18–24 years old, 202 responses are 25–34 years old, and 92 responses older than 35 years. 27 responses did not provide any information regarding their age. Most responses considered their shopping behavior offline-driven (271 customers mentioned that they shop offline weekly).

To analyze the collected data, we conducted a structural equation modelling approach consisting of an outer and an inner model with SmartPLS4 [39]. For the outer model, we checked the outer loadings of the items and their significance. Because of insufficient outer loadings [39], items in the constructs ATI (ATI2 < 0.7) and ease of use (EOU1 < 0.7) had to be eliminated in the model. All other items had sufficient outer loadings > 0.7 and were significant at the 1% level. For the inner model, we checked Cronbach's alpha and composite reliability for the construct reliably and the average variance extracted (AVE). For the construct reliability, all four constructs exceed the recommended threshold of 0.7 for Cronbach's alpha and composite reliability. The calculated AVE coefficient also exceeds the recommended threshold of 0.5 for all four constructs. For the validity, we consider the cross-loadings of the constructs and the Fornell-Larcker criterion. The data support that the cross-loadings and the Fornell-Larcker criterion is fulfilled [39]. We also applied the heterotrait-monotrait ratio of correlations (HTMT) and can confirm the discriminant validity with $HTMT_{85}$ and $HTMT_{90}$ for all constructs [40].

For the assessment of the structural model, we tested for the variance inflation factor (VIFs) of the outer (items) and inner (constructs) models to identify potential multicollinearity, and the adjusted R^2 level. The outer (from 1.640 to 3.989) and inner (from 1.000 to 1.433) VIF model results suggest that multicollinearity is not a concern [39]. For the adjusted R^2 level, the structural model revealed a weak adjusted R^2 level for the intention to use with 43.8% [39]. Furthermore, we quantified how substantial the significant effects are by assessing their effect size f^2 [41]. The bootstrapping analysis of 5000 sub-samples allows for statistical testing of the hypotheses. We can confirm all our hypotheses at the 1% level with a moderate effect size, except for H_2. Additionally, we controlled for a common method bias by checking overlapping items in different constructs [42], the approach of Kock (2015) [43], and the correlation matrix results (r > 0.90) [44]. All results indicated that CMB is not a concern. In the last step, we run a multigroup-analysis to analyze the impact of participants' gender (female vs. male), age (<34 vs. >35) and the customer shopping behavior (frequency and online vs. local) on the intention to use the digital store window. Regarding gender, we find a significantly stronger path coefficient for female customers for the relationship between ease of use and intention to use. Moreover, the relationship between ease of use and intention to use for male users becomes insignificant. The results also show that the relationship between perceived usefulness and intention to use is significantly stronger for male users. The multigroup-analysis for the age revealed that the relationship between ease of use and intention to use is significantly stronger for users over 35 years. For the shopper behavior comparison, the results indicated that low local shoppers have a significantly more robust relationship between ATI for perceived usefulness and ease of use. Interestingly, the relationship between ease of use and intention to use became insignificant irrespectively of the shopper type.

5 Results

With regard to our main RQ, the results revealed that the perceived usefulness and the customer's ATI can be considered as drivers for the adoption. Concerning usefulness, the results confirmed that the perceived customer benefits are critical [4, 24]. In particular, customers valued the functional aspect with an average of 3.0 for increased productivity, 3.3 for time-saving (no need to enter the store) or a better overview of the product variants and 3.4 for easier access to product information (e.g., price) and retailers opening hours and contact details. Especially to get product information outside of opening hours, customers are considered critical (average 3.6). The results showed that our artefact addresses the changing customer behavior and makes shopping possible even if the retailer is closed [4, 7, 24, 31]. Moreover, the results also revealed that the functionalities must be compatible with a smartphone to meet customers' mobile-oriented and omnichannel shopping behavior e.g., [4, 5]. Therefore, the finding extends former results in the field by highlighting the importance of the customer device as a key customer touchpoint. The results for the customer's ATI indicated that customers with a higher level of coping with new technologies positively perceive the ease of use, usefulness, and intention to use. This is in line with the existing research [27, 37]. While ease of use is generally not significant – the multigroup analysis showed that there are subtle differences between the customer. Ease of use is more significant for women and older customers and usefulness for male customers [33]. Furthermore, customers that are more likely to shop online have a higher level of ATI than their offline counterparts. This finding indicated that customers who shop online more often are more likely to use interactive storefront technology, e.g. [45].

5.1 Implications

The results indicated that the artefact could help to retain the "power" of store windows in city centers. But practitioners need to understand that an interactive storefront technology should be mobile responsive and need to provide information that supports customer decision-making. Especially when the store is closed. Second, interactive storefront technology needs to be usable for a broad range of customers. Therefore, practitioners and retailers need to know their audience and provide support measures so that all customers can use the system. Third, the results indicated that interactive storefront technology aligns with online customer behavior. Hence, cities should hire "caretakers" to support retailers marketing measures to regain online customers to show them that they can have a similar shopping experience in the city center.

5.2 Limitation and Future Research

First, we want to modify the artefact to meet customer changing needs. Therefore, it is critical to measure changes in intention to use accordingly. By doing so, we plan to extend our evaluation with further approaches (e.g., Nielsen's system acceptability framework). Second, in the survey, we asked only for the perception of the functionality without considering a specific retailer type. It must be clear that the digital store window is not suitable for every store window type. Alternative forms are possible.

Acknowledgements - Funding. This research was supported by grants awarded from the EFRE-funded "City Lab Südwestfalen" project.

References

1. Deutschland, H.: Eine kleine Kulturgeschichte des modernen Einzelhandels in Deutschland. Callwey, München (2019)
2. Lange, F., Rosengren, S., Blom, A.: Store-window creativity's impact on shopper behavior. J. Bus. Res. **69**, 1014–1021 (2016)

3. Lecointre-Erickson, D., Daucé, B., Legohérel, P.: The influence of interactive window displays on expected shopping experience. IJRDM **46**(9), 802–819 (2018)
4. Pantano, E.: Engaging consumer through the storefront: evidences from integrating interactive technologies. J. Retail. Consum. Serv. **28**, 149–154 (2016)
5. Oh, H., Petrie, J.: How do storefront window displays influence entering decisions of clothing stores. J. Retail. Consum. Serv. **19**, 27–35 (2012)
6. Edwards, S., Shackley, M.: Measuring the effectiveness of retail window display as an element of the marketing mix. Int. J. Advert. **11**, 193–202 (1992)
7. Sen, S., Block, L.G., Chandram, S.: Window displays and consumer shopping decisions. J. Retail. Consum. Serv. **9**, 227–290 (2002)
8. Bitkom - E-Commerce Trends 2021. https://www.bitkom.org/sites/default/files/2021-11/bit kom-charts-pk-e-commerce-trends-2021-18-11-21.pdf. Accessed 20 Feb 2023
9. Hansen, R., Kien, S.S.: Hummel's digital transformation toward omnichannel retailing: key lessons learned. MIS Q. Exec. **14**(2), 51–66 (2015)
10. Roozen, I.: The influence of external design elements on clothing store entry intentions for recreationally and task-oriented female clothing shoppers. Int. Rev. Retail Distrib. Consum. Res. **29**(4), 409–429 (2019)
11. Vinoditha, N.C., Sreeya, B.: Customer perception about window shopping in malls in special reference to Chennai. IJITEE **8**(11), 3180–3183 (2019)
12. Abidin, N.A.Z.Z., Aziz, A.A.: Window display compositions: its influences on youths in Malaysia. Procedia Soc. Behav. Sci. **38**, 355–361 (2012)
13. Sreedhara, R., Agarwal, V.: Visual merchandizing: soul of retailing. Pacific Bus. Rev. Int. **7**(6), 47–54 (2014)
14. Nobbs, K., Foong, K.M., Baker, J.: An exploration of fashion visual merchandising and its role as a brand positioning device. JGFM **6**(1), 4–19 (2015)
15. Somoon, K., Sahachaisaree, N.: Design elements and users' perceptual response: a case of window display design for adolescent merchandising. Procedia Soc **50**, 685–690 (2012)
16. Gudonaviciene, R., Alijosiene, S.: Visual merchandising impact on impulse buying behavior. Procedia Soc. Behav. Sci. **213**, 635–640 (2015)
17. Xing, T.: The effect of complex visual experiences and user interaction on attitudes and intentions in luxury purchase. In: Proceedings of the 3rd International Conference on Big Data and Internet of Things, BDIOT 2019, pp. 131–134 (2018)
18. Mower, J., Kim, M., Childs, M.: Exterior atmospherics and consumer behavior: influence of landscaping and window display. J. Mark. Manag. **16**, 442–453 (2012)
19. Yildirim, K., Akalin-Baskaya, A., Hidayetoglu, M.L.: The effects of the store window type on consumers perception and shopping attitudes through the use of digital pictures. J. Sci. **20**(2), 33–40 (2007)
20. Law, D., Wong, C., Yip, J.: How does visual merchandising affect consumer affective response? An intimate apparel experience. Eur. J. Mark. **46**(1/2), 112–133 (2012)
21. Jain, V., Takayanagi, M., Malthouse, E.: Effects of show windows on female consumers' shopping behavior'. J. Consum. Mark. **31**, 380–390 (2014)
22. Kerfoot, S., Davies, B., Ward, P.: Visual merchandising and the creation of discernible retail brands. Int. J. Retail Distrub. Manag. **31**(3), 143–152 (2003)
23. Reitberger, W., Meschtscherjakov, A., Mirlach, T., Scherndl, T., Huber, H., Tscheligi, M.: A persuasive interactive mannequin for shop windows. ACM **9**(4), 1–8 (2009)
24. Meschtscherjakov, A., Reitberger, W., Mirlacher, T., Huber, H., Tscheligi, M.: AmIQuin - an ambient mannequin for the shopping environment. In: Tscheligi, M., et al. (eds.) AmI. LNCS, vol. 5859, pp. 206–214. Springer, Heidelberg (2009). https://doi.org/10.1007/978-3-642-05408-2_25
25. Campos, P., Campos, M., Freitas, P., Jorge, J.: Foot-turistic multimedia: designing interactive multimedia installations for shoe shops. Multimed. Tools Appl. **61**, 471–487 (2012)

26. Davis, F.D.: Perceived usefulness, perceived ease of use, and user acceptance of information technology. MIS Q. **13**(3), 319–340 (1989)
27. Franke, T., Attig, C., Wessel, D.: A personal resource for technology interaction: development and validation of the affinity for technology interaction (ATI) scale. Int. J. Hum.-Comput. Interact. **35**(6), 456–467 (2018)
28. Bailey, A.A., Pentina, I., Mishra, A.S., Ben Mimoun, M.S.: Mobile payments adoption by US consumers: an extended TAM. IJRDM **45**(6), 626–640 (2017)
29. Johnson, V.L., Kiser, A., Washington, R., Torres, R.: Limitations to the rapid adoption of M-payment services: understanding the impact of privacy risk on M-Payment services. Comput. Hum. Behav. **79**, 111–122 (2018)
30. Klokis, H.: Store windows: dynamic first impressions. Chain Store Age Exec. **62**, 108–109 (1986)
31. Li, Z., Cassidy, T.: Optimum visual angle for fashion retail window display. Int. J. Fash. Des. Technol. Educ. **4**(1), 3–11 (2011)
32. Abrahao, R.d.S., Moriguchi, S.N., Andrade, D.F.: Intention of adoption of mobile payment: an analysis in the light of the UTAUT. RAI **13**, 221–230 (2016)
33. Venkatesh, V., Morris, M.G., Davis, G.B., Davis, F.D.: User acceptance of information technology: toward a unified view. MIS Q. **27**(3), 425–478 (2003)
34. Radner, R., Rothschild, M.: On the allocation of effort. J. Econ. Theory **10**(3), 358–376 (1975)
35. Lewin, K.: Field theory and experiment in social psychology: concepts and methods. Am. J. Sociol. **44**, 868–896 (1939)
36. Kortum, P., Owald, F.L.: The impact of personality on the subjective assessment of usability. Int. J. Hum. Comput. Interact. **34**, 177–186 (2017)
37. Schmettow, M., Drees, M.: What drives the geeks? Linking computer enthusiasm to achievement goals. In: Proceedings of HCI 2014, pp. 234–239 (2014)
38. Straub, D.W., Boudreau, M.-C., Gefen, D.: Validation guidelines for IS positivist research. Commun. Assoc. Inf. Syst. **13**(1), 380–427 (2004)
39. Hair, J.F., Sarstedt, M., Hopkins, L., Kuppelwieser, V.G.: Partial least squares structural equation modeling (PLS-SEM). An emerging tool in business research. Eur. Bus. Rev. **26**(2), 106–121 (2014)
40. Henseler, J., Ringle, C.M., Sarstedt, M.: A new criterion for assessing discriminant validity in variance-based structural equation modeling. JAMS **43**(1), 115–135 (2015)
41. Cohen, J.: Statistical Power Analysis for the Behavioral Sciences. Lawrence Erlbaum Associates, Hillsdale (1988)
42. Conway, J.M., Lance, C.E.: What reviewers should expect from authors regarding common method bias in organizational research. J. Bus. Psychol. **25**, 325–334 (2010)
43. Kock, N.: Common method bias in PLS-SEM. IJeC **11**(4), 1–10 (2015)
44. Bagozzi, R.P., Yi, Y., Phillips, L.W.: Assessing construct validity in organizational research. Adm. Sci. Q. **36**(3), 421–458 (1991)
45. Limayem, M., Hirt, S., Cheung, C.: How habit limits the predictive power of intention: the case of information systems continuance. MIS Q. **31**(4), 705–737 (2007)

ICT Governance and Management

Enriching Enterprise Architecture Stakeholder Analysis with Relationships

Anders W. Tell[ID] and Martin Henkel[✉][ID]

Department of Computer and Systems Sciences, Stockholm University, Stockholm, Sweden
{anderswt,martinh}@dsv.su.se

Abstract. The availability of pertinent, accurate, and useful information has become essential to people and organisations in their collaborations with others. Enterprise architecture provides stakeholder-oriented frameworks and methods supporting producing and consuming information products that satisfy collaborating stakeholders' concerns. However, while stakeholder analysis suggests identifying relationships between stakeholder and their practices, this has not yet been incorporated in the enterprise architecture standard ISO 42010 and frameworks such as TOGAF. The current lack of support for relationships between stakeholder practices limits analysis and right-sizing of the use of information products in a multi-stakeholder environment, where stakeholders collaborate while having different, possibly divergent, interests, work to be done, goals, and information needs over time. This paper presents a situation viewpoint that can be used to extend stakeholder analysis in enterprise architecture framework with relationships to improve the understanding of why and how information products are used in constellations of stakeholders where each stakeholder plays a role. The situation viewpoint aims to improve the relevance, design, tailoring, effectiveness, evolution, and evaluation of information products such as models.

Keywords: Stakeholder analysis · Relationship · Work-oriented Approach · Practice · Enterprise Architecture · Situational Method Engineering

1 Introduction

The availability of information that is relevant and usable is important for organisations and people that collaborate. The design, production, and consumption of information become critical for them when they must consider not only their own activities but also other's points of view and practices.

Enterprise architecture (EA) focuses on working with architectural knowledge and descriptions to manage (information) complexity and address business and IT needs.

A central EA practice is analysing and documenting enterprises according to the world views and the perspectives of different stakeholders' concerns in a holistic way that promises to facilitate the solution of problems and understanding of changes. This is supported by stakeholder analysis and management practices.

Stakeholder analysis typically involves identifying relationships, which refers to how two or more stakeholders are connected, interact or involve each other.

K. Hinkelmann et al. (Eds.): BIR 2023, LNBIP 493, pp. 71–85, 2023.
https://doi.org/10.1007/978-3-031-43126-5_6

The capture of *knowledge of relationships* provides insights into what different stakeholders do with information in relation to each other. Since stakeholders in their practices have their own volition or purpose, points of view, interests, needs, goals, and access to people and data, they can also disagree, leading to potential conflicts. Examining the relationships enables deliberations about alignment, fit, asymmetry, agreement, and knowledge transfer between stakeholders' practices over time which can explain reported problems with stakeholder engagements [27].

However, the application of stakeholder analysis in EA lacks due consideration of *relationships*, such as in practised EA frameworks such as TOGAF architecture development method [47], NAF [30], and in the standardisation of existing enterprise architecture practices by ISO 42010 [25], 42020 [23], 42030 [24], and OMG UAF [22].

Thus, the lack of support for relationships limits the analysis, understanding, and design of situations where stakeholders collaborate using models and diagrams.

This paper presents a problematisation of the lack of support for relationships in EA stakeholder analysis based on problems from an empirical case study and literature studies. The challenges have led to the design of the *Work-Oriented Approach to Information Products* (WOA) and Situation Viewpoint that can represent relationships.

The *Situation Viewpoint* offers to enrich and complement the EA stakeholder analysis by enabling the capture of knowledge about relationships between stakeholders' practices where they use *information products* (IP) such as EA models and diagrams.

The Situation Viewpoint build upon knowledge from the fields of stakeholder analysis [29], practices [4, 31], jobs to be done [48], situational analysis [8], situational method engineering [16], and ISO 42010 [25].

The Situation Viewpoint is demonstrated by the idealisation of two projects, IT portfolio management in a larger university and a research project that created an innovative kind of algorithm for handling sea transports.

The structure of the paper is as follows. Related work and the design science research approach taken are described in Sects. 2 and 3. The problematisation of relationships in EA stakeholder analysis is described in Sect. 4, while the WOA and the Situation Viewpoint are presented in Sect. 5 and demonstrated in Sect. 6. Sections 7 and 8 conclude with a discussion and summary.

2   Related Research

Stakeholder Management. The analysis and management of stakeholders have widely understood concepts and commonly used practices and are well-researched. While there are differences in opinion about the exact definition of a stakeholder, a stakeholder is typically someone that has a stake in the game, someone that affects or is affected by a decision or action [21].

Stakeholder analysis is applied within the field of enterprise architecture, TOGAF architecture development method [47], NAF 4 [30], standardisation of existing EA practices by ISO 42010 [25], 42020 [23], 42030 [24], and OMG UAF [22], systems engineering [17], business modelling [42], and project management [29].

Stakeholder analysis typically includes elements of identification of context and focus (e.g. issue, organisation or intervention) and system boundaries, identification of stakeholders and their stake, categorisation of stakeholders, investigation of relationships between stakeholders and their practices from which interests are derived, and recommendations for future activities and stakeholder engagement [13, 36].

This suggests that EA would benefit from the consideration of relationships between stakeholders that participate in EA activities or are beneficiaries of EA services.

Enterprise Architecture (EA). Today, there are hundreds of EA approaches, frameworks, methods and products such as TOGAF 10 [47], NATO Architecture Framework 4 (NAF) [30], Zachman enterprise ontology for EA [40, 52], and the Unified Architecture Framework (UAF), ISO/IEC 19540:2022 [22], that aims to unify EA Frameworks.

The EA has acquired a tradition and international standards that codifies existing practices; ISO 42010 for architecture descriptions [25], ISO 42020 for architecting processes [23], ISO 42030 for evaluations of architectures [24] and GERAM [18].

ISO 42010 concerns the description of architectures, which are defined as the "fundamental concepts or properties of an entity in its environment and governing principles for the realisation and evolution of this entity and its related life cycle processes." [25].

The ISO 42010 includes definitions of the following concepts:

- **concern**: a matter of relevance or importance to a stakeholder.
- **stakeholder**: role, position, individual, organisation, or classes thereof, having an interest, right, share, or claim, in an entity of interest.
- **stakeholder perspective**: a way of thinking about an entity of interest (3.12), especially as it relates to concerns.
- **viewpoint**: a set of conventions for the creation, interpretation and use of an architecture view to frame one or more concerns.
- **information part**: a separately identifiable body of information that is produced, stored, and delivered for human and machine use. *Note*: can be a model or diagram.

In WOA, an **Information product** is an information part participating in a practice.

Practices. The idea of practice represents the customary, habitual, or expected procedure or way of doing something, including designing and using information. While not supported by a unified practice theory, the study of practices provides insight into human activities and behaviour. Practice theories are part of the field of social sciences [2, 31, 32, 43] and the Schatzki's practice theory [6, 39].

Adler et al. [2] describes a practice as a process and repetition of actions that can be performed correctly or incorrectly and rest on accumulated knowledge.

According to Feldman and Orlikowski [12], there is an essential distinction between the value of technological artefacts and the technology-in-use. It is the ways that technological artefacts are used by agents in their practice that make them resources and meaningful for organisations.

Adjacent to practice theory, there is the jobs-to-be-done theory, as described by Christensen et al. [7] and Ulwick [48], focus on what an individual seeks to accomplish.

In this paper, the concept of practice is used to highlight the perspective that a stakeholder is using information products in their work. Thus, aspects of information products, their use, and stakeholders need to be examined in the context of a practice.

Relationships. Relationships between people, practices, technologies and other entities are considered a key part of social, economic and technical settings and are found in diverse fields, such as stakeholder management [36], actor-network theories [5], situational analysis [8], ontology such as the Unified Foundational Ontology (UFO) [15] that incorporates the 'relator' construct, and institutional logic that considers governance structures, which embody rules for societal behaviour and practices [9].

In other fields, the focus for describing relationships is on exchanges of entities or value between roles, such as consumers (requester) and producers (offerer). Examples include e3Value [51] with the exchange of value between actors, value propositions [34] with gains and gains creators, service-dominant logic (SDL) with the application of skills and knowledge for the benefit of another party [49] and resource-event-agent framework (REA) [14] with the duality of the transfer of resources between agents.

Distinctions between roles can be found in ISO standards ISO 9000 [21] and ISO 15288 [20] that identify roles such as customer, provider, buyer, seller, acquirer, and operator, as well as the duality between roles in ISO 15944 [19].

The aforementioned fields provide convincing arguments that the concepts of relationship and role add aspects that are important to consider for collaborative and servicing practices and their stakeholders. They are therefore incorporated into WOA.

Boundary Object. The concept of boundary object was introduced by Star & Griesemer [41] and examined in the paper "Crossing the line - overcoming knowledge boundaries in enterprise transformation" [1] with respect to models, which can be argued to be devices for alignment between stakeholders.

3 Research Approach

This paper presents a demonstration of results related to the concepts of relationships and roles from the second stage of a design science research (DSR) effort based on Peffers process [35], where the first stage resulted in a dissertation [45] from which the second stage continues.

DSR is carried out to change the state of affairs by designing and evaluating innovative artefacts. The steps in Peffers are 1. Problem identification and motivation, 2. Objectives of a solution, 3. Design and development, 4. Demonstration, and 5. Evaluation.

The research addresses problems relating to differences in perception and use across practices that may hamper the utility of information products over time. The design artefact (WOA) aims to answer the question, How can an information product be represented, designed, used, evolved, and evaluated so that it can participate in different practices and, at the same time, support coherence between collaborative practices within the context of the application of EA methods and frameworks.

4 Problematisation of Relationships in EA Stakeholder Analysis

While EA has matured over the years, where practices and standards have emerged, there remain challenges relating to stakeholders' use and satisfaction with information products. In this section, we identify challenges relating to using information products

(IP) in collaborative practice. The challenges are based on previous research and a case study, literature studies of related fields, and a study of EA evaluations.

4.1 Previous Research

In an empirical case study of the use and utility of an information product - the concept of capability - several problems were identified in relation to work practices [46].

1) Different variations of information products that incorporate the concept of capability were used, and the application and utility varied between work practices. 2) The information products were expected to be used by many people. However, some people use it by referring or linking to others' use, do not use it themselves, or see little utility in using it. 3) The use of an EA framework with a single definition of an information product to integrate different kinds of work products within a project may not lead to a consistent and beneficial use of the information product. 4) The information product was overlaid with non-essential meanings and aspects, and experts added their own relevant meanings.

A review of the case study revealed two additional problems.

5) The interviewees were vague about their experienced or potential use and perceived or expected utility of the information product. The answers became significantly fewer and vaguer when asked about which specific problems and decisions the information product helped with. 6) The interviewees sometimes referred to their own benefits in terms of what others have told them.

a) Thus, there are challenges when an information product does not suit different stakeholder-specific practices in situations where the stakeholders collaborate.

4.2 Challenges from Literature Studies of Related Fields

Relationships Challenges. While relationships between stakeholders and the practices in which they use IP are considered vital in many fields, they are not explicitly supported in stakeholder analysis and management in standards such as ISO 42010 [25], GERAM [18] and EA frameworks such as TOGAF [47], NAF [30], and UAF [22].

Although there exist plentiful techniques to capture knowledge about system users' basic actions and flows, such as use cases, process and goal models, and collaboration diagrams in EA descriptions, they are not used in EA stakeholder analysis.

Knowledge about relationships adds social and co-use aspects in addition to inherent and in-use qualities of IP, in addition to agreements on the knowledge in an IP and how the IP should be interpreted as suggested in SEQUAL [26].

Furthermore, an agreement is one step on the way toward mutually beneficial exchanges over time. Before agreement comes knowledge and training, and after comes intention to use, use, experiences, adoption and advocacy. Misalignment can negatively influence organisational efficiency in an organisation applying work specialisation.

b) Thus, the lack of relational knowledge limits the understanding of and fit, over time, between collaborating stakeholders with diverse and specialised perspectives, interests, work, responsibilities, access to people and data, practices, information needs, use of information products, goals and definitions of success.

A vital relationship to address in EA is found between a stakeholder and an architect. This relationship's imbalances can lead to an architecture-centric situation where architects look at, analyse and evaluate stakeholders instead of a stakeholder-centric situation where architecting is one of many practices in a network of stakeholders all contributing to and servicing an organisation's different parts.

c) Thus, not treating architects' practices in the same way as stakeholders' practices can lead to unbalanced stakeholder analysis in a larger organisational setting where the aggregated utility of architects' and stakeholders' diverse use of information products is not sufficiently considered.

In fields such as innovation, product development, marketing, sales, and start-up, asymmetrical challenges, such as when a business stakeholder once says an architecture model is great but later is not interested in using it any more, are well-known. Transferring knowledge from these fields can explain reported stakeholder problems [27].

d) Thus, the lack of relational knowledge limits the inclusion of knowledge from adjacent fields and analysis of 'cause lead-to effect' in collaborations using IP.

Stakeholder Management Challenges. Stakeholder management in EA is not without problems. In a recent literature and case study from 2021 about "Stakeholder engagement in enterprise architecture practice", 28 inhibitors for engagement were identified [27]. Even though it is unclear if any non-EA stakeholders were interviewed and their reason for being interested in EA was documented, the study points to a remaining mismatch and misalignment between stakeholders and EA practices.

e) Thus, there is a challenge that stakeholders do not engage in EA practices as indented by the applicable EA and stakeholder management approaches.

Practice Challenges. The stakeholder analysis in EA typically does not include identifying and analysing the collaborative stakeholders' practices at a desired level of detail, such as if a model fits with the need for a specific question to be answered.

While ISO 42010 discuss, in theory, the granularity of concerns and that concerns and stakeholder perspectives depend on stakeholders' knowledge, experiences, training, responsibility, authority, needs, goals, and requirements, there are no practical provisions for capturing stakeholder practices in detail. An example is the UAF [22], where concerns are documented with a few words.

f) Thus, the lack of detailed practice knowledge limits detailed analysis, design, evolution, and evaluation of IP in collaborative stakeholder practices.

Evaluation Challenges. The value of an IP can differ depending on who used it. An example is the difference in usability between an EA model that an architect produced and exchanged with a business manager that does not understand the model. A lack of knowledge about relationships limits the evaluation of in-use, co-use, exchange, and network factors that influence the aggregated utility of information products.

g) Thus, the lack of relational knowledge limits the evaluation of information products exchanged and used in different but related stakeholder practices.

Enterprise Modelling Challenges. Even though enterprise modelling is established and included in EA, there are challenges. In the paper "Enterprise Modelling for the Masses – From Elitist Discipline to Common Practice" [38], the authors bring to the surface a challenge - "people refuse to spend time creating and maintaining enterprise models, find modelling and modelling methods complex and cumbersome, or do not immediately see its use for their particular perspective or set of concerns."

h) Thus, even though an IP is intended to be used by many stakeholders, stakeholders may experience challenges relating to an IP and the way it is used depending on the stakeholders' knowledge, skills, attitudes, and jobs to be done.

Boundary Object Challenges. It is easy to imagine that externalised knowledge in EA models can be considered boundary objects when several stakeholders use them. However, do all stakeholders agree that a model is a boundary object?

i) Thus, there is a problem in that information products are thought of as boundary objects when they may not be designed as such and agreed upon by all stakeholders.

Mediation Challenges. Knowledge about a practice and the use of an information product can come from different sources, such as stakeholders describing their own beliefs about themselves, stakeholders describing themself and others, or a mediator analysing and describing multiple stakeholders. When knowledge is mediated by someone other than those who participate in the practice, such as by a business analyst, modeller or architect, biases and undesirable effects can occur if voices from all stakeholders are not heard or if a mediator cannot capture all relevant knowledge.

The consultancy company McKinsey describes in the article "Business's 'It's not my problem' IT problem" what can happen with Business-IT alignment when knowledge is mediated without accountability [28].

j) Thus, the agent that is the source of knowledge about relationships, practices, stakeholders and information products influences the representation, analysis, design, use, evolution, and evaluation of information products in practices.

4.3 Challenges from Enterprise Architecture Evaluation Studies

In an ongoing systematic literature study looking at evaluations of the application of EA and what is evaluated with respect to relationships between stakeholders and their practices, an issue relating to the validity of the results has been found.

Several studies can be argued to be unbalanced since they consider only a few stakeholder groups. An example is found in the paper "An Empirical Investigation of Geographically Distributed Agile Development: The Agile Enterprise Architecture Is a Communication Enabler" [3], where 160 respondents were asked to grade the question "GDAD project meets customer's functional requirements". Unfortunately, only 2 respondents were identified as business stakeholders, leading to questions about the validity with respect to stakeholders. Were they represented, or were architects answering questions about other stakeholders' work?

j) Thus, the validity of evaluations of stakeholders' use of information products can be reduced when a stakeholder answers questions about other stakeholders.

5 Work-Oriented Approach (WOA)

This section describes the Work-oriented Approach solution artefacts, focusing on the Situation viewpoint that directly concerns relationships. The WOA consists of WOA Method chunks [44] and WOA Constructs that aim to address the aforementioned challenges by aiding a designer to construct information products to fit into collaborative practices. This is done by examining the relationships among stakeholders' practices and use of information products. The concepts are described (Sect. 5.1) and used to form a Situation viewpoint that can be utilised to extend EA frameworks (Sect. 5.2).

5.1 Conceptual Model

The WOA is based on a conceptual model that is constructed using OMG Semantics of Business Vocabulary and Business Rules (SBVR) [33], which specifies a rich set of elements that can be used to define meanings, representations, and expressions as well as terminological dictionaries, vocabularies, and rulebooks based on a logical foundation. For the purpose of this paper, key concepts related to relationships are described in this section and illustrated in Fig. 1, but not formally specified.

An **Information product** refers to an information part [25] that participates in a practice as a work product.

An **Agent** refers to an entity or group of entities that can bring about a change in the world, such as stakeholders (a person or organisation that can affect, be affected by, or perceive itself to be affected by a decision or activity [21]) or information systems. Agents can have their own volition or purpose, points of view, responsibilities, interests, needs, goals, and access to people and data, which means they can also disagree, leading to potential conflicts between collaborating agents.

A **Practice** refers to the customary, habitual, or expected procedure or way of doing something [4, 8, 31, 46]. In an organisation, practices often emerge because of work specialisation.

Agents, such as stakeholders, and Entities, such as information products, **participate in a practice** in (thematic) roles. The concept of Participation provides the basis for representing and evaluating in-use and co-use (use in more than one practice) aspects.

A practice can be described in many ways, as demonstrated in Sect. 6. Further examples of how to describe practices in detail are Jobs to be done [48], an actor experiencing a problem or pain [34], or an actor having information needs [17].

A practice can be described at the *desired level of detail* by the addition of statements that each refer to a unit of knowledge relating to the practice, as illustrated in Fig. 2.

A practice can include descriptions of *more than activities*, such as responsibilities, features, questions that can be answered, access to data, needs, and pains that may be deemed relevant for a stakeholder's "what is in it for me" and use of an IP.

A practice can include descriptions of *alternatives* [24] and *relative advantages* [50], which can be relevant for analysing the acceptance of using an IP.

A **Practice Relationship** refers to the way in which two or more practices with their participating agents (e.g. stakeholders) and other entities (e.g. information products) are connected, interact or involve each other. A relationship is an objectified relation and depends on the practices that play roles in the relationship.

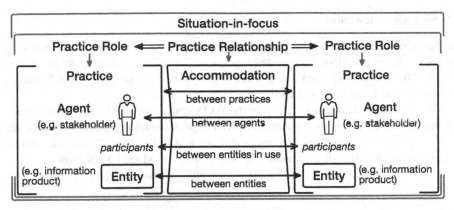

Fig. 1. Illustration of key WOA concepts

A **Practice Role** refers to how practice plays a part, assuming a function or being used in a relationship. The practice role establishes a reference point from which a stakeholder in a practice interpret themselves and entities participating in other practices within the context of the relationship.

The WOA includes the definition of three **archetypical roles** based on the type-instance pattern from the information systems field. In the 'Creator' practice, new types of IP are created, in the 'Producer' practice, IP instances of the type of IP are produced, and in the 'Consumer' practice, the instances are used.

A **Practice Accommodation** refers to how practices and related entities fit or are suitable or congruous, in agreement, or in harmony with each other.

In WOA, the function of accommodation is to with precision characterise a relationship and how entities in practices *structurally and causally fit* each other, the *justification* for how they fit, the *assurance* by argumentation and evidence for the justification, and the *effectuation* of how the fit is (dynamically) achieved through actions over time.

Therefore, WOA enables examination of how an information product produced in one practice fits with the information needs stated in another practice. See Fig. 2 for more examples of fit-cases that may be considered relevant to represent and analyse.

A practice relationship forms a composition of practices and uses of IP with in-use qualities such as usability and satisfaction into a *co-use* situation that enables the calculation of the aggregate utility of the constituent uses of IP.

Situation-in-Focus. The situation-in-focus refers to a portion of reality that is determined to be the study, analysis, design, and/or evaluation object in which a set of practice relationships and practices should be addressed. Typically a situation-in-focus constitutes a portion of a broader situation-of-interest such as a problem-situation.

5.2 Situation Viewpoint

The Situation Viewpoint is a new ISO 42010 Viewpoint that frames relational concerns and establishes conventions for representing a situation-in-focus and with practice relationships. It is part of WOA and is used in the WOA method chunks [44], where Situation views are created, modified and used.

It is constructed from the concepts in the WOA conceptual model and incorporates specifically the concepts of 'situation-in-focus', 'practice relationship' and 'practice role' and references 'practices', represented according to the Work Viewpoint, and an "accommodation". Represented according to the Accommodation Viewpoint.

An in-depth description of the Situation viewpoint is planned as future work.

6 Demonstration

An application of the Situation Viewpoint is demonstrated through a stylised illustration of how an archetypical situation-in-focus can be expressed using text and tables. The demonstration is briefly presented for the purpose and limitations of this paper.

The situation originates from two projects, IT portfolio management in a larger university and a research project that created an innovative kind of algorithm for handling sea transports. Table 1 illustrates the Situation view expressed in table form;

Table 1. Situation View with Relationships and Roles Played by Practices

Name	Archetypical Information Production and Consumption Situation
Situation in focus	An inventor has discovered a new application of mathematical discovery and plans to invent a new type of algorithm and IP kind that are intended to be produced and used to improve decision-making
Identified Practice Roles and Practices	
Creator role	An inventor who creates a new type of algorithm and IP kind
Producer role	A producer who uses the algorithms, rules, and guidance from the created type of algorithm and IP kind to produce an instance based on available data. The instance is then exchanged with the consumer
Consumer role	A consumer who uses the produced IP instance to satisfy their own information needs and to make decisions
Identified Practice Relationships in the Situation-in-focus	
C -> (P-> C)	The creator invents a type of algorithm and IP for participation in a Producer-Consumer relationship
P -> C	The Producer supports Consumers with timely and accurate IP based on an algorithm. The Producer produces an instance and transfers it to the Consumer, who uses it

6.1 Work View with Identified Work Stories

The three (3) practices are expressed by *work stories* using natural language sentences. The following Table 2 and Fig. 2 illustrate two (2) different styles of expressing practices. A work story can also be expressed using canvases with sentences on post-it notes.

The producers' and consumers' work stories illustrate that although they are using the same information product (IP), the work stories are different with different agents, access to data, interests, actions and goals. Thus the aggregated utility of the two uses of the IP in an organisational setting should be calculated based on both uses (co-use).

Table 2. Shortened Creator Work story (due to space considerations of this paper

As a researcher, I invent a new mathematical algorithm and a model kind that can improve the handling of sea transports by an analyst (producer) and a decision maker (consumer). The algorithm and model kind answer question X. Then I document the algorithm and model kind and provide education on their use. [stated by Creator]

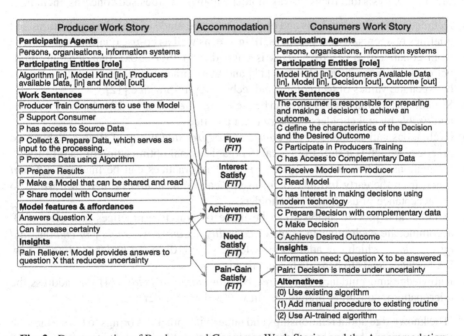

Fig. 2. Demonstration of Producer and Consumer Work Stories and the Accommodation

6.2 Accommodation View

The accommodation view exemplifies 5 kinds of commonly occurring kind of Fit. The length of this paper does not permit a demonstration of the details of How the two sides (causally) FIT each other, nor details about the Justification and Assurance of the FIT and how the FIT are dynamically achieved through actions over time.

7 Discussions

Knowledge about relationships and practices adds additional means for analysing interdependent and collaborating stakeholders in the context of an application of EA where information products (IP) are produced, stored, and exchanged for human and machine use. This includes analysis and explanations of similarities, differences, and fit between practices, stakeholders, and use of information products, as well as management of alignment, (dis)agreements, co-creation and participation in practices at micro and meso levels.

The WOA offer a *neutral* and *balanced* approach to representing, analysing, explaining and evaluating stakeholders' (possible diverging) interests. It is neutral since all stakeholders are treated equally, with no preferential treatment given to any particular group. The neutrality promise to lower the barrier for stakeholders to participate in a balanced dialogue about which information products should be produced and used. These features may improve engagement and satisfaction by business stakeholders.

Knowledge about relationships and practices has a number of advantages over stakeholder analysis that focus on stakeholder and their synthesised concerns, including:

- Detailed and precise analysis and evaluation can be made of the inherent features and qualities of agents, IP and practices, IP in-use, as well as co-use qualities that emerge from collaborative practices. This is aligned with ISO 250xx that separate product qualities from in-use qualities [11] and work practice theories that differentiate between the values of technology and technology-in-practice [12].
- Situational method engineering can be used to *situate* and *tailor* IP to be more r*elevant* and *usable* by stakeholders in their *actual* practices.
- Evaluations can be made of the *co-use* and *aggregated utility* of IP in collaborative practices, which is a shift from local to organisational optimisation of uses of IPs.
- Evaluations of how an IP can be or is used in practices can be made at *different times*, from the early formulation of use by each *stakeholder in their own words* to the acceptance of use by all stakeholders.
- Detailed and precise analysis can be made of *how* two practices and uses of IP accommodate each other in terms of *causality, means-ends, theory of change, and effectuation)*, which can address knowledge gaps [10] in the understanding of how EA Services leads to benefits for an organisation.
- Knowledge and guidance can be *reused from adjacent fields* [34] that address the micropattern, consumer preferences fit with value provider.

The knowledge about relationships and underlying practices brings to the surface the importance of including stakeholders in evaluating the utility, usability, satisfaction, and relative advantage of information products. This supports the argument that *summative participatory evaluations should complement formative expert evaluations* [37].

The ISO 42010 standard does not directly support relationships between stakeholders and their practices. A *design experiment* was conducted indicating that ISO 42010 can be straightforwardly extended with the WOA concepts to enable the standard to benefit from the addition of increased relational and practice knowledge.

8 Summary

This paper presents a novel artefact, Situation Viewpoint resulting from a design science research (DSR) effort based on a problematisation of the lack of support for relationships between stakeholders in EA stakeholder analysis and management.

The incorporation of knowledge about relationships (and practices) promises to enrich EA stakeholder analysis and management by enabling analysis and explanations of similarities, differences, and fit between practices, stakeholders and their use of information products, as well as explicit management of (mis)alignment, (dis)agreements, co-creation and participation in practices at micro and meso levels.

We argue that an application of the Situation viewpoint has the potential to improve the relevance, design, tailoring, effectiveness, coherence, evolution, and evaluation of the co-use of information products such as models by stakeholders in their practices.

Furthermore, the Situation Viewpoint is a part of WOA that offers a *neutral* and *balanced* approach to analysing, explaining and evaluating stakeholders' (possibly diverging) interests.

Limitations: The presented and demonstrated results come from design theory-building activities and must therefore be complemented by theory evaluation(s) of the relevance of the Situation Viewpoint and other WOA artefacts to identified problems. This is according to Peffers iterative process [35], which is planned as future work.

Future Work: An in-depth description of the Situation viewpoint and demonstrations of the other Viewpoints in WOA are planned as future work and paper publications. These demonstrations are planned to include designed canvases that support knowledge capture for each viewpoint. These canvases are used in the WOA Method chunks [44].

In the future work stream lies a completion of the formalisation of the WOA conceptual model, a presentation of integration of WOA with ISO 42010, and an in-depth description of the features and affordances of applying the practice accommodation.

Furthermore, the WOA provide a stepping stone for future empirical research about which relational (and practice) factors contribute to the stakeholders' intention to use, use, co-use, and aggregate utility of information products within the context of relationships and organisation.

References

1. Abraham, R., Aier, S., Winter, R.: Crossing the line: overcoming knowledge boundaries in enterprise transformation. Bus. Inf. Syst. Eng. **57**(1), 3–13 (2015)
2. Adler, E., Pouliot, V.: International practices: introduction and framework. Camb. Stud. Int. Relat. **119**, 3–35 (2011)
3. Alzoubi, Y.I., Gill, A.Q.: An empirical investigation of geographically distributed agile development: the agile enterprise architecture is a communication enabler. IEEE Access **8**, 80269–80289 (2020)
4. Bueger, C., Gadinger, F.: International Practice Theory: New Perspectives. Palgrave Macmillan, London (2014)
5. Bueger, C., Stockbruegger, J.: Actor-Network Theory: Objects and Actants, Networks and Narratives. Routledge, Milton Park (2017)

6. Cetina, K.K., Schatzki, T.R., Von Savigny, E.: The Practice Turn in Contemporary Theory. Routledge, Milton Park (2005)
7. Christensen, C.M., Hall, T., Dillon, K., Duncan, D.S.: Know Your Customers Jobs to Be Done (2016)
8. Clark, A.E., Friese, C., Washburn, R.S.: Situational Analysis: Grounded Theory After the Interpretive Turn. Sage Publications, Thousand Oaks (2018)
9. Dang, D.: Institutional logics and their influence on enterprise architecture adoption. J. Comput. Inf. Syst. 61(1), 42–52 (2021)
10. Drechsler, A., Hevner, A.: Knowledge paths in design science research. Found. Trends Inf. Syst. 6(3), 171–243 (2022)
11. Estdale, J., Georgiadou, E.: Applying the ISO/IEC 25010 quality models to software product. In: Larrucea, X., Santamaria, I., O'Connor, R.V., Messnarz, R. (eds.) EuroSPI. CCIS, vol. 896, pp. 492–503. Springer, Cham (2018). https://doi.org/10.1007/978-3-319-97925-0_42
12. Feldman, M.S., Orlikowski, W.J.: Theorizing practice and practicing theory. Organ. Sci. 22(5), 1240–1253 (2011)
13. Freeman, R.E.: Strategic Management: A Stakeholder Approach. Cambridge University Press, Cambridge (2010)
14. Geerts, G.L., McCarthy, W.E.: An ontological analysis of the economic primitives of the extended-REA enterprise information architecture. Int. J. Account. Inf. Syst. 3(1), 1–16 (2002)
15. Guizzardi, G., Benevides, A.B., Fonseca, C.M., Porello, D., Almeida, J.P.A., Sales, T.P.: UFO: unified foundational ontology. Appl. Ontol. 17(1), 167–210 (2022)
16. Henderson-Sellers, B., Ralyte, J., Ågerfalk, P., Rossi, M.: Situational Method Engineering. Springer, Heidelberg (2014)
17. INCOSE (2023). https://www.sebokwiki.org
18. ISO/IEC: 19439:2006 Enterprise integration - Framework for enterprise modelling (2006)
19. ISO/IEC: ISO 15944-6 Information Technology - Business Operational View - Part 6: Technical Introduction of eBusiness Modelling, 2nd Version. ISO/IEC (2007)
20. ISO/IEC: 15288:2008 System life cycle processes (2008)
21. ISO/IEC: 9000 Quality management systems, Fundamentals and vocabulary (2015)
22. ISO/IEC: 19540:2022 Information technology, Object Management Group Unified Architecture Framework (UAF) (2022)
23. ISO/IEC/IEEE: 42020:2019 Architecture processes (2019)
24. ISO/IEC/IEEE: 42030:2019 Architecture evaluation framework (2019)
25. ISO/IEC/IEEE: 42010:2022 Architecture description (2022)
26. Krogstie, J.: Model-Based Development and Evolution of Information Systems, A Quality Approach. Springer, London (2012)
27. Kurnia, S., Kotusev, S., Shanks, G., Dilnutt, R., Milton, S.: Stakeholder engagement in enterprise architecture practice: what inhibitors are there? Inf. Softw. Technol. 134, 106536 (2021)
28. McKinsey (2023). https://www.mckinsey.com/capabilities/mckinsey-digital/our-insights/businesss-its-not-my-problem-it-problem
29. Missonier, S., Loufrani-Fedida, S.: Stakeholder analysis and engagement in projects: from stakeholder relational perspective to stakeholder relational ontology. Int. J. Project Manage. 32(7), 1108–1122 (2014)
30. NATO: NATO Architecture Framework - NAF 4. NATO (2018)
31. Nicolini, D.: Practice Theory, Work, and Organization: An Introduction. Oxford University Press, Oxford (2012)
32. Nicolini, D.: Practice theory as a package of theory, method and vocabulary: affordances and limitations. In: Jonas, M., Littig, B., Wroblewski, A. (eds.) Methodological Reflections on Practice Oriented Theories, pp. 19–34. Springer, Cham (2017). https://doi.org/10.1007/978-3-319-52897-7_2

33. Group OM: Semantics of Business Vocabulary and Business Rules (SBVR) v1.5 (2019)
34. Osterwalder, A., Pigneur, Y., Bernarda, G., Smith, A.: Value Proposition Design: How to Create Products and Services Customers Want. Wiley, Hoboken (2015)
35. Peffers, K., Tuunanen, T., Rothenberger, M.A., Chatterjee, S.: A design science research methodology for information systems research. J. Manage. Inf. Syst. 24(3), 45–77 (2007)
36. Reed, M.S., et al.: Who's in and why? A typology of stakeholder analysis methods for natural resource management. J. Environ. Manage. 90(5), 1933–1949 (2009)
37. Sager, F., Mavrot, C.: Participatory vs Expert Evaluation Styles. Sage Handbook of Policy Styles. Routledge, London (2021)
38. Sandkuhl, K., et al.: Enterprise modelling for the masses – from elitist discipline to common practice. In: Horkoff, J., Jeusfeld, M.A., Persson, A. (eds.) PoEM. LNBIP, vol. 267, pp. 225–240. Springer, Cham (2016). https://doi.org/10.1007/978-3-319-48393-1_16
39. Schatzki, T.R.: Where the action is (on large social phenomena such as sociotechnical regimes). Sustainable Practices Research Group, Working Paper 1 (2011)
40. Sowa, J.F., Zachman, J.A.: Extending and formalizing the framework for information systems architecture. IBM Syst. J. 31(3), 590–616 (1992)
41. Star, S.L., Griesemer, J.R.: Institutional ecology, translations' and boundary objects: amateurs and professionals in Berkeley's Museum of Vertebrate Zoology, 1907–39. Soc. Stud. Sci. 19(3), 387–420 (1989)
42. Stirna, J., Persson, A.: Enterprise Modeling, Facilitating the Process and the People. Springer, Cham (2018)
43. Swanson, E.B.: Technology as routine capability. In: Academy of Management Proceedings, vol. 10605. Academy of Management Briarcliff Manor (2016)
44. Tell, A.: A situating method for improving the utility of information products. In: 25th International Conference on Enterprise Information Systems, ICEIS, pp. 589–599. SciTePress (2023)
45. Tell, A.W.: Designing Situated Capability Viewpoints: Adapting the general concept of capability to work practices. Dissertation, Stockholm University (2018)
46. Tell, A.W., Henkel, M.: Capabilities and work practices - a case study of the practical use and utility. In: Rocha, Á., Adeli, H., Reis, L.P., Costanzo, S. (eds.) WorldCIST 2018. AISC, vol. 745, pp. 1152–1162. Springer, Cham (2018). https://doi.org/10.1007/978-3-319-77703-0_112
47. Group the Open: The TOGAF Standard, 10th edn (2023)
48. Ulwick, A.W.: Jobs to Be Done: Theory to Practice. Idea Bite Press (2016)
49. Vargo, S.L., Lusch, R.F.: Service-dominant logic: continuing the evolution. J. Acad. Market. Sci. 36(1), 1–10 (2008)
50. Venkatesh, V., Morris, M.G., Davis, G.B., Davis, F.D.: User acceptance of information technology - toward a unified view. MIS Q. 27(3), 425 (2003)
51. Weigand, H.: The E3value ontology for value networks-current state and future directions. J. Inf. Syst. 30(2), 113–133 (2016)
52. Zachman John, A. (2023). https://www.zachman.com/about-the-zachman-framework

Developing Digital Competencies in Small and Medium-Sized Enterprises Through Microlearning Applications: A Research Agenda

Ekaterina Veldyaeva[✉] 📵, Lukas R. G. Fitz📵, and Jochen Scheeg

Department of Business and Management, Brandenburg University of Applied Sciences, Magdeburger Str. 50, 14770 Brandenburg an der Havel, Germany
{veldyaev, fitz, scheeg}@th-brandenburg.de

Abstract. This article presents a research outline on the use of microlearning applications to develop digital competencies in Small and Medium-sized Enterprises (SMEs). The digital transformation of businesses has become essential for their survival, and SMEs need to develop digital competencies (DC) to remain competitive in the market. Microlearning (ML), a form of learning that involves small, bite-sized learning modules, has been gaining popularity in recent years as a way to efficiently and effectively develop skills. Through a semi-systematic literature review approach, our study examines prevalent knowledge in the area of ML and DC and discusses interrelations. As a result, we propose a research roadmap consisting of six research questions targeting four dimensions of ML for DC development in SMEs: 1) context, 2) formats, 3) reward system, and 4) complexity level.

Keywords: Digital Competencies · Microlearning · SME

1 Introduction

The significance of Digital Transformation (DT) for small and medium-sized enterprises (SME) has been highlighted in recent years by information systems scholars [1, 2]. DT refers to change processes within a company through the integration of new digital technologies, typically intending to enhance business performance or leverage new strategies or business models [2]. Many incumbent companies have been outperformed by innovative digital businesses in the past and consequently struggled to keep up with the development [3]. SMEs constitute over 99% of all businesses in the EU and serve as the foundation of the European economy [4]. DT is considered a paradigm to SMEs' future readiness. Implicitly, the introduction of digital technology in SMEs is expected to lead to strategic advantage and improve future-readiness in areas such as Industry 4.0 [5]. Recent research has tackled several problems regarding SMEs' engagement in DT. A primary objective, though, is to develop innovative capabilities and approach DT initiatives strategically [6]. According to the European Commission's definition, SMEs employ fewer than 250 persons, have an annual turnover not exceeding €50 million, or

K. Hinkelmann et al. (Eds.): BIR 2023, LNBIP 493, pp. 86–104, 2023.
https://doi.org/10.1007/978-3-031-43126-5_7

have an annual balance sheet total not exceeding €43 million [7]. Hence, taking into account SMEs' limited resources, lacking knowledge and biased understanding of new digital technologies [5], acquiring digital competencies (DC) is becoming both essential [8] and challenging for SMEs. Although some findings indicate that the practical use of technology inherently develops organizational DC [9], the question remains how learning concepts may be designed to enable SME actors to leverage the full DT potential in a self-efficate manner.

In this article, we focus on the concept of Microlearning (ML) as an emerging global topic, which is considered a promising research direction [10]. In essence, ML can be described as a technology-enhanced learning concept [11], in which smaller segments of e-Learning content are comprehensively delivered in very short time [12]. Such segments as learning objects, created in the ML context, are called microcontents. Through these, competencies may be put across in only three to five minutes [13]. Researchers also mention the important role of technology in the development of ML [10]. Electronic microcontents are often informal and can be separated to form new learning paths and patterns [14]. Conducting a literature review, this article aims to shed light onto the current state of research regarding DC development in SMEs for DT. Consequently, it highlights research gaps and develops new research avenues contributing to theoretical information systems (IS) research in the conjunction of small business, e-learning and gamification.

2 Background and Related Work

SMEs differ from large companies in terms of their characteristics, but also regards behavior. Table 1 summarizes and describes considerable key limitations of SMEs, which are often mentioned in literature contextualized with DT.

Researchers suggest that a primary objective is to enhance SMEs' digital skills and workforce [8]. Implicitly, there is a need to improve training and educational systems at all levels and SMEs must ensure that their training aligns with best practices for successful DT. Proper training might not only develop necessary skills but also employees' sense of ownership in the company's success [8].

Previous research also identified the need for an information culture in SMEs, whereby the quality and relevance of information shared between employees is of importance [20]. For instance, internal organizational knowledge can build a sustainable competitive advantage for enterprises [25, 26] and is considered a strategic resource for the formation of organizational DCs [20]. SMEs pursuing such developments are typically facing the challenging decision whether to further invest in training of prevalent staff or in the acquisition of new, digitally affine specialists [27]. New digital skills helping to overcome DT barriers are often a part of DC concepts proposed in the literature [28–31]. The researchers mostly underline the importance of ensuring DC for every individual in a digitalized world [28]. They also state that the successful use of information and communication technology (ICT) could be facilitated if SMEs had employees mastering one or two DC areas. This would help them acquire sufficient knowledge, skills, and attitudes [32] in parallel. In addition, DCs are also considered increasingly relevant for the development of other competencies in general [30].

Table 1. Characteristics of SMEs from the literature

SME characteristics	Description	Source
Lack of resources and financing	SMEs have limited financial and human resources to invest in DT initiatives	[9, 15–18]
Limited (IT) knowledge and skills	Employees have insufficient digital skills and it is difficult for SMEs to attract new staff with sufficient knowledge and skills in IT due to limited networks and small companies' size	[5, 8, 9, 15, 19, 20]
Low awareness	There is a lack of digital awareness in SMEs, low awareness of the importance of (IT) skills development, and lacking access to infrastructure	[5, 21]
Entrepreneurial orientation	SME managers and owners are often involved in processes and decision-making relying on their vision; managers often lack knowledge of change and digital innovation	[8, 17, 22, 23]
Flexibility and agility	SMEs are more agile and adaptable to changing market conditions than larger companies due to their smaller size, which can be leveraged through DT initiatives	[17, 24]

In response to these challenges, ML is considered an appropriate concept for work-based learning [12]. According to pre-pandemic statistics, ML was used by 27 percent of all retail companies in North America in 2017, as well as by 25 percent of manufacturing and logistics enterprises, finance and insurance organizations [33]. Statistics however do not provide any data on the size of these companies. In a worldwide survey in 2019, only nine percent of enterprises were about to explore ML platforms as a new learning tools [34]. Along with the introduction of ML, researchers often propose a concept of competency-based learning, which is often used the context of students' learning. However, Camacho and Legare [35] refer to the Micro-e-Learning conception also for professional development, deeming that a competency-based approach was more robust than a traditional learning system [36]. Moreover, the learning culture in enterprises can be improved by applying ML [37]. Other techniques such as subscription learning within a competence-based ML strategy for organizations may be used to enhance the performance of employees [13].

In the current body of literature, only few articles discuss the development of DCs in SMEs. For instance, Plattfaut and Borghoff [38, 39] conducted action studies with cooperating SMEs and found that external support was needed to establish adequate mindsets and skills. Their ongoing research targets the implementation of workshops and process digitalization to tackle the issue, since the lack of digital skills among SME employees was found to limit the company's capabilities for change and innovation. Asadullah et al. [9] observed SMEs "going online" in the digital platform economy. Through interviews, the authors took a learning perspective and investigated the development of organizational capabilities by using digital platforms. They found that digital platforms may help SMEs to develop operational and dynamic innovation capabilities based on accumulated experience, socializing and development of new skills. Furthermore, the SMEs learned from educational materials provided by the platform providers. However, if such resources were too basic and did not contain any advanced content, it could also hinder learning. The use of inaccurate information and the equivocality of the learning process on the platforms could also inhibit DC development in SMEs.

Another relevant dimension to DC development is decision-making in SMEs. The need to acquire new skills is of particular interest for small business managers if they intend to consider multiple knowledge-generation options [27]. Weigel et al. [40] examined IT competence profiles of 19 SME leaders and found that DCs might be subdivided into explicit knowledge and mere experience with IT. According to the authors, DT navigated by leaders without explicit IT skills may still be successful if they were flexible, adaptable, and able to profit from learning structures and cooperation. Within such cooperation, trust was identified as a major decisive factor, since confidence when selecting external partners also depended on IT experience.

Interestingly, change readiness and capabilities are often taken into account when evaluating competency-building effort. For instance, [9, 38, 39] draw upon the concept of dynamic capabilities, meaning capabilities aiming a strategic change within an organization [41], to describe SMEs' abilities between sensing a need for change and taking transformative action. Song and Qureshi [42] developed their own "IT Therapy" framework suggesting external IT intervention to start from "problematization" and translating onwards to "interessement", "enrollment" and finally "mobilization" of micro-firms towards technology adoption and training. A so-called therapeutic phase was also recommended by Deegan et al. [43]: workshops and a mentoring program were set up and evaluated as measures for local government IT intervention. It was concluded that individual factors such as lacking IT skills and knowledge could be addressed by Basic IT Use workshops while mentoring programs were rather suitable to promote organizational factors such as efficiency.

In sum, the importance of organizational knowledge [25] and DC is described in the literature, and researchers propose cross-disciplinary studies in the context of applying ML in an organizational environment for workplace learning [10]. Nevertheless, it seems like little focus had been set on learning concepts targeting DCs for SMEs in practice. Therefore, we manifest the relevance and rigor of this article by proposing the following research question (RQ): *How can ML applications be designed to help SMEs develop DCs?*

3   Research Model

In response to the RQ and considering the nascent state of research around the identified research gap, we apply a twofold research approach featuring a semi-systematic literature review (SSLR) followed by a research outline proposal and discussion. For a broad understanding of the constraints in this research direction, we investigate two streams in IS and Business research: 1) ML applied in practice, to develop an understanding of related work and identify helpful concepts for our topic; 2) variety and characteristics of DC concepts, to derive a set of potential target DCs for SMEs.

The semi-systematic approach [44, 45] was considered most effective to gain an overview of relevant research and its progression over time [44, 45]. This approach presents a type of literature review that includes a systematic search extraction process, however, it does not lead to a fully systematic analysis. Instead, it aims to identify and understand all potentially relevant research traditions that have implications for the topic of our study and summarize them using meta-narratives rather than measuring effect size [45].

Moreover, our SSLR can be characterized as a scoping review, drawing upon the typology of Paré et al. [46]. Such reviews focus on breadth rather than depth of coverage, and the synthesized evidence may be presented in tabular form using thematic analysis. As proposed by Webster and Watson [46], key findings will be summarized in a concept-centric manner.

4   Literature Review

In the course of conducting this SSLR, we followed a four-step approach for comprehensive search strategy as proposed by Snyder [44]. In the first phase, which has yet been described, we designed our research by defining the aims of the research, a research question, and methodology. Now, after specifying the search strategy, we conduct the literature search and analyze the search results. In the final stage, all information is structured and synthesized. First, we aimed to overview the existing concepts of applying ML in practice. Secondly, a review centered around DC concepts was conducted. The subsequent analysis focused on the themes and patterns that emerged from the literature, as well as the gaps and inconsistencies that were identified.

4.1   Search

The databases searched included ACM Digital Library, AIS e-Library, IEEE Xplore, and Springer Link. Only full texts in English were included. Forward and backward searches were conducted to find background literature, primary sources, or findings built upon the collected papers. The keywords and extraction criteria applied for each search direction will be explained in the following.

The research dynamics on ML show an increasing number of relevant papers. For instance, more than 50% of the papers provided by IEEE Xplore based on the keyword "micro learning" have been published in the last four years. Results from ACM Digital Library on the same keyword showed an increasing amount of papers since 2019, which account for almost 30% of the total outcome. In our SSLR, the keywords "micro learning" and "microlearning" were used. Thematically, our search aimed at practical application scenarios in which ML had been implemented and studied. Therefore, all papers concerning ML system architecture, learning algorithms, improvement of technical features, micro assessment, or "mobile learning" without "micro" specification were excluded.

The search on the keyword "digital competenc*" returned papers from different research fields and most of the found studies were conducted in education research. In IEEE Xplore, more than 60% of the papers mentioning DC were published in the last four years. Given our interest in "IT therapy" for SMEs, papers dealing with DC development were particularly extracted. After selecting relevant papers, an additional backward search was conducted, since most of the identified articles were strongly related to older literature.

4.2 Results on Applied ML

Six concepts centered around applied microlearning in practice have been found and thematically grouped as proposed by Webster and Watson [46]. Table 2 lists the identified concepts and references the papers assigned.

Table 2. Concepts in Research regarding ML

Concept		References
C1.1	Language Teaching	[47–52]
C1.2	Professional Training (work-related)	[11–13, 53–65]
C1.3	Mobile Feature in e-Learning	[49, 54–58, 60, 62, 64, 66, 67]
C1.4	Tackling Human Learning Problems	[68–73]
C1.5	Integration with Social Web	[51, 52, 73–76]
C1.6	Enabler for Gamification Approaches	[54, 55, 68, 77]

- **Mobile Feature in e-Learning.** For about twenty years, ML has been regarded as a special type of e-learning [78]. We find that a majority of papers were concerned with online or e-learning in environments like higher education, schools, or MOOCs. Therein, ML solutions were proposed, designed, or used as a mobile extension, adaption, or alternative to traditional technology-enhanced learning. Since researchers targeted the development of e-Learning towards a more ubiquitous learning environment through mobile ML features, this concept was considered relevant to stand separately.
- **Professional Training.** This concept groups papers about ML solutions training users' knowledge, capabilities, or competencies in a professional, work-related context. While some authors address the topic on a general level, more specific target domains included medical education, health care, and IT-related skills.

- **Language Teaching.** Studies, which used ML in the specific context of language teaching, are allocated to this concept. Five out of six articles dealt with vocabulary training, and one with intonation.
- **Tackling Human Learning Problems.** In contrast to the other concepts, which are mainly aimed at enhancing traditional learning through ML, this concept attempts to limit human learning problems in various contexts. We found that such hindering factors include procrastination, low attention or distraction, low motivation, difficult learning environments, or mental burnout.
- **Integration with Social Web.** The common concept of the papers allocated here is the idea of integrating ML features in social web environments like social media feeds or messengers. It aims at enhancing learning progress or frequency. Such channels included Telegram, Facebook, and text messages.
- **Enabler for Gamification Approaches.** Serious games researchers utilize the ML components as an enabling format for mobile gamified learning. Gamification-related papers are grouped in this concept.

Regarding our research focus and research questions, this part of the SSLR confirmed the outcome of Busse et al. [11], who found that IS research has barely touched ML in the context of building DC. While individual IT capabilities like programming [62] or operating system basics [60] were taught via ML formats in the context of professional training, no authors studied such competency development in an organizational, business-related context. Nevertheless, this review shows that a lot of conceptual work around ML utilization in education itself is still to be done.

The work of Busse et al. [11] seems especially relevant for our research. Among all ML-supported competencies identified by the authors, digital competence and professional competence stick out in particular as relatable to the SME context. First of all, the empirical study confirmed that digital competence can be developed as a side effect of different media usage and application of ML together with other e-Learning formats. In return, the use of ML applications also requires some level of digital competence. On top of that, employees found embedded ML in a learning concept more useful for developing basic professional knowledge compared to understanding complex topics in a whole. In more recent research, Busse et al. [79] present design patterns for enterprise ML solutions. Therein, they propose the use of micro contents, which are expected to be especially beneficial when integrated in employees' everyday-work routines.

At this stage of our SSLR, we could not determine any recent typology of ML formats. According to the variety in the collected body of literature, ML can be applied, for instance, in form of short videos, game-based entities, or textual blocks. However, we find that the latest general classification of ML types dates back to 2005 [80] and can barely be applied in modern research regarding new emerging formats, also considering the rapid development of digital technology in the past two decades. This indicates another possible research gap in the area of ML, since a structured typology of existing formats would be helpful, particularly for practice-oriented case studies.

4.3 Results on DCs

This section presents eight DC-related concepts from the extracted literature and discusses its understanding from an individual and organizational perspective. Table 3 lists the identified concepts [46] and references the papers assigned.

Table 3. Concepts in Research regarding DC

Concept		References
C2.1	Organizational Competencies	[20, 29, 31, 32, 81]
C2.2	Professional Expertise	[20, 31, 32, 82]
C2.3	Mindset	[28, 30, 32, 83–85]
C2.4	Communication and Social Competencies	[28, 30, 32, 82, 85]
C2.5	Technical Skills	[28, 29, 31, 32, 83]
C2.6	Learning	[28–32, 83, 85]
C2.7	Use of Technology	[20, 31, 32, 81, 84, 85]

- **Organizational Competencies.** This concept includes competencies, which are important for businesses in an organizational context. Amongst the most mentioned are process design, allocation of resources, governance, organizational culture and strategic alignment. Other organizational competencies concern financial aspects such as ICT investment and capturing value thereof.
- **Professional Expertise.** This concept summarizes methodical and professional expertise of employees, their self-competence, key skills for work, and knowledge.
- **Mindset.** The DC mindset concept refers to a set of cognitive, affective, and behavioral dispositions that influence how individuals process and respond to information and experiences. This includes attitudes toward learning, critical thinking skills, creativity, and problem-solving abilities. It can also include beliefs about intelligence, motivation, and effort, as well as the ability to adapt to changing situations and persevere in the face of challenges.
- **Communication and Social Competencies.** Most studies included the ability to communicate and cooperate both virtually and in real life. Though, the use of digital tools for communication is also considered an essential DC element. This concept also includes social intelligence, social understanding, and an intercultural attitude.
- **Technical Skills.** As one of the core DC concepts, this one is centered around individual and organizational technical skills on different levels. Most often, these are instrumental and advanced skills of employees, for instance in media application, learning, and information management as well as ICT-handling and further e-skills.
- **Learning.** This concept refers to the synthesis of information and knowledge for training, learning, and education of employees.
- **Use of Technology.** The prevalence and development of digital infrastructure in enterprises, and the self-efficacious participation in a digitalized culture, form this concept.

The use of digital technologies is an essential part of digital integration in studies on DC.

ICT skills and competencies in SMEs have been discussed in academic literature since the 1980s [31]. However, the analysis of DCs especially in SMEs often lacks structure [31] and there is no consistent nor agreed definition of DCs in previous research [86]. Moreover, researchers emphasize a need for empirical research on DCs in SMEs [82]. Current research rather provides a wide overview and comparison of DC concepts [32, 82, 83] and an understanding of DC from different perspectives. In the current state of literature, researchers do not agree on one consistent definition of DC. However, two definitions proposed in previous studies are cited the most in individual and organizational, SME-related contexts: the definition of DC for SMEs proposed by Vieru et al. [32] is fundamentally similar to the DC understanding for individuals by Ferrari [83]. Building upon both definitions, the central aspects of DC are (1) the use of digital technology, (2) critical thinking and evaluation, (3) building/developing knowledge and digital skills and (4) solving emerging problems. The terms capabilities and competencies may also be distinguished, as proposed by Lehner et al. [31]. According to the authors, capabilities were core competencies of an enterprise, while individual abilities of employees were called skills and competencies. In fact, individual employees' skills were essential components of the earlier DC framework, too [29].

In sum, we derive from the SSLR that individual competencies should be considered as an essential part of organizational DCs. Almost all concepts proposed in an organizational, SME-related context, are rooted in such individual competencies, skills, capabilities, and personal knowledge of employees [20, 29, 31, 32], or self-competence [82]. Among the concepts in Table 3, C2.2-C2.5 refer to individual competencies of employees and represent their skills and abilities (C2.3, C2.5), expertise (C2.2), and attitudes (C2.3). C2.6 includes personal knowledge and self-determined learning of employees, which builds organizational knowledge in SMEs. C2.7 has elements of personal competencies, such as individual ability and motivation to use technology, which can form overall organizational digital integration and technology adoption. C2.1 summarizes DCs, which are relevant at the overall organizational level.

4.4 Summary

Although different concepts for applying ML in various contexts already exist in the research landscape, our SSLR confirms that ML has not yet been discussed as a solution for building DCs in SMEs yet. We therefore derive a limited validation of our RQ from the SSLR. Another research gap concerns the development of DCs, especially in SMEs [32], in spite of mentioning a problematic lack of ICT skills [31], training and education [32] in SMEs. Furthermore, it was often agreed that there is a need for new learning culture and learning strategies [8, 9, 15, 19]. Also, both definitions of DC most cited in literature [30, 32] mention building or developing knowledge as an essential goal of an individual or an organization. Overall, DC is considered important for enterprises, as it positively affects the whole organizational performance [81, 87]. Since Vieru et al.'s [32] conceptualization of DC was particularly focused on SMEs, while we could not identify any deviating aspects in the remaining literature, it seems viable to build upon Vieru et al. when developing a future research outline.

5 Discussion and Future Research Outline

Referring to the initially determined SME characteristics, SME requirements for ML solutions to overcome DT barriers may be summarized as follows. SMEs require 1) financial support and acquiring qualified human resources, 2) development of digital skills and knowledge of employees, and 3) increase of digital awareness among employees and managers. In the light of ML-based DC development in SMEs and potential future research opportunities in this direction, we argue that target dimensions 2) and 3) are especially relevant. Based on the SSLR outcome in conjunction with these SME requirements, we propose and elaborate on two hypotheses in this section. Figure 1 shows the proposed links between DC and ML dimensions derived from the SSLR and thereby visualizes the meta-narrative of our hypotheses, too.

Hypothesis 1 (H1): Implementation of ML in SMEs can enhance DCs of employees in regards of knowledge, skills, and attitudes to support DT.

One of the most studied SME challenges in overcoming DT barriers is the need to compensate a lack of digital skills, knowledge, and qualified employees. One might argue that it is generally possible to apply ML as a strategy with an educational objective to develop skills and knowledge of employees. Moreover, our review of existing ML concepts showed that ML has already been applied to limit human learning problems. Previous research confirmed that the implementation of ML can deal with procrastination, low attention, and distraction, low motivation, or mental burnout [68–73]. However, the learning process itself requires specific ways of thinking, behavior, and motivation of employees [32]. On top of that, the learning culture within small organizations is often not optimal. We assume that the application of ML techniques could consequently be used to shape attitudes in SME employees towards DT. Thus, an essential base for their DC development would be formed. Due to the low amount of time resources needed to consume micro contents, and values-added such as gamification elements, the implementation of ML in SMEs could maintain higher motivation and higher mental focus. For instance, as ML has already been applied as an enabler of gamification approaches, it could be beneficial for enterprises to implement micro-gamification elements in their learning strategy. Creating a competitive environment among employees using gamified ML techniques could increase motivation to learn even more, thus have an additional impact on attitudes towards DT.

Hypothesis 2 (H2): Implementation of ML for DT in SMEs must aim at both DC and social competency development.

Previous research on both ML and DC underlines the relevance of social aspects in multiple concepts. For instance, ML could help developing social competencies in organizations, in which the social learning environment and social communication tools play important roles [11]. Moreover, social competencies are also part of the three competence areas constituting integrative DCs proposed by Vieru et al. [32]. Such DCs with social import are online collaboration and communication, or engagement in digital networks and communities. In addition, learning domains proposed in the research include the knowledge of collaborative networking, skills of information sharing, and motivation to take action in collaborative environments. Therefore, ML for DC development must as well consider target users and the embedding into a community's environment, in which learning takes place. Also, the quantity and quality of possible interactions between SME employees should be considered, in addition to any external stakeholders, which are also characterized as communication partners in DC archetypes [32]. When developing DCs of SME managers [40], the contextual goal of implementing ML may also lie in developing flexibility. One possible technological way of ML application in the social context, which has shown throughout the SSLR, is to integrate ML in the social web [51, 52, 73–76]. For instance, Kovacs [52] studied the implementation of ML content in the Facebook feed and tried to complement in-feed messages with small, encouraging learning tasks to foster micro-exercising habits. In a comparable way, ML could be integrated in social apps used in particular SMEs.

To finalize this discussion, we synthesize the obtained knowledge on SME-specific requirements in the face of DT, applied ML concepts and DC concepts within four main parameters. We suggest that these are relevant for the determination of an ML implementation strategy for DC development in SMEs. On top of that, we formulate exemplary RQs, which constitute recommendations for a future research outline, which we intend to provide with this paper.

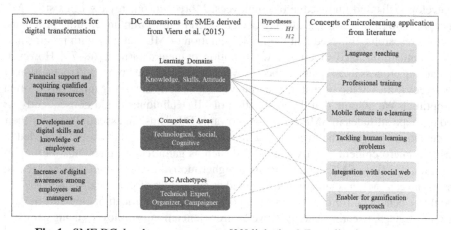

Fig. 1. SME DC development concepts [23] linked to ML application concepts

- **Context.** ML is considered to be highly adaptable to various contexts, which allows the creators to design microcontents for any special needs of the environment [55]. Towards both H1 and H2, future researchers, who determine a ML strategy in SMEs, could study the following exemplary research question (RQ1): *What characterizes a suitable ML context for DC development in SMEs?*
- **Formats.** Although our SSLR does not yield any concrete typology of ML formats, the samples of ML applied in practice show there is a greater variety of formats to

fit micro contents in. Short videos, game-based elements, and textual blocks were among the most often applied. Despite the appearance of micro contents, formats are also defined by the way how contents are conveyed. For instance, ML can be integrated into digital platforms as learning-enabling mechanisms [9] or into internal workshops [38, 43] in SMEs. What is more, the learning process can occur on different interaction levels, with one or more employees participating in learning activities at the same time. The format might also be influenced by users themselves, taking into account individual needs and context. In addition, ML could either be considered as a tool for dynamic learning on-demand or as a static long-term educational strategy. Future research could therefore focus on ML formats to answer the following research question (RQ2): *Which ML formats are suitable for organizational and individual learning toward DC development in SMEs?* In 2005, Hug [80] proposed seven dimensions for designing ML lessons, which included a process for various forms of interactions. Later studies confirmed that such forms of interactions, namely learner-to-content, learner-to-expert, and learner-to-learner, are an indispensable part of ML contents [65, 88–90]. Furthermore, feedback and evaluation functionalities are considered essential in digital learning [65, 91]. Previous studies on ML quiz-formats suggest providing feedback from colleagues and managers right after each session [65, 90, 91]. The following research question (RQ3) might be studied for an enhanced understanding of the significance of learners' interaction in SMEs with a DC development goal: *How should the interaction within learning formats in ML for DC development in SMEs be designed?*

- **Reward system.** Several studies suggested using ML as an enabling approach for gamification, leveraging learning success [54, 55, 68, 77]. These authors consider reward systems an important part of the learning strategy. For instance, a gamification technology, which includes awarding points and badges to learners, could increase motivation to learn [55]. Other scholars propose the creation of a playful learning environment using gamification techniques for unconscious learning while keeping the students engaged in the process [68]. Against the backdrop of H1, ML could therefore enhance DCs of SME employees by addressing their individual motivation. An answer to the following exemplary RQ4 would consequently lead to valuable insights: *How can different rewarding systems be implemented in ML for successful learning towards DC development in SMEs?*

- **Complexity level.** Current research does not provide enough empirical evidence from SMEs regarding the complexity of micro contents used in ML for DC development. Asadullah et al. [9] claim that complexity of content used for learning purposes should not be on a too basic level, as it can hinder the learning process in SMEs. At the same time, Busse et al. [11] deem that ML was most suitable for gaining only basic knowledge in an organizational context. We assume that this factor could also be strongly influenced by the individual employee's entry level of digital affinity and ML design should therefore be dynamically adapted to the context. In addition, ML could help improve the personalization of a learning process, as it might allow users to dynamically choose the desired content [65]. The answer to the following research question (RQ5) could help to define a complexity-sensitive ML strategy for SMEs: *How can the complexity of ML for DC development in SMEs be managed?*

Altogether, interdependencies between the ML dimensions are not studied yet and open the field for future research (RQ6) on applying ML for competence development in organizations: *How are context, learning level, reward system, and formats of ML for DC development in SMEs interrelated?*

6   Conclusion

Apart from the research outline, some questions in the context of our study have not been thoroughly studied and should be taken into consideration for future research. The question, whether the implementation of ML can entirely replace traditional learning approaches in SMEs, or whether they should be employed as an additional learning tool, remains a subject of debate. As of yet, there is insufficient empirical evidence to make a definitive claim regarding the efficacy of ML as a sole learning approach in comparison to traditional methods. As such, further research is necessary to determine the role and potential impact of ML in the context of DT initiatives. Furthermore, our study did not focus on the costs and efficiency of self-development of ML content in contrast to the purchasing of ready-made solutions. Especially in the context of SMEs, which often lack financial resources and skilled employees, future research should examine and evaluate these options. However, the overall goal of this paper is to expose the cornerstones of a research outline towards adequate ML application design to help SMEs develop DCs. SSLR and scoping review methods were used to identify and understand prevalent research on applied ML and DC. As a result of this study, we have proposed two hypotheses on ML application for DC development in SMEs and suggested a research outline consisting of 6 research questions regarding four main parameters of ML: 1) context, 2) formats, 3) reward system, and 4) complexity level.

Our research has several limitations. First, our selected methods involve, to a considerable extent, subjective interpretation. Scoping reviews, while useful for providing a broad overview of a topic, lack the rigor of systematic reviews and may not fully capture the nuances and complexities of the literature. Second, our results are not yet supported by empirical data, but are of logi-theoretical character. However, this opens up new possibilities for practice-oriented studies to evaluate the findings using empirical data and refine the interrelationships between ML and DC dimensions discussed here. After all, this study contributes to IS research, especially in the areas of e-learning, serious games and design. It also has some implications for practitioners. First, it summarizes and presents the state-of-art literature concepts and fills a research gap by exploring the correlation between ML and DC. Second, it can provide insights to practitioners in designing ML applications for work-related learning in SMEs.

References

1. Hönigsberg, S., Dias, M., Dinter, B.: Design principles for digital transformation in traditional SMEs - an antipodean comparison. In: Chandra Kruse, L., Seidel, S., Hausvik, G.I. (eds.) The Next Wave of Sociotechnical Design. DESRIST 2021. LNCS, vol. 12807, pp. 375–386. Springer, Cham (2021). https://doi.org/10.1007/978-3-030-82405-1_36

2. Vial, G.: Understanding digital transformation: a review and a research agenda. J. Strateg. Inf. Syst. **28**, 118–144 (2019). https://doi.org/10.1016/j.jsis.2019.01.003
3. Verhoef, P.C., et al.: Digital transformation: a multidisciplinary reflection and research agenda. J. Bus. Res. **122**, 889–901 (2021)
4. Eurostat: Small and medium-sized enterprises: an overview. https://ec.europa.eu/eurostat/web/products-eurostat-news/-/ddn-20200514-1. Accessed 28 Feb 2023
5. Chonsawat, N., Sopadang, A.: Defining SMEs' 4.0 readiness indicators. Appl. Sci. **10**, 8998 (2020). https://doi.org/10.3390/app10248998
6. Canhoto, A.I., Quinton, S., Pera, R., Molinillo, S., Simkin, L.: Digital strategy aligning in SMEs: a dynamic capabilities perspective. J. Strateg. Inf. Syst. **30**, 101682 (2021). https://doi.org/10.1016/j.jsis.2021.101682
7. European Commission: Commission Recommendation of 6 May 2003 concerning the definition of micro, small and medium-sized enterprises (Text with EEA relevance) (notified under document number C(2003) 1422). (2003)
8. Rupeika-Apoga, R., Bule, L., Petrovska, K.: Digital transformation of small and medium enterprises: aspects of public support. J. Risk Financ. Manag. **15**, 45 (2022). https://doi.org/10.3390/jrfm15020045
9. Asadullah, A., Faik, I., Kankanhalli, A.: Can Digital platforms help SMEs develop organizational capabilities? A qualitative field study. In: ICIS 2020 Proceedings, p. 12 (2020)
10. Leong, K., Sung, A., Au, D., Blanchard, C.: A review of the trend of microlearning. J. Work-Appl. Manag. **13**, 88–102 (2020). https://doi.org/10.1108/JWAM-10-2020-0044
11. Busse, J., Lange, A., Briesemeister, M., Schumann, M.: Become competent in 15 minutes?- The suitability of micro learning for competence development. In: Proceedings of the 28th European Conference on Information Systems (ECIS), An Online AIS Conference (2020)
12. Jomah, O., Masoud, A.K., Kishore, X.P., Aurelia, S.: Micro learning: a modernized education system. BRAIN. Broad Res. Artif. Intell. Neurosci. **7**, 103–110 (2016)
13. Emerson, L.C., Berge, Z.L.: Microlearning: knowledge management applications and competency-based training in the workplace. Knowl. Manag. E-Learn. **10**, 125–132 (2018). https://doi.org/10.34105/j.kmel.2018.10.008
14. Sánchez-Alonso, S., Sicilia, M.-A., García-Barriocanal, E., Armas, T.: From microcontents to micro-learning objects–which semantics are required?(semantics for microlearning). Micromedia E-learn. **2**, 295–303 (2006)
15. Vey, K., Fandel-Meyer, T., Zipp, J.S., Schneider, C.: Learning & development in times of digital transformation: facilitating a culture of change and innovation. Int. J. Adv. Corporate Learn. **10** (2017). https://doi.org/10.3991/ijac.v10i1.6334
16. Zhu, Y., Warner, M., Sardana, D.: Internationalization and destination selection of emerging market SMEs: issues and challenges in a conceptual framework. J. Gen. Manag. **45**, 206–216 (2020). https://doi.org/10.1177/0306307020903530
17. OECD: The Digital Transformation of SMEs. Organisation for Economic Co-operation and Development, Paris (2021)
18. Drechsler, A., Hönigsberg, S., Watkowski, L.: What's in an SME? Considerations for Scoping Research on Small and Medium Enterprises and Other Organisations in the IS Discipline. ECIS 2022 Research Papers, p. 50 (2022)
19. Schröder, C.: The Challenges of Industry 4.0 for Small and Medium-sized Enterprises. Friedrich-Ebert-Stiftung, Bonn, Germany. (2016)
20. González-Varona, J.M., López-Paredes, A., Poza, D., Acebes, F.: Building and development of an organizational competence for digital transformation in SMEs. J. Ind. Eng. Manag. **14**, 15–24 (2021). https://doi.org/10.3926/jiem.3279
21. Chonsawat, N., Sopadang, A.: The development of the maturity model to evaluate the smart SMEs 4.0 readiness. In: Proceedings of the International Conference on Industrial Engineering and Operations Management, pp. 354–363 (2019)

22. Deakins, D., Freel, M.: Entrepreneurship and Small Firms 6e. McGraw Hill Education, Berkshire (2012)
23. Li, W., Liu, K., Belitski, M., Ghobadian, A., O'Regan, N.: e-Leadership through strategic alignment: an empirical study of small-and medium-sized enterprises in the digital age. J. Inf. Technol. **31**, 185–206 (2016). https://doi.org/10.1057/jit.2016.10
24. Faherty, U., Stephens, S.: Innovation in micro enterprises: reality or fiction? J. Small Bus. Enterp. Dev. **23**, 349–362 (2016). https://doi.org/10.1108/JSBED-11-2013-0176
25. Davenport, T., Prusak, L.: Working Knowledge: How Organizations Manage What They Know. Harvard Business Press, Brighton (1998). https://doi.org/10.1145/348772.348775
26. Norveel, J., Gonzalez, R., Presthus, W.: Basic digital competence in Norwegian banking. Procedia Comput. Sci. **196**, 183–190 (2022). https://doi.org/10.1016/j.procs.2021.12.004
27. Trenkle, J.: Survival in the digital age–a framework for formulating a digital transformation strategy in SME. In: Proceedings of the 19th International Conference on Electronic Business, pp. 428–442 (2019)
28. Ala-Mutka, K.: Mapping digital competence: towards a conceptual understanding. Sevilla: Institute for Prospective Technological Studies, pp. 7–60 (2011)
29. Caldeira, M.M., Ward, J.M.: Using resource-based theory to interpret the successful adoption and use of information systems and technology in manufacturing small and medium-sized enterprises. Eur. J. Inf. Syst. **12**, 127–141 (2003). https://doi.org/10.1057/palgrave.ejis.3000454
30. Ferrari, A., Punie, Y.: DIGCOMP: A framework for developing and understanding digital competence in Europe (2013)
31. Lehner, F., Sundby, M.W.: ICT skills and competencies for SMEs: results from a structured literature analysis on the individual level. In: Harteis, C. (ed.) The Impact of Digitalization in the Workplace. Professional and Practice-based Learning, vol. 21, pp. 55–69. Springer, Cham (2018). https://doi.org/10.1007/978-3-319-63257-5_5
32. Vieru, D., Bourdeau, S., Bernier, A., Yapo, S.: Digital competence: a multi-dimensional conceptualization and a typology in an SME context. In: 2015 48th Hawaii International Conference on System Sciences, pp. 4681–4690 (2015). https://doi.org/10.1109/HICSS.2015.557
33. Axonify: Share of companies in North America using microlearning in 2017, by industry. https://www.statista.com/statistics/952602/microlearning-usage-industry-north-america/. Accessed 03 Nov 2022
34. Sierra-Cedar: Share of organizations exploring new learning tools worldwide in (2019). https://www.statista.com/statistics/1085909/organizations-exploring-learning-tools/. Accessed 03 Nov 2022
35. Camacho, D.J., Legare, J.M.: Shifting gears in the classroom-movement toward personalized learning and competency-based education. J. Competency-Based Educ. **1**, 151 (2016)
36. Williams, M.: Competency-based learning: proof of professionalism. Editor. Board **4**, 10 (2013)
37. Poulin, M.: In learning, size matters. Chief Learn. Off. **12**, 38–56 (2013)
38. Plattfaut, R., Borghoff, V.: Developing digitalization mindset and capabilities: preliminary results of an action research study. In: Ahlemann, F., Schütte, R., Stieglitz, S. (eds.) Innovation Through Information Systems. WI 2021. LNISO, vol. 48, pp. 155–161. Springer, Cham (2021). https://doi.org/10.1007/978-3-030-86800-0_12
39. Plattfaut, R., Borghoff, V.: Capabilities for digital process innovation: results of an ongoing action research study. In: Marrella, A., Weber, B. (eds.) Business Process Management Workshops. BPM 2021. LNBIP, vol. 436, pp. 232–242. Springer, Cham (2022). https://doi.org/10.1007/978-3-030-94343-1_18
40. Weigel, A., Heger, O., Hoffmann, J., Röding, K.: CEOs of SMEs: how IT-governance compensates the lack of digital competencies. ECIS 2020 Research Papers, p. 61 (2020)

41. Helfat, C.E., Peteraf, M.A.: Understanding dynamic capabilities: progress along a developmental path (2009)
42. Song, C., Qureshi, S.: The role of an effective IT intervention for microenterprises. Inf. Syst. Quant. Anal. Fac. Proc. Present. **34** (2010)
43. Deegan, G., Fernando, A.T., Ratsch, G.: Local government interventions for facilitating SME IT innovation. In: PACIS 2015 Proceedings, p. 82 (2015)
44. Snyder, H.: Literature review as a research methodology: an overview and guidelines. J. Bus. Res. **104**, 333–339 (2019). https://doi.org/10.1016/j.jbusres.2019.07.039
45. Wong, G., Greenhalgh, T., Westhorp, G., Buckingham, J., Pawson, R.: RAMESES publication standards: meta-narrative reviews. J. Adv. Nurs. **69**, 987–1004 (2013). https://doi.org/10.1111/jan.12092
46. Webster, J., Watson, R.T.: Analyzing the past to prepare for the future: writing a literature review. MIS Q. **26**, xiii–xxiii (2002)
47. Dingler, T., Weber, D., Pielot, M., Cooper, J., Chang, C.-C., Henze, N.: Language learning on-the-go: opportune moments and design of mobile microlearning sessions. In: Proceedings of the 19th International Conference on Human-Computer Interaction with Mobile Devices and Services, pp. 1–12 (2017). https://doi.org/10.1145/3098279.3098565
48. Edge, D., Cheng, K.-Y., Whitney, M., Qian, Y., Yan, Z., Soong, F.: Tip tap tones: mobile microtraining of mandarin sounds. In: Proceedings of the 14th International Conference on Human-Computer Interaction with Mobile Devices and Services, pp. 427–430 (2012)
49. Edge, D., Fitchett, S., Whitney, M., Landay, J.: MemReflex: adaptive flashcards for mobile microlearning. In: Proceedings of the 14th International Conference on Human-Computer Interaction with Mobile Devices and Services, pp. 431–440 (2012)
50. Edge, D., Searle, E., Chiu, K., Zhao, J., Landay, J.A.: MicroMandarin: mobile language learning in context. In: Proceedings of the SIGCHI Conference on Human Factors in computing Systems, pp. 3169–3178 (2011)
51. Javorcik, T.: Flashcards as a microlearning tool in English language teaching. In: Rocha, Á., Adeli, H., Dzemyda, G., Moreira, F., Ramalho Correia, A.M. (eds.) Trends and Applications in Information Systems and Technologies. WorldCIST 2021. AISC, vol. 1367, pp. 113–122. Springer, Cham (2021). https://doi.org/10.1007/978-3-030-72660-7_12
52. Kovacs, G.: FeedLearn: using facebook feeds for microlearning. In: Proceedings of the 33rd Annual ACM Conference Extended Abstracts on Human Factors in Computing Systems, pp. 1461–1466 (2015). https://doi.org/10.1145/2702613.2732775
53. Butgereit, L.: Gamifying mobile micro-learning for continuing education in a corporate IT environment. In: 2016 IST-Africa Week Conference, pp. 1–7 (2016). https://doi.org/10.1109/ISTAFRICA.2016.7530597
54. Decker, J., Wesseloh, H., Schumann, M.: Anforderungen an mobile micro learning Anwendungen mit gamification-elementen in Unternehmen. In: Knoll, M., Meinhardt, S. (eds.) Mobile Computing. Edition HMD, pp. 851–865. Springer Vieweg, Wiesbaden (2016). https://doi.org/10.1007/978-3-658-12029-0_12
55. Díaz Redondo, R.P., Ktena, A., Kunicina, N., Zabasta, A., Patlins, A., Mele, D.E.: Advanced practices: micro learning, practice oriented teaching and gamified learning. In: 2020 IEEE 61th International Scientific Conference on Power and Electrical Engineering of Riga Technical University (RTUCON), pp. 1–7 (2020). https://doi.org/10.1109/RTUCON51174.2020.9316555
56. Gill, A.S., Irwin, D.S., Ng, R.Y., Towey, D., Wang, T., Zhang, Y.: The future of teaching post-COVID-19: Microlearning in product design education. In: 2020 IEEE International Conference on Teaching, Assessment, and Learning for Engineering (TALE), pp. 780–785. IEEE, Takamatsu, Japan (2020). https://doi.org/10.1109/TALE48869.2020.9368322

57. Hegerius, A., Caduff-Janosa, P., Savage, R., Ellenius, J.: E-Learning in pharmacovigilance: an evaluation of microlearning-based modules developed by uppsala monitoring centre. Drug Saf. **43**, 1171–1180 (2020). https://doi.org/10.1007/s40264-020-00981-w

58. Leela, S., Chookeaw, S., Nilsook, P.: An effective microlearning approach using living book to promote vocational students' computational thinking. In: Proceedings of the 2019 The 3rd International Conference on Digital Technology in Education, pp. 25–29 (2019). https://doi.org/10.1145/3369199.3369200

59. Manning, K.D., Spicer, J.O., Golub, L., Akbashev, M., Klein, R.: The micro revolution: effect of Bite-Sized Teaching (BST) on learner engagement and learning in postgraduate medical education. BMC Med. Educ. **21**, 1–11 (2021). https://doi.org/10.1186/s12909-021-02496-z

60. Polasek, R., Javorcik, T.: Results of pilot study into the application of microlearning in teaching the subject computer architecture and operating system basics. In: 2019 International Symposium on Educational Technology (ISET), pp. 196–201. IEEE, Hradec Kralove, Czech Republic (2019). https://doi.org/10.1109/ISET.2019.00048

61. Simons, L., Foerster, F., Bruck, P.A., Motiwalla, L., Jonker, C.M.: Microlearning mApp raises health competence: hybrid service design. Health Technol. **5**, 35–43 (2015). https://doi.org/10.1007/s12553-015-0095-1

62. Skalka, J., et al.: Conceptual framework for programming skills development based on microlearning and automated source code evaluation in virtual learning environment. Sustainability **13**, 3293 (2021). https://doi.org/10.3390/su13063293

63. Walaszczyk, L., Dingli, S.: Business models for management and entrepreneurs as a tool for survival and success. Found. Manag. **12**, 249–260 (2020). https://doi.org/10.2478/fman-2020-0019

64. Wasiuk, C., Soper, K., McAllister-Gibson, C., Meadows, C.: 1minuteCPD: connecting digital presence and professionalism through experiments in micro-learning. Spark UAL Creat. Teach. Learn. J. **2**, 160–166 (2017)

65. Zhang, J., West, R.E.: Designing microlearning instruction for professional development through a competency based approach. TechTrends **64**, 310–318 (2020). https://doi.org/10.1007/s11528-019-00449-4

66. Aitchanov, B., Zhaparov, M., Ibragimov, M.: The research and development of the information system on mobile devices for micro-learning in educational institutes. In: 2018 14th International Conference on Electronics Computer and Computation (ICECCO), pp. 1–4. IEEE (2018). https://doi.org/10.1109/ICECCO.2018.8634653

67. Bothe, M., Renz, J., Rohloff, T., Meinel, C.: From MOOCs to micro learning activities. In: 2019 IEEE Global Engineering Education Conference (EDUCON), pp. 280–288. IEEE, Dubai, United Arab Emirates (2019). https://doi.org/10.1109/EDUCON.2019.8725043

68. De Troyer, O., Maushagen, J., Lindberg, R., Muls, J., Signer, B., Lombaerts, K.: A playful mobile digital environment to tackle school burnout using micro learning, persuasion & gamification. In: 2019 IEEE 19th International Conference on Advanced Learning Technologies (ICALT), pp. 81–83. IEEE (2019). https://doi.org/10.1109/ICALT.2019.00027

69. Draxler, F., Schneegass, C., Niforatos, E.: Designing for task resumption support in mobile learning. In: Proceedings of the 21st International Conference on Human-Computer Interaction with Mobile Devices and Services, pp. 1–6 (2019). https://doi.org/10.1145/3338286.3344394

70. Hersh, M.: Evaluating ICT based learning technologies for disabled people. In: Miesenberger, K., Fels, D., Archambault, D., Peňáz, P., Zagler, W. (eds.) Computers Helping People with Special Needs. ICCHP 2014. LNCS, vol. 8548, pp. 315–322. Springer, Cham (2014). https://doi.org/10.1007/978-3-319-08599-9_48

71. Inie, N., Lungu, M.F.: Aiki-turning online procrastination into microlearning. In: Proceedings of the 2021 CHI Conference on Human Factors in Computing Systems, pp. 1–13 (2021). https://doi.org/10.1145/3411764.3445202

72. Kävrestad, J., Nohlberg, M.: Using context based micro training to develop OER for the benefit of all. In: Proceedings of the 15th International Symposium on Open Collaboration, pp. 1–10 (2019). https://doi.org/10.1145/3306446.3340814

73. Kizilcec, R.F., Chen, M.: Student engagement in mobile learning via text message. In: Proceedings of the Seventh ACM Conference on Learning@ Scale, pp. 157–166 (2020). https://doi.org/10.1145/3386527.3405921

74. Aldosemani, T.I.: Microlearning for macro-outcomes: students' perceptions of telegram as a microlearning Tool. In: Väljataga, T., Laanpere, M. (eds.) Digital Turn in Schools—Research, Policy, Practice. LNET. Springer, Singapore (2019). https://doi.org/10.1007/978-981-13-7361-9_13

75. Göschlberger, B.: A platform for social microlearning. In: Verbert, K., Sharples, M., Klobučar, T. (eds.) Adaptive and Adaptable Learning. EC-TEL 2016. LNCS, vol. 9891, pp. 513–516. Springer, Cham (2016). https://doi.org/10.1007/978-3-319-45153-4_52

76. Hahn, N., Iqbal, S.T., Teevan, J.: Casual microtasking: embedding microtasks in Facebook. In: Proceedings of the 2019 CHI Conference on Human Factors in Computing Systems, pp. 1–9 (2019). https://doi.org/10.1145/3290605.3300249

77. Agbo, F.J., Oyelere, S.S., Suhonen, J., Laine, T.H.: Co-design of mini games for learning computational thinking in an online environment. Educ. Inf. Technol. **26**, 5815–5849 (2021). https://doi.org/10.1007/s10639-021-10515-1

78. Hug, T.: Microlearning. In: Encyclopedia of the Sciences of Learning, pp. 2268–2271. Springer, Cham, US, Boston, MA (2012). https://doi.org/10.1007/978-3-031-13359-6

79. Busse, J., Schumann, M.: Towards a pedagogical pattern language for micro learning in enterprises. In: 26th European Conference on Pattern Languages of Programs, pp. 1–8. Association for Computing Machinery, New York, NY, USA (2022). https://doi.org/10.1145/3489449.3489973

80. Hug, T.: Micro learning and narration. Exploring possibilities of utilization of narrations and storytelling for the designing of "micro units" and didactical micro-learning arrangements. In: Fourth Media in Transition Conference (2005)

81. Yu, J., Moon, T.: Impact of digital strategic orientation on organizational performance through digital competence. Sustainability **13**, 9766 (2021). https://doi.org/10.3390/su13179766

82. Hubschmid-Vierheilig, E., Rohrer, M., Mitsakis, F.V.: Digital competence and SMEs: review of the relevant literature. In: 20th International Conference on Human Resource Development Research and Practice across Europe (UFHRD) (2019)

83. Ferrari, A.: Digital competence in practice: an analysis of frameworks. Sevilla JRC IPTS **10**, 82116 (2012). https://doi.org/10.2791/82116

84. Ilomäki, L., Paavola, S., Lakkala, M., Kantosalo, A.: Digital competence – an emergent boundary concept for policy and educational research. Educ. Inf. Technol. **21**, 655–679 (2016). https://doi.org/10.1007/s10639-014-9346-4

85. Hartmann, W., Hundertpfund, A.: Digitale Kompetenz. Was die Schule dazu beitragen kann, p. 1 (2015)

86. Oberländer, M., Beinicke, A., Bipp, T.: Digital competencies: a review of the literature and applications in the workplace. Comput. Educ. **146**, 103752 (2020). https://doi.org/10.1016/j.compedu.2019.103752

87. Ravichandran, T.: Exploring the relationships between IT competence, innovation capacity and organizational agility. J. Strateg. Inf. Syst. **27**, 22–42 (2018). https://doi.org/10.1016/j.jsis.2017.07.002

88. Job, M.A., Ogalo, H.S.: Micro learning as innovative process of knowledge strategy. Int. J. Sci. Technol. Res. **1**, 92–96 (2012)

89. Baumgartner, P.: Educational dimensions of microlearning–towards a taxonomy for microlearning. Designing Microlearning Experiences (2013)

104   E. Veldyaeva et al.

90. Alqurashi, E.: Microlearning: a pedagogical approach for technology integration. Turk. Online J. Educ. Technol. **16**, 942–947 (2017)
91. Berge, Z.L.: Active, interactive, and reflective elearning. Q. Rev. Dist. Learn. **3**, 181–190 (2002)

Exploring Smart Meters: What We Know and What We Need to Know

Shashini Rajaguru$^{(\boxtimes)}$, Björn Johansson , and Malin Granath

Linköping University, Linköping, Sweden
{shashini.rajaguru,bjorn.se.johansson,malin.granath}@liu.se

Abstract. Implementation of smart meters is revolutionizing traditional energy grids, promoting energy efficiency, and enabling two-way communication between energy suppliers and consumers. This paper presents a scoping review of smart meters investigating functional and non-functional expectations, benefits, drawbacks, and factors influencing implementation of smart meters. The study aims at providing an overview of existing research in this area and identify gaps and limitations in literature, especially in between smart meter literature and how consumers perceive smart meters. Through a scoping review process, 16 articles were selected for analysis. The findings highlight the importance of real-time information, remote monitoring, accuracy, privacy, and security in smart meter functionality. The benefits encompass improved customer awareness, energy efficiency, and grid stability, while the drawbacks include privacy concerns and limitations in current standards. Factors influencing adoption include cost-benefit analysis, regulatory policies, consumer awareness, and technical considerations. The study reveals research gaps related to long-term performance, social and psychological factors, diverse consumer segments, privacy and data security, economic viability, regional contexts, and stakeholder dynamics. Addressing these gaps will contribute to maximizing benefits of smart meters, informing policymakers, utility companies, and researchers for effective strategies in energy management and sustainability. The paper concludes with recommendations for future research and underscores the need to understand consumers' perspectives on smart meters.

Keywords: Smart Meter · Scoping Review · Smart Meter Consumer

1 Introduction

The smart meter phenomenon is a significant move towards the digitalization of traditional energy grids and promoting energy saving and efficiency. The term "smart meter" has multiple definitions provided by academia and the global energy sector, but fundamentally smart meters are described as an advanced metering device that enables two-way communication between the energy supplier and the consumer by measuring and reporting energy consumption [1–3].

The implementation of smart meters worldwide has been driven by various factors, including the need to improve energy efficiency, reduce costs, and support the demand response management [4, 5].

© The Author(s), under exclusive license to Springer Nature Switzerland AG 2023
K. Hinkelmann et al. (Eds.): BIR 2023, LNBIP 493, pp. 105–120, 2023.
https://doi.org/10.1007/978-3-031-43126-5_8

Sweden was one of the first countries in Europe to introduce smart meters and stands out as a global leader in smart meter implementation. The Swedish government introduced a mandatory rollout of smart meters in 2009, which has been highly successful in achieving near-universal deployment. Swedish Energy Markets Inspectorate (EI) has developed a new regulation introducing five minimum functional requirements for all the electricity meters in the low voltage network, to be achieved by 2025 [6]. In the United States, smart meters have been rolled out on a large scale that in 2021, U.S. electric utilities had about 111 million smart metering infrastructure installations which was equal to about 69% of total electric meters installations [7]. Similarly, Europe has been at the forefront of smart meter adoption, with countries such as Germany and the United Kingdom setting ambitious targets for deployment. The German government has adopted a draft law to digitalize its energy transition and accelerate the rollout of smart metering by spring of 2023 [8]. At the end of 2021, there were 27.8 million smart and advanced meters in Great Britain in homes and small businesses [9].

As smart meter technology continues to evolve, it is also becoming an interesting, timely and a crucial topic to explore this phenomenon further since it provides an insight to understand what makes electricity meters smart and how the smart meters are expected to function in relation to traditional non-smart meters. To get further insights, it is also interesting to explore what are the benefits or drawbacks and expectations associated with smart meters and what sort of collaboration or interaction it requires from the users or consumers in order to reach its goals. In this research we attempt to encapsulate all these questions from a consumer perspective to understand if any gaps exist in the current literature.

In accordance with these questions, we attempt to explore, functional requirements of smart meters referring to specific features and capabilities that users expect from smart meters, such as accuracy and timeliness of measurement, compatibility with other smart devices, and user-friendly interfaces and non-functional requirements which are considered broader qualities and characteristics that users expect from smart meters, such as reliability, security, privacy, and ease of installation. We believe this exploration can help us understand expectations associated with smart meters. We also aim to investigate benefits, drawbacks and factors associated with adoption/utilization of smart meters.

To do this we used a scoping method to examine current literature identifying key themes and insights related to smart meter expectations (functional and non-functional), benefits, drawbacks, and adoption/utilization factors.

Through this investigation, we hope to provide an overview of the existing research in this area and identify any gaps and limitations in literature, especially in between smart meter literature and how consumers perceive smart meters. We believe this investigation will help stakeholders to develop more effective strategies for promoting smart meter adoption and maximizing benefits of this technology for energy management and sustainability.

The next section of this paper will provide a brief overview of the methodology followed during the scoping review. Then we present our extensive literature review based on the scoping method that will be followed by an analytical discussion of the key themes and insights identified from the scoping review, including functional and non-functional requirements, benefits and drawbacks of smart meters, and factors influencing adoption. The final section will summarize the main findings of the study and discuss their implications for policymakers, utility companies, and consumers and gaps identified during the scoping review. The paper will conclude with recommendations for future research in this area.

2   A Scoping Review on Smart Meters

When conducting the scoping review, we followed the five stages of the framework developed and adopted by Arksey and O'Malley [10] further refined by Levac et al. [11]. This means that the scoping review was conducted according to the following stages: 1) Identifying the research question, 2) Identifying relevant studies, 3) Study selection, 4) Charting the data, 5) Collating, summarizing, and reporting the results.

The search strategy was developed based on the research aims and relevant keywords. A total of 20 keywords (Smart meter, Smart electricity meter, Advanced electricity meter, Advanced metering infrastructure, Advanced energy meter, Smart metering systems, Expectation formation, Technological expectations, Smart meter adoption, Consumer expectations, Smart meter rollouts, Attitudes toward smart meters, Smart meter implementation, User expectations, Smart meter benefits, Perceived risks, Smart meter privacy, User trust, Energy efficiency goals and User engagement) were used to guide the search in various combinations.

To begin this literature review, five search strings were created using the 20 keywords in various combinations. The search was carried out in two major academic databases: Web of Science and Scopus. The initial search was limited to English review articles published between 2013 and 2023 that have been cited, allowing us to synthesize comprehensive insights into the field of smart meters. Following that, 366 articles were exported to the Endnote reference manager for further review. Following the removal of duplicates, 195 articles were left for title screening. The inclusion criteria for the title screening were to select topics that explicitly presented the smart electricity meter or events from the context, which led to a selection of 36 results. The next step involved a thorough analysis of the abstracts of the selected articles. This analysis aimed to identify journal articles and conference papers that discussed functional and non-functional requirements associated with implementation, benefits and drawbacks of smart meters and factors influencing adoption/utilization of smart meters. After abstract analysis and a thoroughly review based on the research aims a final selection of 16 articles were made. The final analysis included reviewing selected articles thematically using a descriptive approach. In the next section we present the findings of the scoping review in a narrative synthesis format.

3   Findings on What is Known About Smart Meters

The selection of 16 articles and retrieved data from them was qualitatively evaluated in order to find patterns, themes, and commonalities. Findings were then thematically grouped to provide a clear and simple summary. By analyzing a wide range of studies and research findings, this review seeks to establish a robust foundation and identify gaps in knowledge for future research.

3.1 Functional and Non-Functional Requirements

Smart meters have emerged as essential tools in measuring and communicating real-time electricity usage, providing valuable insights into energy consumption patterns for both consumers and utility providers. The functional requirements associated with smart meters are multifaceted and have been examined by several researchers.

Bahmanyar, Jamali [12] emphasize that accurate measurement of electricity consumption and generation is a fundamental functional requirement of smart meters. They provide specific examples of off-the-shelf, or prototype smart meters being tested in the ongoing European project FLEXMETER, showcasing their potential in enabling accurate measurement. Furthermore, Chakraborty and Sharma [13] discuss the importance of design requirements, hardware and software specifications, and communication protocols as non-functional requirements for smart meters. They delve into the technological aspects and communication protocol developments associated with smart meters, highlighting their significance in achieving efficient implementation.

Subhash and Rajagopal [14] emphasize that one of the primary functional requirements is the provision of real-time information on energy usage, enabling consumers to monitor and control their electricity consumption more effectively. Their study conducted a survey among residential customers with smart meters and found that 70% of respondents considered real-time information as the most useful feature of smart meters. This real-time feedback empowers consumers to make informed decisions about energy usage and adjust their behavior to optimize energy efficiency. In addition to real-time information, smart meters facilitate remote monitoring and control of power consumption. Subhash and Rajagopal [14] explain that this feature enables utilities to detect and respond to abnormal usage patterns, improving grid stability and reliability. Moreover, smart meters enable accurate billing by eliminating the need for manual meter readings, reducing human errors and disputes over energy bills [15].

Opriş et al. [16] highlight the importance of real-time information provided by smart meters, which allows consumers to monitor their energy usage and make informed decisions regarding their consumption patterns. The authors discuss that smart meters facilitate energy efficiency by providing accurate data for demand response programs, allowing consumers to participate in energy-saving initiatives and adjust their consumption during peak periods. They conducted a case study involving 60 households and found that the implementation of smart meters led to a 15% reduction in overall energy consumption. This functionality not only reduces strain on the power grid but also contributes to significant energy savings by empowering consumers to adopt demand-side behaviors that promote energy efficiency and reduce greenhouse gas emissions.

While the functional benefits of smart meters are evident, non-functional aspects and concerns associated with their implementation of smart meters have received attention in the literature. Privacy and data security are significant considerations in the adoption of smart metering systems. Yesudas [17] emphasize that consumers express concerns about the data collected by smart meters and the potential for unauthorized access to personal information. Their qualitative study conducted interviews with residential customers and identified privacy as a major concern. Participants expressed worries about their energy usage data being misused or shared without consent. The authors emphasize that adequate measures must be in place to protect consumer privacy and ensure the secure handling of data and addressing these concerns is crucial for building trust and ensuring widespread acceptance of smart meters.

Furthermore, Yesudas and Clarke [18] highlight the need to address consumer concerns regarding the loss of control over energy usage and data privacy. Their study found that participants felt uneasy about their energy usage being monitored remotely and the potential for third-party access to their data. It is essential to establish mechanisms that empower consumers to have control over their energy usage data and provide transparency in data handling processes.

Yesudas and Clarke [19] argue that some consumers perceive smart meters as infringing upon their interests and rights, as they may feel that their energy usage is being monitored and controlled by external entities. Overcoming this perception requires designing smart metering systems that incorporate controls and choices for consumers, empowering them to maintain a sense of control over their energy usage.

Understanding and addressing these concerns is essential in terms pf assurance for minimizing resistance to smart meter adoption. A summary of functional and non-functional expectations is presented in Table 1.

Table 1. Functional and non-functional expectations associated with smart meters

Functional expectations
Accurate measurement of electricity consumption and generation are a fundamental requirement [12]
Real-time information provision enables consumers to monitor and control their electricity consumption effectively [14]
Remote monitoring and control of power consumption enable utilities to detect and respond to abnormal usage patterns, improving grid stability and reliability [14]
Smart meters facilitate accurate billing by eliminating the need for manual meter readings, reducing human errors and disputes over energy bills [17, 20]
Smart meters provide accurate data for demand response programs, enabling consumers to participate in energy-saving initiatives and adjust consumption during peak periods, contributing to energy efficiency and reducing greenhouse gas emissions [16]
Non-Functional expectations
Design requirements, hardware and software specifications, and communication protocols are essential non-functional requirements for smart meters [13]
Privacy and data security are significant concerns, requiring measures to protect consumer privacy and ensure secure handling of data [19]
Consumer concerns include loss of control over energy usage and data privacy, necessitating mechanisms to empower consumers and provide transparency in data handling [18]
Consumer perception of smart meters infringing upon their interests and rights can be addressed by designing systems that incorporate controls and choices for consumers, enabling them to maintain a sense of control over their energy usage [15]
Potential health risks associated with radiofrequency electromagnetic fields require understanding and addressing to minimize resistance to smart meter adoption [17]

3.2 Benefits and Drawbacks

Smart meters offer a wide range of benefits across different stakeholders that contribute to improved energy management, efficiency, and environmental sustainability. The literature highlights these benefits from various perspectives.

Subhash and Rajagopal [14] emphasize the advantage of enhanced customer awareness of energy usage and associated costs. Their study found that consumers who had access to real-time energy data through smart meters were more likely to adopt energy-saving behaviors. By providing real-time information on energy consumption patterns and usage information, smart meters empower consumers to track their electricity usage, identify energy-intensive appliances, and make informed choices about their energy consumption resulting in potential energy savings that lead to optimizing energy efficiency. This increased awareness leads to reduced energy wastage and cost savings for consumers.

Energy efficiency is another significant benefit of smart meters. Opriş et al. [16] emphasize that real-time information and feedback provided by smart meters enable consumers to adopt energy-saving behaviors, leading to a reduction in overall energy demand. This does not only benefits individual consumers by lowering their energy bills but also contributes to environmental sustainability by reducing greenhouse gas emissions. Opriş and Caracasian [21] emphasize that smart meters provide real-time data on electricity usage, enabling more efficient management of consumption, increased energy efficiency, and reduced greenhouse gas emissions. To illustrate the benefits, they provide specific examples of how real-time information available through smart metering systems enables more efficient management of electricity consumption, thus contributing to stable and economically profitable electricity generation, transmission, and distribution. Additionally, Malik et al. [22] highlight the advantages of smart meters in optimizing heavy-load devices and supporting the integration of renewable energy sources into the grid. They present research on development of a wireless smart metering system that enables real-time monitoring of significant devices in a home, emphasizing importance of energy control and optimization.

Furthermore, implementation of demand response programs through smart meters enables consumers to actively participate in energy conservation. Opriş et al. [16] highlight that smart meters allow consumers to adjust their energy consumption during peak periods or in response to price fluctuations, thus reducing strain on the power grid and promoting a more stable and efficient energy system. Their study conducted a field experiment involving 200 households and found that participants who engaged in demand response programs achieved an average reduction of 20% in their electricity bills.

Additionally, benefits of smart meters extend to environmental sustainability. Opriş et al. [16] note that by promoting energy-conscious behaviors, smart meters contribute to reduced greenhouse gas emissions and align with global efforts to mitigate climate change. Their study conducted a simulation analysis and estimated that implementation of smart meters could lead to a 10% reduction in carbon dioxide emissions.

However, alongside the numerous benefits, smart meters also present certain drawbacks. Privacy and data security concerns are paramount and have been extensively discussed by various authors. Subhash and Rajagopal [14] emphasize that the collection and sharing of detailed data about usage raise questions about individual privacy rights and data breaches. Their study highlighted the need for robust data encryption and access control measures to protect consumer information. Yesudas and Clarke [18] highlight the need to address these concerns to overcome resistance to smart meter adoption. Bahmanyar et al. [12] also raise concerns regarding data privacy and security threats as significant challenges. They emphasize need for further research and development to address these drawbacks and to ensure protection of consumer data. Bugden and Stedman [23] highlight high cost of implementation and maintenance as a potential barrier to widespread adoption. They discuss the ambivalence and negative attitudes of ratepayers towards smart meters, emphasizing the need for effective communication strategies to overcome these challenges and increase adoption rates. Therefore, ensuring that smart metering systems incorporate controls and choices for consumers, as well as robust data security measures, can help mitigate these drawbacks.

In addition, perceived health risks associated with smart meter radiation with electromagnetic fields emitted by smart meters have been a subject of discussion. While scientific evidence supports the safety of smart meters within established standards, Opriş et al. [16] and Yesudas [17] highlight that despite scientific evidence suggesting that radiation levels from smart meters are within acceptable limits, some individuals still express concerns regarding potential health effects. Opriş et al. [16] conducted a survey among residents living near smart meters and found that while a majority had no health concerns, a small percentage reported symptoms they attributed to the presence of smart meters. Addressing these concerns through public awareness campaigns and providing accurate information about the safety of smart meters can help alleviate apprehensions and encourage wider acceptance of smart meters.

Another drawback identified is the potential for limitations in the current standards and feedback devices of smart metering systems. Pullinger et al. [24] argue that the existing standards and feedback mechanisms may not effectively incorporate the latest research findings, hindering the ability of smart metering programs to achieve their objectives in reducing energy demand and spending. Enhancing the feedback mechanisms and aligning them with specific energy usage practices of consumers can further improve effectiveness of smart meters in promoting behavioral changes and demand reduction.

Moreover, perceived loss of control over energy usage and data privacy can generate skepticism among consumers and hinder widespread adoption. Subhash and Rajagopal [14] emphasize the need to develop mechanisms that empower consumers to have control over their energy usage data and ensure transparency in data handling processes. Incorporating user-friendly interfaces and clear communication about data privacy measures can enhance consumer confidence and acceptance of smart meters. A summary of identified benefits and drawbacks is presented in Table 2.

3.3 Factors Influencing Smart Meter Implementation and Awareness

The implementation of smart meters and its awareness is influenced by a multitude of factors that shape consumer acceptance and overall market penetration. Researchers have identified several key factors that play a significant role in influencing smart meter implementation and awareness.

Table 2. Benefits and drawbacks of smart meters

Benefits
Enhanced customer awareness of energy usage and associated costs, leading to energy-saving behaviors and cost savings for consumers [14]
Energy efficiency through real-time information and feedback, resulting in reduced energy demand, lower bills, and reduced greenhouse gas emissions [16, 21]
Optimization of heavy-load devices and support for the integration of renewable energy sources into the grid [22]
Active participation in demand response programs, enabling consumers to adjust energy consumption and achieve cost savings [16]
Contribution to environmental sustainability through energy-conscious behaviors and reduced greenhouse gas emissions [16]
Drawbacks
Privacy and data security concerns, necessitating robust encryption and access control measures[12, 14, 18, 25]
High implementation and maintenance costs, potential resistance, and negative attitudes towards smart meters [23]
Perceived health risks associated with smart meter radiation, despite scientific evidence suggesting their safety [16, 17]
Limitations in current standards and feedback mechanisms, hindering the achievement of energy demand reduction goals [24]
Perceived loss of control over energy usage and data privacy, requiring mechanisms for consumer empowerment and transparent data handling [14]

Bahmanyar et al. [12] highlight economic incentives, consumer education, and regulatory policies as key factors that promote adoption. They emphasize the importance of economic incentives in incentivizing consumers to adopt smart meters. Gumz and Fettermann [26] identifies factors that influence acceptance, such as familiarity with the technology and positive attitudes towards smart meters. They provide some specific examples, where factors like better energy management through feedback, eco-concern, and the requirement of financial gain were found to drive acceptance. They also highlight barriers such as security threats, unfamiliarity, and associated costs, which can hinder adoption rates.

Cost-benefit analysis plays a crucial role in the decision-making process of both consumers and utilities. Yang et al. [27] emphasizes that cost of smart meters and related infrastructure, along with potential financial benefits for consumers, influence their willingness to adopt smart meters. Utilities also consider long-term cost savings and operational efficiencies associated with smart meters when determining their adoption strategies. Pullinger et al. [24] highlight importance of evaluating financial implications of smart meter implementation. Their study conducted a cost-benefit analysis of smart meter deployment in a large utility company and found that while there were initial investment costs, the long-term benefits in terms of operational efficiency, accurate billing, and reduced meter reading expenses outweighed the upfront expenses. Consumers need to assess potential energy savings and long-term cost-effectiveness, while utility providers must consider investment costs and benefits in terms of operational efficiency and grid management. Understanding financial implications from various perspectives is essential for informed decision-making regarding smart meter adoption.

Regulatory policies and government support play a significant role in driving smart meter adoption. Yang et al. [27] highlights the importance of government policies and regulations that promote and incentivize deployment of smart meters. These policies can include financial incentives, regulatory frameworks, and mandates that encourage utilities and consumers to embrace smart metering technologies. Subhash and Rajagopal [14] emphasize the role of government regulations and incentives in shaping the land-scape of smart meter deployment. Their study examined impact of regulatory mandates on smart meter adoption in different countries and found that countries with supportive policies experienced higher rates of adoption. Supportive policies can create a favorable environment for utilities to invest in smart meters, and regulatory mandates can drive the adoption of the technology. Moreover, government initiatives to provide subsidies or incentives for consumers to adopt smart meters can accelerate their uptake.

Consumer awareness, education, and acceptance are crucial factors in smart meter adoption. Opriş et al. [16] emphasize importance of consumer knowledge and awareness of smart meters as a need for consumers to actively engage in the planning process of smart meter implementation, as their involvement leads to better acceptance and adoption of the technology and lack of information or misconceptions can hinder adoption. Their study found that consumers who were well-informed about functionalities and benefits of smart meters were more likely to adopt them. Educating consumers about benefits, functionalities, and potential cost savings of smart meters through targeted campaigns and educational programs can enhance their acceptance and willingness for adoption. More-over, educating consumers about benefits and functionality of smart meters, addressing privacy and security concerns, and providing clear communication regarding data usage and control can enhance consumer acceptance and adoption rates [19].

Technical considerations are crucial in successful implementation of smart meters. Compatibility and integration of smart meters with existing infrastructure and communication technologies are important factors to ensure seamless operation. Subhash and Rajagopal [14] highlight the significance of technical feasibility, including network connectivity and interoperability, in determining effectiveness of smart meter deployment. Their study emphasizes the need for robust communication protocols and standardized interfaces to facilitate integration of smart meters into existing energy infrastructure. Compatibility with different communication technologies, such as wire-less networks or powerline communication, should also be considered to ensure reliable data transmission. Furthermore, ongoing research and development are necessary to improve inter-operability and scalability of smart meters, ensuring their compatibility with future advancements in energy management systems and smart grid technologies.

Socio-economic factors also play a role in smart meter adoption. Bugden and Stedman [23] mention that factors such as familiarity, age, and income level influence consumer acceptance of smart meters. Their study conducted a survey among residential consumers and found that younger generations, particularly the Web 2.0 generation, were more receptive to technological advancements and may embrace smart meters more readily. Additionally, income levels can affect affordability of smart meters and influence consumer decision-making. Utility companies and policymakers need to consider the socio-economic context and potential disparities in access to smart meters to ensure equitable deployment and adoption.

Furthermore, presence of supportive infrastructure and stakeholder collaboration are important factors in facilitating smart meter adoption. Pullinger et al. [24] highlight the significance of establishing a robust communication network and backend systems to support functionalities of smart meters. Additionally, effective collaboration between utility providers, regulators, and technology vendors is crucial for successful implementation. This collaboration can ensure alignment of goals, address regulatory requirements, and streamline the deployment process. A summary of factors is shown in Table 3.

Table 3. Factors influencing smart meter implementation and awareness

Economic Incentives
Economic incentives, consumer education, and regulatory policies promote adoption [12]
Familiarity with technology and positive attitudes towards smart meters drive acceptance [26]
Cost-benefit analysis influences consumer willingness to adopt smart meters [27]
Cost-Benefit Analysis
Long-term cost savings, operational efficiencies, and potential financial benefits influence adoption [24]
Regulatory Policies ([27]
Government policies, regulations, and mandates drive smart meter adoption [14, 27]
Consumer Awareness
Consumer knowledge and awareness positively impact acceptance [16]
Educating consumers about benefits, functionalities, and cost savings enhances acceptance [15, 16]
Technical Considerations
Technical feasibility, compatibility, and interoperability are crucial for successful implementation [14]
Socio-Economic Factors
Factors such as familiarity, age, and income level influence acceptance [23]
Socio-economic context and disparities in access should be considered [23]
Supportive Infrastructure
Robust communication network and backend systems are essential [24]
Stakeholder collaboration facilitates successful implementation [24]

4 Analyzing Scoping Review Themes on Smart Meters

This scoping review provided an overview of literature on smart metering systems, with a focus on functionality and non-functionality, benefits and drawbacks, factors influencing adoption, and associated policies and technologies. We were able to identify several key themes that emerged from the scoping review as presented in Tables 1, 2 and 3.

To begin, according to the review, functional expectations for smart meters include real-time measurement, remote monitoring, two-way communication, and integration with other systems, while non-functional expectations include security, privacy, dependability, and compatibility. According to the literature, smart meters can provide real-time information on energy consumption, allowing consumers to monitor and adjust their behavior accordingly. Remote monitoring allows energy providers to manage energy supply and demand more effectively, resulting in increased efficiency and cost savings. Two-way communication enables more precise energy management and integration of other systems, such as renewable energy sources.

Second, while smart meters provide benefits such as increased accuracy, better energy management, and increased efficiency, they also have drawbacks such as privacy concerns, implementation costs, and compatibility issues. These drawbacks are mainly associated with the lack of functionality of smart meters. Smart meters' accuracy enables more precise billing and better energy management, resulting in cost savings. However, implementation costs can be high, and there may be compatibility issues when integrating with existing infrastructure. Concerns about privacy are also a significant disadvantage, as sharing detailed energy use data can reveal information about people's personal lives and infringe on their sense of autonomy, choice, and control.

Third, regulatory requirements, consumer education, and cost, as well as familiarity, perceptions of climate change risk, smart meter acceptance, age, and other factors, all influence smart meter implementation and awareness. Smart metering system implementation and consumers awareness can be influenced by policies and regulations. Consumer education is also essential for raising awareness and understanding of advantages and disadvantages of smart meters. Another important consideration is cost, as smart meters can be prohibitively expensive for some consumers. Other factors influencing adoption include familiarity with technology, perceptions of the risk of climate change, and age.

Fourth, smart metering system design, hardware, software, and communication protocols are critical components of the smart grid, and data security and privacy issues must be addressed by implementing appropriate communication protocols and technological solutions. Smart metering system design and components must be robust and reliable, and communication protocols must be secure to ensure privacy and prevent cyberattacks. Data security and privacy are critical issues that must be addressed with appropriate technological solutions.

Finally, user perceptions and acceptance are critical for smart meter implementation success, and policymakers must consider these factors when promoting their adoption. In countries like Sweden, where smart meters have been mandated, these considerations should be measured in order to raise consumer awareness levels and promote better utilization. Building user trust is critical for addressing privacy concerns and encouraging participation in smart local energy systems. End-user engagement is critical for smart metering success, especially in terms of consumers' social, economic, and behavioral factors. Consumer education and awareness are also critical for increasing acceptance and understanding of the benefits and drawbacks of smart meters.

5 Discussing Identified Research Gaps

This study was an attempt to provide a comprehensive overview of existing research on smart meter technology while identifying any gaps and limitations, particularly concerning the connection between smart meter literature and consumer perceptions. Our primary objective was to delve into the consumer perspective by exploring their expectations, benefits, drawbacks, and adoption factors related to smart meters. Through our investigation, we aimed to pinpoint any gaps in the current literature. However, our findings highlighted a significant oversight in understanding how consumers perceive smart meters, their user experience, and the overall significance of incorporating the consumers' viewpoint into this technology. This led us to identify a notable research gap, wherein the dominance of a top-down approach and policymakers' perspective in smart meter literature primarily focuses on the functional aspects of the technology. Insufficient attention has been devoted to exploring consumers' perceptions, user experience, and the crucial importance of understanding their perspective within the realm of smart meters.

It is important to explore smart meters from a user perspective to understand what factors influence awareness and interactions between consumers and smart meters.

Addressing these research gaps will contribute to a more comprehensive understanding of smart metering systems, their implementation, and their impact on energy consumption, consumer behavior, and the overall energy landscape. It will also provide insights and recommendations for policymakers, utilities, and researchers to maximize the benefits and address the challenges associated when implementing smart meters.

While literature provides valuable insights into functional and non-functional expectations, benefits and drawbacks, and factors influencing smart meter implementation there are several research gaps that need to be addressed. Firstly, there is a need for further investigation into the long-term performance and reliability of smart meters. While studies have explored functional expectations of smart meters, there is a lack of comprehensive analysis on their durability and accuracy over extended periods. Research could focus on assessing the longevity of smart meters in real-world scenarios, considering factors such as environmental conditions, maintenance requirements, and technological obsolescence. This creates a need for more research on the long-term behavioral changes and energy-saving outcomes resulting from smart meter implementation. While studies highlight the potential for energy savings, more research is needed to understand the sustained impact and effectiveness of smart meters in promoting long-term energy efficiency.

Secondly, the social, cultural and psychological factors that impact smart meter adoption/utilization require deeper exploration. While studies have discussed the benefits and drawbacks of smart meters, there is limited understanding of how individuals and communities perceive and experience these technologies. Future research could investigate the psychological factors influencing consumer acceptance and engagement with smart meters, including factors such as privacy concerns, trust, and the impact on energy-saving behaviors. Understanding how social norms, beliefs, and attitudes influence consumer acceptance, adoption and utilization of smart meters can provide valuable insights for designing effective communication and engagement strategies.

Thirdly, literature reveals a lack of comprehensive studies focusing on specific needs and requirements of different consumer segments. While benefits of smart meters for individual consumers and utility companies have been well-documented, there is a lack of research on impact of widespread smart meter adoption on the overall energy grid and energy systems. Therefore, more research is needed to understand broader systemic effects of smart meter implementation. Yesudas [17] highlights the importance of identifying consumer segments based on their energy behaviors and requirements to tailor smart metering strategies accordingly. Future research should address the diverse needs of various consumer groups, including low-income households, elderly individuals, and those with special energy requirements. Future studies could also focus on analyzing implications of smart meters on grid stability, energy demand patterns, and integration of renewable energy sources at a larger scale.

There is also a critical need for continuous evaluation and improvement of privacy and data security measures in smart metering systems. Given the evolving nature of technology and potential cybersecurity threats, ongoing research and development should focus on enhancing the privacy and security features of smart metering systems. This includes exploring advanced encryption methods, robust authentication mechanisms, and establishing clear guidelines and regulations for data collection, storage, and usage.

Furthermore, additional research is needed to assess the economic viability and cost-effectiveness of smart metering systems in different contexts. Cost-benefit analysis should consider not only immediate financial implications but also long-term benefits in terms of energy savings, grid stability, and environmental impact.

Moreover, in terms of smart meter literature, more studies are required from a consumer perspective to enrich literature and control its dominant nature discussing smart meters based on a top-down approach to a well-balanced one where it also discusses smart meters from a user level approach.

Additionally, there is a need for research that examines the specific challenges and opportunities of smart meter adoption in different geographical contexts and socioeconomic settings. Studies have primarily focused on developed countries, and there is limited research on the unique challenges faced by developing regions in implementing smart metering systems. The literature would benefit from more comparative studies that analyze experiences from different countries or regions in implementing smart metering programs. Such studies can shed light on the contextual factors, policy frameworks, and regulatory approaches that contribute to successful smart meter adoption and identify best practices that can be shared and replicated. Future research could investigate cultural, economic, and infrastructural factors that influence smart meter implementation in diverse contexts.

Finally, the role of stakeholders, such as policymakers, regulators, and energy service providers, in facilitating smart meter adoption warrants further investigation. Understanding the dynamics and interactions among various stakeholders is crucial for effective policy formulation and implementation. Future studies could explore the decision-making processes, policy frameworks, and collaborative approaches that support successful smart meter deployment and adoption.

A summary of the key points and gaps in knowledge regarding smart meter implementation is presented in Table 4.

Table 4. Summary of key points and knowledge gaps

Key points
Valuable literature on requirements, benefits, drawbacks & adoption factors
Smart meters offer real-time measurement, remote monitoring, & improved efficiency
Drawbacks include privacy concerns, implementation costs,& compatibility issues
Adoption influenced by regulatory requirements, consumer education, cost, familiarity
Design, hardware, software, and communication protocols are critical for smart meters
Gaps in Knowledge
Long-term performance and reliability of smart meters
Social, cultural, and psychological factors impacting adoption
Specific needs of different consumer segments and broader systemic effects
Continuous evaluation and improvement of privacy and data security
Economic viability and cost-effectiveness in different contexts

6 Concluding Remarks

This scoping review gave a thorough assessment of the literature on smart meters. It has emphasized the potential benefits and downsides of smart meters, as well as the factors that impact their acceptance. It has identified crucial smart grid components as well as data security and privacy issues that must be addressed for the successful implementation of smart meters. When supporting the use of smart meters, policymakers must consider user views and acceptability, because creating user trust is crucial for addressing privacy concerns and encouraging participation. Energy providers can employ smart meters to better control energy supply and demand, resulting in enhanced efficiency and cost savings. Future research should address privacy and security problems, interoperability challenges, and customer acceptance to assure the successful implementation of smart meters and the realization of their potential benefits.

This study identified major gaps in smart meter literature especially in terms of how consumers perceive smart meters. This scoping review has provided a comprehensive analysis of the existing literature, providing a solid base and a good understanding to conduct further investigation that will offer further insights into the perspectives of smart meter consumers in the real world.

The potential results of a larger study could provide significant insights into the expectations, benefits, and drawbacks of smart meters, as well as the factors influencing smart meters implementation and awareness. Future research in line with findings from this study will be valuable to policymakers, industry stakeholders, and researchers in the field of information systems, and will contribute to a better understanding of the implementation, awareness and use of smart metering systems.

Acknowledgement. This work has been conducted within the program "Resistance and Effect – on the smart grid for the many people" funded by the Kamprad Family Foundation.

References

1. Mohassel, R.R., et al.: A survey on advanced metering infrastructure. Int. J. Electr. Power Energy Syst. **63**, 473–484 (2014)
2. Ehrhardt-Martinez, K., Donnelly, K.A., Laitner, S.: Advanced metering initiatives and residential feedback programs: a meta-review for household electricity-saving opportunities. American Council for an Energy-Efficient Economy Washington, DC (2010)
3. Barai, G.R., Krishnan, S., Venkatesh, B.: Smart metering and functionalities of smart meters in smart grid-a review. In: 2015 IEEE Electrical Power and Energy Conference (EPEC). IEEE (2015)
4. Corbett, J., Wardle, K., Chen, C.: Toward a sustainable modern electricity grid: the effects of smart metering and program investments on demand-side management performance in the US electricity sector 2009–2012. IEEE Trans. Eng. Manag. **65**(2), 252–263 (2018)
5. Anda, M., Temmen, J.: Smart metering for residential energy efficiency: the use of community based social marketing for behavioural change and smart grid introduction. Renew. Energy **67**, 119–127 (2014)
6. Huang, Y., et al.: Smart meters in Sweden-lessons learned and new regulations. Current Futur. Chall. Energy Secur. **177** (2018)
7. (EIA), U.S.E.I.A. Frequently asked questions (faqs) (2022). https://www.eia.gov/tools/faqs/faq.php?id=108&t=3. Accessed 12 Mar 2023
8. McCann, K.: Germany moves to make smart metering rollout mandatory by 2025 (2023). https://www.iotinsider.com/smart-cities/germany-moves-to-make-smart-metering-rollout-mandatory-by-2025. Accessed 12 Mar 2023
9. Gov.uk, Statutory framework for the Early Years foundation stage - gov.uk. 2021
10. Arksey, H., O'Malley, L.: Scoping studies: towards a methodological framework. Int. J. Soc. Res. Methodol. **8**(1), 19–32 (2005)
11. Levac, D., Colquhoun, H., O'Brien, K.K.: Scoping studies: advancing the methodology. Implement. Sci. **5**, 1–9 (2010)
12. Bahmanyar, A., et al. Emerging smart meters in electrical distribution systems: opportunities and challenges. In: 2016 24th Iranian Conference on Electrical Engineering (ICEE). IEEE (2016)
13. Chakraborty, A.K., Sharma, N.: Advanced metering infrastructure: technology and challenges. In: 2016 IEEE/PES Transmission and Distribution Conference and Exposition (T&D). IEEE (2016)
14. Subhash, B., Rajagopal, V.: Overview of smart metering system in Smart Grid scenario. In: 2014 Power and Energy Systems Conference: Towards Sustainable Energy, PESTSE 2014 (2014)
15. Yesudas, R., Clarke, R.: Consumer concerns about smart meters. In: Streitz, N., Markopoulos, P. (eds.) Distributed, Ambient, and Pervasive Interactions. DAPI 2015. LNCS, vol. 9189, pp. 625–635. Springer, Cham (2015). https://doi.org/10.1007/978-3-319-20804-6_57

16. Opriş, I., et al.: The household energy consumer in a smart metering environment. In: 2015 9th International Symposium on Advanced Topics in Electrical Engineering (ATEE). IEEE (2015)
17. Yesudas, R.: A consumer friendly framework for smart grid initiatives. In: TENCON 2015–2015 IEEE Region 10 Conference. IEEE (2015)
18. Yesudas, R., Clarke, R.: Architecture and data flow model for consumer-oriented smart meter design (2014)
19. Yesudas, R., Clarke, R.: Identifying consumer requirements as an antidote to resistance to smart meters. In: IEEE PES Innovative Smart Grid Technologies Conference Europe (2015)
20. Freitas, J., et al.: Smart electricity metering systems for smart grids: technologies, choices, and deployment experiences. In: 2021 IEEE PES Innovative Smart Grid Technologies Conference-Latin America (ISGT Latin America). IEEE (2021)
21. Opriş, I., Caracasian, L.: On the implementation of the functionalities of smart metering systems. In: 2013 8Th International Symposium on Advanced Topics in Electrical Engineering (Atee). IEEE (2013)
22. Malik, J.S., Verma, R.K., Gupta, G.: Development of smart meter. In: 2015 4th International Conference on Reliability, Infocom Technologies and Optimization: Trends and Future Directions, ICRITO 2015 (2015)
23. Bugden, D., Stedman, R.: A synthetic view of acceptance and engagement with smart meters in the United States. Energy Res. Soc. Sci. **47**, 137–145 (2019)
24. Pullinger, M., Lovell, H., Webb, J.: Influencing household energy practices: a critical review of UK smart metering standards and commercial feedback devices. Technol. Anal. Strateg. Manag. **26**(10), 1144–1162 (2014)
25. Vigurs, C., et al.: Customer privacy concerns as a barrier to sharing data about energy use in smart local energy systems: a rapid realist review. Energies **14**(5), 1285 (2021)
26. Gumz, J., Fettermann, D.C.: Better deployments come with acceptance: an investigation of factors driving consumers' acceptance of smart meters. Current Sustain. Renew. Energy Rep. 1–13 (2023)
27. Yang, B., et al.: Smart metering and systems for low-energy households: challenges, issues and benefits. Adv. Build. Energy Res. **13**(1), 80–100 (2019)

Exploring Techno-Invasion and Work-Life Balance on Digital Platforms: A Preliminary Study with Amazon MTurk's Gig Workers

Hasan Koç$^{(\boxtimes)}$ ⓘ and Chingiz Gasimov

Berlin International University of Applied Sciences, Salzufer 6, 10587 Berlin, Germany
{koc,chingizgasimov}@berlin-international.de

Abstract. The rapid advances in technology and COVID-19 lockdown measures transformed the way of working and paved the way for the rise of digital platform work. Although potentially expanding employment opportunities and introducing many beneficial aspects, digital platform work is also associated with exposure to stress due to various factors. Technostress is one such area of concern for platform workers. This preliminary study focuses on a single technostressor, techno-invasion, which refers to the perceived intrusion of technology into personal life, and investigates the impact of techno-invasion on the work-life balance of digital platform workers. Testing six hypotheses, the research surveyed 30 Amazon MTurk workers to measure techno-invasion and work-life balance. The results reveal a significant positive linear relationship between techno-invasion and work interference with personal life, indicating that greater perceived intrusion of technology leads to lower work-life balance. Additionally, female workers experience higher levels of techno-invasion compared to their male counterparts, potentially due to additional caregiving responsibilities. Acknowledging limitations due to the small sample size drawn solely from Amazon MTurk, the preliminary study suggests that digital platforms should implement measures to reduce techno-invasion, such as offering training and support to enhance workers' digital literacy as well as actively seeking feedback from platform workers.

Keywords: Platform Business Model · Technostress · Online Platform Work · Work-life Balance · Wellbeing · Techno-invasion · Gig Economy

1 Introduction

In today's world, information and communication technologies (ICTs) have become an indispensable aspect of people's everyday work and private life. This transformation had a profound impact on various sectors, and one notable area where it has revolutionized the business is the platforms and online labour markets. A platform business is "a business creating significant value through the acquisition matching and connection of two or more customer groups to enable them to transact" [1, p.22]. The platform business model is prevalent among the largest global companies, top-5 most valuable brands worldwide in 2022 adopt platform-powered business models [2].

© The Author(s), under exclusive license to Springer Nature Switzerland AG 2023
K. Hinkelmann et al. (Eds.): BIR 2023, LNBIP 493, pp. 121–132, 2023.
https://doi.org/10.1007/978-3-031-43126-5_9

Platform businesses rely on of two or more distinct types of affiliated customers [3], enabling value-creating interactions between external producers and consumers [4]. From a taxonomical perspective, the format of labour provision differentiates "online" (UpWork, 99Designs) and "on-location" (Uber, Deliveroo) platforms. The external producers are termed as *gig workers* [5] or *digital platform workers* [6] in online platforms, and they "provide labour intermediated with a greater or lesser extent of control via a digital labour platform, regardless of [the] legal environmental status." [6, p.5]. In this sense, and for this study, an online labour market - also referred to as digital labour platforms or online marketplaces - is understood as a market consisting of platform-mediated work that is conducted remotely via the Internet [7].

For online/digital platform work, the significance of technologies cannot be overstated as individuals increasingly embrace enhanced internet connectivity and the widespread availability of advanced data storage and processing capabilities. [8] reports that 5–9% of adult Internet users work through online platforms every week. Moreover, a recent study estimates that there are 163 million profiles registered on online platforms, and around 12% have obtained work through the platform at least once [9]. The main potential advantages tied to platform work are flexibility and the reduction of work-family conflict [8]. Nevertheless, digital platform work is also associated with exposure to stress due to various factors (see Sect. 2.1), and technostress is one such area of concern for platform workers.

Technostress is "stress that users experience as a result of their use of information systems (IS) in the organizational context" [10, p.103]. There are five technostress creators; techno-overload, techno-complexity, techno-invasion, techno-insecurity, and techno-uncertainty [11]. Technostress has gained interest among IS researchers [12, 13], with techno-invasion being one of the most extensively studied construct [14]. Yet not much has been said about the impact of technology in the context of gig workers' well-being. Digital platform workers experience technostress [15], and this exploratory investigation focuses only on a particular technostressor "techno-invasion", aiming to answer the researcher question "What is the relationship between techno-invasion and digital platform workers' work-life balance?" For this purpose, Sect. 2 explains the theoretical background of gig workers' work-life balance and technostress. Section 3 mentions the research method adopted in the study, Sect. 4 presents the results, Sect. 5 discusses the findings, and Sect. 6 informs of the limitations and future research.

2 Background and Literature Review

2.1 Online Platform Work and Technostress

With the rise of the digital economy, the pervasiveness of technology, and the introduction of COVID-19 lockdown measures, platforms and online platform work gained significant relevance. A comprehensive study conducted by the International Labour Organization (ILO) in 2021 provides an estimate of the annual revenue generated by online digital labour platforms, standing at $2.5 billion [16]. As for the count of platform workers, various statistics are available. For instance, it is approximated that 9.7% of the adult population in the EU has earned income from a digital platform [17]. According to a survey conducted by the Pew Research Center in 2021, 16% of Americans have engaged in earning money through an online gig platform [18]. Although precise figures are lacking, there has been a rapid growth in the number of digital labour platforms and platform workers over the past decade.

Various terms have been used in the literature to denote platform work, e.g., gig worker [5], digital platform worker [6] or platform worker [8]. Although a thorough discussion of these concepts would extend the boundaries of this study, it is acknowledged that those "digital public squares" [15] have an impact on economic processes in terms of the creation and delivery of services. Also, there is an agreement on the recurring characteristics of online platform work, which are intermediation by a digital labour platform, triangular relationship (between platform, worker, and client), piece-rate pay and temporary nature of work, the use of digital technologies, non-standard working arrangements and shifting the risks to the digital platform worker [6].

From a terminological perspective, [19] argues that online platform work denotes all labour provided through, on, or mediated by online platforms, including the both digital and manual provision of work. Yet, for this exploratory study, the focus is on the digital provision form and excludes on-location/on-site (e.g., TaskRabbit, Uber, Deliveroo) platform work. Hence, we follow the definition provided in [6, p.8], "online platform work refers to tasks that are matched with workers online and are performed only or mostly virtually on an electronic device at any location".

A latest study mentions that there are 351 online freelancing platforms, with a predicted number of 163 million registered profiles [9]. Digital platforms' core task is matchmaking the users, allowing them to interact and create value for both parties. In this sense, more than the number of registered users, activity and interaction between them are what matters [4]. Thus, the same study also reveals that "approximately 19 million of [digital platform workers] have obtained work through the platform at least once, and 5 million have completed at least 10 projects or earned at least $1000", emphasizing the relevance of online platform work [9, p.1].

From an occupational safety and health perspective, digital platform workers are exposed to factors that increase the chances of experiencing stress, such as employment status, digital surveillance [6], isolation, job instability, low salaries [20], poorly arranged workstations, and high pace of work [5]. A major threat is the high dependency on ICTs and the risks tied to precarious working conditions [21]. In this context, technostress is mentioned as one important psycho-social risk for online platform workers [15, 22], which is the stress that users experience as a result of their use of ICTs [10]. Consequences of technostress can be physiological, psychosocial, organizational, and societal [23]. It can lead to burnout [10, 24], lower performance [25], low job satisfaction [11], poor sleep quality [24], and work-family conflict [10, 12]. Therefore, it is essential for employers and policymakers to take steps to mitigate the risks of technostress and promote the well-being of digital platform workers.

2.2 Techno-Invasion and Work-Life Balance

Technostress comprises five dimensions. Techno-overload "describes situations where the use of IS forces professionals to work more and work faster". Techno-invasion "describes situations where professionals can be reached anywhere and anytime". Techno-complexity "describes situations where the complexity associated with IS forces professionals to spend time and effort in learning and understanding how to use new applications". Techno-insecurity "emerges in situations where users feel threatened about losing their jobs to other people who have a better understanding of new [IS]", techno-uncertainty refers to contexts where continuing changes and upgrades to [IS] do not give professionals a chance to develop a base of experience for a particular application or system [26].

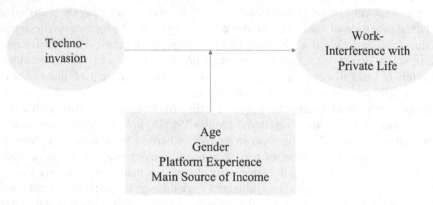

Fig. 1. Research model.

To get more clients and increase their income, digital platform workers have an always-on mindset, work faster, and strive to be available at all times [6, 15, 19]. Technology plays a central part in the activities of online platform workers. Interviewing 30 workers, Lehdonvirta [8] mentions that half of the informants utilise software technologies to enhance their work, for example by monitoring tasks that match certain criteria available or displaying earnings. One informant, alarmingly, mentions being chained to the computer endlessly in the search for the next tasks. This is consistent with the findings of [27], where 55% of platform workers reported to having worked long hours and at a high intensity, which can harm work-life balance.

Although platform workers most possibly experience every dimension of technostress, this preliminary study focuses on techno-invasion and how it impacts the well-being of platform workers. This is mainly against the background that techno-invasion "refers to constant connectivity of being 'always exposed' that blurs desired boundaries between work and personal life" [28, p.454], and that techno-invasion, one of the mostly studied constructs in technostress research [14], is shown to have a negative impact on work-family conflict [29]. Hence, we hypothesize, that (H1) Techno-invasion is positively associated with work interference with life. In addition to techno-invasion and work-life balance, further variables such as age and gender are important measures when examining the impact of technostressors [12, 14, 30]. Studies show that platform workers are generally younger than non-platform workers [5, 17]. As technostress decreases with increasing age [11], we hypothesize (H2) that age and techno-invasion are significantly correlated, such that younger digital workers experience more techno-invasion.

Research on technostress and gender is limited and has contrasting findings. Ragu-Nathan et. al. [11] reports more technostress among men whereas [31] does not detect any significant effect. [32] breaks down the effects and finds that men are more affected by techno-invasion, [33] shows that females tend to experience increased technostress. Against this background, we hypothesize (H3) gender and techno-invasion are significantly correlated such that female workers experience higher techno-invasion. Furthermore, comparing both groups, (H4) the association between techno-invasion and work-life interference is significantly higher for the female workers. Online work is usually perceived as a source of supplementary income [9]. Hence, we further hypothesize that (H5) digital platform work as the main source of income moderates the relationship between techno-invasion and work interference with life, i.e., workers who are dependent on platform work experience a significantly stronger impact of technology invasion on their private life. Technology self-efficacy is known to reduce the amount of technostress [34], with the experience of platform work, the frequency of technology use and level of technology self-efficacy increases. We thus hypothesize (H6) experience with platform work moderates the relationship between techno-invasion and work interference with life in the sense that the impact of techno-invasion on private life is lower for experienced workers. The next section discusses the research method utilized to investigate the aforementioned hypotheses.

3 Research Method

To explore the relationship between techno-invasion and work-life balance, a survey[1] was performed with 30 digital platform workers. For assessing the work-life balance, we asked seven questions from Work Interference with Personal Life (WIPL), a first-level construct from the Measure of Work-Life Balance (WLB) scale [35]. An exemplary question was "My personal life suffers because of work". Techno-invasion was measured using the technostress creators inventory [25] (e.g. "I spend less time with my family due to this technology."). All questions were measured using a 5-point Likert scale (1 = strongly disagree, 5 = strongly agree). The research model is shown in Fig. 1. Moreover, the demographics of the participants were measured by inquiring about their age (in years), gender, experience as a platform worker, and whether the platform labor is their main source of income (see Table 1). The survey was prepared on Google Forms and disseminated among 30 digital platform workers of Amazon MTurk. The data was analyzed using R Studio (2023.03.1).

---

[1] The survey can be accessed at https://bit.ly/3NBQyki.

Table 1. Sample characteristics

Variable	Values	% of respondents
Age	18–24	10%
	25–34	50%
	35 or over	40%
Gender	Female	46.7%
	Male	52.3%
Platform as the main source of income	Yes	86.7%
	No	13.3%
Experience as a platform worker	6.53 (years)	n/a

4 Findings

Due to the small sample size for this preliminary study, and the fact that the normality assumption is violated, we used robust methods with bootstrapping to analyze the relationships between the variables. The correlation matrix is shown in Table 2. (Note that * $p \leq 0.05$, ** $p \leq 0.01$, *** $p \leq 0.001$, **** $p \leq 0.0001$, WIPL = Work Interference with Personal Life, TINV = Techno-invasion).

Table 2. Correlation matrix

	WIPL	TINV	Platform Experience	Age	Gender
WIPL	1				
TINV	0.81****	1			
Platform Experience	0.10	−0.16	1		
Age	0.15	0.05	0.54***	1	
Gender	-0.28	−0.44**	0.21	−0.27	1

Among the variables, only Techno-invasion was found to have a highly significant and very strong positive relationship with Work Interference with Personal Life ($r_{pb} = 0.81, p \leq 0.0001$). Platform Experience, Age, and Gender have all weak and insignificant associations with Work Interference with Personal Life. However, there is a significant and negative moderate relationship between a platform workers' gender (0 = female, 1 = male) and how much techno-invasion they experience ($r_{pb} = 0.54, p \leq 0.001$), suggesting that female digital platform workers are exposed to more techno-invasion as compared to their male counterparts.

Based on this finding, we compared the correlations between the investigated variables and checked whether there is a difference when bringing in the gender aspect. Our results showed that the correlation between the levels of Techno-invasion and Work Interference with Personal Life significantly differ in female and male groups, showing a very strong positive correlation in the former group ($r_{pb} = 0.96$, p ≤ 0.05). This suggests that the strong positive correlation between Techno-invasion and Work Interference with Personal Life is even higher for female platform workers as compared to male platform workers.

We fitted a robust linear regression model using the *lmRob* function to predict the outcome variable (Work Interference with Private Life) with Techno-invasion as the predictor. The model estimates were obtained using robust methods, which account for potential outliers and violations of the classical assumptions. The model explains a substantial proportion of variance ($R2 = 0.61$, p < .001) in predicting Work Interference with Private Life. As shown in Table 3, the effect of Techno-invasion on Work Interference with Private Life was statistically significant and positive (beta = 0.69, std. Beta = 0.61, p < 0.0001, 95% std. CI [0.38, 0.83]). In other words, if Techno-invasion is increased by one standard deviation, then our model predicts that WIPL increases by 0.61 standard deviations.

Table 3. The robust linear regression model

	Estimates	std. Beta	CI	std. CI	p
Intercept	1.14	1.35	0.63–1.64	0.64–2.06	.0001
Techno-invasion	0.69	0.61	0.53–0.84	0.38–0.83	< .0001

Table 4. Hypotheses

Hypothesis	Result
H1. Techno-invasion is positively associated with work interference with life	Supported
H2. Age and techno-invasion are significantly correlated, such that younger digital workers experience more techno-invasion	Not supported
H3. Gender and techno-invasion are significantly correlated such that female workers experience higher techno-invasion	Supported
H4. The association between techno-invasion and work-life interference is significantly higher for the female workers	Supported
H5. Digital platform work as a main source of income moderates the relationship between techno-invasion and work interference with life	Not supported
H6. Experience with platform work moderates the relationship between techno-invasion and work interference with life	Not supported

To test H5 and H6, we ran two analyses. None of the robust models shows a significant moderation effect, $b = -0.026$, 95% CI [−0.17, 0.12], $t (26) = −.367$, $p > 0.05$ for platform experience and $b = −.082$, 95% CI [−3.35, 3.18], $t (26) = -0.052$, $p > 0.05$ for having the platform work as a main source of income respectively.

5 Discussion

The proliferation of smart devices, data-driven algorithms, and rapid technological advancements have contributed to the rise of the platform economy and platform work. Both from regulatory and organizational health and safety perspectives, digital platform work has become a topic of intense debate lately. Particularly, online platform workers belong to a vulnerable workforce, since they are professionally isolated, subject to monitoring surveillance, and review systems. Furthermore, online platform workers have lower autonomy, less access to social protection, and insecure income, which forces them to work faster and accept more jobs. As such, they face high risks of stress, and technostress is one such health risk. This preliminary study focuses on techno-invasion, a technostressor, and its impacts on online platform workers' private life.

The study has several contributions. From a theoretical aspect, there is a necessity to investigate the impact of technostress and its moderators in various usage contexts. According to [30], previous technostress research has predominantly focused on organizational environments, neglecting the importance of studying work-from-home arrangements. As highlighted in the comprehensive systematic review conducted by LaTorre et al. [12], technostress affects workers engaged in diverse types of work that are closely intertwined with ICT usage. It is particularly crucial to examine the effects of technostress on emerging professional categories, as these workers are even more extensively exposed to the pervasive influence of ICT. Moreover, the inclusion of potential moderators, such as self-efficacy, individual differences, or organizational demands, is suggested in the investigation of technostressors' impact [36]. Our exploratory study makes a valuable contribution to the existing literature by examining how techno-invasion impacts the work-life balance of digital platform workers, while also considering additional moderating variables, e.g., experience with platform work and the significance attributed to platform work from an income perspective.

The results suggest that there is a significant positive linear relationship between techno-invasion and work-life balance, supporting H1 and indicating that the more platform workers perceived their personal lives to be invaded by technology, the more likely they were to experience work interference with personal life. Specific design and technical features of technologies, such as push notifications, information feeds [37] or nudges [6] as well as the tendency to react immediately [38] might trigger techno-invasion, which can lead to time-management problems, exhaustion and loss of concentration among online platform workers. It is important for digital platform workers to take steps to protect their well-being, such as setting boundaries between work and personal life, taking breaks, and seeking help if they are experiencing stress. Digital platforms are thus recommended to implement measures to reduce the amount of techno-invasion. For example, they can offer training and education programs to enhance users' digital literacy and time management skills. Providing support on how to effectively use the platform, manage time, and set boundaries between work and personal life can help users cope with techno-invasion more effectively.

In addition to techno-invasion and work-life balance, variables such as age, gender, and individuals' experience in platform work were also measured when examining the relationship between techno-invasion and work-life balance. We did not find any support for H2, as age and techno-invasion did not have a meaningful relationship. Although the samples were not limited to platform workers, this contradicts the findings of [11, 39] where younger employees reported lower technostress levels. Variables such as job characteristics, work demands, or technological proficiency, which were not included or adequately controlled for in this study, could be influencing the relationship.

Our investigation has revealed that in comparison to male digital platform workers, female workers are encountering a considerably higher degree of techno-invasion, which supports H3. These findings contradict the results presented in [32], which indicate that men are more affected by techno-invasion than women. However, our findings are consistent with [33], which suggests that females experienced increased technostress. This can be attributed to caregiving responsibilities that women often undertake, such as childcare and household tasks, which restrict the time available for female online platform workers to complete their work-related duties, and thus force them to multi-task during the day [40], supporting H4. To buffer against the higher impact of techno-invasion on work-life balance, platforms are recommended to actively seek feedback from female workers to understand their experiences and challenges related to techno-invasion. Furthermore, based on the feedback, platforms should assess specific types of demands and resources these groups possess to understand the impact of techno-invasion on the work-life balance. Incorporating workers' input into platform design can help address specific issues and tailor solutions that are more responsive to platform workers' needs.

Literature suggests that gig workers who have chosen to work on the platforms are likely to experience less negative outcomes compared to the ones who participate in there out of economic necessity (pull vs. push factors) [41]. However, our findings indicate that the perceived status of platform work as the primary income source does not impact the relationship between techno-invasion and work-life balance. While it is important to consider individual coping mechanisms, personal adaptation factors and support systems, we acknowledge that the disproportionate allocation of online platform workers in our sample (see Table 1) may have influenced this outcome. Furthermore, the significant relationship between techno-invasion and work interference with private life is found to be consistent across different platform experience levels, leading to the rejection of H6.

6 Summary, Limitations and Outlook

As noted in [8], platform workers praise the flexibility of working schedules and mention that platform work allows them to balance work with other activities. Our initial findings show that i) techno-invasion negatively impacts work-life balance, ii) female workers experience higher techno-invasion, and iii) the association between techno-invasion and work-life interference is significantly higher for female workers. Hence, techno-invasion, especially with female digital platform workers, might increase the gap between the expectations of the worker, and experienced distress, resulting in lower satisfaction and performance levels.

The present study is preliminary in nature, and subject to several limitations. First, it focuses on a single technostressor (techno-invasion), one of the most extensively studied construct in the Technostress Creators Inventory [14]. Second, the generalizability of the findings is limited due to the small sample size. Third, the respondents were drawn from Amazon MTurk's platform worker pool, which may not represent the entire population of digital platform workers. Last but not least, the analysis does not account for the preferences, interests, motivations, and nature of work (such as precarity or job insecurity) among online platform workers. Considering these limitations, and the promising results obtained in this study, we are currently developing a more comprehensive investigation. This forthcoming study will encompass additional technostressors (such as challenge and hindrance technostressors), outcome variables (such as wellbeing and exhaustion), and moderators (such as technology self-efficacy, technology-enabled performance, job support, autonomy, skill/task variety) using a larger sample. Thus, our future research aims to explore the specific characteristics of digital technologies for online platform workers, examine the factors that may induce eustress and distress, and provide insights into the advantages and disadvantages of engaging in online platform work.

References

1. Reillier, L.C., Reillier, B.: Platform strategy. How to unlock the power of communities and networks to grow your business. Routledge, New York (2017)
2. Interbrand: Leading brands worldwide in 2022, by brand value (in billion U.S. dollars) (2022), https://www.statista.com/statistics/264826/most-valuable-brands-worldwide-in-2009/
3. Hagiu, A., Wright, J.: Multi-sided platforms. Int. J. Ind. Organ. **43**, 162–174 (2015). https://doi.org/10.1016/j.ijindorg.2015.03.003
4. Parker, G., van Alstyne, M., Choudary, S.P.: Platform revolution. How networked markets are transforming the economy - and how to make them work for you. W.W. Norton, New York, London (2017)
5. Tran, M., Sokas, R.K.: The gig economy and contingent work: an occupational health assessment. J. Occup. Environ. Med. **59**, e63–e66 (2017)
6. Lenaerts, K., Waeyaert, W., Smits, I., Harald, H.: Digital platform work and occupational safety and health: a review. European Risk Observatory Report (2021)
7. Stephany, F., Kässi, O., Rani, U., Lehdonvirta, V.: Online Labour Index 2020: new ways to measure the world's remote freelancing market. Big Data Soc. **8**, 205395172110432 (2021)
8. Lehdonvirta, V.: Flexibility in the gig economy: managing time on three online piecework platforms. N. Technol. Work. Employ. **33**, 13–29 (2018). https://doi.org/10.1111/ntwe.12102
9. Kässi, O., Lehdonvirta, V., Stephany, F.: How Many Online Workers are there in the World? A Data-Driven Assessment (2021)
10. Tarafdar, M., Pullins, E.B., Ragu-Nathan, T.S.: Technostress: negative effect on performance and possible mitigations. Inf. Syst. J. **25**, 103–132 (2015). https://doi.org/10.1111/isj.12042
11. Ragu-Nathan, T.S., Tarafdar, M., Ragu-Nathan, B.S., Tu, Q.: The Consequences of Technostress for End Users in Organizations: Conceptual Development and Empirical Validation. Inf. Syst. Res. **19**, 417–433 (2008)
12. La Torre, G., Esposito, A., Sciarra, I., Chiappetta, M.: Definition, symptoms and risk of technostress: a systematic review. Int. Arch. Occup. Environ. Health **92**, 13–35 (2019). https://doi.org/10.1007/s00420-018-1352-1
13. Pflügner, K.: Technostress Management at the Workplace: A Systematic Literature ReviewLiterature Review. In: Wirtschaftsinformatik 2022 Proceedings. Association for Information Systems (2022)
14. Marsh, E., Vallejos, E.P., Spence, A.: The digital workplace and its dark side: an integrative review. Comput. Hum. Behav. **128**, 107118 (2022). https://doi.org/10.1016/j.chb.2021.107118

15. Garben, S.: Protecting Workers in the Online Platform Economy: an overview of regulatory and policy developments in the EU. European Risk Observatory Executive summary (2017)
16. International Labour Office: World Employment and Social Outlook. the role of digital labour platforms in transforming the world of work. International Labour Office, Geneva (2021)
17. Pesole, A., Urzi Brancati, M.C., Fernandez Macias, E., Biagi, F., Gonzalez Vazquez, I.: Platform Workers in Europe Evidence from the COLLEEM Survey. Publications Office of the European Union, Luxembourg (2018)
18. Anderson, M., McClain, C., Faverio, M. and Gelles-Watnick, R.: The State of Gig Work in 2021 (2021), https://www.pewresearch.org/internet/2021/12/08/the-state-of-gig-work-in-2021/
19. Garben, S.: The regulatory challenge of occupational safety and health in the online platform economy. Int. Soc. Secur. Rev. **72**, 95–112 (2019)
20. Freni-Sterrantino, A., Salerno, V.: A plea for the need to investigate the health effects of Gig-Economy. Front. Oublic Health **9**, 638767 (2021)
21. Wood, A., Lehdonvirta, V.: Platforms disrupting reputation: precarity and recognition struggles in the remote gig economy. SSRN J. 00380385221126804 (2022)
22. Umair, A., Conboy, K., Whelan, E.: Understanding the influence of technostress on workers' job satisfaction in Gig-economy: an exploratory investigation. In: ECIS 2019 proceedings. Research-in-Progress Papers. Association for Information Systems, Erscheinungsort nicht ermittelbar (2019)
23. Bondanini, G., Giorgi, G., Ariza-Montes, A., Vega-Muñoz, A., Andreucci-Annunziata, P.: Technostress dark side of technology in the workplace: a scientometric analysis. Int. J. Environ. Res. Public Health **17**, 8013 (2020)
24. Barber, L.K., Santuzzi, A.M.: Please respond ASAP: workplace telepressure and employee recovery. J. Occup. Health Psychol. **20**, 172–189 (2015). https://doi.org/10.1037/a0038278
25. Tarafdar, M., Tu, Q., Ragu-Nathan, T.S.:Impact of technostress on end-user satisfaction and performance. J. Manag. Inf. Syst. **27**, 303–334 (2010)
26. Tarafdar, M., Tu, Q., Ragu-Nathan, T.S., Ragu-Nathan, B.S.: Crossing to the dark side. examining creators, outcomes, and inhibitors of technostress. Commun. ACM **54**, 113–120 (2011). https://doi.org/10.1145/1995376.1995403
27. Graham, M., Lehdonvirta, V., Wood, A., Barnard, H., Hjorth, I., Simon, P.D.: The risks and rewards of Online Gig Work at the global margins (2017), https://www.oii.ox.ac.uk/wp-content/uploads/2017/06/gigwork.pdf
28. Chen, Y., Wang, X., Benitez, J., Luo, X., Li, D.: Does techno-invasion lead to employees' deviant behaviors? J. Manag. Inf. Syst. **39**, 454–482 (2022). https://doi.org/10.1080/07421222.2022.2063557
29. Cho, S., Kim, S., Chin, S.W., Ahmad, U.: Daily effects of continuous ICT demands on work-family conflict: negative spillover and role conflict. Stress Health J. Int. Soc. Invest. Stress **36**, 533–545 (2020). https://doi.org/10.1002/smi.2955
30. Grummeck-Braamt, J.-V., Nastjuk, I., Najmaei, A., Adam, M.: A bibliometric review of technostress: historical roots, evolution and central publications of a growing research Field. In: Bui, T. (ed.) Proceedings of the 54th Annual Hawaii International Conference on System Sciences, 6621–6630 (2021)
31. Wang, K., Shu, Q., Tu, Q.: Technostress under different organizational environments: an empirical investigation. Comput. Hum. Behav. **24**, 3002–3013 (2008)
32. Marchiori, D.M., Mainardes, E.W., Rodrigues, R.G.: Do individual characteristics influence the types of technostress reported by workers? Int. J. Human Comput. Interact. **35**, 218–230 (2019). https://doi.org/10.1080/10447318.2018.1449713
33. D'Arcy, J., Gupta, A., Tarafdar, M., Turel, O.: Reflecting on the "Dark Side" of Information Technology Use. CAIS, vol. 35 (2014). https://doi.org/10.17705/1CAIS.03505

34. Truța, C., Maican, C.I., Cazan, A.-M., Lixăndroiu, R.C., Dovleac, L., Maican, M.A.: Always connected @ work. Technostress and well-being with academics. Comput. Human Behav. **143**, 107675 (2023)
35. Agha, K., Azmi, F.T., Khan, S.A.: Work-Life Balance: Scale Development and Validation. In: Heras, M.L., Chinchilla, N., Grau, M. (eds.) The Work-Family Balance in Light of Globalization and Technology, pp. 109–130. Cambridge Scholars, Newcastle upon Tyne, UK (2017)
36. Tams, S.: Challenges in Technostress Research: Guiding Future Work Emergent Research Forum papers. In: AMCIS 2015 Proceedings. Association for Information Systems (2015)
37. Becker, J., Berger, M., Gimpel, H., Lanzl, J., Regal, C.: Considering Characteristic Profiles of Technologies at the Digital Workplace: The Influence on Technostress. In: ICIS 2020 Proceedings (2020)
38. Ghislieri, C., Emanuel, F., Molino, M., Cortese, C.G., Colombo, L.: New technologies smart, or harm work-family boundaries management? gender differences in conflict and enrichment using the JD-R theory. Front. Psychol. **8**, 1070 (2017)
39. Fischer, T., Reuter, M., Riedl, R.: The digital stressors scale: development and validation of a new survey instrument to measure digital stress perceptions in the workplace context. Front. Psychol. **12** (2021)
40. Gerber, C.: Gender and precarity in platform work: old inequalities in the new world of work. New Technol Work Employ **37**, 206–230 (2022). https://doi.org/10.1111/ntwe.12233
41. Keith, G.M., Harms, D.P., Long, C.A.: Worker Health and Well-Being in the Gig Economy: A Proposed Framework and Research Agenda. In: Perrewé, P.L., Harms, P.D., Chang, C.-H. (eds.) Entrepreneurial and small business stressors, experienced stress, and well being. Research in occupational stress and well being, pp. 1–33. Emerald Publishing, United Kingdom (2020)

An Approach for Knowledge Graphs-Based User Stories in Agile Methodologies

Marco Mancuso and Emanuele Laurenzi$^{(\boxtimes)}$ (iD)

FHNW University of Applied Sciences and Arts Northwestern Switzerland, Riggenbachstrasse 16, 4600 Olten, Switzerland
marcocarmelo.mancuso@students.fhnw.ch, emanuele.laurenzi@fhnw.ch

Abstract. In this paper, we present AOAME4UserStories, a modelling and ontology-based approach that enables the creation of visual user stories grounded in a knowledge graph. The approach includes an ontology-based domain-specific modelling language - User Story Modelling & Notation (USMN) - and resolves the problem of creating inconsistent user stories in agile software development methodologies such as Scrum. The Design Science Research methodology was followed for the creation of USMN and its implementation in the modelling tool AOAME. The evaluation was conducted by first creating a visual user story reflecting a real-world use case and then by proving the consistent production of knowledge graphs for the given visual story.

Keywords: Agile software development · Scrum · visual user stories · knowledge graphs · USMN · domain-specific modelling language (DSML) · ontology-based meta-modelling · AOAME4UserStories

1 Introduction

Agile software development methods are increasingly adopted across industries for their user-centricity and avoidance of sequential steps. The Scrum framework is an agile method that helps a team (i.e., the Scrum team) solve complex software development problems by decomposing them into small work units, which are processed in short time frames, typically called sprints [1]. Each sprint aims to generate added value for the targeting stakeholders, which can manifest in a product feature. Hence, a product is developed iteratively through sprints by starting from the needs of the stakeholders and ending with their evaluation. In contrast to traditional software development methodologies, where the needs or requirements of the stakeholders (or end users) are reported in written natural language and lengthy documents, Scrum indicates such requirements in the form of user stories [2]. The latter consolidates the requirements in a state that is quicker to express and easier to understand by stakeholders.

As of today, however, there is no consistent way to express user stories, which vary across companies and the specifications are often left up to the experience of the product owner (PO) or requirements engineers (RE) [3].

K. Hinkelmann et al. (Eds.): BIR 2023, LNBIP 493, pp. 133–141, 2023.
https://doi.org/10.1007/978-3-031-43126-5_10

To overcome this issue, in this paper we create a domain-specific modelling language (DSML) which could start setting the basis for creating a visual standard for user stories. Furthermore, in order to make the user stories interpretable and interchangeable across systems, the proposed DSML is grounded in a knowledge graph.

The remainder of the paper is as follows: Sect. 2 describes the related work; Sect. 3 explains the followed methodology; the suggested DSML is described in Sect. 4, and the evaluation is in Sect. 5. Section 6 concludes this paper and points to future work.

2 Related Work

Floruț and Buchmann [4] proposed a modelling approach that offers a visual alternative to JIRA as a diagrammatic model utilising modelling standards like BPMN and UML. The approach integrates the modelling standards with issue-tracking technologies, enabling explicit links between user stories, software artefacts, and business processes. Although the approach uses modelling standards, it does not offer a modelling construct tailored to the representational requirements of user stories in Scrum.

Athiththan et al. [5] introduced Sponto, a software process automation ontology approach that makes use of user stories to produce various software artefacts. Different from our approach, Sponto addresses the absence of artefact traceability issues in the agile software development process.

Nasiri et al. [6] were using NLP technology. The USon ontology allows the automatic creation of UML Class Diagrams from user stories. The authors [6] argue that their approach promises to lower error rates, improve teamwork, and gain time. Differently our knowledge-driven approach aims to create consistent and machine-interpretable user stories.

Thamrongchote and Vatanawood [7] propose a Business Process Ontology to store user stories as a knowledge base and allow for archiving and reuse. The authors used a user story template suggested by Zeaaraoui et al. [8] to incorporate role-action-object relations into the mapping of user stories to the ontology schema. The approach, however, does not have a visual representation that targets Scrum practitioners.

Murtazina and Avdeenko [9] proposed an ontology-based method for agile requirements engineering that makes it easier to track the relationships between user stories and evaluate their quality, importance, and risk. Differently, our approach also enables the visualisation of user stories.

Lucassen et al. [10] have created an NLP-based tool called Visual Narrator, to produce outputs for the ontology visualisation of user stories. The tool can find dependencies and redundancies by extracting conceptual models from user stories. However, a combination of tools and knowledge is needed to easily access conceptual models.

Further research by the same researchers [11] highlighted the advantages of visualising user story requirements at various levels of granularity. Furthermore, according to Lucassen et al. [11] it makes it easier to fully comprehend needs, which is helpful when dealing with many different requirements and concepts.

However, user stories must be written and kept within a repository and then processed using the Visual Narrator tool, which was previously mentioned [10].

In contrast, our method makes it easier to create user stories by incorporating all of their essential elements into a user-friendly modelling environment and storing them in a knowledge graph.

3 Methodology

In this work, the ontology-based DSML and related models about user stories have been developed by conducting one additional iteration of the Design Science Research (DSR) methodology [12] from the approach presented in [13].

The problem understanding was deepened by conducting a literature review and was supplemented by interviews with Scrum specialists to elicit domain-specific requirements elicitation. The latter activity is consistent with the best practices for creating DSMLs [14, 15]. In total, five semi-structured interviews were conducted with four Product Owners and one Scrum Master. The elicitation of requirements was done by analysing the answers of the specialists. Findings from both literature and the primary data served as a basis for the development of the DSML and involved determining, comprehending, and documenting the needs, expectations, and constraints that the DSML should meet. Table 1 shows two of the overall 26 requirements gathered.

Table 1. Gathered requirements towards a DSML for user stories.

Requirement number	Requirement description	categorisation
#03	The DSML should provide an extension mechanism to cover all possible applications within its domain. It should allow adding new elements as needed by the scrum team or stakeholders [14]	general
#12	The DSML should support defining acceptance criteria	functional

The below sections elaborate on the suggestion, implementation and evaluation phases, respectively.

4 AOAME4UserStories

This section describes the solution AOAME4UserStories, which includes the DSML that we call "User Story Modelling & Notation" (USMN) and its implementation in AOAME for creating visual user stories using domain-specific modelling constructs.

4.1 Our Proposed DSML: The User Story Modelling & Notation (USMN)

The DSML User Story Modelling & Notation (USMN) was created by addressing requirements elicited in the awareness of problem phase of the DSR methodology.. Figure 1 depicts the meta-model. The metamodel consists of several different classes and relationships. For example, the class "Actor" represents the acting person within a user story. The class "Reason" illustrates the motivation of a user – the "why" a user story should be implemented in a software system. The focus is on the user story class as it is focal in the DSML.

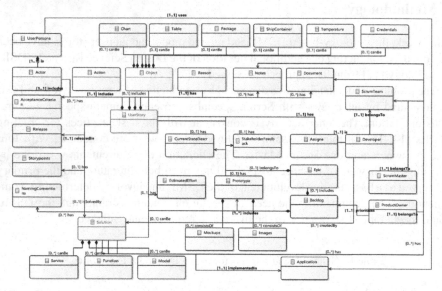

Fig. 1. Metamodel of the User Story Modelling Language & Notation (USMN)

Table 2 shows an excerpt of the constraints for the USMN. The graphical notation is displayed directly in the evaluation chapter.

Table 2. An excerpt of the constraints for USMN

Constraints	Description	Arise from requirement
#01	Every user story must consist of at least an actor, an action, and a reason	#01, #08, #09, #10, #11, #14, #18, #23
#02	A user story should have acceptance criteria	#01, #12, #18

4.2 AOAME - The Modelling Environment

The metamodel is implemented in AOAME since it has extension mechanisms and allows for an easy-to-use approach to creating ontology-based metamodels [13].

AOAME also fulfils several requirements towards the USMN, for instance, the need to extend the DSML based on the requirements of a specific domain (requirement #03) or the need to link several other models, respectively, sources of information to the user story (requirements #17 and #22).

Therefore, an ontology is created representing the metamodel of the USMN that is implemented in AOAME.

4.3 Implementation in AOAME

The initial step of the implementation of USMN consists of developing a grounding ontology with all relevant relations to match the above-suggested metamodel. The ontology allows for structuring the elements of DSML effectively and for building upon this foundation, ensuring that the extension is coherent and consistent. Once the ontology of the USMN is implemented, the visual representation elements mapped to the ontology entities are implemented in the palette of AOAME. This leverages the existing infrastructure of the modelling environment and facilitates the inclusion of visual components.

The user story class is the core class of the User Story Ontology and has been implemented in the ontology Turtle (ttl) format.

The constraints shown in Table 2 ensure that every user story consists of semantically correct information.

More constraints are implemented in the user story ontology by creating different types of object properties that are constructs of the RDF, respectively, the OWL syntax. Figure 2 illustrates the connection of the user story class to the other proposed entities from the metamodel, which are connected through object properties within the ontology file.

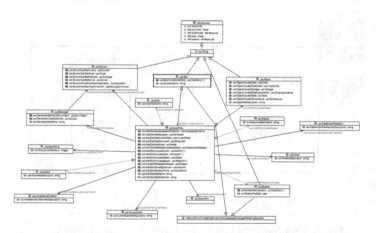

Fig. 2. Class Diagram of the User Story Ontology

The second and third step of the implementation phase within the DSR cycle consists of extending the already existing palette ontology and the modelling language ontology of AOAME and including a visual representation of each created class within the ontology that needs to be represented in the DSML.

5 Evaluation

5.1 User Story Creation

A use case scenario for the USMN evaluation replicates a user story utilising the created DSML within AOAME. To do this, an example user story is picked, and the user story sentence that corresponds to it is shown in AOAME with the corresponding modelling language created.

To evaluate the utility of the proposed approach, the real-world use case scenario has been implemented in AOAME to prove the visual creation of a user story. First, the evaluation assesses how well the notation captures and reflects the key components of the user story by visualising and replicating the user story in the DSML. Secondly, the proof of the produced ontology for the given user story is shown by showing the query results over the knowledge graph-based user story in the triple store of AOAME.

The following user story serves as an evaluation example:

"As a CRM user I want to log in into the CRM system using my username and password to create a safer system environment."

The sample user story will only be accepted by an acceptance criterion that states: *"The log in with corresponding username and password is successful and the user is logged in in the CRM system."* Fig. 3 shows the user story implemented in AOAME with our USMN.

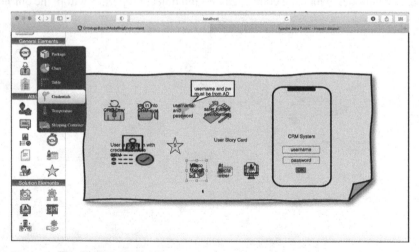

Fig. 3. User Story use case created with the USMN in AOAME

The figure shows a created user story with the DSML. Within the picture the entities "Actor", "Action" "Object" or more specific "Credentials", "Reason", "Acceptance" Criterion", "Story Points", "Assignee", "Release", "Application" and some subclasses of "Prototype" can be seen as part of the wanted solution to the user story. The elements correspond with the entities in the suggested metamodel, derived from the requirements.

The knowledge graph which is built through the environment and logics implemented in AOAME can be retrieved with a SPARQL-Query that uses the ontologies' prefix.

Fig. 4. SPARQL query results performed in the triple store of AOAME showing the instances created from the visual user story.

Figure 4 shows the query results, proving that the ontology instances are created automatically from the visual representation of the user story using USMN. The visual representation of the USMN allows for the creation of visual user stories, which are stored in a knowledge graph, allowing the creation directly within AOAME. Users of the USMN face the benefit of having predefined modelling elements which give direction of how to extend and specify the user story correctly.

5.2 Comparison to Domain-Specific Requirements

To prove the correctness of the implemented artefact in AOAME, a comparison of the gathered requirements and the implemented concrete syntax is made. This comparison illustrates how the requirement is implemented in the USMN. The following table shows an excerpt of the comparison and how the elicited requirements are fulfilled with the USMN (Table 3).

Table 3. Excerpt of requirements comparison

Requirement	Fulfilment	Description
The DSML should provide extension mechanisms to cover all possible applications within its domain. It should allow adding new elements as needed by the Scrum team or stakeholders	Covered by extension mechanisms of AOAME	AOAME allows for: Extending, editing, hiding, and deleting modelling constructs
The DSML should support defining acceptance criteria	Covered with element "Acceptance Criterion"	The palette element "Accpentace Criterion" can be used to model an acceptance criterion

6   Conclusion

In this paper we presented an approach for the creation of visual user stories in the context of the Scrum framework for agile software development. A DSML has been created called USMN – User Story Modelling & Notation. The language is grounded in an ontology, thus enabling machine interpretability of the visual user stories. USMN and the respective model have been implemented in the modelling tool AOAME through the Design Science Research methodology, which led to the instantiation of the modelling tool into AOAME4UserStories.

Future work revolves around the extension of the presented approach towards ontology-based case-based reasoning to the retrieval of the most similar user stories of past successful projects to support the creation of well-formed user stories and in the retrieval of possible documentation of the stored user stories since the focus in agile methodologies is on cooperation instead.

References

1. Schwaber, K., Sutherland, J.: The scrum guide the definitive guide to scrum: the rules of the game (2020)
2. Russo, D.: The agile success model. ACM Trans. Softw. Eng. Methodol. (TOSEM) **30** (2021). https://doi.org/10.1145/3464938
3. Cohn, M.: User Stories Applied: For Agile Software Development. Addison-Wesley Professional, Boston (2004)
4. Floruţ, C., Buchmann, R.A.: Modeling tool for managing requirements and backlogs in agile software development (2022)
5. Athiththan, K., Rovinsan, S., Sathveegan, S., Gunasekaran, N., Gunawardena, K.S.A.W., Kasthurirathna, D.: An ontology-based approach to automate the software development process. In: 2018 IEEE International Conference on Information and Automation for Sustainability (ICIAfS), pp. 1–6 (2018). https://doi.org/10.1109/ICIAFS.2018.8913339

6. Nasiri, S., Rhazali, Y., Lahmer, M., Adadi, A.: From user stories to UML diagrams driven by ontological and production model. Int. J. Adv. Comput. Sci. Appl. **12** (2021). https://doi.org/10.14569/IJACSA.2021.0120637

7. Thamrongchote, C., Vatanawood, W.: Business process ontology for defining user story. In: 2016 IEEE/ACIS 15th International Conference on Computer and Information Science, ICIS 2016 - Proceedings. Institute of Electrical and Electronics Engineers Inc. (2016).https://doi.org/10.1109/ICIS.2016.7550829

8. Zeaaraoui, A., Bougroun, Z., Belkasmi, M., Toumi, B.: User stories template for object-oriented applications (2013). https://doi.org/10.1109/INTECH.2013.6653681

9. Murtazina, M.S., Avdeenko, T.V: Ontology-based approach to the requirements engineering in agile environment. In: 2018 XIV International Scientific-Technical Conference on Actual Problems of Electronics Instrument Engineering (APEIE), pp. 496–501 (2018). https://doi.org/10.1109/APEIE.2018.8546144

10. Lucassen, G., Robeer, M., Dalpiaz, F., van der Werf, J.M.E.M., Brinkkemper, S.: Extracting conceptual models from user stories with visual narrator. Requir Eng. **22**, 339–358 (2017). https://doi.org/10.1007/s00766-017-0270-1

11. Lucassen, G., Dalpiaz, F., van der Werf, J.M.E.M., Brinkkemper, S.: Visualizing user story requirements at multiple granularity levels via semantic relatedness. In: Comyn-Wattiau, I., Tanaka, K., Song, I.-Y., Yamamoto, S., Saeki, M. (eds.) ER 2016. LNCS, vol. 9974, pp. 463–478. Springer, Cham (2016). https://doi.org/10.1007/978-3-319-46397-1_35

12. Vaishnavi, V.K., Kuechler, W.: Design research in information systems (2004)

13. Laurenzi, E., Hinkelmann, K., van der Merwe, A.: An agile and ontology-aided modeling environment. In: Buchmann, R.A., Karagiannis, D., Kirikova, M. (eds.) PoEM 2018. LNBIP, vol. 335, pp. 221–237. Springer, Cham (2018). https://doi.org/10.1007/978-3-030-02302-7_14

14. Frank, U.: Domain-specific modeling languages: requirements analysis and design guidelines. In: Reinhartz-Berger, I., Sturm, A., Clark, T., Cohen, S., Bettin, J. (eds.) Domain Engineering. Springer, Berlin, Heidelberg, pp. 133–157 (2013). https://doi.org/10.1007/978-3-642-36654-3_6

15. Cho, H., Gray, J., Syriani, E.: Creating visual domain-specific modeling languages from end-user demonstration. In: 2012 4th International Workshop on Modeling in Software Engineering (MISE), pp. 22–28. IEEE (2012)

AI Applications and Use Cases
in Business

Morphological Box for AI Solutions: Evaluation and Refinement with a Taxonomy Development Method

Jack Daniel Rittelmeyer[1]([✉]) [iD] and Kurt Sandkuhl[1,2] [iD]

[1] Institute of Computer Science, University of Rostock, Albert-Einstein-Str. 22, 18057 Rostock,
Germany
{jack.rittelmeyer,kurt.sandkuhl}@uni-rostock.de,
kurt.sandkuhl@ju.se
[2] School of Engineering, Jönköping University, Jönköping, Sweden

Abstract. Investigations into the organisational uptake of artificial intelligence (AI) solutions confirm that there is a growing interest in enterprises and public authorities to use AI. In this context, the lack of understanding of AI concepts in organisations is a significant challenge. As a contribution to addressing this issue, we previously developed and evaluated a morphological box for AI solutions. To further refine this morphological box, the paper follows a well-established scientific method for this purpose: This paper presents the application of a taxonomy development method to our morphological box. We use this method to determine a meta-characteristic, identify the target audience, project the use of the morphological box, and define both subjective and objective ending conditions. We describe several iterations of the development and evaluation loops and present our final results. Our analysis demonstrates the effectiveness of the taxonomy development method in refining and enhancing the morphological box for AI solutions. We further present the application of the morphological box for classifying AI projects with four initial case studies, discuss the results as well as further development directions and potentials of the box.

Keywords: Morphological Box · Artificial Intelligence · Taxonomy
Development · Organisational AI Solutions · AI Context

1 Introduction

Recent investigations into the organisational uptake of artificial intelligence (AI) solutions confirm that there is a growing interest in enterprises [1] and public authorities [2] to use AI for, e.g., the automation of routine tasks, implementing process innovation, changes in the business model, or entirely new products and services [3]. However, at the same time, research in organisational readiness for AI solutions [4], innovation management and change processes [5] confirms that in particular small and medium-sized enterprises still have problems grasping the potential of AI [6] and deciding under what conditions AI is useful, what actual solution to select and how to introduce solutions [7].

© The Author(s), under exclusive license to Springer Nature Switzerland AG 2023
K. Hinkelmann et al. (Eds.): BIR 2023, LNBIP 493, pp. 145–157, 2023.
https://doi.org/10.1007/978-3-031-43126-5_11

AI technologies are different from other IT technologies due to the capability to perform cognitive functions in a way that resembles a human-like manner and the ability to learn and self-correct [8]. Thus, the introduction of AI solutions differs from other IT introduction processes.

One reason for this problem is seen in the variety of different AI approaches and difficulties distinguishing the suitability of these approaches for enterprise problems. Machine learning [9], deep learning [10], support vector machines [11] or principle component analysis [12] to take only some examples, might all be applicable to the same organisational problem. If you start from the technical task to be solved, like classification of data, information extraction or pattern recognition, the same variety of solution potential exists that has to be taken into account in the organizational adoption journey [5].

In this context, we argue that systematizing features of AI solutions might help organizations in their decision processes or even in conducting introduction processes. As a contribution to this systematization, we developed in earlier work a morphological box (see Sect. 2.1) by deriving it from own experiences, expert knowledge and systematic evaluations. First experiences in applying the morphological box (MB) showed its utility but also resulted in the question when the MB is mature enough and does not need further refinement. One option to answer this question is the use of development approaches for taxonomies as morphological boxes and taxonomies share many characteristics.

In this paper we aim to investigate if approaches for developing taxonomies are suitable for guiding the MB development, how the level of maturity of our MB is from the perspective of taxonomy development and what improvements have to be made. To address this aim, the paper is structured as follows: Sect. 2 presents the theoretical background for our work from taxonomy development methods and the previously achieved results for the MB for AI solutions. Section 3 discusses the potential of applying the taxonomy development method for the MB. Section 4 investigates improvement potentials of the MB on the basis of the empirical-to-conceptual development path from taxonomy development, including the resulting improved MB version. Section 5 discusses the findings of our work and potential future activities.

2   Theoretical Background and Related Work

In this chapter we summarize the necessary background regarding the morphological box for AI solutions and the taxonomy development method by [13] that will be used in this paper.

2.1   Morphological Box for AI Solutions

In accordance with [14], a morphological box is a product development tool that can facilitate problem-solving by breaking down problems into smaller components, each with its own solution. These individual solutions can then be viewed as features for which values should be provided. Typically, a morphological box takes the form of a table, with features listed in the first row and corresponding values in the rows below.

The process begins with a problem statement, followed by the collection of an initial set of features and values.

In a previous study [15], we introduced a morphological box designed to support the development and integration of AI solutions within companies (refer to Fig. 1). This box was built using four distinct industrial use cases for AI solutions from various domains of application. Furthermore, we applied the box to the AI context model outlined in [16] and demonstrated that it could aid in the introduction of AI by enhancing various steps in the context model. The application of the box resulted in more comprehensive requirements for AI solutions. Nevertheless, the box's development was based solely on four use cases, and its application revealed potential areas for improvement. As a result, we sought to augment the box's empirical foundation by conducting expert interviews as a qualitative approach [17]. The primary objective was to evaluate the completeness of the box and identify any potential redundancies, which resulted in a revised version of the box (see Fig. 1). We further explained possibilities to support the organizational introduction of AI solutions by applying the box to the different development phases and steps shown in [18]. The results showed the most application potential in the phases of decision making (analysis of AI potential, feasibility analysis, readiness check), specification (specify operational integration) and contracting and realization (make or buy decision, development and integration of AI solution). It can further support the introduction phase with earlier planning of potential end-users and required training [17].

Feature	Values						
AI Focus	Processing input		Generating output			Computing task	
End-User	IT-Expert		IT-Savvy			No IT-Knowledge	
Computing Source	Cloud		Local computing center		End-Device		Hybrid
Time to Decision	Real-time		Near Real-Time		Several Hours		Later
Special Hardware Required	Computing		Data Capture		Data Visualization		Data Output
Reliability and Precision of Results	~ 99,9 % Required		Defined by Enterprise		Defined by Domain		Defined by Competitors
Point in Time of AI Use in Solution Development	Design-Time		Runtime		Accompanying runtime		Hybrid
Primary Purpose	Assistance		Decision Making	Forecasting		Classification	Anomaly Detection
Data Source	Own Data		Augmented Data	Open Data		Commercial Collection	Synthetic Data
Data Quantity	Very High		High	Moderate		Low	Very Low
Maturity	COTS		Commercial Components	Open Source Components		Prototype	Individual
Data and Model Update Frequency	Continuously		In Case of Changes in Regulation	In Case of New Documents/Data		In case of Changes in Customer Behavior	In Case of Quality Problems
Extent of Effect on Enterprise	Isolated Solution		Single Process	Workflow		Work System	Business Model
Communication	Frequent & detailed, active collaboration		Regular, some collaboration	Minimal, min. collaboration		Specific moments	None
Primary Data Type	Audio	Video	Raster Image		Vector Image	Transaction Records	Time Series Data
Data Quality	Inconsistent	Duplicate	Incomplete	Outdated	Biased	Noisy	Corrupted
Data Security	Compliance	Data Encryption	Access Control	Data Integrity	Data Privacy	Incident Management	Audit & Monitoring

Fig. 1. Morphological box for AI solutions [17].

2.2 Taxonomy Development Method for Information Systems

Nickerson, Varshney and Muntermann presented a taxonomy development method for information systems with several process steps (see Fig. 2) that can be used not only for taxonomies but for similar artifacts in general [13]. They claim that their method supports the development of useful taxonomies, not necessarily the best or correct ones. The method starts with the determination of a meta-characteristic, which should be based on the purpose of the taxonomy as well as its potential users, target audience and projected use. In the second step, the ending conditions for the taxonomy development process should be determined, differentiating between subjective and objective ending conditions. They propose that a useful taxonomy has to be concise, robust, comprehensive, extendible and explanatory (subjective ending conditions). They further present eight general objective ending conditions which are not exhaustive [13]:

- All objects or a representative sample of objects have been examined
- No object was merged with a similar object or split into multiple objects in the last iteration
- At least one object is classified under every characteristic of every dimension
- No new dimensions or characteristics were added in the last iteration
- No dimensions or characteristics were merged or split in the last iteration
- Every dimension is unique and not repeated (i.e., there is no dimension duplication)
- Every characteristic is unique within its dimension (i.e., there is no characteristic duplication within a dimension)
- Each cell (combination of characteristics) is unique and is not repeated (i.e., there is no cell duplication)

After those two preparation phases, the actual development of the taxonomy starts with the decision of the approach that should be used in the first iteration of the process: Empirical-to-conceptual (steps 4e to 6e) or conceptual-to-empirical (steps 4c to 6c). They recommend to use the empirical-to-conceptual approach if the researcher has a lot of data but not much knowledge about the domain and vice versa for the conceptual-to-empirical approach [13].

The empirical-to-conceptual approach starts with the identification of (new) subsets of objects. The researcher should use a set of familiar objects that should be classified. In the next step one should search for common characteristics of those objects. The characteristics should be "logical-consequences of the meta-characteristic". However, it is highly important that a characteristic discriminates between the objects, meaning that not all objects should have the exact same value for a specific characteristic. In the last step the characteristics should be grouped into dimensions to create or revise (for later loops) the taxonomy [13].

The conceptual-to-empirical approach starts with the conceptualization of (new) characteristics and dimensions of objects based on his/her own knowledge and understanding of the domain. The characteristics of the dimensions should again be "logical consequences of the meta-characteristic". After that, the researcher should choose objects that should be examined for the conceptualized characteristics and dimensions to evaluate and review them. It is emphasized that "each dimension must contain characteristics that are mutually exclusive and collectively exhaustive". This then results in a first or revised version of the taxonomy similar to the conceptual-to-empirical approach [13].

After one of the two approaches are accomplished, the last step is to check if the ending conditions are met or not. Both the objective as well as the subjective ending conditions must be met. If they are met, the process is done and the taxonomy is finished. If the conditions are not met, the process goes back to the third step and the empirical-to-conceptual or conceptual-to-empirical approach should be run through again. Those loops are run through until the ending conditions are met. In each loop it is allowed to choose either of the two approaches [13].

The paper also gives a short outlook about what should be done after the method is finished. The most important aspect is to evaluate the developed taxonomy for its usefulness. One important question that should be evaluated is if the user's purpose can the accomplished with the taxonomy. To achieve that, interviews or questionnaires could be used to ask potential users could be asked if and how they would use the taxonomy. Additionally, the taxonomy could be evaluated while the researchers accompany real use-cases where the taxonomy will be used and applied in practice [13].

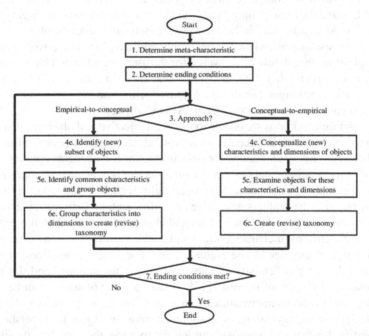

Fig. 2. Taxonomy development method by Nickerson, Varshney and Muntermann [13].

3   Application of the Taxonomy Development Method on the Morphological Box for AI Solutions

On the one hand, we want to use the taxonomy development method by [13] to evaluate our previous approach for developing a morphological box for AI solutions. On the other hand, we intent to further follow the approach to revise and finish our morphological box. Firstly, it should be stated that we can use the taxonomy development method also for a morphological box because [13] specifically said that they created their method in such an open way that it can be used not only for taxonomies but also for typologies, frameworks, classifications or similar artefacts.

First, with our meta-characteristic we define that all characteristics of our artefact should be "relevant factors that highly influence the success or failure of introducing AI applications in companies" (step 1). Potential users of the box should be enterprises that want to implement and use AI. Particularly, we want to create an artefact that is useful for non-IT companies that lack the necessary knowledge to successfully introduce AI in their companies. Therefore, the target audience are General users but it can also be used by IT-experts in the companies. The projected use of the artefact is that it helps its users to understand the topic of introducing AI better and to not miss any highly relevant factors that could significantly influence the successful introduction of AI as early as possible, in the best case already at the beginning while evaluating a possible AI usage. The main questions that should be answered for the users are what do I have to consider, what must I not forget, where should I start, what should I focus on? It is intended to provide a decision-making aid so that an AI introduction can be successful or so that a consideration can be made as to whether an AI is worthwhile or not.

For our ending conditions we decide to use the subjective and objective ending conditions named in chapter II. B. (step 2). Because we already developed an artefact, we can directly check the ending conditions for our current version of the morphological box. For the subjective ending conditions, we argue that the box is already concise, robust and extendible. It is concise because it is meaningful without being too overwhelming. It is robust because the features and values can differentiate between objects. In our case features and values are the dimensions and characteristics. Further, it is extendible because new dimensions or characteristics can be added easily. The conditions comprehensive and explanatory need to be evaluated first. For comprehensiveness it needs to be checked if the box can "classify all known objects in the domain" and if it includes "all dimensions of objects of interest" [13]. If the box is explanatory can be checked "if someone knows the characteristics of an object, he/she will find the object in an identifiable spot in the taxonomy, or if someone finds an object [...], he/she will be able to identify the characteristics without having to know the complete details of the object" [13]. For the objective ending conditions, we argue from our observings that the following four conditions are already met and that the remaining conditions are not met yet:

- No dimensions or characteristics were merged or split in the last iteration
- Every dimension is unique and not repeated (i.e., there is no dimension duplication)
- Every characteristic is unique within its dimension (i.e., there is no characteristic duplication within a dimension)

- Each cell (combination of characteristics) is unique and is not repeated (i.e., there is no cell duplication)

Now, we want to map the steps of the taxonomy development method on our previous steps for developing the morphological box. So far, we cycled through three loops of the method (step 3). In the first and third cycle, we used the conceptual-to-empirical approach. In the second cycle, we chose the empirical-to-conceptual approach.

At the beginning of the development, we chose the conceptual-to-empirical approach because we had accumulated a lot of experience and knowledge about the introduction of AI solutions in companies and only a small amount of data available during that time. We then proceeded to conceptualize potential characteristics and dimensions of objects (step 4c), which can be found in chapter 3.2 in [15]. After that, we examined objects for the characteristics and dimensions by deploying our initial set of them to our context modelling method [16] as explained in chapter 4 in [15] (step 5c). Finally, we were able to create an initial version of our morphological box, that was presented in [15] (step 6c). After checking the ending conditions, we can summarize that they were not met yet (step 7).

According to the method, we went back to step three but chose the empirical-to-conceptual approach this time. In this second run, we wanted to gather more data to also have a quantitative basis for our research project. To gather data, we decided to conduct expert interviews with experts that have experience with introducing AI solutions in companies. We chose not to go for a questionnaire because of the required knowledge for the topic of AI introduction. The expert interviews helped us to identify new subsets of objects (step 4e). We then used the interviews findings to identify common characteristics and grouped objects (step 5e), followed by grouping the characteristics into dimensions to revise taxonomy (step 6e). Arguably, the steps 4e to 6e and the resulting revised taxonomy were presented in [17]. Again, not all of the ending conditions were met, leading to the third run.

This time we used the conceptual-to-empirical approach again, because we used a literature search to find and conceptualize new values respectively characteristics as described in chapter six of [17] (step 4c). Then we examined objects in form of outlining the application potential of the box with its current and new features and values along the IS development process as explained in chapter seven of [17] (step 5c). At the end of the third run, we had revised version of our morphological box (step 6c), which was the current version presented in II. A. The ending conditions that are currently met, as described earlier in this chapter, are also deduced from this version of the box. Because still not all objective and subjective ending conditions were met, we had to go back to step three and choose one of the two approaches. This newest iteration will be described in the following chapter.

4   Classifying Objects with the Morphological Box and Discussion

For the next iteration that is presented in this paper for the first time, we decided to switch to the empirical-to-conceptual approach again. First, we describe how we conducted the classification (Sect. 4.1), followed by the discussion of its results (Sect. 4.2).

4.1 Classification of Objects from AI Use Cases

We want to test if our box is able to classify objects, starting with some AI use cases we also used for the initial version of the box. Because of that, the box should be able to classify those projects. Similarly to table nine in Nickerson et al. [13], we want to classify our objects with our morphological box. Our four projects (i.e. our objects) are from the following areas and cover the described AI solutions:

Table 1. Analysed industrial case studies with AI solution.

Case	Domain	AI solution	Literature
A	Clean room and air conditioning	Energy optimization on fleet level; anomaly detection on facility level	[15]
B	Financial industries	Fraud detection for instant payments	[19]
C	Marketing	AI for Object Recognition and Marketing Support	[20]
D	Garden products	Forecast of transaction development; anomaly detection	[21]

We then used our own experience, records and recorded data from those projects to check which value of each feature is true for each project. The results of this classification process are shown in Tables 2 and 3. Each "X" shows which of the values of a feature applies to a use case. For every feature one value was chosen with the exception of data security in use case B. In this case two data security aspects were highly relevant and had to be met/considered. According to Nickerson et al. normally only one value should be chosen for each feature but in this case, it seems to make sense that several security aspects can be relevant for an AI solution. Similarly to the feature "computing source", a "hybrid" value could be added as well but in this case it is not clear which of the values are meant with "hybrid". Because of that, we suggest to offer to possibility to choose several values for this feature of the morphological box.

The goal should be that for each value an object can be identified because if there is not a single object with a specific value, this value seems to be irrelevant. Although there still are several values without an identified object, we argue that they can still be relevant because the initial set of just four objects is very small. In future research the goal should be to classify a significant number of objects/projects to truly identify which values are relevant and which are not relevant.

4.2 Discussion

Despite the relatively small number of objects some tendencies can be seen. Firstly, in three of four use cases the main AI focus was a computing task and in only one case the focus was to generate output and in zero cases to process input.

The planned end-user was distributed nearly evenly among all values. Only the end-user with no it-knowledge at all was chosen two times.

Table 2. Classification of AI projects using the morphological box (part 1).

Features	Values / Industrial Cases	Clean Room and Air Conditioning (A)	Financial Industries (B)	Marketing (C)	Garden Products (D)
AI Focus	Processing Input				
	Generating Output			x	
	Computing Task	x	x		x
End-User	IT-Expert			x	
	IT-Savy		x		
	No IT-Knowledge	x			x
Computing Source	Cloud	x			x
	Local Computing-Center		x	x	
	End-Device				
	Hybrid				
Time to Decision	Real-Time				
	Near Real-Time		x		
	Several Hours	x		x	x
	Later				
Special Hardware Required	Computing		x	x	
	Data Capture	x			x
	Data Visualization				
	Data Output				
Reliability & Precision of Results	~ 99,9 % Required				
	Defined by Enterprise	x			x
	Defined by Domain		x		
	Defined by Competition			x	
Point of Time of AI Use in Solution Development	Design Time				
	Runtime		x		
	Accompanying runtime	x			
	Hybrid			x	x
Primary Purpose	Assistance	x			
	Decision Making		x		
	Forecasting				x
	Classification			x	
	Anomaly Detection				
Data Source	Own Data	x	x		x
	Augmented Data				
	Open Data				
	Commercial Collection			x	
	Synthetic Data				
Data Quantity	Very High		x		
	High			x	x
	Moderate	x			
	Low				
	Very Low				

For the computing source all use cases are split up between cloud computing and local computing centres but there were no cases of end-devices or hybrid options for the computing source.

Very interesting was also the distribution of the feature time to decision because one could assume that most of the time decisions of AI solutions have to be delivered immediately but in our industrial cases it was acceptable to receive the results after several hours and only in the financial industry case it was necessary to receive them near real-time.

The required special hardware was also split up evenly between hardware for computing and data capturing tasks only.

Reliability and precision of results showed a very intriguing result because in none of the cases a percentage of around 99,9% was required. In two cases the required reliability and precision were determined by the enterprise and in one case by the domain and competitors each. One reason for this result could be that none of the use cases was from a sector or solution that could potentially risk human lives as in medicine or nuclear power plants. But on the other side in the use cases of air conditioning and in the financial industries one could have expected a required percentage of 99,9%.

In two cases the AI solution was used in more than one of the different development phases (hybrid) and one was used during runtime and one was accompanying runtime.

The primary purpose varied between all use cases and ranged from assistance and decision making to forecasting or classification leaving only anomaly detection open.

Another result we want to highlight is that in three of four cases the own data of the company was used and only in the marketing use case a commercial collection was bought what makes sense because with data from outside it is possible to learn new marketing techniques or strategies not already present in the company. But on the other side it is noticeable that only data from outside was used and no own data. The remaining values did not apply to the presented use cases.

Table 3. Classification of AI projects using the morphological box (part 2).

Features	Values / Industrial Cases	Clean Room and Air Conditioning (A)	Financial Industries (B)	Marketing (C)	Garden Products (D)
Maturity	COTS				
	Commercial Components		X		X
	Open Source Components	X		X	
	Prototype				
	Individual				
Data & Model Update Frequency	Continuously				
	In Case of Changes in Regulation		X		
	In Case of New Documents/Data	X			
	In Case of Changes in Customer Behavior				
	In Case of Quality Problems			X	X
Extent of Effect on Enterprise	Isolated Solution				
	Single Process				
	Workflow		X		
	Work System	X			X
	Business Model			X	
Communication	Frequent & detailed, active collaboration				
	Regular, some collaboration		X	X	
	Minimal, min. collaboration	X			X
	Specific Moments				
	None				
Primary Data Type	Audio				
	Video			X	
	Raster Image				
	Vector Image				
	Transaction Records		X		X
	Time Series Data	X			
Data Quality	Inconsistent		X		X
	Duplicate				
	Incomplete	X			
	Outdated				
	Biased				
	Noisy			X	
	Corrupted				
Data Security	Compliance		X		
	Data Encryption				
	Access Control				X
	Data Integrity				
	Data Privacy		X	X	
	Incident Management	X			
	Audit & Monitoring				

As expected, the required amount of data was either very high (one case), high (two cases) or at least moderate (one case). During the application of this feature the question arose what counts as e.g., moderate? Here it should be evaluated if a possibility exists that can distinguish more clearly between the different options and that would make it easier for the users of the box to choose their required value.

For the maturity in all cases collections of configurable components were used. It is noteworthy that the project partners would have preferred commercial off-the-shelf (COTS) solutions but such were not available for their cases. On the other side, they did not want to start completely from scratch, hence they decided to use either commercial (B, D) or open-source components (A, C). These findings also open the question if "prototype" is a useful value because it is difficult to imagine that a prototype for a specific AI solution exists somewhere except for if you start a new project based on an old project or if you are really lucky to find a prototype of a similar topic online.

Surprisingly, it was not necessary to update the data and model of any of the AI solutions continuously. They only need to be updated when specific events occur like a change in regulation (B), when new documents need to be processed (A) or when quality problems occur (C, D).

Additionally, in all of the cases the AI solution had a medium to large effect on the whole enterprise. In case B, a workflow was changed. In case A and D, a work system was affected and in case C the whole business model of the company was adapted. It seems like that in all of these projects, the AI solutions were of high importance and led to major changes in the companies.

The communication in the projects between the developers (either internal or external ones) and the affected business units was either minimal with minimum collaboration (A, D) or regular with some collaboration (B, C). Similarly to the data quantity, the question arose how to measure the degree of communication and collaboration if possible. Another question for us was what differentiates minimal communication from communication only in specific moments? For us the difference is that for minimal communication not much communication is required during the whole development and implementation process but with specific moments a lot of communication could be required but only in very specific and short moments during the process, for example only at the beginning and the end of a project and no to minimum communication in between.

The primary type of data that should be processed in the projects were video (C) and time series data (A) and transaction data (B, D).

The data quality feature describes potential data quality issues of the available datasets of a company. Those issues can be handled in two ways: Either the data has to be cleaned before using it for the AI solution or the AI solution has to be able to handle and process the data successfully despite its quality issues. In cases B and D, the available data was inconsistent whereas in case A the data was incomplete and in case C it was noisy.

As discussed earlier, the data security feature showed the anomaly that in case B compliance as well as data privacy were highly important and required for the to-be-developed AI solution. The focus in the other projects laid more on incident management (A), access control (D) and also data privacy (C). This shall not mean that for example data privacy played no role in projects A and D. It should rather help to figure out and to make clear which are the most important data security aspects for an AI solution during the planning of its development.

5 Conclusion and Future Work

At the beginning of this paper, we showed how the taxonomy development process by Nickerson, Varshney and Muntermann [13] could be applied to the development process of our morphological box so far by mapping our process steps to the steps of the taxonomy development process. This showed that we did not meet our chosen ending conditions and hence decided to use an empirical-to-conceptual approach for the next iteration by classifying past AI solution development projects from us as objects.

In conclusion, the classification of our four projects showed that the box works and that it can classify AI solutions respectively the development projects for AI solutions successfully. But it also revealed that a few aspects of the box require more clarity, which would be beneficial for potential users. Thus, our ending conditions are still not met because some values need to be tweaked leading us back to step three (see Fig. 2).

Despite that only four use cases were analysed, some first tendencies could be recognised regarding which values seem to be more common for some features. But if those tendencies are true needs to be evaluated with a considerably larger set of data, maybe in form of a survey. With more data, it could also be analysed if for example in specific domains or when using specific AI technologies (e.g. neural networks, rule-based systems, support-vector-machines), specific values occur significantly more often than others. Based on this data it probably could be possible to give recommendations for each feature based on the application domain or AI technology. When thinking really far ahead, one could think about using the box and this data to train an AI that recommends how to develop an AI, i.e., which values of the box are recommended for each feature.

In work about quantifying the costs and benefits of AI we realized that there is a lack of cost/benefit or business case approaches tailored to the specifics of AI projects. Established approaches for IT projects in general do not sufficiently consider the costs of acquiring datasets or training machine learning approaches. The morphological box could be a suitable means to support cost/benefit investigations as the different features of AI solutions potentially affect their costs and benefits. However, this requires thorough investigation and will be part of future work.

Another future approach could be to evaluate if the knowledge included in the box can help with the successful implementation of an AI project when it is present from the beginning of the project. We see the main potential for the box in its usage during the requirements engineering phase of the development process because we argue that it could help to get an overview about important aspects that should be taken into consideration when thinking about the possible use of an AI solution. Thereby, it could prevent to miss important aspect and hence it could improve the success rate for implementing AI solutions. But it should be emphasised that at this moment, these ideas are just considerations for discussions and require excessive research in the future.

References

1. Eurostat: Use of artificial intelligence in enterprises (2022). https://ec.europa.eu/eurostat/statistics-ex-plained/index.php?title=Use_of_artificial_intelligence_in_enterprises#Enterprises_using_artificial_intelligence_technologies
2. Mikalef, P., et al.: Examining how AI capabilities can foster organization-al performance in public organizations. Gov. Inf. Q. 40(2), 101797 (2023)
3. Mariani, M.M., Machado, I., Nambisan, S.: Types of innovation and artificial intelligence: a systematic quantitative literature review and research agenda. J. Bus. Res. 155, 113364 (2023)
4. Jöhnk, J., Weißert, M., Wyrtki, K.: Ready or not, AI comes—an interview study of organizational AI readiness factors. Bus. Inf. Syst. Eng. 63, 5–20 (2021)
5. Uren, V., Edwards, J.S.: Technology readiness and the organizational journey towards AI adoption: an empirical study. Int. J. Inf. Manage. 68, 102588 (2023)

6. Sandkuhl, K.: Putting AI into context-method support for the introduction of artificial intelligence into organizations. In: 2019 IEEE 21st Conference on Business Informatics (CBI), vol. 1, pp. 157–164 (2019)
7. Hansen, E.B., Bøgh, S.: Artificial intelligence and internet of things in small and medium-sized enterprises: a survey. J. Manuf. Syst. **58**, 362–372 (2021)
8. Russell, S.J.: Artificial intelligence a modern approach. Pearson Education, Inc. (2015)
9. Mahesh, B.: Machine learning algorithms-a review (2020)
10. Pouyanfar, S., et al.: A survey on deep learning. ACM Comput. Surv. **51**, 1–36 (2019). https://doi.org/10.1145/3234150
11. Suthaharan, S.: Support Vector Machine Machine Learning Models and Algorithms for Big Data Classification, pp. 207–235. Springer, Boston, MA (2016). https://doi.org/10.1007/978-1-4899-7641-3_9
12. Bro, R., Smilde, A.K.: Principal component analysis. Anal. Methods **6**, 2812–2831 (2014). https://doi.org/10.1039/C3AY41907J
13. Nickerson, R.C., Varshney, U., Muntermann, J.: A method for taxonomy development and its application in information systems. Eur. J. Inf. Syst. **22**, 336–359 (2013). https://doi.org/10.1057/ejis.2012.26
14. Zwicky, F.: Discovery, Invention, Research through the Morphological Approach (1969)
15. Rittelmeyer, J.D., Sandkuhl, K.: Features of AI Solutions and their Use in AI Con-text Modeling. Gesellschaft für Informatik e.V (2022)
16. Sandkuhl, K., Rittelmeyer, J.D.: Use of EA Models in Organizational AI Solution Development, pp. 149–166. Springer, Cham (2022). https://doi.org/10.1007/978-3-031-11520-2_10
17. Rittelmeyer, J.D., Sandkuhl, K.: Morphological Box for AI Solutions: Development, Evaluation and Application Options Hybridaims Workshop Proceedings 2023
18. Rittelmeyer, J.D., Sandkuhl, K.: Effects of artificial intelligence on enterprise architectures - a structured literature review. In: 2021 IEEE 25th International Enterprise Distributed Object Computing Workshop (EDOCW). IEEE (2021). https://doi.org/10.1109/edocw52865.2021.00042
19. Diadiushkin, A., Sandkuhl, K., Maiatin, A.: Fraud detection in payments transactions: Overview of existing approaches and usage for instant payments. Complex Syst. Inf. Model. Q. **20**, 72–88 (2019)
20. Reiz, A., Albadawi, M., Sandkuhl, K., Vahl, M., Sidin, D.: Towards more robust fashion recognition by combining of deep-learning-based detection with se-mantic reasoning. In: AAAI Spring Symposium: Combining Machine Learning with Knowledge Engineering (2021)
21. Sandkuhl, K., Shilov, N., Seigerroth, U., Smirnov, A.: Towards the quantified product - product lifecycle support by multi-aspect ontologies. In: Yuval, C. (ed.) Proceedings 14th IFAC Workshop on Intelligent Manufacturing Systems. IFAC (2022)

Explainable AI for the Olive Oil Industry

Christian Schmid[1], Emanuele Laurenzi[1]($\boxtimes$) (iD), Umberto Michelucci[2] (iD), and Francesca Venturini[3] (iD)

[1] FHNW University of Applied Sciences and Arts Northwestern Switzerland, Olten, Switzerland
christian.schmid2@students.fhnw.ch, emanuele.laurenzi@fhnw.ch
[2] Lucerne University of Applied Sciences and Arts, Lucerne, Switzerland
umberto.michelucci@hslu.ch
[3] Zurich University of Applied Sciences, Winterthur, Switzerland
francesca.venturini@zhaw.ch

Abstract. Understanding Machine Learning results for the quality assessment of olive oil is hard for non-ML experts or olive oil producers. This paper introduces an approach for interpreting such results by combining techniques of image recognition with knowledge representation and reasoning. The Design Science Research strategy was followed for the creation of the approach. We analyzed the ML results of fluorescence spectroscopy and industry-specific characteristics in olive oil quality assessment. This resulted in the creation of a domain-specific knowledge graph enriched by object recognition and image classification results. The approach enables automatic reasoning and offers explanations about fluorescence image results and, more generally, about the olive oil quality. Producers can trace quality attributes and evaluation criteria, which synergizes computer vision and knowledge graph technologies. This approach provides an applicable foundation for industries relying on fluorescence spectroscopy and AI for quality assurance. Further research on image data processing and on end-to-end automation is necessary for the practical implementation of the approach.

Keywords: Knowledge Graph · Computer Vision · Olive Oil · Quality Assessment · Fluorescent Spectroscopy · Fluorescent Images

1 Introduction

Olive oil as a consumer product has been experiencing steady market growth worldwide for decades, of which 80% is produced in approximately 12,000 European based factories. Besides positive health effects, such as strengthening the immune system or fighting heart attacks, olive oil also contributes to a cultural heritage and an anchored economy in the rural areas of the Mediterranean region [1,42]. As a consequence, consumers are demanding more and more high-quality products, putting pressure on producers to align their activities with standards to improve quality [26]. Although the International Olive Oil Consortium (IOC)

K. Hinkelmann et al. (Eds.): BIR 2023, LNBIP 493, pp. 158–171, 2023.
https://doi.org/10.1007/978-3-031-43126-5_12

sets and regulates the quality characteristics of olive oil and requires extensive chemical and organoleptic testing by official laboratories for appropriate quality labelling [2,4], the authenticity of food and the traceability of quality characteristics is still a global issue, not only to prevent mislabelling, but also to avoid endangering public health [1]. Accordingly, there is a considerable need to reduce the time and effort required for these analyses, especially because of the many different properties and parameters that need to be tested simultaneously [2]. Recent promising fluorescent spectroscopic analysis techniques offer therefore rapid real-time monitoring of olive oil quality [26] and with the inclusion of machine learning (ML), predictions can even be made reliably about various quality parameters and the quality grade of olive oil (extra-virgin, virgin, lampante) [5]. Meanwhile, small, minimalist sensor designs can take fluorescent images of olive oil test samples and classify them within seconds using a trained ML-model [6].

However, with the emergence of artificial intelligence systems in the olive oil sector [7], there is still limited focus on making the increasingly complex algorithms explainable to humans [8]. One rising approach is the use of knowledge graphs (KG) as a representation for input and output information of ML-algorithms. KGs offer the advantage of capturing compositional behaviour and data structures in AI systems to improve their explainability. Such graphs can be used to process texts as well as images with the aim of drawing conclusions [9].

The use of KGs in combination with image recognition methods is already being used in agriculture, but primarily focuses on RGB-images (red, green, blue) of, for example, olive trees for the detection of dirt and diseases [10]. By contrast, for fluorescent images, which offer quality characteristics for processed olive oil, it remains unresolved how and with which methods conclusions can be drawn for olive oil producers in order to preserve the highest quality of olive oil.

To tackle this challenge, we present a hybrid artificial intelligent system that ultimately supports olive oil producers in their quality assessment by answering relevant questions. In particular, firstly, a Machine Learning-based image recognition technique is used to identify relevant quality attributes from fluorescent images of olive oil test samples. Secondly, these attributes are injected into a domain knowledge graph for the support of quality assessment.

The paper is structured as follows: Sect. 2 elaborates on the background and related work. The methodology is described in Sect. 3. Next, Sect. 4 introduces our proposed solution and the evaluation is reported in Sect. 5. Finally, Sect. 6 concludes the paper.

2   Background and Related Work

First of all, the EU sets clear marketing standards for the distribution of olive oil in its regulations No. 1308/2013, No. 29/2012 and No. 2568/91. By all means, Olive oil producers must comply with these framework conditions and standards. The first regulation regulates the market organisation and policy, including, for example, which aid programs can be used under certain conditions, or the implementation of testing procedures. No. 29/2012, on the other hand, regulates marketing standards, including how olive oil can be packaged and labelled. The third regulation sets specific, characteristic standards for each category of olive oil including analytical procedures. Every country in the EU has to carry out annual controls in the market to determine whether the standards are being met including risk analyses for all production steps, consumer complaints and operator characteristics [39]. In particular, Regulation No.2568/91 sets essential characteristics and procedures for quality testing to guarantee the purity and quality of olive oil products. Both chemical-physical and organoleptic characteristics are specified with precise thresholds and classifications. For chemical-physical analyses, for which, in some cases several, comprehensive procedures and threshold values are described. Quality characteristics include acidity (%), peroxide values, extinction coefficients K232 and K270, delta-k value and fatty acid ethyl ester values. In addition, purity characteristics are evaluated for classification, including several fatty acid contents (%), total translinoleic (%), stigmastadienes, 2-glyceril monopalmitate (%) and several sterol compositions (%). Official laboratories as well as producers are guided by specific decisions trees for all the comprehensive evaluation procedures [40]. Given this background, it is important for olive oil producers to have a clear strategy for handling test samples in order to map traceability correctly, not only to meet the requirements of the laboratories, but also to ensure the protection of one's own product. In this context, supporting guidance can be found in series of instructions and standards by the IOC as well as the HACCP principles, ISO22000, ISO90001 [26,27]. At an operational stage, there are different maturities for quality assurance in the industry, ranging from manual inspection to automatic monitoring of individual process steps. Framework concepts such as lean management, total quality management and zero defect management are used, all with the aim of ensuring the highest possible quality of olive oil [28]. For example, an analysis of the quality management of SMEs in southern Italy confirms that quality certificates and quality traceability systems play an important role for both companies and potential customers with a high impact to export activities. As the flow of information in agri-food supply chains is often one-way, i.e. only from sender to receiver, the traceability of olive oil quality is an essential element for customers when making purchasing decisions. Unfortunately, it is precisely these small and medium-sized enterprises that find it difficult to obtain such certificates due to the lack of control and overview of the companies own entire value chain [29]. An analytical technique for assessing and supporting olive oil quality is fluorescence spectroscopy, which uses the ability of atoms and molecules to absorb light at a certain electromagnetic wavelength and then re-emit it at a longer wavelength. Not all types of molecules are fluorescent, but olive oils have some components that can be mapped by fluorescence spectra, mainly chlorophyll. A measurement result is displayed in an EEM matrix, whereby fluorescent zones have a high colour intensity, mostly in reddish discolouration. An example of a test sample, which was classified as EVOO, shows two emission peaks one at about

650–700 nm (nanometer) and a weaker signal at about 300nm. Depending on the quality of the olive oil and its progressing ageing, these signal ranges shift and lose intensity [30]. Although recent spectroscopic analysis methods offer rapid real-time monitoring of the olive oil quality without destroying the samples, these spectral measurements are complex and require high expertise [26]. A promising emerging enhancement under the use of machine learning algorithms offers simple classification of fluorescent images into one of three quality level (EVOO, VOO, LOO) and gives predictions about chemical parameters (acidity, peroxide value, K232, K270, and ethyl ester values) [6]. Despite this progress, results from fluorescent spectroscopy in combination with machine learning is not a complete alternative to the regulatory comprehensive analytical tests carried out by certified laboratories. In this context, the question arises how the test results, and thus the contents of fluorescent images, can be interpreted and exploited by local producers in the hope of ensuring continuous monitoring, guaranteeing quality assurance and reducing the need to use the expensive laboratories [6]. From the producers' point of view, reasons for the ageing process of olive oil are complex, light, heat and air have a strong influence on the olive oil quality and thus lead to a reduction of fluorescent elements in fluorescent images [31].

For one thing, interpretation of images can be supported by employing ML-based computer vision (CV) techniques, with specific task such as object detection and labelling, image classification, or scene understanding. For example, CV can detect olives in a image of an olive tree and label them accordingly [18]. However, such systems, which are based on neural networks, are black boxes and offer comparatively weak explanations for the results and transparency for the end users [41]. In this regard, KGs offer themselves for the abstraction and structuring of knowledge by taking up relationships between different entities and sources. By providing knowledge described in KGs as input, they are also starting to play a crucial part in describing information collected by AI systems and for enhancing the predictions of these systems [9].

Regarding CV and its application in the food industry, such CV systems are meanwhile widely used and support entire process chains in quality assessment [7]. However, in the olive sector, the technology is only found in specific applications. One example uses a simple camera that takes pictures of fresh batches of olives. In contrast to olives picked directly from the olive tree, olives picked from the ground can have high acidity levels due to dirt. CV identifies different types of dirt, colours and textures, and finally classifies the olives for further processing. Such sorting systems achieve high classification accuracy, replace manual inspection before the olives are even pressed [20] and allow adjustments to the production chain for optimal processing of the olives at hand [21]. Likewise, results using the similar CV techniques and batch monitoring of whole olive fruits show promising correlation results between the content image data and the acidity index, peroxide values, ethyl esters, polyphenols, chlorophylls and carotenoids [34]. Another example in the olive oil industry uses CV and image analysis using dieletric spectroscopy during the storage [33]. Although all the results described can be used to predict chemical values and classify images into a specific category, they do not provide conclusive information about the compositional content of the images and its relation to the domain. On a technical level, there are various models with different architectures and layers, namely CNNs, RNNs, Yolo, LSTM, GANs and many more that are applied for different CV-tasks [22]. One example and solution concept uses a YOLOv5 model for object detection in infrared images in order to cope with the higher noise and poorer spatial resolution in the images [24]. Focusing on the analysis of fluorescent images, CV offers the possibility of a controllable environment by using pre-trained data sets that are tailored to the specifically defined task. Predictions on new images can thus be made very quickly, since the model is already pre-trained and no parameter optimisation is necessary. The most common models for microscopy images are supvervised learning models, which use labelled data to make more precise predictions and are easier to interpret [25].

Regarding the use of KG applications, it is noticeable that although the food sector has manifold uses for KGs, the olive sector, despite its multifaceted characteristics, has not yet targeted the explaining capabilities of KGs for ML-algorithms. A KG technology that takes up the compositional properties in images is referred to as Scene Graph (SG). A SG picks up objects in images and establishes a semantic relationship between them. This procedure enables cause-and-effect reasoning, for example. However, the basic prerequisite for this procedure is that the objects present in the images have an internal relationship such as a farmer picking an olive [9]. Fluorescent images, on the other hand, mainly show the chlorophyll content of olive oil and do not contain any real relationship between objects [31]. Nonetheless, KGs offer an opportunity to integrate, organise and draw conclusions from a wide range of business information [9]. Exemplary, a KG created as a complement to a decision tree of an ML algorithm in combination with grain-related text data from the industry shows that the network type structure of KGs can provide clear and comprehensive information to more accurately estimate grain loss. ML in agriculture often use black-box models that do not allow insight into the internal process or factors, making it difficult to verify causes, gain analytical insights or make recommendations [16]. Particularly significant in this context are explainable AIs, which are used especially for decision support in economically sensitive domains [35]. Moreover, domain-specific knowledge graphs have become easier to construct since recent technological advances, along with the help of domain experts, human knowledge can be mapped in an abstracted way, making conclusions by a machine possible [17]. In order for a KG to be able to pursue the set goals and enable appropriate inferences, the design of a knowledge-based system (KBS) including appropriate knowledge acquisition, validation and representation is necessary [11]. A suitable basis for this is provided by the prior design of an ontology in order to map the domain characteristics in a way that is appropriate for the addressees and to make explicit knowledge machine-readable [13].

Overall, as AI technologies are increasingly used in agriculture and also in the olive oil industry [7], the question is how to combine ML-based results with domain knowledge to support quality decisions in a more informed way. With the development of ML-based small portable instruments, fluorescence spectroscopy is taking on a new dimension in improving the time- and resource-intensive quality assessment of olive oil test samples, opening up the possibility of establishing direct links to production and highlighting dependencies [5]. However, for this further endeavour, the combination of ML-based results, such as by CV, and the explicit knowledge mapping by a KG is necessary.

3   Methodology

For the research design, a systematic design science research (DSR) approach was chosen to develop practical solutions for the domain and at the same time expanding the existing knowledge base. DSR focuses on the development and evaluation of a design solution or artefact based on a sophisticated understanding of the problem and the needs of the relevant stakeholders [38]. In order to address the research problem, an iterative six-step process is used, consisting of problem identification (*awareness phase*), definition of solution goals (*suggestion phase*), design and development (*development phase*), demonstration, evaluation (*evaluation phase*) and finally communication [37].

In order to approach the problem situation of the domain more explicitly and to gain a comprehensive understanding of the quality assessment of olive oils, semi-structured interviews with domain experts from Spain and Italy are conducted. The consultation of domain experts in the olive oil sector addresses organisational, procedural and technological aspects in the quality assessment of the product. In addition, the interview should reveal possible shortcomings and unforeseen issues so that the effectiveness of the solution design can be assessed. For a comprehensive picture of the sector, interview partners from SMEs as well as large companies from Europe are targeted based on the company presentation on the internet and the offers and size shown. A further interview is conducted with a technical expert who understands and is able to interpret a dataset of fluorescent images of olive oil, which were made available by the ZHAW as part of the ARES project [3]. All responses are transcribed, coded and analysed with the application Atlas.ti with the help of the environmental attributes of the DSR framework so that structured information is available for the suggestion and development phase of the artefact. Further, a data set of fluorescence images is obtained and examined for their quality in order to assess and propose implementation options later. Closing the awareness phase, and in order to obtain a targeted understanding of the requirements, a use case diagram is created, which is used to record and visualise the interactions and functions in the quality assessment of olive oil. From the diagram, requirements can be extracted, requirements recorded and directions communicated. In the suggestion phase, a specific proposal is made including a description of how the new artefact will support the quality assessment with the help of image recognition techniques on the basis of the created use case. More precisely, an ontology as a basis for a KG is proposed for the perceived domain specificities including some informal competency question that shall be adressed and what axioms apply to it. For the fluorescence images considered, a proposal is made as to which features and attributes should be picked up with computer vision techniques and in what way these can be included in a KG. Subsequently, in the development phase, a prototype consisting of a CV model in combination with a domain-specific KG is created iteratively and presented. Finally, the result is assessed on the basis of CV performance criteria, the informal competency questions set and additional KG-specific evaluation criteria.

4   Computer Vision Based Knowledge Graph Framework

Regarding the exploitation of relevant quality attributes through CV-application in fluorescent images, three supervised CV-tasks are proposed using a provided dataset of 240 images. On the one hand, the two fluorescent regions are to be detected and framed so that the user is directed to the relevant content in the image. Furthermore, the colour intensities of these two zones are to be displayed in a diagram so that the user can understand simplified changing events. A third task is dedicated to the idea of classifying a fluorescent image into one ageing step (0–9). A user can then easily compare different samples over a period of time and get a single simplified indication of whether the olive oil has aged. All three tasks pursue the goal of making the contents of fluorescence images more comprehensible to the user and preparing them in a supportive form. For one thing, the objective is to show the user which areas in the image are important for the quality assessment. For another thing, the CV-tasks should simplify and display results for the user to recognise and classify changing properties. For implementation, a YOLOv8 model is used. Yolo models have an uncomplicated architecture based on a single neural network and a single pipeline. This makes these models easier to understand, implement and train. The latest model Yolov8 from Ultralytics, in particular, no longer uses predefined anchor points to predict the position and size of objects in an image. This means that overlapping prediction boxes can be removed more quickly, which shortens calculations and speeds up predictions. The YOLO models offer a suitable functional abstraction also in connection with the fluorescence images, where the content objects represent special colour-intensive zones. Even if an object frame is misplaced, it will still be close to the real object due to the anchor structure [36].

On the other hand, a domain-specific ontology will be created that addresses three domain functions of a medium-sized enterprise (quality manager, quality tester, production worker) and maps the output of the CV task as well as ML-based prediction- and chemical analysis results. The ontology should include important chemical parameters such as free-fatty acidity (FFA), ethyl esters, K270, K232, peroxide value and phenolic components and their measurement systems. It should be possible to distinguish between predictions of fluorescent spectroscopy and direct measurement results of other chemical analysis methods. From a process perspective, the ontology should map the production processes, as well as the post production processes before marketing, so that the results can be

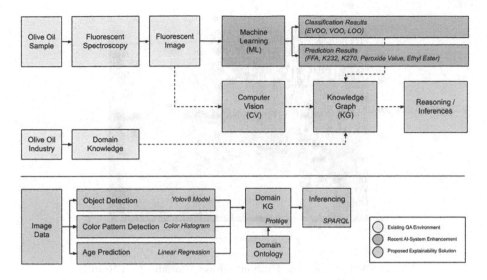

Fig. 1. Methodology Pipeline

linked to the corresponding internal decision stages. This should also include, for example, storage conditions of containers and batches. Furthermore, the ontology should provide information about responsibilities, completed activities and dependencies. All with the aim of increasing traceability and providing easier conclusions for quality reporting. In this context, it is necessary to define certain rules. An olive oil that has quality results EVOO should receive a corresponding precautionary post-procedure status. Other elements such as organoleptic properties are not included, as the focus is on chemical relationships for the time being. Figure 1 below abstracts the aforementioned domain situation surrounding the quality assessment of olive oil test samples and presents a suggestion for overcoming the problem situation (marked in grey).

5   Evaluation

5.1   CV Information Extraction

For the development of the CV-Model, the programming language Python as well as the YOLO implementation library provided by Ultralytics is used. Further libraries used are OpenCV for image processing, NumPy for mathematical functions, Matplotlib for visualisation, Pandas for data analysis. By extending the data with 200 more images, manual annotation and a data split for training, validation and testing (87%, 8%, 5%), the YOLO model was created, which can identify the two fluorescent zones. The following graph shows the object identification results of an olive oil test sample "O" with confidence level of the two detected regions.

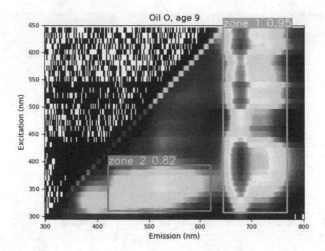

Fig. 2. CV Development Python: Object Classification Result

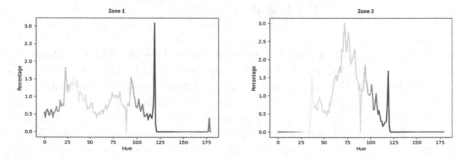

Fig. 3. CV Development Python: Color Intensities

For the *Image Analysis:* Based on the colour content of the two zones, the colours were extracted in a Hue histogram with the help of the Python library Matplot. For this purpose, the zones were additionally extracted and converted from a BGR format (Blue, Green, Red) into a HSV format (Hue, Saturation, Value). Figure 3 shows the colour distribution and intensity of the two zones. Colour shifts within the zones can be easily detected. Further, first results show an image classification for the ageing stage with an accuracy of 97%. The test sample from Fig. 2 was assigned the correct ageing level 9. Consequently, all results of the three CV tasks were integrated into a domain-specific ontology. For this purpose, instances were created for the fluorescent images and the confidence levels, the red intensities based on a threshold value, and the classified ageing level were stored as attributes.

Figure 4 depicts the developed ontology with its classes and sub-classes. Marked in orange are the two main elements, the quality assessment and the necessary olive oil test samples after which decisions are made. Both, individual

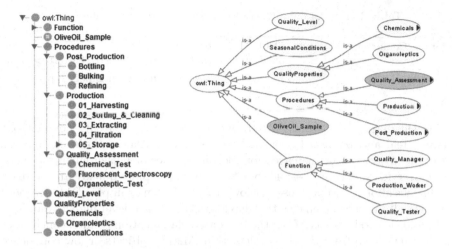

Fig. 4. Ontology Development: High-Level Hierarchy

Fig. 5. Ontology Development: Property Assertion for Images

instances for olive oil sample as well as fluorescent images can be stored under the respective class, all equipped with a time stamp. In addition, both instances hold extensive attributes from the AI-results and the direct chemical measurements. In the same way, person-related instances are stored for the functions mentioned, along with rules for responsibilities. In this way, individual activities carried out can be traced back and compared with the individual instances checked. Figure 5 shows the different data properties of a single fluorescent image enriched by ML predictions, CV results and quality classification.

Table 1. Evaluation: 3 Query Results for Competency Question

Informal Competency Question	SELECT ?a ?b WHERE { ?a oliveontology:hasAgeingStep ?b. FILTER (?b > "5")}
Execution Results	Fluorescent_Image_4 8 Fluorescent_Image_3 6

On this basis, extensive SPARQL queries can be carried out. Comparisons between real and predicted measured values can be drawn. Entire summaries of sample arrays can be displayed for specific batches or measurement systems. These overviews make it possible to detect anomalies more quickly and to draw conclusions about possible causes. Below in Table 1 is an example SPARQL query that lists all fluorescent images that have reached an age level higher than 5.

In addition to inferences from the CV-based classification results, conclusions can also be drawn from the object detection. Missing objects or low confidence numbers indicate that the test was performed incorrectly, as the object detection insists on olive oil and would not detect other objects from other oils with different fluorescent behaviour. The same applies to diluted olive oil. Further inferences allow first simplified indicators of deteriorating quality to be derived from the changing colour intensities. Using limit values, for example, a decreasing red content can be stored as a warning signal.

6   Conclusion

The presented approach addresses and connects practical business problems in the quality assessment of olive oil and missing reasoning from emerging AI systems. Furthermore, the KG-framework allows to link prediction and classification results of ML-models of fluorescent spectroscopy with domain-specific properties and other and comprehensive measurement systems - all with the aim to draw multifaceted conclusions to sustain and support high olive oil production. The proposed artefact primarily supports the quality assessment of olive oil by improving clarity, traceability of results and integrity in an organisation. Personal, time and equipment-related data are integrated into the ontology, so that responsibilities and individual activities related to the fluorescent images are arranged in a structured way. Although the presented KG as a starting point enables supporting inferences for the quality assessment of olive oil, it would be interesting to connect further comprehensive measuring systems directly and automatically in order to verify the practical suitability. For practical operation, both a user-friendly front end and easy implentability in the traditional olive oil environment are necessary and must still be considered, for example through action-research and real-time responses by quality managers. The artefact could be further strengthened by addressing anomalies or pattern recognition of monocultures, for example. More specific, comprehensive data sets would be needed for this task. Both types of information from the fluorescence images could provide better information about high-quality products and help producers maintain biodiversity and heritage.

In addition, the prototype can also be used as a starting point for other industries that have to fulfill similar extensive quality criteria, sell products with similar ageing behaviour and rely on fluorescence spectroscopy.

References

1. De Leonardis, A.: Food and Beverage Consumption and Health Virgin Olive Oil Production, Composition, Uses, and Benefits for Man. Nova Publisher, New York (2014)
2. Barjol, J., Aparicio, R.: Handbook of Olive Oil Analysis and Properties (2013)
3. Venturini, F., Fluri, S., Baumgartner, M.: Dataset of fluorescence EEM and UV spectroscopy data of olive oils during ageing. Data **8**, 81 (2023). https://doi.org/10.3390/data8050081
4. European Commission: On the characteristics of olive oil and olive-residue oil and on the relevant methods of analysis (1991)
5. Venturini, F., Sperti, M., Michelucci, U., Gucciardi, A., Martose, V., Deriu, M.: Physico-chemical properties extraction from the fluorescence spectrum with 1D-convolutional neural networks: application to olive oil (2022)
6. Venturini, F., et al.: Exploration of Spanish olive oil quality with a miniaturized low-cost fluorescence sensor and machine learning techniques (2021)
7. Benos L., Tagarakis A.C., Dolias, G., Berruto, R., Kateris, D., Bochtis, D.: Machine learning in agriculture: A comprehensive updated review, MDPI AG (2021)
8. Lecue, F.: On The Role of Knowledge Graphs in Explainable AI (2020)
9. chaudhri, V., et al.: Knowledge graphs: Introduction, history, and perspectives, AI Magazine (2022)
10. Khan, A., Mukhtar, H., Saba, T., Riaz, O., Ghani, M., Bahaj, S.: Scene Graph Generation with Structured Aspect of Segmenting the Big Distributed Clusters (2022)
11. Kendal, S., Creen, M.: An Introduction to Knowledge Engineering. Springer, London (2006). https://doi.org/10.1007/978-1-84628-667-4
12. Liebowitz, J.: Knowledge Management: Learning from Knowledge Engineering. CRC Press, Boca Raton (2001)
13. Russell, S., Norvig, P.: Artificial Intelligence - A Modern Approach. Pearson, Harlow (2021)
14. Studer, R., Benjamins, V., Fensel, D.: Knowledge engineering: principles and methods. Data Knowl. Eng. **25**, 161–197 (1998)
15. Ehrlinger, L., Wöss, W.: Towards a definition of knowledge graphs. SEMANTiCS (Posters Demos SuCCESS) **2**(48), 1–4 (2016)
16. Zhao, L., Li, B., Mao, B.: Communications in Computer and Information Science - Decision Tree and Knowledge Graph Based on Grain Loss Prediction. Springer, Singapore (2020)
17. Kejriwal, M.: Domain-Specific Knowledge Graph Construction. SCS, Springer, Cham (2019). https://doi.org/10.1007/978-3-030-12375-8
18. Szeliski, R.: Computer Vision. Springer, London (2011)
19. Voulodimos, A., Doulamis, N., Doulamis, A., Protopapadakis, E.: Deep learning for computer vision: a brief review. Comput. Intell. Neurosci. **2**(2018), 1–13 (2018)
20. Aguilera Puerto, D., Cáceres Moreno, O., Martínez Gila, DM., Gómez Ortega, J., Gámez García, J.: Online system for the identification and classification of olive fruits for the olive oil production process. J. Food Measur. Charact. **2**(13), 716–727 (2019)

21. Navarro Soto, J., Satorres Martínez, S., Martínez Gila, D., Gómez Ortega, J., Gámez García, J.: Fast and reliable determination of virgin olive oil quality by fruit inspection using computer vision. Sensors **2**(18), 3826 (2019)
22. Goodfellow, I., Bengio, Y., Courville, A.: Deep Learning. The MIT Press, Cambridge (2016)
23. Girshick, R., Donahue, J., Darrell, T., Malik, J.: Rich feature hierarchies for accurate object detection and semantic segmentation. In: 2014 IEEE Conference on Computer Vision and Pattern Recognition, pp. 580–587 (2014)
24. Li, S., Li, Y., Li, Y., Li, M., Xu, X.: YOLO-FIRI: improved YOLOv5 for infrared image object detection. IEEE Access **2**(9), 141861–141875 (2021)
25. Zinchuk, V., Grossenbacher Zinchuk, O.: Machine learning for analysis of microscopy images: a practical guide. Cell Biol. **2**(86), e101 (2020)
26. Kiritsakis, A.K., Shahidi, F.: Olives and Olive Oil as Functional Foods. John Wiley & Sons, Oxford (2017)
27. Parra-López, C., Hinojosa-Rodríguez, A., Carmona-Torres, C., Sayadi, S.: ISO 9001 implementation and associated manufacturing and marketing practices in the olive oil industry in southern Spain (2015)
28. Martínez G., Diego M., Navarro Soto, J., Satorres Martínez, S., Gómez Ortega, J., Gámez García, J.: The Advantage of Multispectral Images in Fruit Quality Control for Extra Virgin Olive Oil Production (2020)
29. Riganelli, C., Marchini, A.: The Quality Management in the Olive Oil SMEs: An Analysis in the Southern Italy Olive oil analysis through scanner data View project Innovation in olive oil sector View project (2015)
30. Sikorska, E., Khmelinskii, I., Sikorski, M.: Analysis of Olive Oils by Fluorescence Spectroscopy: Methods and Applications (2012)
31. Sikorska, E., et al.: Fluorescence spectroscopy in monitoring of extra virgin olive oil during storage (2008)
32. Chaudhri, V., et al.: Knowledge graphs: Introduction, history, and perspectives (2022)
33. Sanaeifar, A., Jafari, A., Golmakani, M.: Fusion of dielectric spectroscopy and computer vision for quality characterization of olive oil during storage (2018)
34. Soto, J., Martinez, S., Gila, D., Ortega, J., Garcia, J.: Fast and Reliable Determination of Virgin Olive Oil Quality by Fruit Inspection Using Computer Vision (2018)
35. Schoenke, J., et al.: Gaia-AgStream: an explainable AI platform for mining complex data streams in agriculture. In: Boumerdassi, S., Ghogho, M., Renault, É. (eds.) SSA 2021. CCIS, vol. 1470, pp. 71–83. Springer, Cham (2021). https://doi.org/10.1007/978-3-030-88259-4_6
36. Terven, J., Cordova-Esparza, D.: A Comprehensive Review of YOLO From YOLOv1 to YOLOv8 and Beyond (2023)
37. Peffers, K., Tuunanen, T., Rothenberger, M., Chatterjee, S.: A design science research methodology for information systems research (2007)
38. Hevner, A., March, S., Park, J., Ram, S.: Design Science in Information Systems (2004)
39. European Commission: on the characteristics of olive oil and olive-residue oil and on the relevant methods of analysis (1991)

40. European Union: Commission Regulation (EEC) No 2568/91 on the characteristics of olive oil and olive-residue oil and on the relevant methods of analysis (1991)
41. Xu, F., Uszkoreit, H., Du, Y., Zhao, D., Zhu, J.: Explainable AI: A Brief Survey on History. Research Areas, Approaches and Challenges (2019)
42. Banias, G., Achillas, C., Vlachokostas, C., Moussiopoulos, N., Stefanou, M.: Environmental impacts in the life cycle of olive oil: a literature review (2017)

A Flexible, Extendable and Adaptable Model to Support AI Coaching

Ritu Duhan⬚, Charuta Pande$^{(\boxtimes)}$⬚, and Andreas Martin⬚

Intelligent Information Systems Research Group, FHNW University of Applied
Sciences and Arts Northwestern Switzerland, Riggenbachstrasse 16, 4600 Olten,
Switzerland
{charuta.pande,andreas.martin}@fhnw.ch

Abstract. We present a model based on coaching definitions, concepts, and theories to support AI coaching. The model represents the evidence-based coaching practice in different coaching domains by identifying the common elements in the coaching process. We then map the elements of the coaching model with Conversational AI design and development strategies to highlight how an AI coach can be instantiated from the model. We showcase the instantiation through an example use case of an HIV coaching chatbot.

Keywords: Coaching · Conversational AI Design · AI Coaching · Coaching Model · Chatbot

1 Introduction

Coaching as a profession finds application in various domains like healthcare, organization, sports, and education. Digitalization of coaching can lead to several benefits - increasing the accessibility, affordability, and availability of coaching and reducing the burden on coaches [25,32]. Conversational agents or chatbots provide an effective way to digitalize natural language communication and can also be applied to coaching. Due to the highly skilled, complex, and non-standard nature of coaching, it is challenging to emulate the coaching process through conversational agents.

In the context of organizational coaching, Strong and Terblanche [28] have identified the requirements of an AI coach chatbot. Terblanche [30] has further proposed approaches to designing an AI coach. However, it is not clear how a mapping between human coaching and AI coaching can be established. Grassman et al. [12] define AI coaching as "*a machine-assisted systematic process to help clients set professional goals and construct solutions to efficiently achieve them*". In order to align with this definition, it is recommended that the design of AI-based coaching conversations should be informed by coaching models and theories as in human coaching. The main point of consideration in doing so is to recognize the perspectives presented in established theories and the structural stages outlined in coaching models which can serve as a framework for creating AI-based coaching conversations.

Clutterbuck [8] suggests four levels of AI-enabled coaching based on "the potential to replace or enhance humans". Levels 1 and 2 focus on basic coach bots that either ask "diagnostic" questions or imitate simple human-like coaching conversations. For e.g., coach bots that follow the GROW (Goal, Reality, Options, Will) model of coaching [34] can effectively demonstrate these initial levels of AI-enabled coaching, as established through the experiments performed by Terblanche et al. [31,32] in organizational coaching. Level 3 involves more human-like capabilities like better semantic understanding and communicative abilities through the use of sentiments and empathy, whereas level 4 takes these human-like capabilities even further, thus forming a partnership between a coach and AI. In our research, we explore how a coach-AI partnership can be realized given a concrete coaching scenario.

We consider AI-based coaching as a hybrid intelligent system in which humans, organizations, AI and non-AI components participate. We regard the partnership between a coach and AI as a collaborative environment where both contribute to each other's learning and performance to deliver a quality service to coachees. The proposed model is a starting point for coaches to define and customize their partnership with AI.

The main goal of our research is to support coach-AI partnership and thus enhance the coaching process using AI, specifically Conversational AI, which targets natural language communication between humans and machines. We propose a coaching model as a bridge between human and AI coaching. The model provides an abstraction to represent the coaching process in different domains. The model is created to be flexible, extendable, and adaptable to meet the unique needs of each coaching domain. Further, we demonstrate how our coaching model can be instantiated using Conversational AI design and development strategies through a use case of HIV coaching in the healthcare domain. We limit our work to text-based conversational agents.

This paper is structured as follows: we discuss related work in Sect. 2 and our research method in Sect. 3. Section 4 describes the elements of the coaching model and its evaluation. Sections 5 and 6 describe the mapping and instantiation of the coaching model using Conversational AI design strategies followed by a discussion in Sect. 7. Section 8 outlines the future work and conclusion.

2   Related Work

The ongoing trend towards digitalization and automation of coaching practices aims at focused support towards pursuing goals and self-sufficiency by providing motivation [15]. Conversational AI agents are being designed and developed in diverse coaching domains to achieve faster, more efficient, and more effective sharing of knowledge. To fully realize the potential of the coach-AI partnership, it is essential to integrate new technology into coaching practice. Delegating tasks that AI is proficient at can free the coaches to focus on other value-added activities involving human judgment and discretion [33]. AI coaching has the potential to transform the coaching profession by offering low-cost and readily available services to a broader audience [12]. AI-based coaching agents can facilitate decision-making, ask reflective questions, and explore options for achieving goals [19]. Mai et al. [20] mention that coachees intend to use coaching chatbots due to the ability to express themselves more openly. Woebot and Coach Vici are examples of AI chatbots developed based on established coaching theories and models.

Woebot [10] is an AI-powered chatbot that provides users with mental health coaching and support. The platform uses Cognitive Behavioral Therapy techniques to help users manage anxiety, depression, and other mental health issues. The therapeutic process-oriented features of Woebot include empathic responses, tailoring, goal-setting, accountability, reflection, motivation, and engagement.

Coach Vici [32] has been developed using goal theory and helps to set realistic goals, plan achievable actions, discuss issues, and track progress. The framework used to develop Coach Vici is based on evidence-based coaching theories and also uses human coaching aspects connected with Conversational AI design strategies [30]. Encouraging results were achieved in the study, underlining scalability and cost-effectiveness as the main advantages of using this technology [32].

For effective implementation, Conversational AI coaching agents should adhere to the same standards and codes, and be guided by the same coaching theories and models as human coaches [20,28]. For example, Pereira et al. [27] have proposed an integrative model that incorporates Positive Psychology and Solution-focused approaches with cognitive-behavioral coaching.

Kamphorst [15] has proposed design guidelines for systems to be involved in coaching, which mention that AI coaching agents should -

- be dialog-based for user engagement
- have the social ability to create mutually shared relationships
- be context-aware
- have the ability to ask questions and provide personalized feedback
- follow some type of behavior-change model
- have the ability to guide in planning
- proactively encourage reflection
- have the capacity to interface with various sources of information to provide a broad range of inputs

A typical chatbot functions by receiving inputs in natural human language, linking those inputs to a knowledge base, and providing a corresponding response [29]. Montenegro et al. [24] have implemented the GROW coaching model by developing a proactive conversational agent, for helping the elderly improve their life quality, that can guide the conversations toward the achievement of goals. The ability of an AI conversational agent to be proactive results in more fluid and natural conversations [23] and enhances coaching sessions by assisting coachees in their thinking and reflection process [6]. Proactivity is a part of conversational intelligence and can be achieved by including strategies like *maintaining conver-*

sational context and flow, particularly by including *topic suggestions, follow-up questions, and initiating exchanges* in the conversation design [6,14].

Table 1. Mapping Core Coach Competencies to Conversational AI Strategies

Core Coach Competencies (ICF)	Conversational AI Design Strategies	How AI can support the human coach
Ethical practice - maintain confidentiality - appropriate, respectful language	Personification - define bot persona [6]	Onboard and gain trust of the coachee
Coaching mindset - flexible and reflective practice	Personalization - remember preferences [14]	Encourage a non-judgemental approach. [8]
Coaching agreements	Onboarding - ethical AI design [12] - disclosure [2]	Share limitations and relevant information. [2]
Supportive environment	Encouraging, empathetic, and supportive responses [36]	Encourage openness through anonymity [19]
Coach presence	Personification - include greetings, small-talk and humor [14] Handle fallback scenarios [14]	Choose a desired coach persona (avatar)
Effective communication	Communication techniques [6] - follow turn-taking etiquette - maintain conversational flow Personalization - sentiment-based response [14]	Keep focus on the issue [8] Stick to the objectives and not digress [8] Formulate the next question [24]
Facilitate learning and growth	Design based on coaching theories [29,36] Proactivity [24] Behavior analysis [5] Follow-up on status quo [36] Share relevant resources [16]	Analyze conversations [8] and use insights to - set goals - automate feedback - decision-making - monitoring progress

Design strategies like *repeating or rephrasing*, and *confirmation messages* using the same language as the coachee [18], exhibit understanding on the part of the chatbot. In Conversational AI, *sentiment analysis* is used as a design approach to extract feelings and opinions from textual data, as demonstrated by Montenegro et al. [24]. Using sentiment analysis, AI chatbot can detect positive, negative, or neutral emotions in the conversations, and the gathered data can be used to help coachees reflect on behaviors that support or limit their goal-attainment efforts, following the principles of the cognitive-behavioral approach.

The positive psychology approach focuses on the strengths of individuals and can use Conversational AI design strategies like *personalized responses, positive feedback*, and *encouraging, empathetic, and supportive statements* [6,23] leading to increased user engagement. Beinema et al. [4] have suggested that along with goal agreement and task agreement, building a personal bond influences the quality of the coach-coachee alliance leading to desired coaching outcomes.

Apart from the above-mentioned attributes, certain design strategies are critical for building a relationship and improving engagement and credibility in Conversational AI. These are fundamental components of coaching practice. Creating an identity and a personality for the chatbot, *personification*, leads to trust [29]. Explicitly defining data privacy and confidentiality agreements as a part of the *onboarding phase*, and adhering to *ethical AI design* guidelines are required to establish a strong coach-coachee alliance [12]. *Fallback scenarios*, such as conversational flow failures, should be handled in a seamless and agreeable manner [14]. Transparency in a coach-coachee relationship is established as *disclosure* by clearly specifying the capabilities and limitations of Conversational AI agents (not being human) [14,29]. Based on the discussion above, Table 1 summarises the design strategies of Conversational AI with core coach competencies, as found in the relevant research studies.

3   Method

To design a coaching model, it is important to understand what a coach needs for informed coaching practice. Following the iterative phases of Design Science Research methodology, we studied literature for relevant research works on coaching definitions, concepts, theories, and the so-called 'evidence base' in the practice of coaching. To understand how AI technology is developing in the field of coaching, recommendations on design propositions, features, and use cases of AI coaching agents were researched, as well as ethical challenges and limitations in the design and usage of these agents.

After the literature review, a first draft of the coaching model was designed and presented to four expert coaches (one from the organizational coaching domain, one from the sports domain, and two from the education domain with experience in conversational AI designing), and further empirical insights were gathered. The qualitative data collected from the literature review and semi-structured interviews with expert coaches were analyzed and an updated version of the coaching model (Fig. 1) was designed. The selection criteria of expert coaches was an important agenda of the study to get a holistic picture of the coaching process and the feasibility of integrating human coaching strategies with Conversational AI design strategies.

To evaluate our coaching model's flexibility, adaptability, and extendability, we chose six experts from different domains of coaching. The evaluation methodology is described further in Sect. 4.4.

4   Model for AI Coaching

To derive our coaching model, we primarily referred to three different definitions of coaching - by the International Coaching Federation (ICF)[1], Cox [9] and Kamphorst [15]. The definitions are broadly divided into three parts, where the first part is about establishing a coach-coachee partnership, the second part highlights the coaching process with coaching strategies, tools, and techniques as common elements, and the final part focuses on the outcomes like improving performance and achieving goals.

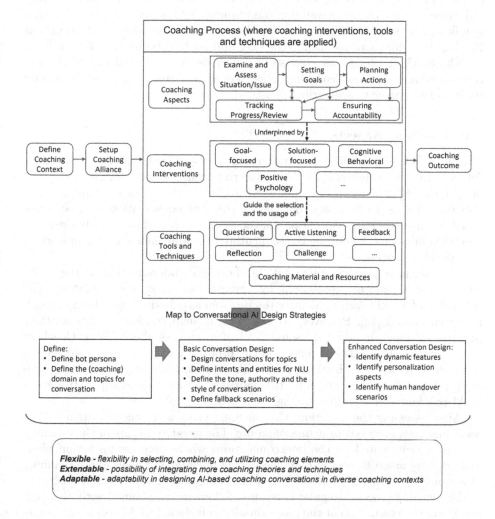

Fig. 1. Model to support AI Coaching

---

[1] https://coachingfederation.org/about.

The essence of coaching lies in the coaching process. Therefore, the coaching process conceptualized by Bachirova [3] was investigated. It comprises four fundamental elements common to the above-mentioned definitions - dialog, collaborative learning, coaching interventions, and tools and techniques. The coaching dialog comprises specific steps that facilitate collaborative learning and personal growth. These steps were adapted from ICF core competency model and identified as coaching aspects.

Based on the discussion above, we propose a coaching model as shown in Fig. 1. The overall phases in coaching can be depicted as a set of sequential steps. The context of coaching is defined in the first step, where the coaching objectives are set by understanding the requirements of the coachee. This step is followed by setting up the coaching alliance, where an agreement on details like logistics, duration, payment, schedule, and confidentiality may be reached.

The coaching process as a phase in the model is conducted iteratively and comprises three sections - coaching aspects, coaching interventions, and coaching tools and techniques, as described below.

4.1   Coaching Aspects

Coaching dialog [3] is a means to realize coaching and hence should be meaningful and of value to the coachee. This concern becomes more relevant in the case of AI coaching. Therefore, it is important to have a theme for coaching dialogs. Our coaching model proposes that the AI coaching conversations can be structured around coaching aspects as conversation themes. The coaching aspects identified in our model outline the sequential steps and their interdependence in the coaching process.

The coaching process starts with a thorough understanding of the problem/current situation, represented by *examine/assess current situation*. The capability of an AI coach to identify the problem as effectively as a human coach has been argued [12]. However, AI coaches can help coachees reflect on their problems if they already have some level of awareness about them. Coachees can work with AI coaches to reflect on the problem and progress toward setting goals in such cases. Technological aids like videos, podcasts, mind-maps, predesigned questionnaires, and reflective journals can be used as supporting tools in AI coaching conversations to analyze a problem [16].

After assessing the situation, the coaching process commences with *setting goals* and then proceeds to *action planning*. The iterative nature of the coaching process is represented by the interconnections where progress on action plans and *tracking progress/review*, may necessitate redefining of goals and replanning of actions. *Ensuring accountability* is a crucial aspect that applies at each step of the coaching process. Regular check-ins, follow-ups on planned activities, and reviewing the status quo of the goals should be included in AI coaching conversations to promote a sense of accountability on the part of the coachees [10].

The coaching aspects are underpinned by coaching interventions as evidence-based coaching relies on the application of theory and empirical knowledge [11].

Therefore, AI coaching sessions should be guided by established coaching interventions so as to increase their meaningfulness and reliability.

4.2 Coaching Interventions

Through literature review and insights gained from expert coaches, we learned that experienced coaches often incorporate a combination of perspectives from different coaching theories rather than adhering to a single coaching model. The flexibility and adaptability provided by integrating relevant theories characterize human coaching as a highly specialized skill. Consequently, our coaching model also suggests incorporating such integration into AI coaching. Moreover, it is possible to extend our model by including other relevant coaching interventions supported by empirical research depending on the coaching domain.

According to the selected coaching aspect, an AI coach can take the initiative to suggest relevant and suitable conversations based on the coachee's specific situation [4]. For example, an AI coach can adopt a *Positive Psychology* approach emphasizing individual strengths to build positive motivation. The *cognitive-behavioral* approach can be employed to provide support and guidance in handling stigma or challenging situations. The GROW model has been suggested as the underpinning intervention for the goal-focused approach. It is an established coaching model that provides a structure to the coaching session and helps the coachee set goals, evaluate options, and create a plan for implementing solutions. An AI coach can focus on discussing concrete action plans based on the selected intervention, enabling the coachee to implement practical steps toward their goals. The solution-focused approach complements by helping the coachee focus on the present and the future to co-create the solutions. By combining these approaches, adherence, and engagement can potentially be increased by providing users with relevant tools and information that directly apply to their needs [4]. Hence, the proposed coaching model makes these coaching interventions explicit as used in human coaching practice.

4.3 Coaching Tools and Techniques

This section corresponds to the communication techniques used during coaching. The coaching interventions guide the selection and usage of coaching tools and techniques, such as - *questioning, listening, challenge, feedback and reflection, and sharing coaching resources.* As identified in Sect. 2 and Sect. 5, each coaching tool and technique can be mapped to an appropriate Conversational AI design strategy.

The coaching model provides flexibility to select and add various coaching tools and techniques, suggested and guided by established coaching interventions. Section 6 illustrates some examples of AI coaching conversations (excerpts taken from the HIV Coach chatbot) that show the usage of coaching interventions, tools, and techniques, as proposed by our coaching model.

4.4 Evaluation

For the final evaluation of our coaching model, six expert coaches were interviewed. Our criteria for selecting experts were – a. certified coaches from different domains and b. senior researchers in Conversational AI. Thus, our evaluators included two senior researchers in Conversational AI also coaching in the education domain, one certified systemic and design thinking coach, and three ICF-certified executive coaches, also doing transformational and life coaching. The feedback of the coaches was collected through semi-structured interviews followed by a questionnaire that included a mix of questions with a 5-point Likert scale and open-ended questions. The coaches were encouraged to provide their opinion on the chosen score on the Likert scale. The open-ended questions were used to gather overall feedback on the coaching model's design, its practical usefulness, and potential challenges in guiding the design of AI coaching conversations.

Finding a certified coach who also has experience with designing Conversational AI is a limitation faced during this research study. Although coaches from varied domains were interviewed, interviewing a fairly sufficient number of coaches from more diverse coaching domains is needed to further strengthen the validity and applicability of the findings.

5   Mapping Coaching Model to Conversational AI Strategies

A step towards instantiating our coaching model is to map the coaching phases to specific Conversational AI design and development strategies. We refer to the Conversational AI Life-Cycle framework by Martin [21,22] to suggest concrete activities to implement an AI coach chatbot; our focus is more on the design-related phases than the operational phases of the framework.

The Define phase involves creating a persona for the chatbot by taking into account the coaching domain and the coaching needs of the coachees, e.g., choosing a name, visualization, and other characteristics of the chatbot. Further, the topics of coaching are identified such that one topic addresses one or more coaching needs/goals. The topics are derived from the coaching intervention used by the coach as well as the coaching aspects. For e.g., a topic based on *Cognitive Behavioral Theory* corresponding to the coaching aspect *Examine and Assess Situation/Issue* could be a wellness survey to determine the level of well-being in a coachee.

In the Design phase, actual conversations are developed taking into account the information to be shared with coachees, appropriate tone, authority, and relevant coaching techniques. In this phase, a decision regarding the dialog management strategy of the chatbot is made, e.g., rule-based, frame-based, etc. as proposed by Pande et al. [26]. Depending on the interaction required for a topic, AI components like intents and entities are defined. Additionally, fallback scenarios are identified and handled appropriately in the conversation design.

The enhanced conversation design focuses on identifying dynamic features like storing user information, scheduling appointments, and sharing relevant resources like videos, etc. Personalization aspects are designed into the conversations based on the captured user information, and conversational history. Coaching techniques like feedback and reflection can be effectively applied by identifying further relevant AI components like sentiment detection, emotion recognition, response generation, etc. Additionally, situations where human handover is required are also identified and an appropriate mechanism to contact humans is defined, for e.g., notification via email, SMS, a phone call, or by scheduling an appointment.

Table 2. Mapping Coaching Model to Conversational AI Strategies.

Coaching Process	Desired attributes in AI coaching agent	Conversational AI design strategies
Coaching interventions:		
Goal-focused (GROW)	Proactive behavior Session structure	Maintain conversational context Maintain conversational flow with follow-up questions
Solution-focused	Insightful, solution-focused questions	Repeating and rephrasing Confirmation messages to exhibit understanding Sharing resources
Cognitive-behavioral	Analyse behavior and thinking patterns Empathetic responses	Sentiment analysis Emotion detection and empathetic responses Personalization
Positive-psychology	Strength-focused approach Emotional intelligence leading to motivation	Positive attitude, polite, respectful, and friendly conversations Tone, authority, and style of conversation Encouraging and supportive statements, positive and motivational responses
Coaching tools and techniques:		
Questioning	Insightful questions	Formulate the next relevant question, questions to collect information
Active Listening	Exhibit understanding for better engagement	Repeat, summarise, confirm
Feedback, reflection, and challenge	Detect behavior patterns, sentiments, and emotions	Collect data and present with analysis and description Personalized messages and prompts Regular check-ins and follow-ups
Coaching material and resources	Detect coaching needs and share relevant resources	Share resources like online tools, tutorials, videos, blogs, websites, etc.

The Define and Design phases are best carried out as a collaborative activity between coaching experts and Conversational AI developers.

Further mapping between the coaching model elements, the desired attributes of AI coaching agents, and the Conversational AI design strategies is shown in Table 2.

6   Instantiation of Coaching Model

AI-based coaching can aid individuals in achieving their self-improvement objectives by providing a diverse range of techniques and strategies, especially in the healthcare domain [15]. Additionally, this approach has demonstrated significant potential in supporting and promoting behavioral change [35]. We demonstrate how our coaching model can be realized into an AI coach using the case of an HIV Health Coach chatbot.

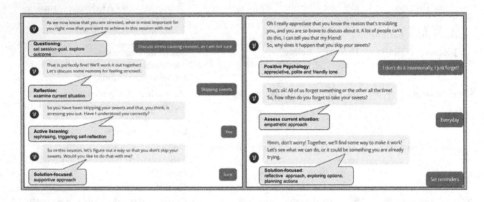

Fig. 2. Instantiation of Coaching Model: HIV Coach Chatbot Example 1

Figures 2 and 3 show examples of dialogs that integrate elements of Cognitive Behavioral, Positive Psychology, and Solution-focused approaches with a focus on meeting the desired goal. A session structure is followed to set goals, explore the current situation, discuss various options, and plan activities to realize the goal.

The coachee being stressed is the problem situation identified. Coaching starts with setting the focus on what to achieve in the session. This involves proactive behavior on the part of the AI coach chatbot by framing relevant, insightful questions. Encouraging, supportive and friendly statements are used to show a positive attitude. Negative sentiments are identified and handled based on a cognitive-behavior approach, also using an empathetic tone and style of conversation. Politely giving feedback to trigger reflection is another technique used in the dialog. The Positive Psychology approach is used to focus on strengths and preferences for further motivation toward achieving the goal/s. Active listening is exhibited by summarising and confirming with the coachee. Figure 3 also shows the analysis of the wellness survey [17], where the coachee is empathetically advised professional help, which demonstrates human intervention as part of ethical design practice. In addition to the shown example, story-telling is another approach used in the dialogs. Also, relevant resources, like videos, websites, etc. are shared with the coachee as and when required.

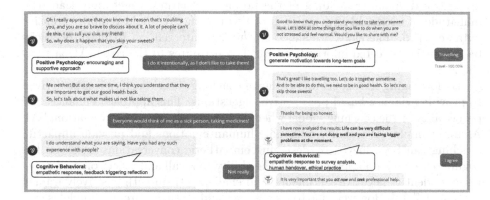

Fig. 3. Instantiation of Coaching Model: HIV Coach Chatbot Example 2

The above use case has been derived from our in-progress research. The Health Coach chatbot will be accessed over WhatsApp. The requirements, technical details, and ethical considerations regarding the development of this chatbot have been described in our previous work [26].

7   Discussion

In the evaluation, the coaches confirmed that the coaching model helps in making the knowledge about coaching theories and techniques explicit. The concept of transitioning the coaching sessions from being intuitive to being deliberate or evidence-based makes it possible to have a concrete implementation as a tool. The integration of theoretical principles from underpinning theories is considered a good starting point by the experts. An area of further development is foreseen in terms of simplification and translation of these principles so that they can be effectively implemented in AI coaching by aligning them with Conversational AI design strategies.

Overall, the experts found the coaching model to be a helpful resource for reflecting on and improving their coaching practices. As for its applicability to AI-based coaching conversations, the expert coaches found the model useful for providing a clear theoretical foundation and effective implementation of early steps in the identified coaching aspects. For the more advanced coaching stages, the coaches observed that it can guide the design of a rich, more effective coaching approach. One feedback highlighted that incorporating such an approach can help design coaching conversations where coachees are forced to reflect and explore options. The discussion regarding deeper aspects of coaching that involve delving into underlying beliefs, values, and motivations of the coachee, helped to understand not just the potential capabilities but also limitations of AI coaching.

As a limitation, AI coaching conversations cannot fully replicate human coaching skills. The coaching aspect 'examine and assess current situation' involves a deep understanding of the problem situation, which may lead to a multitude of issues. Identifying each of them using AI would require extensive data sets [12]. Therefore, we suggest a human intervention to make decisions based on the collected information, which contributes to the coach-AI partnership.

By leveraging the expert knowledge of coaching theories, rules can be derived to provide evidence-based prescriptive suggestions. This approach enhances the practicality of the coaching model when designing rule-based Conversational AI. As an example, AI's ability to handle human emotions and provide impactful coaching can be achieved by designing empathetic conversations based on the cognitive-behavioral approach, with the ability to recall and reflect on past experiences, identify negative sentiments, and challenge them with positively framed content [1,7,13]. However, due to its abstract and static nature, the model is currently limited in representing such prescriptive elements that simulate implicit decision-making in coaching. We address this limitation by providing concrete mappings between the elements of the model with Conversational AI design strategies (see Sect. 5).

Another point of discussion is the situation where the coachee deviates from the structure of the conversation. One way to address this issue is by implementing AI design techniques such as 'fallback' options and providing clear information about AI capabilities. This would help manage the coachee's expectations around the technology's capabilities and limitations. In cases where an AI coach is unable to handle a specific scenario, human coaching intervention may be recommended. In addition to handling simple, reflective, and repetitive tasks, more complex conversations would require training the coach chatbot on larger data sets using machine learning techniques.

Although the model was evaluated with coaches from different domains, there is still a need to validate it further with more experts as well as by instantiating the model for different use cases in coaching.

8   Future Work and Conclusion

We presented a coaching model which helps in making the knowledge about coaching explicit and thus guide the creation of AI coaches.

The coaching model consolidates diverse perspectives, tools, and techniques from various coaching interventions for coaches to incorporate into their sessions. The model provides flexibility in selecting and combining the elements of coaching depending on the requirements of coaching. Additionally, the model can be extended to include other theories and techniques making it applicable across different coaching domains. The adaptability of the model lies in transferring its elements into designing AI coaches for diverse coaching domains while drawing on the same evidence base as human coaching.

Our coaching model offers a constructive beginning and provides insights to inform and direct future research work on evidence-based AI coaching by contributing to an effective partnership between human coaches and AI. In its current state, the model relies on the coaches to make decisions on what elements can be incorporated into AI coaching.

Our future work will involve supporting coaches further in designing AI coaches. Additionally, we will continue to validate the model by instantiating it for different coaching scenarios similar to that of the HIV Coach bot. This will help in distinguishing the overlapping and non-overlapping domain-specific aspects of coaching and the measures needed to incorporate these aspects using Conversational AI design strategies.

Acknowledgements. The use case for demonstrating this work has been derived from the research project "Researching intelligent chatbots as healthcare coaches" funded by the Swiss National Science Foundation (SNSF) under grant IZSTZ0_202602 within the Swiss Programme for International Research by Scientific Investigation Teams (SPIRIT).

References

1. Alazraki, L., Ghachem, A., Polydorou, N., Khosmood, F., Edalat, A.: An empathetic AI coach for self-attachment therapy. In: 2021 IEEE Third International Conference on Cognitive Machine Intelligence (CogMI), pp. 78–87. IEEE (2021). https://doi.org/10.1109/CogMI52975.2021.00019
2. Amershi, S., et al.: Guidelines for human-AI interaction. In: Proceedings of the 2019 Chi Conference on Human Factors in Computing Systems, pp. 1–13 (2019). https://doi.org/10.1145/3290605.3300233
3. Bachkirova, T.: Developing a knowledge base of coaching: questions to explore. The SAGE Handbook of Coaching, pp. 23–41 (2017)
4. Beinema, T., Op den Akker, H., Hermens, H.J., van Velsen, L.: What to discuss?- A blueprint topic model for health coaching dialogues with conversational agents. Int. J. Hum. Comput. Interact. **39**(1), 164–182 (2023). https://doi.org/10.1080/10447318.2022.2041884
5. Chatterjee, A., Gerdes, M., Prinz, A., Martinez, S.: Human coaching methodologies for automatic electronic coaching (eCoaching) as behavioral interventions with information and communication technology: systematic review. J. Med. Internet Res. **23**(3), e23533 (2021). https://doi.org/10.2196/23533
6. Chaves, A.P., Gerosa, M.A.: How should my chatbot interact? A survey on social characteristics in human-chatbot interaction design. Int. J. Hum. Comput. Interact. **37**(8), 729–758 (2021). https://doi.org/10.1080/10447318.2020.1841438
7. Chew, H.S.J.: The use of artificial intelligence-based conversational agents (chatbots) for weight loss: scoping review and practical recommendations. JMIR Med. Inf. **10**(4), e32578 (2022). https://doi.org/10.2196/32578
8. Clutterbuck, D.: The future of AI in coaching. In: Greif, S., Möller, H., Scholl, W., Passmore, J., Müller, F. (eds.) International Handbook of Evidence-Based Coaching, pp. 369–379. Springer, Cham (2022). https://doi.org/10.1007/978-3-030-81938-5_30

9. Cox, E., Clutterbuck, D.A., Bachkirova, T.: The complete handbook of coaching. The Complete Handbook of Coaching, pp. 1–504 (2014)
10. Fitzpatrick, K.K., Darcy, A., Vierhile, M.: Delivering cognitive behavior therapy to young adults with symptoms of depression and anxiety using a fully automated conversational agent (Woebot): a randomized controlled trial. JMIR Ment. Health 4(2), e7785 (2017). https://doi.org/10.2196/mental.7785
11. Göldi, A., Rietsche, R.: Whereto for automated coaching conversation: Structured intervention or adaptive generation? ECIS 2023 Research-in-Progress Papers (2023)
12. Graßmann, C., Schermuly, C.C.: Coaching with artificial intelligence: concepts and capabilities. Hum. Resour. Dev. Rev. 20(1), 106–126 (2021). https://doi.org/10.1177/1534484320982891
13. Hildebrandt, F., Lichtenberg, S., Brendel, A.B., Riquel, J., Dechant, D., Bönig, F.: Conversational agents in service context: towards a classification of human-like design expectations. In: Proceedings of the 29th Americas Conference on Information Systems (AMCIS) (2023)
14. Jain, M., Kumar, P., Kota, R., Patel, S.N.: Evaluating and informing the design of chatbots. In: Proceedings of the 2018 Designing Interactive Systems Conference, pp. 895–906 (2018). https://doi.org/10.1145/3196709.3196735
15. Kamphorst, B.A.: E-coaching systems: what they are, and what they aren't. Pers. Ubiquitous Comput. 21(4), 625–632 (2017). https://doi.org/10.1007/s00779-017-1020-6
16. Kanatouri, S.: Digital coaching: A conceptually distinct form of coaching? (2020). https://doi.org/10.13109/9783666407420.40
17. Kroenke, K., Spitzer, R.L., Williams, J.B.: The PHQ-9: validity of a brief depression severity measure. J. Gen. Intern. Med. 16(9), 606–613 (2001). https://doi.org/10.1046/j.1525-1497.2001.016009606.x
18. Lee, S.T.: Solution Focused Briefly Illustrated. Partridge Publishing, Singapore (2021)
19. Mai, V., Richert, A.: AI coaching: effectiveness factors of the working alliance in the coaching process between coachbot and human coachee-an explorative study. In: EDULEARN20 Proceedings, pp. 1239–1248. IATED (2020). https://doi.org/10.21125/edulearn.2020.0411
20. Mai, V., Wolff, A., Richert, A., Preusser, I.: Accompanying reflection processes by an AI-Based StudiCoachBot: a study on rapport building in human-machine coaching using self disclosure. In: Stephanidis, C. (ed.) HCII 2021. LNCS, vol. 13096, pp. 439–457. Springer, Cham (2021). https://doi.org/10.1007/978-3-030-90328-2_29
21. Martin, A.: The conversational AI life-cycle (2019). https://doi.org/10.5281/zenodo.7991800
22. Martin, A.: The conversational AI life-cycle - version 2 (Apr 2023). https://doi.org/10.5281/zenodo.7992227
23. Medhi Thies, I., Menon, N., Magapu, S., Subramony, M., O'Neill, J.: How do you want your chatbot? An exploratory Wizard-of-Oz study with young, Urban Indians. In: Bernhaupt, R., Dalvi, G., Joshi, A., Balkrishan, D.K., O'Neill, J., Winckler, M. (eds.) INTERACT 2017. LNCS, vol. 10513, pp. 441–459. Springer, Cham (2017). https://doi.org/10.1007/978-3-319-67744-6_28
24. Montenegro, C., et al.: A dialogue-act taxonomy for a virtual coach designed to improve the life of elderly. Multimodal Technol. Interact. 3(3), 52 (2019). https://doi.org/10.3390/mti3030052

25. Mrazek, M., O'Neill, F.: Artificial intelligence and healthcare in emerging markets (2020)
26. Pande, C., Martin, A., Pimmer, C.: Towards hybrid dialog management strategies for a health coach chatbot. In: Proceedings of the AAAI 2023 Spring Symposium on Challenges Requiring the Combination of Machine Learning and Knowledge Engineering (AAAI-MAKE 2023). vol. 3433. CEUR-WS.org (2023)
27. Pereira Dias, G., Palmer, S., Nardi, A.E.: Integrating positive psychology and the solution-focused approach with cognitive-behavioural coaching: the integrative cognitive-behavioural coaching model. Eur. J. Appl. Positive Psychol. **1**, 1–8 (2017)
28. Strong, N., Terblanche, N.: Chatbots as an instance of an artificial intelligence coach. Coaching im digitalen Wandel, pp. 51–62 (2020). https://doi.org/10.13109/9783666407420.51
29. Terblanche, N.: The coaching model derivation process: combining grounded theory and canonical action research for developing coaching models. Coaching: Int. J. Theor. Res. Pract. **13**(1), 45–60 (2020). https://doi.org/10.1080/17521882.2019.1619794
30. Terblanche, N.: A design framework to create artificial intelligence coaches. Int. J. Evid. Coaching Mentoring **18**(2), 152–165 (2020). https://doi.org/10.24384/b7gs-3h05
31. Terblanche, N., Kidd, M.: Adoption factors and moderating effects of age and gender that influence the intention to use a non-directive reflective coaching chatbot. SAGE Open **12**(2), 21582440221096136 (2022). https://doi.org/10.1177/21582440221096136
32. Terblanche, N., Molyn, J., de Haan, E., Nilsson, V.O.: Comparing artificial intelligence and human coaching goal attainment efficacy. Plos one **17**(6), e0270255 (2022). https://doi.org/10.1371/journal.pone.0270255
33. Upadhyay, A.K., Khandelwal, K.: Artificial intelligence-based training learning from application. Dev. Learn. Organ. Int. J. (2019). https://doi.org/10.1108/DLO-05-2018-0058
34. Whitmore, J.: Coaching for Performance: The Principles and Practice of Coaching and Leadership FULLY REVISED 25TH ANNIVERSARY EDITION. Hachette UK (2010)
35. Wolever, R.Q., Moore, M.A., Jordan, M.: Coaching in healthcare. The Sage Handbook of Coaching, pp. 521–543 (2017)
36. Zhang, J., Oh, Y.J., Lange, P., Yu, Z., Fukuoka, Y.: Artificial intelligence chatbot behavior change model for designing artificial intelligence chatbots to promote physical activity and a healthy diet. J. Med. Internet Res. **22**(9), e22845 (2020). https://doi.org/10.2196/22845

Predicting Patterns of Firms' Vulnerability to Economic Crises Using Open Data, Synthetic Minority Oversampling Technique and Machine Learning

Mohsan Ali$^{(\boxtimes)}$ ⓘ, Euripidis Loukis ⓘ, and Yannis Charalabidis ⓘ

University of the Aegean, Samos, Greece
{mohsan,eloukis,yannisx}@aegean.gr

Abstract. One of the most serious problems of the market-based economies are the instabilities of the economic activity (business cycles), which are sometimes large and lead to recessionary economic crises of different intensities, geographical scopes and durations, and have quite negative consequences for firms. Governments, in order to reduce these negative consequences of economic crises, which can lead to high levels of unemployment and poverty, as well social unrest and political extremism, undertake various interventions, such as large-scale economic stimulus programs. However, in order to maximize their cost-effectiveness, as well as the economic and social value they generate, it is necessary that they are properly targeted and directed to/focused on the most vulnerable firms to the economic crisis. This paper describes a methodology that can be quite useful for this: it enables the prediction of multi-dimensional patterns of individual firms' vulnerability to economic crisis with respect to the main aspects of their financial situation. For this purpose, Machine Learning algorithms are used, in combination with the Synthetic Minority Oversampling Technique (SMOTE) for increasing their performance, which are trained using open government data from Statistical Authorities. Furthermore, a first application/validation of the proposed methodology is presented, using open data from the Greek Statistical Authority about 363 firms for the severe Greek economic crisis period 2009–2014, which gave satisfactory results.

Keywords: Economic Crises · Open data · Machine Learning

1 Introduction

One of the most serious problems of the market-based economies are the instabilities of economic activity (business cycles), which sometimes can be large and result in recessionary economic crises of different intensities, geo-graphical scopes and durations [1–7]. These economic crises have quite negative consequences for society and the economy [1, 2, 8–11]. Due to the decrease of overall economic activity and incomes during economic crises leads most firms face a deterioration in many important aspects

K. Hinkelmann et al. (Eds.): BIR 2023, LNBIP 493, pp. 188–196, 2023.
https://doi.org/10.1007/978-3-031-43126-5_14

of their economic situation: most firms experience decrease of their sales, and therefore their revenue and their liquidity, increase of their debts, and reductions investments and personnel employment, while some firms cannot survive and go bankrupt. However, these negative impacts of economic crisis differ significantly among firms [1–3, 12]: some firms exhibit higher capabilities to cope with the economic crises and therefore higher vulnerability to them, while some other firms cannot sufficiently cope with the crises and are more vulnerable.

So, it is one of the most important challenges of governments face to reduce as much as possible these severe negative consequences for the society and the economy of the economic crises that repeatedly appear, which can result in high levels of unemployment, poverty and social exclusion, as well social unrest, and political extremism. For this purpose, governments undertake huge interventions, such as large-scale economic stimulus programs, which include the provision to firms of tax rebates, financial assistance, subsidies, financial support for investments, low-interest (or even no-interest) loans, etc. [13–16]. These important government interventions, and especially the large-scale economic stimulus programs, are more cost-effective and generate more economic and social value if they are properly targeted and directed to/focused on the most vulnerable firms to the economic crisis.

This paper describes a methodology that can be quite useful for achieving this focus: it enables the prediction of the multi-dimensional 'patterns' of individual firms' vulnerability to economic crisis with respect to the main aspects of their financial situation (such as sales revenue, liquidity, debts, investment, employment, etc.). For this purpose, we employ Artificial Intelligence (AI) algorithms from the area of Machine Learning (ML) [17, 18], which are used in order to construct a set of prediction models of the vulnerability to economic crises of an individual firm with respect the main aspects of their financial situation (i.e. the degree of deterioration of each of them during an economic crisis); as independent variables are used the characteristics of each individual firm. For the training of these prediction models are used open government data (OGD) [19, 20] from Statistical Authorities. Furthermore, a first application/validation of the proposed methodology is presented, which gives satisfactory results.

Our paper consists of four sections. In the following Sect. 2 the proposed methodology is described, and then in the Sect. 3 the abovementioned application of it is presented; lastly, the conclusions are summarized in the final Sect. 4.

2 Proposed Methodology

The proposed methodology aims to predict the multi-dimensional 'pattern of vulnerability' to an economic crisis (VEC) of an individual firm, which is defined as a vector having as components the degrees of deterioration of the main aspects of firm's financial situation, such as sales revenue, liquidity, debts, investment, employment, etc. (they can be measured in a 5-levels Likert scale: not at all, small, moderate, large, very large), during an economic crisis (Fig. 1):

$$VEC = [VEC_1, VEC_2, \ldots, VEC_N]$$

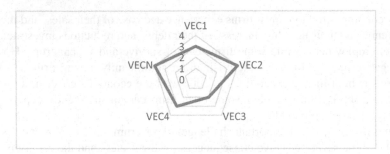

Fig. 1. Multidimensional Pattern of Firm's Vulnerability to Economic Crisis

So, for each of these components/dimensions of firm's vulnerability to economic crisis VEC_1, VEC_2, ..., VEC_N we construct a prediction model of it (having it as dependent variable). In order to determine the appropriate independent variables of these prediction models we have been based on theoretical foundations from management sciences. In particular, several frameworks have been developed concerning the main elements of a firm that determine its performance, with the 'Leavitt's Diamond' framework being the most widely recognized one, which includes five main elements: strategy, processes, people, technology, and structure [21, 22]. We can expect that these five main elements of the 'Leavitt's Diamond' framework will be the main determinants of the performance of a firm both in normal economic periods and in economic crisis ones.

So, the prediction models of firm's economic vulnerability concerning the main aspects of its financial situation VEC_i will include five corresponding groups of independent variables concerning:

a) strategy (e.g., degree of adoption of the main competitive advantage strategies, such as cost leadership, differentiation, focus, innovation, etc.)
b) processes (e.g., main characteristics of firm's processes, such as complexity, flexibility, etc.)
c) people (e.g., shares of firm's human resources having different levels of education or specific skills, certifications, etc.)
d) technology (e.g., use of various production technologies, digital technologies, etc.)
e) structure (e.g., main characteristics of firm's structure, degree of adoption of 'organic' forms of work organization, such as teamwork, etc.)

and also, a sixth group of independent variables concerning general information about the firm, such as size, sector, comparative performance vis-à-vis competitors, etc.

The structure of the prediction models of firm's crisis-vulnerability dimensions' VEC_i (dependent and independent variables) is shown in Fig. 2.

For the construction of each of these prediction model we can use the main supervised ML algorithms described in relevant literature [17, 18], such as Decision Tree (DT), Random Forest (RF), Logistic Regression (LR), Support Vector Machines (SVM), and Multilayer Perceptron (MLP), and then compare the prediction performances of the corresponding prediction models, and finally select the one with the highest prediction performance. For training them we can use relevant OGD for economic crisis periods provided by Statistical Authorities; the available dataset will be divided into two parts:

the 'training dataset', which is used for constructing the prediction model, and the 'test dataset', in which the prediction performance of this model is evaluated, by calculating its prediction accuracy, precision, recall, and F-Score are calculated.

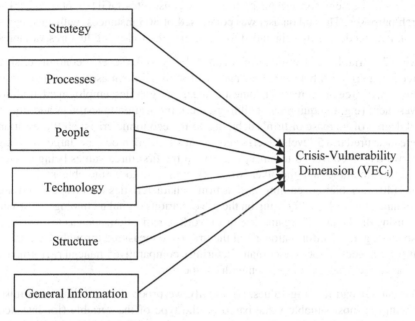

Fig. 2. Structure of the prediction models of firm's crisis-vulnerability dimensions

However, the abovementioned datasets we use for the construction of the models usually a) have missing values, b) their size can be not large enough to train a healthy and accurate ML model, and c) are unbalanced with respect to the classes (they include small numbers of observations/samples for some of the classes, and much larger numbers of observations/samples for some other classes); these can result in prediction models with lower prediction performance and also biased. In order to address problems b) and c) our methodology includes a pre-processing of these datasets using the Synthetic Minority Oversampling Technique (SMOTE) [23]; this technique increases the number of samples of the dataset using the existing samples of the classes (oversampling), balances the dataset with respect to the number of samples of each class, fills missing values, which enable the estimation of better prediction models with higher prediction performance. Furthermore, our methodology includes an initial Exploratory Data Analysis (EDA) in order to get a first insight of the data through visualizations, and make some necessary transformations, and then a Principal Component Analysis (PCA) in order to analyze the importance of the features, and select the eliminate the important ones, and eliminate the ones that are not important, which helps to improve performance and reduce training time.

3 Application

A first application/validation of the proposed methodology was made using a dataset that was released by the Greek Statistical Authority on request by the authors, and after signing an agreement concerning its use, so it constitutes OGD freely available for research purposes. The full dataset was comprised of 363 instances, with each instance being an independent firm. It included for each firm the following features/variables:

a) seven (7) variables concerning firm's vulnerability to the severe economic crisis that Greece experienced between 2009 and 2014 with the main aspects of its economic situation: degree of decrease of domestic sales, foreign sales, employment, traditional investment (e.g. in equipment, buildings, etc.), innovation investment and liquidity, and degree of increase of firm's debt, due to the economic crisis; all these variables were measured in a 5-levels Likert scale (not at all, small, moderate, large, very large), and were then converted to binary ones (with the first three values being converted to 'non-vulnerable' and the other two being converted to 'vulnerable');
b) forty (40) variables concerning various firm's characteristics with respect to strategy, personnel, technology (focusing on the use of various digital technologies), structure (focusing on the use of organic' forms of work organization, such as teamwork) and also some general information about the firm (size measured through the number of employees, sector (services or manufacturing), comparative financial performance in the last three years in comparison with competitors).

The dataset had missing values, so initially we proceeded to filling each missing value with the most suitable value based on the type of the variable (for instance, if the variable was ordinal, then the missing values were filled with the highest relative frequency value of this variable). Then exploratory data analysis (EDA) was applied in order to gain a better insight into the data through visualizations and make some necessary transformations. As a next step, since the size of our data set (which included data for 363 firms as mentioned above) did not allow constructing/training supervised ML prediction models with good prediction performance, we used the abovementioned oversampling and class-balancing algorithm SMOTE. Finally, the dataset was divided into a training dataset including 66% of the samples and a testing dataset including 33% of the samples. The former was used for the training of ML models with the following algorithms: Decision Tree (DT), Random Forest (RF), Logistic Regression (LR), Support Vector Machines (SVM), and Multilayer Perceptron (MLP); the latter was used for assessing the prediction performance of these ML models. We can see the results (prediction accuracy, precision, recall and F-score) in Table 1 (with bold are shown for each dimension of crisis-vulnerability the results for the best performing algorithm).

We can see that for two dimensions of firm's vulnerability to economic crisis, concerning foreign sales and employment (degree of decrease of foreign sales and degree of decrease of employment due to the economic crisis), we have a high prediction performance (prediction accuracy 89% and 85% respectively). For two more dimensions of firm's vulnerability to economic crisis, concerning debt and liquidity (degree of increase of debt and degree of decrease liquidity due to the economic crisis), we have a lower – but still high - prediction performance (prediction accuracy 79% for both). For the remaining three dimensions, concerning domestic sales, traditional investment, and innovation

Table 1. Prediction Performance of AI/ML Algorithms for each Crisis-Vulnerability Dimension

Crisis – Vulnerability Dimension	AI/ML Algorithm	Accuracy	Precision	Recall	F-score
Domestic Sales Crisis Vulnerability	Decision Tree	0.67	0.66	0.67	0.66
	Random Forest	0.76	0.75	0.76	0.75
	Logistic Regression	0.62	0.60	0.60	0.60
	SVM	**0.77**	**0.76**	**0.76**	**0.76**
	MLP	0.68	0.64	0.63	0.64
Foreign Sales Crisis-Vulnerability	Decision Tree	0.76	0.75	0.75	0.75
	Random Forest	**0.89**	**0.90**	**0.87**	**0.88**
	Logistic Regression	0.65	0.64	0.61	0.60
	SVM	0.87	0.88	0.85	0.86
	MLP	0.73	0.72	0.69	0.69
Employment Crisis-Vulnerability	Decision Tree	0.74	0.74	0.74	0.74
	Random Forest	**0.85**	**0.85**	**0.85**	**0.85**
	Logistic Regression	0.65	0.64	0.65	0.65
	SVM	0.77	0.76	0.74	0.75
	MLP	0.69	0.67	0.66	0.67
Traditional Investment Crisis-Vulnerability	Decision Tree	0.71	0.70	0.71	0.70
	Random Forest	0.76	0.78	0.73	0.73
	Logistic Regression	0.62	0.62	0.62	0.62
	SVM	**0.74**	**0.74**	**0.72**	**0.72**
	MLP	0.62	0.61	0.58	0.56
Innovation Investment Crisis-Vulnerability	Decision Tree	0.60	0.62	0.60	0.61
	Random Forest	0.74	0.74	0.74	0.74
	Logistic Regression	0.60	0.61	0.60	0.60
	SVM	**0.76**	**0.75**	**0.76**	**0.75**
	MLP	0.64	0.64	0.64	0.64
Debt Crisis-Vulnerability	Decision Tree	0.68	0.68	0.68	0.68

(continued)

Table 1. (*continued*)

Crisis – Vulnerability Dimension	AI/ML Algorithm	Accuracy	Precision	Recall	F-score
	Random Forest	**0.79**	**0.79**	**0.79**	**0.78**
	Logistic Regression	0.64	0.63	0.64	0.62
	SVM	0.77	0.79	0.77	0.76
	MLP	0.64	0.64	0.64	0.62
Liquidity Crisis-Vulnerability	Decision Tree	0.70	0.71	0.70	0.70
	Random Forest	**0.79**	**0.78**	**0.79**	**0.78**
	Logistic Regression	0.63	0.64	0.63	0.63
	SVM	0.75	0.76	0.75	0.76
	MLP	0.56	0.54	0.56	0.55

investment, we had slightly lower prediction performance (prediction accuracy 77%, 76% and 74% respectively).

Overall, the results of this first application of the proposed methodology (prediction performances) can be regarded as satisfactory, taking into account the small size of the dataset we have used (data from 363 firms), and provide a first validation of this methodology; we expect that using a larger dataset (as governments have such data for quite large numbers of firms) will allow training crisis-vulnerability prediction models with higher prediction performances.

4 Conclusion

In the previous sections of this paper has been described a methodology for predicting the whole pattern of vulnerability to economic crisis of individual firms, which respect to the main aspects of their financial situation (such as sales, liquidity, debt, investment, employment, etc.); for this purpose are used AI/ML techniques, in combination with SMOTE in order to increase their performance, which are trained using OGD from Statistical Authorities. The proposed methodology aims to support and enhance/augment (in order to increase its effectiveness) one of the most important and costly kinds of interventions that governments have to make: the interventions they undertake in tough times of economic crises in order to reduce their negative consequences, and especially the large-scale economic stimulus programs.

The research presented in this paper has some interesting implications for research and practice. With respect to research, it makes a significant contribution to two highly important research streams. First, to the growing research stream investigating the use of AI in government, by developing a novel approach for a highly beneficial use of AI/ML for supporting and enhancing/augmenting a critical activity of government with quite high economic/social importance and financial magnitude. Second, to the research stream investigating OGD research stream, by providing an approach for increasing the economic/social value generation form the OGD through advanced processing of them using AI/ML techniques. With respect to practice, it provides a useful tool to government agencies that are responsible for the design and implementation of economic stimulus programs aiming to reduce the negative consequences of economic crises.

However, further research is required in the following directions: a) further application of the proposed methodology, using larger datasets, and in various national and sectoral contexts (experiencing different types and intensities of economic crises); b) investigate the use of other pre-processing algorithms (e.g., oversampling and class-balancing algorithms) as well as AI/ML algorithms (deep learning ones); c) investigate the combination of such OGD with other sources of data about firms (e.g. from other government agencies, from private firms, such as private business information databases), in order to obtain more information about firms that might improve the performance of the prediction of their pattern of vulnerability to economic crises.

Acknowledgments. This research has been conducted as part of the project ODECO that has received funding from the European Union's Horizon 2020 research and innovation program under the Marie Skłodowska-Curie grant agreement No 955569.

References

1. OECD. Responding to the Economic Crisis Fostering Industrial Restructuring and Re-newal (2009a)
2. Keeley, B., Love, P.: From Crisis to Recovery: The Causes, Course and Consequences of the Great Recession (2010)
3. Knoop, T.A.: Recessions and Depressions: Understanding Business Cycles (2015)
4. Allen, R.E.: Financial Crises and Recession in the Global Economy, 4th edn (2016)
5. Saifi, S., Horowitz, J.: Blackouts and soaring prices: Pakistan's economy is on the brink (2023)
6. Loukis, E., Arvanitis, S., Myrtidis, D.: ICT-related behavior of Greek banks in the economic crisis. Inf. Syst. Manag. **38**, 79–91 (2021)
7. Baldwin, R., di Mauro, B.W.: Mitigating the COVID Economic Crisis: Act Fast and Do Whatever It Takes (2020)
8. Oliveras, L., et al.: Energy poverty and health: trends in the European union before and during the economic crisis, 2007–2016. Health Place **67**, 102294 (2021)
9. Dagoumas, A., Kitsios, F.: Assessing the impact of the economic crisis on energy poverty in Greece. Sustain. Cities Soc. **13**, 267–278 (2014)
10. Stylidis, D., Terzidou, M.: Tourism and the economic crisis in Kavala, Greece. Ann. Tourism Res. **44**, 210–226 (2014)
11. Das, M.: Economic crisis in Sri Lanka causing cancer drug shortage. Lancet Oncol. **23**, 710 (2022)
12. Arvanitis, Sp., Loukis, E.: Factors explaining ICT investment behavior of firms during the 2008 economic crisis. Inf. Syst. Manag. 1–22 (2023). https://doi.org/10.1080/10580530.2023.2213839
13. Khatiwada, S.: Stimulus Packages to Counter Global Economic Crisis
14. Coenen, G., Straub, R., Trabandt, M.: Gauging the effects of fiscal stimulus packages in the Euro area
15. Kalinowski, T.: Crisis management and the diversity of capitalism: fiscal stimulus packages and the East Asian (neo-)developmental state. Econ. Soc. **44**, 244–270 (2015)

16. Taylor, J.B.: Fiscal Stimulus Programs During the Great Recession (201AD)
17. Witten, I.H., Frank, E., Hall, M.A.: Data Mining: Practical Machine Learning Tools and Techniques. Morgan Kaufmann (2011)
18. Russell, S.J., Norvig, P., Davis, E.: Artificial Intelligence: A Modern Approach. Pearson (2015)
19. Gao, Y., Janssen, M., Zhang, C.: Understanding the evolution of open government data research: towards open data sustainability and smartness. Int. Rev. Adm. Sci. **89**, 59–75 (2023)
20. Charalabidis, Y., et al.: The world of open data: Concepts, methods, tools and experiences. In: Public Administration and Information Technology, vol. 28, pp. 1–194 (2018)
21. The Corporation of the 1990s: information technology and organizational transformation. Oxford University Press (1991)
22. Applied organizational change in industry: Structural, technological and humanistic approaches, Handbook of organizations. Routledge (2013)
23. Dudjak, M., Martinović, G.: In-depth performance analysis of SMOTE-based oversampling algorithms in binary classification. Int. J. Electr. Comput. Eng. Syst. **11**, 13–23 (2020)

Business and IS Development

Improving IT Governance, Security and Privacy Using Fractal Enterprise Modeling: A Case of a Highly Regulated Company

Steven Leego[1,2]([✉]) and Ilia Bider[1,3]

[1] Department of Computer Science, University of Tartu, Tartu, Estonia
{steven.leego,ilia.bider}@ut.ee
[2] Digiarhitekt OÜ, Tartu, Estonia
[3] Computer and System Sciences, Stockholm University, Stockholm, Sweden

Abstract. The article presents a practical case of using a modelling technique called Fractal Enterprise Modelling (FEM) to improve a highly regulated financial sector company in the EU. The company had the practical goals of achieving compliance and improving operations in three closely related areas - IT governance, information security management, and privacy management. The project also had an unusual constraint, as it was not possible to use visual models for communication in the project. We decided to use design science principles to investigate whether FEM could be useful within this scenario and its limitations.

It turned out that the conceptual structure of FEM fits quite well with the concepts of the three areas, and it was possible to use FEM despite the constraint on its usage. This led to the invention of a new analysis approach to go around the restriction. It included translating patterns defined with FEM into mind maps that were used for conducting interviews. FEM enabled the analyst to systematically, flexibly and quickly explore and understand the company and its state in the three areas. The paper aims to provide practically useful insights to practitioners that want to drive innovation, improve security or achieve compliance.

Keywords: Model evaluation · IT governance · Security management · Privacy management · GDPR · Compliance handling · Fractal enterprise model

1 Introduction

IT governance, information security management and privacy management are three closely related areas. At the core, they are about the handling of information – the first is about enabling the creation, processing, storing, retrieving, and exchanging of data and information through technology [1], and the latter two are about maintaining security [2] and privacy [3] in these activities. This paper presents a practical case where the first author's task was to substantially improve the handling of these areas in a highly regulated financial industry company in the EU. It was decided to handle these areas in a single consultancy project because: (1) all three areas needed urgent handling due to the need for compliance with the regulations and the growth of the company, (2) the number of stakeholders was relatively small, and the existing practices in these areas were not deeply ingrained; thus, the handling of these areas together was feasible, and (3) the first author had knowledge, skills and experience in all three areas, and saw an overlap between the areas and potential for synergy in a combined approach.

To fulfil the project goals, various tools were needed to analyze the company. There are lots of well-established business analysis techniques [4], and many have been used in this project, such as interviewing, observation, document analysis, mind mapping, among others [4]. In addition to the established methods, a novel technique called Fractal Enterprise Modelling (FEM) was used as a facilitator for an agile approach in the project. FEM is a relatively new enterprise modelling technique which can be used to quickly and efficiently analyze and model an organization. It was first introduced in detail in [5]. Even though it has been tested in several research-oriented and practical projects [6–8], its capabilities and limitations have not been thoroughly investigated. Filling this gap is a long-term research goal of the authors, especially regarding FEM's usefulness in planning and implementing change. Thus, we use this case to evaluate FEM's effectiveness and suitability and expand its knowledge base.

Initial work revealed an important restriction for the project – the main stakeholder, the IT manager, did not believe in visual modelling and prohibited using them. He felt they would not produce long-lasting value and was ultimately only interested in achieving practical project results. Thus, FEM could not be used in its usual way of producing and presenting visual diagrams to the stakeholders. This called for an alternative approach. We decided to research how suitable FEM is for the purposes of the project and how FEM can be used within the restrictions. We established three research questions:

- *RQ1 How do FEM's concepts relate to the areas of IT governance, information security management, and privacy management?*
- *RQ2 How can FEM be used when there is a restriction to not produce visual models for communication?*
- *RQ3 How useful is FEM in achieving compliance and improving operations in the three areas?*

The rest of the paper is structured as follows. Section 2 describes the background of the three areas of concern, the FEM technique and the research methodology. Section 3 discusses the case and its motivation, context, limitations and activities. Section 4 covers the relationship between FEM and the three areas (RQ1), the application of FEM in the case (RQ2) and its usefulness for the practical goals (RQ3). Section 5 includes concluding remarks and areas for future research.

2 Background

2.1 Management of IT, Information Security and Privacy

There are several common terms that are related to the "handling of IT matters" in an organization – *IT governance, IT service management* and *IT management*. According to one of the influential frameworks in the field, COBIT [9, 10], governance is about the higher-level setting of objectives and direction and monitoring their performance and compliance, while management is about planning, building, running and monitoring activities that correspond to the objectives and direction. Another well-known framework is ITIL [1] which describes best practices in IT service management. ITIL is designed to ensure a system for the effective governance and management of IT-enabled services. According to the framework, an IT service is based on information technology, and they assume that almost any service in today's world utilizes IT.

The frameworks provide practical guidance and know-how in areas related to IT governance and management. Both of them identify the components of the environment to be controlled, provide principles to be followed, discuss various governance and management practices and objectives, and establish guidelines towards adopting the frameworks. At the centre of the frameworks lies the concept of aligning business and IT and ultimately creating value.

ISO/IEC 27000-series is the most well-known family of standards in *information security management*. It consists of numerous individual standards for different purposes, and the most widely used are ISO/IEC 27000 [11], which provides an overview and vocabulary, ISO/IEC 27001 [2], which provides requirements for an information security management system, and ISO/IEC 27002 [12], which provides controls for responding to risks. The standard [11] defines information security as the "preservation of confidentiality, integrity and availability of information". At the core of information security management is the management of risks that should be tightly integrated with the organization's processes and overall management [2]. Another useful information security material is CIS (Critical Security Controls) Version 8 [13], which aims to provide a prescriptive, prioritized, highly focused set of actions for organizations.

One of the most influential and comprehensive regulations on *privacy* is the General Data Protection Regulation (GDPR) [3]. This regulation addresses privacy and concerns personal data, which is defined as "any information relating to an identified or identifiable natural person". The regulation aims to regulate the processing of personal data, and processing is defined as "any operation or set of operations which is performed on personal data". The regulation outlines generic principles and specific rules for various aspects of the processing, and it demands that the data controller demonstrate compliance. The main principles outline that personal data shall be: (1) processed lawfully, fairly and transparently; (2) collected for a specific purpose; (3) adequate, relevant and limited to what is necessary; (4) accurate and up-to-date; (5) kept only as long as necessary; (6) processed in a manner that ensures security.

2.2 Fractal Enterprise Model

Each of the three areas mentioned in the previous section must be considered in an enterprise context. Thus, improving them requires understanding the enterprise. Enterprise modelling can help in this area, and for our project, we chose a novel technique called Fractal Enterprise Modelling (FEM) [5]. FEM is a technique that includes a modelling method to depict information graphically and procedures for producing FEM models. It is used to represent concepts of an enterprise in a high-level, simple, abstract way, and it helps to find and depict interconnections between the concepts. A FEM toolkit [14] has been built on a metamodelling platform called ADOxx [15] to support producing the models. Over time, additional elements have been added to the technique and toolkit, such as the relationship *Monitoring*. This relationship has a significant role in this project, which is discussed in Sect. 4.1.

FEM presents an enterprise in the form of a directed graph consisting of three types of elements – processes and assets as nodes of the graph, and relations between them as edges. Visually, the processes are depicted as ovals and assets – as rectangles. An example of a FEM diagram can be seen in Fig. 1.

If we compare FEM with one of the well-known enterprise modelling languages, Archimate [16], then FEM's processes represent behavioural elements, and assets represent structural elements. Assets in FEM depict sets of things; what that set consists of is defined by the label assigned to it and the roles it plays in processes. The depiction of an asset or a process in a model might represent a concrete instance (e.g., a specific application or the development of a specific application), or it might be a generalization, group or pool, e.g., all the company's IT applications and infrastructure, or a group of processes included in the provision of services.

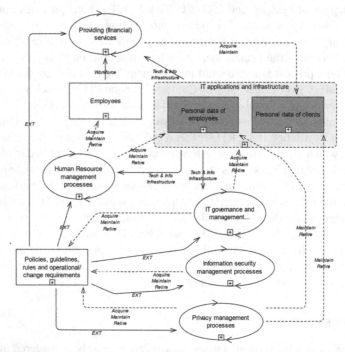

Fig. 1. Simplified model of FEM depicting the three areas in the context of an enterprise. Ovals represent processes, rectangles present assets, dashed lines the "process-*manages*-asset" relationship, regular lines the "asset-*used by*-process" and red color indicates assets which classify as personal data.

The relationships have two main types: *used in* and *managed by*. A *used in* relationship is directed from an asset to a process, and it means that the asset plays a role in the process; the abstract label on the arrow explains in which way/capacity the asset is used in the process. For example, in Fig. 1, the asset *Policies, guidelines, rules and operational/change requirements* is used as an EXecution Template (EXT) for the processes *Providing (financial) services* and management processes, while the asset *IT applications and infrastructure* plays the role of Technical & info infrastructure in the same processes. Several other categories are defined for *used in* relations, such as *workforce, partner,* and *stock*. A *managed by* arrow is directed from a process to an asset, meaning that the process manages the assets in some way. An abstract label depicts the type of management on the arrow, i.e., *Acquire, Maintain,* or *Retire*. The process either adds something to a set, changes the state of set elements or removes things from a set accordingly. For example, in Fig. 1, assets *Employees* are managed by the *Human Resource management* processes. When setting labels, specific business terminology can be used for naming processes and assets. For example, specific processes for employee management would often be called hiring/onboarding for *Acquire,* training/ motivating for *Maintain* and firing/terminating employment/off-boarding for *Retire*.

The building of FEM models is usually initiated from an organization's primary processes or services and figuring out which kind of assets are needed for these. Subsequently, each asset needs to have some management processes to ensure that there are enough assets for the processes and that they are operational. Going one level deeper, these processes once again need to have assets to carry them out and so on. This recursively repeating pattern is the origin of the term "Fractal" in the modelling technique. Referring to the example in Fig. 1, you need a workforce and IT systems to provide financial services. HR processes manage the workforce, and for the HR processes, there is a need for more specific assets, such as HR specialists and specialized HR software.

The building of the models can also start from any place, such as an asset type of *organizational infrastructure,* to figure out in which processes a specific department is engaged. This pattern was, for example, used to holistically analyze a water utility company [6]. Further information on FEM can be found in [17].

2.3 Research Approach

This paper is part of a larger research initiative that follows the Design Science (DS) [18, 19] research paradigm, which aims to find generic and useful solutions to known and unknown problems. As DS is about generating and testing hypotheses for generic solutions, it requires researchers to be active in both the real world of specific situations, problems, and solutions, as well as the abstract world of generic situations, problems, and solutions [18]. The research part of the project, more specifically, follows the Action Design Research (ADR) method, which is about generating design knowledge through building and evaluating artefacts in an organizational setting [20].

FEM is an already developed modelling technique with a tool to support it; thus, from the Design Science perspective, our larger undertaking is to justify FEM's value and evaluate its usefulness. We do that by testing it in practice and conducting case studies. We use the results of these studies to identify the appropriate environments where it can be applied, generate new knowledge on how to use FEM and get feedback for the development and refinement of FEM. In theory, the suitability of a modelling language to a certain problem can be checked by analyzing whether it has concepts for covering the details that are important for the task. However, if a modelling language employs high-level abstract concepts (as UML [21], ArchiMate [16], and partly, FEM do), such a test might be positive for any purpose. Still, it would not guarantee suitability or usefulness for a specific purpose. The final test comes only from using a language in a practical project. As the saying goes, "the proof of the pudding is in the eating".

From the perspective of the Design Science Research Knowledge Contribution Framework [22], the current project belongs to a relatively low-maturity application domain. We could not find any literature discussing combining the handling of all three areas – IT governance, information security management and privacy management. We did, though, identify literature discussing combining either privacy and security management [23, 24] or security and IT management [25–27]. Thus, as we used FEM in a new domain and invented a new approach to using it, our knowledge contribution classifies as both Invention and Exaptation [22].

When investigating organizational problem-solving, it is important to consider the problems in a context of a typical practical project (see, for example, [6]). This includes characteristics, constraints and limitations to the specific project and organization at the specific time point of investigation. Furthermore, in the domain of modelling [28], there is a recommendation to systematically explore models at work and describe the scenario in which they are produced. Following the ADR method [20], we describe the problems and the project-specific context in Sect. 3, how the artefacts were designed, built and used in the case in Sects. 4.1 and 4.2, and reflect on the experience and generalize the results in Sect. 4.3. As the first author carried out the project, the research results and insights were obtained by studying interview notes, analyzing project documents, and reflecting on the experience following the Practitioner's Reflections concept [29].

3   Case Description

This chapter describes the case at hand, namely: (1) why the project was approached in a certain way, (2) what was the context and limitations, and (3) what was done during the project. The company has not given a permission to share details about its operations. Therefore, the company is not named, and some details that could reveal its identity have been omitted.

3.1   The Motivation Behind the Project

The project was initiated by the company's IT manager, who contacted the first author with a request to update the existing IT documentation to make it compliant with the GDPR. Further discussions revealed that the existing documentation had only been addressed from one office's perspective, included only IT management, and was out-of-date. Also, progress in GDPR compliance was almost non-existent, except for a few country offices trying to handle things themselves. Thus, it was decided that the new IT documentation should involve offices from other countries and also handle information security and privacy management. Becoming up-to-date in this scenario meant updating the existing documentation with the latest business information and implementing current best practices. It also became clear that the GDPR was not the only regulation dictating what should be handled.

The project concerned an international financial company operating in Europe. This means that the company needs to follow numerous rules specific for the countries where the company has operations, and EU-wide rules. Furthermore, there are rules specifically for the financial sector [30]. The rules cover multiple areas of operation, but the project's goal was to handle only areas related to IT, information security and privacy. The European Banking Authority and local regulators have released guidelines for companies, and these guidelines consider IT and information security in tandem [31]. The privacy side is mostly regulated by the GDPR [3]. The rules define what needs to be achieved but, for the most part, do not give specific instructions on how to ensure compliance. Information about what should be done and best practice guidelines on getting there can be found in respective fields' standards and frameworks [1, 2, 9–13]. These standards and frameworks still do not dictate the specific methods to use, and there is little guidance on how different areas could be handled together.

Due to the compliance pressure, the first author's previous experience in all the fields and the small number of stakeholders involved, the decision was made to handle all three areas in one project. Thus, the task was to understand the current state, the regulatory rules that apply and the best practices, and subsequently derive the policies, guidelines, rules and requirements for establishing appropriate future operations.

3.2 Project Context, Limitations and Activities

As in any practical project, some project's decisions and some of its actions were dictated by the context, i.e. the company itself and the project settings. To start with, the first author, entering the project as a consultant, did not have any previous experience with the business domain or the actual company. Also, while the author understood the requirements set by the three relevant areas, there was no understanding of how they were applied in the company nor how well the compliance requirements were fulfilled. The documentation describing these aspects was almost non-existent, and information was spread among stakeholders. The company's international scope further complicated things, as all three areas need to consider each country's operation's specifics.

Furthermore, there were many constraints set by the project organization – the budget was limited, the results were expected quickly, and the availability of the stakeholders to participate in the project was limited. The main stakeholder, the IT manager, was especially overloaded with everyday tasks; therefore, there was a clear expectation for the project to include only activities that would produce practical results.

In addition, of the three relevant areas, only the area of IT had a prior governance/management structure in place. This structure, though, was mostly of reactive nature; it consisted of responding to requests from the business management while ignoring best practices in the field and the compliance requirements. Information security management had mostly been a grey area with no systematic, holistic approach. The IT manager handled some cybersecurity areas, while other areas were either unaddressed or handled by the business management on an ad-hoc basis. The area of privacy management was almost completely unaddressed, with some initial steps taken by the management and a few isolated local initiatives within some country offices.

The project team was also quite small, consisting of the IT manager, a few IT specialists responsible for specific areas, a group-level manager and a few local managers that had done some work on GDPR compliance. A colleague of the first author also participated in the project by helping the company in achieving GDPR compliance.

The first large phase of the project included **getting an initial understanding** of the domain, the business and the existing materials. This was achieved by simultaneously carrying out interviews and workshops and analyzing existing documentation, regulations, standards and best practice frameworks. The gathered information was contextualized and tied together using FEM.

The second phase included **carrying out a deeper analysis within the three areas**. The important topics relevant to the three areas were analyzed more deeply with the help of a FEM-inspired metamodel. This metamodel was used as a template to help systematically go through relevant components and identify their current state, the privacy and security risks involved and potential areas for improvement. IT and information security matters were mainly discussed with IT staff, and privacy matters with managers. However, all three areas were kept in mind during all the discussions.

The third phase included **preparing the documents** to cover all goals that were initially set. The gathered information was used to establish governance and management systems and create documents required or suggested by the regulations, standards and frameworks [1–3, 9–13, 30, 31]. Figure 1 shows that all three areas contribute to the internal pool of policies, guidelines, rules and operational/change requirements. This pool establishes how the business should operate to be both compliant and efficient. The information gathered in the previous phase was sufficient for the first author and his colleague to prepare the initial drafts of the documents by themselves. The documents were finalized and validated in cooperation with the company stakeholders.

4 Using FEM in the Project

4.1 FEM's Relation to the Three Areas

This section answers the question RQ1, and it presents how FEM's concepts relate to the concepts of the three areas – IT governance, information security management and privacy management. A generic metamodel depicting the essence of these areas is presented in Fig. 2. In the center, there is a class of relevant *assets*, and these assets are used in *various processes*. Furthermore, these assets need to be *managed*, and to do this effectively, the management processes use information gathered by processes that *monitor* the state of the assets and their usage. Table 1 gives examples of how FEM's concepts correspond to the central concepts of the relevant areas. This correspondence was identified by conducting a thorough analysis of the relevant literature in the three areas [1–3, 9–13, 30, 31] and mapping the findings to the FEM's concepts and capabilities.

The *monitor* relationship is a new concept to FEM, and while not yet discussed in the research literature, it exists in the latest version of the FEM toolkit [14]. We also identified three generic sub-types of monitoring: (1) keeping an overview of the asset(s), (2) monitoring the state and usage of the asset(s), and (3) identifying any issues and tasks related to the asset(s). Risk management is another important concept for the three areas. It can also be treated as a monitoring process as it gathers information about assets and processes, identifies potential issues and creates tasks for the management processes, which serve as control elements (EXT) for them (see Fig. 2).

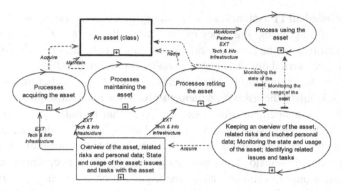

Fig. 2. A metamodel depicting key concepts of the three areas using FEM

Table 1. Correspondence between concepts of FEM and the three areas

FEM concept	Corresponding concepts
Asset (set of things)	People, organizations (incl. partners, suppliers), organizational structures, IT infrastructure (incl. personal computers, smart/mobile devices, network devices, server hardware, sensors/IoT devices, virtual resources), software (applications), information/data (incl. databases, documents, tacit knowledge, personal data), networks, firewalls, access controls, digital identities, backups, event/incident logs, management systems, policies and regulations, goals/strategies, requirements, tasks, equipment, buildings
Process (behaviour)	Process, value stream, service, processing, activity, function
Assets->used in->processes relationship	A person acts as *workforce*, a laptop is used as *tech & info infrastructure*, a logistics company is used as a *partner*, a policy/procedure document is used as an *EXecution Template*
Processes->manage->assets relationship	Development/building/implementing processes, purchasing/acquiring processes, deployment/delivering processes, maintenance/management/servicing/supporting processes, continual improvement, change management, workforce management, supplier/third-party management
Processes->Monitor->assets/processes relationship	Knowledge management, measurement and reporting, risk management, maintaining overviews (incl. usage of personal data), portfolio/project management, strategy management, capacity and performance management, monitoring/evaluating/assessing, incident/problem management, architecture management, continuity management

4.2   Application of FEM in the Case

This section presents an overview of how FEM was applied in the project and how it was used to overcome the restriction of not using visual models, which answers the question RQ2. FEM was used in a traditional way during the first phase of the project. It followed the generic principles described in Sect. 2.2 and was used for internal experimentation to tie separately collected pieces of information together. This helped to understand the business, the domain and the types of assets involved. We started with the primary services of the business and expanded the model by adding the assets used in the services.

The assets included all IT systems and technical infrastructure, the physical infrastructure, all roles of employees, the types of customers, the stock for service provision, any partners involved in the services and any execution templates that dictate how the services should be carried out. A simplified model is presented in Fig. 1.

Furthermore, following the FEM's patterns, we went one, sometimes two, layers deeper to contextualize the asset management processes and, subsequently, the assets included in those management processes. The areas that included personal data processing were highlighted using a red background color. These models were made for internal use; they were messy and difficult to comprehend for an outsider. Nevertheless, they helped discuss ideas inside the consultant group, obtain a conceptual understanding of the company's business model and domain, get a high-level understanding of the current state, and identify topics that needed further analysis. A polished version that contained all the main elements was presented to the IT manager, but he did not find it useful. Considering the project's focus on practical output, achieving quick results and optimizing the work efforts by treating the three areas of concern together, there was a need for a new approach for carrying out a deeper analysis in the second phase.

A new way of using FEM was invented to overcome these obstacles. The new approach takes the shortcut of not creating a full FEM model and not using FEM for communicating with stakeholders. Instead, it uses FEM's powerful conceptual structure in combination with mind mapping. The approach was inspired by the first author's habit of taking notes of every meeting in a mind-mapping tool. The FEM metamodel presented in Fig. 2 was used as a template to create mindmap questionnaires. These questionnaires were used to structure the interviews and to help gather information about matters relevant to the three areas. In essence, they consider a certain set of assets or a generic asset class from Table. 1 and systematically ask questions about the assets.

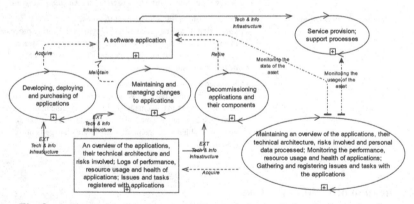

Fig. 3. An example of the metamodel instantiation at the level of an asset class

Before translating to a mind map, the generic metamodel of Fig. 2 needs to be considered with specific classes of assets. An example of instantiating the metamodel for the class *software application* is presented in Fig. 3. As the terminology used in Fig. 2 is unusual for business practice, the process and asset names have to be modified to correspond to the terms commonly used in practice. For example, *acquire* means development and deployment for in-house software applications, while for out-of-the-box or SaaS applications, *acquire* is purchasing and setting up/configuring. When considering a specific asset, such as the company website, the terminology can become even more specific and narrowed down, which can be seen in Fig. 4. With specific assets, additional relevant information can be identified that corresponds to the actual context. This is done by using FEM process-asset patterns/archetypes [5]. The extension might include identifying the *workforce*, external *partners*, *infrastructure* used in the process, or *policies* that dictate *execution* rules for the management and monitoring processes.

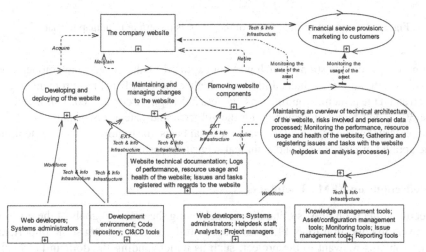

Fig. 4. An example of the metamodel instantiation at the level of a specific asset

To create a mindmap questionnaire based on the metamodel, we considered a given asset class and investigated which particular assets of that class existed in the actual scenario. Then, we asked more specific questions for each asset, such as how it was used, monitored and managed. An excerpt of the questionnaire produced for the asset class *(software) Application* and a specific application *The company website* is presented in Fig. 5. We asked open-ended questions according to the metamodel to find out relevant information, such as the related processes and their *workforce*, used *technology*, and identify potential problems. The received answers were immediately written behind the questions. This format allowed us to discuss the issues as long as needed to gather relevant information and to include new discussion topics as they surfaced. While some information was gathered in the first phase of the project, details were obtained and confirmed in the second phase.

The mind map was used to systematically investigate all issues relevant to the three areas by choosing an appropriate asset or asset class as a basis for investigation. Most of the assets were relevant to both IT governance and information security management, as the first area is primarily concerned with acquiring, retiring and keeping operational any assets that handle information, while the latter was concerned with keeping the handled information safe. Also, some specific assets, such as personal data, required

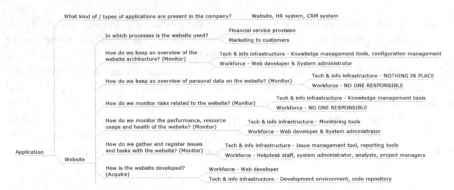

Fig. 5. A fragment of an example of the analysis pattern in mindmap format

asking more specific questions, which was not captured by the generic metamodel. For example, specific questions helped identify whether the GDPR [3] requirements were followed and if the principles outlined in Chapters 2–5 [3] were considered. This included Article 30, which required documenting the subjects and categories of personal data, whether external parties received the data, the legal basis, the requirements for retention and the applied organizational and technical security measures.

4.3 Reflections on FEM's Usefulness

This section reflects on FEM's suitability for achieving the practical goals of the project and answers the question RQ3. FEM was successfully used in solving some important general problems relevant to the project, such as understanding the domain [1, 4, 9], business context [1, 2, 4, 9, 32] and business operations [1, 2, 4, 9, 32], as well as managing project information [1, 2, 4, 9] and eliciting requirements [1, 2, 4, 9, 32]. FEM also helped to complete the project despite some constraints, such as limited time and resources, the low quality of the existing documentation and a restriction on the usage of visual models in communication with the stakeholders.

In the first phase of the project, FEM was primarily used as an analysis tool to help contextualize information gathered from interviews and document analysis. FEM was also used for communication inside the consultants' team. Even though FEM has been previously used for communication with stakeholders [6], an attempt to use it for this purpose in this project failed. This does not concern FEM as such, but any kind of visual modelling. We also produced and presented some Archimate models to show the business model and connections between business areas and IT, but none of them were accepted as useful. This was due to the IT manager's desire to get practical results quickly and his opinion that visual modelling does not help achieve them. He claimed that it is better to represent the connections between business and IT in a configuration management database. He believed that visual models would become out-of-date too quickly and that updating them would require too much work.

In the second phase of the project, FEM was used to produce a rich set of relevant questions by creating a metamodel of Fig. 2, and the concepts map of Table 1, which were used to generate a mindmap questionnaire and carry out semi-structured interviews. The approach enabled a flexible but systematic way to gather information. In this project, the metamodel was combined with the mind mapping technique, but it may also work as a simple mental model to guide discussions or be used to create a questionnaire to be filled in by the stakeholders.

The approach of using only the mindmap for investigation also has some negative aspects. As it does not follow the usual, holistic, systematic visual exploration, there is a risk that some important information is missed in the analysis. Also, FEM does not help to thoroughly map the interconnections between an asset's components (parts or set elements) and direct relationships between the assets. Creating and maintaining these mappings requires a different approach. Another modelling language, such as Archimate, or a special tool like a configuration management database might suit the task.

Had there been more resources and fewer constraints, fully-fledged models of FEM could have been helpful as well. The models could have been used to communicate information, e.g. to explain general concepts to someone who does not understand a specific area or to convey the organization-specific context. Furthermore, they could have helped create a systematic inventory of assets, processes and their connections, as the FEM toolkit helps track occurrences of the same element across multiple models. Additionally, FEM could have been used for business improvement (model the *to-be*).

It is clear that using FEM still helped fulfil the initial practical project goals. The information gathered was useful as it was sufficient to create the necessary documentation that covers the relevant topics identified in the literature [1–3, 9–13, 30, 31]. Tackling the three areas in one initiative saved the company time and resources, and FEM was shown to be a useful tool for this due to its conceptual compatibility with the areas. Had these areas been approached in isolation, then each time, the business context and the state of assets with overlapping relevance to areas would have needed to be explored once more. Furthermore, as the areas are tightly interconnected, handling them separately might result in incoherent, inefficient, bureaucratic rulesets and processes.

An important thing to note is that FEM was used in combination with other, sometimes more established techniques, such as interviewing, mind mapping, document analysis, observation and other modelling techniques. The use of abstract and less-structured techniques was made possible by the first author's previous experience in numerous similar projects, knowledge of the three areas, and a deep understanding of analysis techniques and FEM. A novice analyst or one experienced only in a subset of the areas might need to adjust the approach and cooperate with other experts. Making visual models might be particularly useful for communication in this case.

5 Research Contributions and Plans for the Future

From the research point of view, this paper presents the evaluation of the FEM technique in a practical case where three areas – IT governance, information security management and privacy management – have been approached together in order to improve operations and achieve compliance with regulations. We first investigated how FEM relates to the three areas and found that at a generic level, the most important concepts are matching (RQ1). A metamodel was created to illustrate the shared concepts, which is presented in Fig. 2. We further used the conceptual mapping to overcome an unusual restriction of not using visual models for communication. This resulted in the invention of a new way to use FEM by combining its conceptual structure with the mind-mapping technique to create questionnaires (RQ2). The creation and usage of the new approach are detailed in Sect. 4.2. The results show that FEM enables quick but structured information gathering, particularly within this project's constraints (RQ3). This application of FEM provides an interesting observation that a modelling technique does not have to be used fully explicitly to be helpful for information gathering.

A future research direction could be as follows. (1) To use the generic FEM meta-model of Fig. 2 and the concept of monitoring to identify relevant questions for other areas important for an organization. Other types of business activity probably also need to maintain an overview of assets, monitor their state, manage risks and identify tasks to be completed. An output of such research could be a reusable, generic questionnaire for systematic information gathering. (2) The same approach of using concepts from a modelling language without building visual models might be applicable to other languages and worth investigating. For example, following Archimate's [16] core layers, one could ask *which applications through which technology serve our business.*

Acknowledgments. The first author's work was fully supported, and the second author's work was partly supported by the Estonian Research Council (grant PRG1226).

References

1. AXELOS. ITIL foundation, ITIL 4 edition. TSO The Stationery Office (2019)
2. ISO. ISO/IEC 27001:2013 Information technology - Information technology - Security techniques - Information security management systems - Requirements (2013)
3. European Union. General Data Protection Regulation, Regulation (EU) 2016/679 (2016). https://eur-lex.europa.eu/eli/reg/2016/679/oj. Accessed 16 July 2023
4. IIBA, BABOK v3 A Guide to the Business Analysis Body of Knowledge (2015)
5. Bider, I., Perjons, E., Elias, M., et al.: A fractal enterprise model and its application for business development. Softw. Syst. Model. **16**, 663–689 (2017)
6. Leego, S., Bider, I.: Using fractal enterprise model in technology-driven organisational change projects: a case of a water utility company. In: 2021 IEEE 23rd Conference on Business Informatics (CBI), pp. 107–116 (2021)
7. Bider, I., Lodhi, A.: Moving from Manufacturing to Software Business: A Business Model Transformation Pattern (2020)
8. Henkel, M., Koutsopoulos, G., Bider, I., Perjons, E.: Using the Fractal Enterprise Model for Inter-organizational Business Processes (2019)
9. ISACA. COBIT 2019 Framework: Introduction and Methodology (2018)
10. ISACA. COBIT 2019 Framework: Governance and Management Objectives (2018)
11. ISO. ISO/IEC 27000:2018 Information technology – Security techniques – Information security management systems – Overview and vocabulary (2018)
12. ISO. ISO/IEC 27002:2013 Information technology – Security techniques – Code of practice for information security controls (2013)
13. Center for Internet Security. CIS Controls Version 8 (2021)
14. FEM toolkit. www.fractalmodel.org/fem-toolkit/. Accessed 16 July 2023
15. ADOxx.org, ADOxx. https://www.adoxx.org. Accessed 16 July 2023

16. The Open Group. ArchiMate® 3.1 Specification (2019). https://pubs.opengroup.org/architect ure/archimate3-doc/. Accessed 16 July 2023
17. FEM website. www.fractalmodel.org/. Accessed 16 July 2023
18. Bider, I., Johannesson, P., Perjons, E.: Design science research as movement between individual and generic situation-problem-solution spaces. In: Baskerville, R., De Marco, M., Spagnoletti, P. (eds.) Designing Organizational Systems. An Interdisciplinary Discourse, pp. 35–61. Springer, Heidelberg (2013). https://doi.org/10.1007/978-3-642-33371-2_3
19. Hevner, A.R., March, S.T., Park, J., Ram, S.: Design science in information systems research. MIS Q. 28(1), 75–105 (2004)
20. Sein, M., Henfridsson, O., Purao, S., Rossi, M., Lindgren, R.: Action design research. MIS Q. 35(1), 37–56 (2011). https://doi.org/10.2307/23043488
21. OMG, Unified Modeling Language (UML), Version 2.5.1. https://www.omg.org/spec/UML/. Accessed 16 July 2023
22. Gregor, S., Hevner, A.: Positioning and Presenting Design Science Research for Maximum Impact, White Paper submitted for publication (2011)
23. Soldatos, J. (ed.): Security Risk Management for the Internet of Things (2020)
24. Tsohou, A., et al.: Privacy, security, legal and technology acceptance elicited and consolidated requirements for a GDPR compliance platform (2020)
25. Gehrmann, M.: Combining ITIL, COBIT and ISO/IEC 27002 for structuring comprehensive information technology for management in organizations. Navus: Revista de Gestão e Tecnologia 2, 66–77 (2012)
26. Sheikhpour, R., Modiri, N.: A best practice approach for integration of ITIL and ISO/IEC 27001 services for information security management. Indian J. Sci. Technol. 5, 2170–2176 (2012)
27. Al Faruq, B., Herlianto, H., Simbolon, S., Utama, D., Wibowo, A.: Integration of ITIL V3, ISO 20000 & ISO 27001: 2013 for IT services and security management system. Int. J. Adv. Trends Comput. Sci. Eng. (2020)
28. Models at Work website. www.models-at-work.org. Accessed 16 July 2023
29. Mott, V.: Knowledge comes from practice: reflective theory building in practice. In: Rowden, R.W. (ed.) Workplace Learning: Debating Five Critical Questions of Theory and Practice, pp. 57–63. Jossey-Bass, San Francisco (1996)
30. European Union. Proposal for a regulation of the European Parliament and of the Council on digital operational resilience for the financial sector. COM/2020/595 final (2020). https://eur-lex.europa.eu/legal-content/EN/TXT/?uri=CELEX:52020PC0595. Accessed 16 July 2023
31. European Banking Authority. Final report on guidelines on ICT and security risk management (2019). https://www.eba.europa.eu/regulation-and-policy/internal-governance/gui delines-on-ict-and-security-risk-management. Accessed 16 July 2023
32. Dumas, M., La Rosa, M., Mendling, J., Reijers, H.A.: Fundamentals of Business Process Management. Springer, Heidelberg (2018). https://doi.org/10.1007/978-3-662-56509-4

Model-Based Digital Business Ecosystems: A Method Design

Chen Hsi Tsai[✉] ⓘ, Jelena Zdravkovic ⓘ, and Janis Stirna ⓘ

Department of Computer and Systems Sciences, Stockholm University, Stockholm, Sweden
{chenhsi.tsai,jelenaz,js}@dsv.su.se

Abstract. In traditional business models, organisations typically work independently and have limited interactions with other entities in the network. In contrast, Digital Business Ecosystems (DBE) foster collaboration, responsibility-taking, and resource sharing between multiple actors, enabling them to leverage their capabilities. Such characteristics require in return well-thought approaches for identification and design of the DBE components and tasks unified in an underlying digital environment. In this study, we address this challenge by proposing a modular model-based method for design of DBE that uses Situational Method Engineering as the underlying methodology and meta-models that describe the concepts and relationships on the modular level. We have illustrated some applications of the method and design task with existing enterprise architecture and enterprise modelling approaches.

Keywords: Enterprise Modelling · Digital Business Ecosystem · Method Engineering

1 Introduction

A DBE is defined as: "a socio-technical environment, enabled by shared digital platforms and ICTs, where loosely-coupled interdependent organisations and individuals in an economic community deliver, consume, or exchange resources and co-evolve their capabilities and roles [1]." Depending on the maturity level, a DBE can be in three different phases. *Design phase* is the initiation phase of a DBE focusing on designing of the structure, such as architectures or platforms, and how the structure supports the integration of capabilities, core services or products, and DBE actors. A DBE becomes more stable during *deployment phase* when improvements are supported by analysis of its different aspects. During *management phase*, a stablised DBE is continuously monitored and actively managed to facilitate changes leading to a more resilient system.

The unique characteristics, namely the *digital environment, heterogeneity, symbiosis, co-evolution, and self-organisation*, makes this type of multi-actor constellation stand out and contribute to the novel digital business ecosystem theory. Using the theory as lenses, various business models and networks [2–4] can be investigated and assessed focusing on the resilience aspect of a system in relation to the characteristics mentioned above. An example of a business network which is not considered a DBE is the Swedish alcohol

K. Hinkelmann et al. (Eds.): BIR 2023, LNBIP 493, pp. 214–228, 2023.
https://doi.org/10.1007/978-3-031-43126-5_16

company (Systembolaget) and various alcohol providers and wine importers which it collaborates with. This network does not focus on the onboarding of heterogeneous actors, the co-evolution of participating actors, and the adaptation according to internal or external environment. Analysing it using the digital business ecosystem theory can identify improvements needed for ensuring its resilience.

DBEs are highly complex constellations of actors and hence their design, analysis, and management requires a support for viewing them from a certain perspective or aspect. As part of a design science research [5] project, this paper presents work on modelling method intended to support these tasks. The envisioned method is modular – consisting of a number of components (method chunks) that are configurable depending on the designers' intentions. In previous work, we have explicated the problem and elicited and analysed requirements for the design artefact [4, 6] and presented the overall way of working and intentions for modelling in the form of method maps [7], DBE analysis procedures [7], and the modelling constructs of the method [1]. The goal of this paper is to integrate the method maps with the meta-model for the envisioned modelling method in order to establish a self-contained core method for the purpose of modelling DBE. We have also specified the potential application of existing enterprise architecture and enterprise modelling approaches to the maps and method chunks of the envisioned modelling method.

The rest of the paper is structured as follows. Section 2 presents background to DBE resilience and typical roles in DBEs as well as provides background to situational method engineering and method modularisation. Section 3 presents the elaboration of the method chunks together with the modelling constructs they require. Section 4 discusses the application of the method. Concluding remarks are suggested in Sect. 5.

2 Background

Resilience of a DBE concerns *"its ability to remain or recover to a stable state to continuously operate during and after threats, opportunities, or changes [1]."* The four pillars of resilience are *diversity, efficiency, adaptability, and cohesion* (c.f. [1] for more information of these four pillars).

DBE roles and their corresponding responsibilities are significant for the design of a DBE and its resilience, concerning the continuous operation of the DBE. The eight DBE roles, namely *Driver, Aggregator, Modular Producer, Complementor, Customer, End-User, Governor*, and *Reputation Guardian*, and their responsibilities are described in detail in [7].

Situational Method Engineering (SME) [8] is a framework that provides theory and guidance for the design of methods that are situation-specific and configurable. SME has been adopted for constructing the DBE method [7] because of its key feature, the support for method modularity as method chunks of various granularities. This feature supports the need of addressing the multiple perspectives and dynamics in a DBE and the feasibility of the DBE method. A method, including its *process* and *product*, is composed of modules of method chunks – each contains parts of the process and product. With the *Map* approach [9], parts of the process related to method chunks of a method are presented in terms of engineering *intentions* (i.e., the engineering goal; shown as green-coloured ellipse nodes in "Process" in Table 2 for example) and alternative *strategies* (shown as black-coloured arrow edges between nodes in "Process" in Table 2 for example) for achieving these intentions. In total, 11 maps, representing the process of the DBE method, have been constructed. Five maps, namely scope and boundaries (S-map), actors and relationships (A-map), interchangeability of capabilities (C-map), interchangeability of resources (R-map), and digital infrastructures (D-map) are considered as baseline maps for the DBE method. The other six maps are integration of processes (IP-map), policies and regulations (PR-map), domain specific concerns (DSR-map), communication channel and information sharing (CCIS-map), KPIs, indicators, and actors' performance (KIP-map), and runtime management (RM-map). *Baseline* means that a map is necessary to be used when adopting the DBE Method. As shown in Table 1, three types of dependencies are implemented for the maps.

Table 1. Dependency types and their description

Name	Description
Condition	It means that a map is a perquisite of another map
Include	It means that a map requires the execution of the included map
Feedback	It means that the execution of a map may suggest returning to one or more previously performed map(s)

The 11 maps, showing the process parts of the DBE method, are intended to provide users with an agile way of using the method. This means that users could use several of the maps simultaneously or in the users' preferred order based on their preferences and needs. The baseline maps and the dependencies, nevertheless, provide a general structure of how the method can be applied by means of these maps.

The product part of the DBE method is defined according to the meta-model for a digital business ecosystem presented in [1]. The meta-model is divided into three aspects - *actor & role*, *goal & performance*, and *fitness & qualification* (also shown in this study as Fig. 1, Fig. 2, and Fig. 3) and described in detail in [1].

3 Results

The DBE modelling method is envisioned to consist of method components that can be assembled and tailored depending on the needs of a project. Hence, the specifications concern high-level modularity and low-level modularity of the DBE method. The high-level modularity is supported by the 11 maps as mentioned in Sect. 2.2. Each map, as a module, targets a design/ structural concern of a DBE. The specifications for these 11 maps take into account of the design/structural concerns and describe the situations when they can be applied in the different phases of a DBE. The dependencies among these maps provide general guidance on how they can be applied in terms of timely order (c.f. Sect. 2.2). The low-level modularity is supported by the method chunks in these maps. These method chunks target more specific modelling purposes, which means they are more often reusable in different situations and phases of a DBE. This way of differentiating the specification of high- and low-level modularity of the DBE methods supports the extension of the method. Because method chunks (strategies and intentions) suited for the way how the DBE actors behave, interact, and react to each other in specific dynamic situations when considering a specific design/ structural concern can be added.

The examples of three specifications of maps concerning the high-level modularity (Table 2, 3 and 4) and three of method chunks concerning the low-level modularity (Table 5, 6 and 7) are presented in the following Sects. 3.1 and 3.2.

3.1 High-Level Modularity

The objective of the actors and relationships (A-map) module (Table 2) is to support DBE designers, analysts, managers, individual companies participating in DBEs, consultants to gain insight concerning a DBE's actors, roles, and relationship network and to reuse existing actor models.

As shown in Table 2, the situation specifies when a module can be used. The A-map as a module can be applied to a DBE in the design, deployment, and management phases. In practice, it is often the use of other modules (maps), which triggers the application of the A-map module in the management phase. The intention describes all the intentions being part of a module – in this case, *I2 Identify actors*, *I6 Identify relationships between actors*, and *I7 Analyse DBE's relationship network*. The related method chunk(s) further specifies all related intentions with achieving strategies – as shown here < <consists> > means the intentions and the different strategies used to achieve them as constituents of a module. A module's dependency considering the three types (as presented in Sect. 2.2) is listed under the dependency. The existing method(s) potential application describes some of the known methods which can be adopted when performing a module. For the A-map module, modelling methods such as 4EM [10] and ArchiMate [11] can be used to identify actors and their relationships and further extended to accommodate the need of identifying DBE roles and responsibilities. The stakeholder map in TOGAF's Architecture Vision [12] could also, in some extent, be applied for identifying DBE actors. The interface defines the situations and intentions in the process (shown as a map) and related product part (as meta-model) of a module.

Table 2. Specification of the actors and relationships (A-map) module

Module	Content
Name	Actors and relationships (A-map)
Situation	Design phase: In the beginning of emergence and formation of a DBE, the module is used for structuring the initial design of actors, roles, their relationships, and their DBE roles and responsibilities in a DBE. Deployment phase: In case of actors joining, elimination, or context changes affecting actors and relationships in a DBE, the module is used for adjusting current or new actors, roles, their relationships, and their DBE roles and responsibilities in a deployed DBE; In case of the need of understanding actors and relationships in a DBE before making decisions regarding actor recruitment or elimination, the module is used for analysing the current DBE relationship network or the new network relationships in terms of connections or attractiveness. Management phase: DSC-map, KIP-map, RM-map may trigger the use of A-map during this phase in terms of the following - continually readjust and manage current or new actors, roles, their relationships, and their DBE roles and responsibilities in a DBE during runtime; continually analyse and monitor the current runtime DBE relationship network or the new network relationships in terms of connections or attractiveness.
Intention	Identify actors, roles, their relationships, and their DBE roles and responsibilities and analyse the relationship network in a DBE
Dependency	Baseline: The A-map is a baseline map
Related method chunk(s)	<<consists>> *I2 Identify actors* by Driver-first DBE role-based discovery/ by new actor discovery/ by modelling /by reuse existing actor model; <<consists>> *I6 Identify relationships between actors* by Driver-centred/ by single actor's viewpoint/ by modelling/ by reuse existing actor model; <<consists>> *I7 Analyse DBE's relationship network* by model analysis/ by attractiveness analysis
Existing method(s) potential application	4EM (actor resource), ArchiMate, TOGAF–Architecture Vision – Stakeholder map
Interface	<(situation – problem statement), discover and analyse actors and their relationship network >

Process (for the product part see the meta-model on Fig. 1)

The connection among the specification for actors and relationships module, the A-map showing the process, and the meta-model as the product part in Fig. 1 can be observed. The classes and associations in the meta-model (Fig. 1) reflect the intentions and strategies of the module.

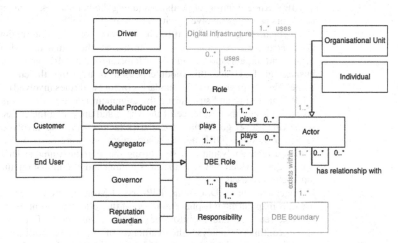

Fig. 1. Meta-model supporting the actors and relationships (A-map) module

The objective of the scope and boundaries (S-map) module (Table 3) is to support DBE designers, analysts, managers, individual companies participating in DBEs, consultants to capture the high-level goals, meaning scope, and the actors and roles involved, meaning boundaries, and structure the goal alignment and gain insight concerning a DBE's resilience.

Table 3 reads in the same way as Table 2. The dependency of including the A-map in the S-map module suggests that it is required to perform the A-map module after commencing the S-map module. Therefore, all the related method chunks of the A-map module are also considered as constituents of this module. The listed existing methods, BMM [13], 4EM [10], ArchiMate [11], and TOGAF's Business Architecture [12], can be applied for goal modelling purposes concerning the intention of aligning DBE actors' goals.

As shown in Fig. 2, the classes DBE Boundary, Actor, Role, DBE Role, Scope, and Ecosystem Goal in the meta-model reflect the intention of delimiting a DBE's scope and boundaries. This reflection between the five classes and the intention is illustrated in a more general way here for the S-map. Note that this intention leads to the use of A-map where the connection between its process and product part exists in a more detailed way. The classes Resilience Goal, Ecosystem Goal, and Business Goal and the associations among them reflect the intention of aligning DBE actors' goals. This means, for example, that business goal instances can be modelled and aligned with the ecosystem goal instances which they support. The classes Resilience Goal, DBE Role, Resilience Indicator, Ecosystem Goal, and Business Goal and the associations among them reflect the intention of analysing a DBE's resilience. These reflections highlight the connection among the scope and boundaries module, its process, and its product part.

Table 3. Specification of the scope and boundaries (S-map) module

Module	Content
Name	Scope and boundaries (S-map)
Situation	Design phase: When initiating a DBE, this module is used for outlining a DBE's scope (high-level goals), including the boundaries, meaning the actors and roles involved (with the use of the A-map).
	Deployment phase: During this phase, more concrete information about actors can be captured – for instances, the actual individual actors and organisational units participating in a DBE and their business goals. Hence, this module is used for adjusting the current scope (high-level goals) and boundaries (actors and roles involved) of a DBE; analysing and structuring the alignment among DBE actors' goals; analysing the resilience of the DBE; and analysing the current scope (high-level goals) and boundaries (actors and roles involved) related to a single DBE actor. When mismatches are suspected or observed after analysing and structuring the alignment among DBE actors' goals, which may lead to actors joining and/or elimination, this module is also used.
	Management phase: DSC-map, KIP-map, RM-map may trigger the use of S-map during this phase in terms of the following - continually analyse, readjust, and monitor the alignment among DBE actors' goals; continually analyse the resilience of the DBE; continually analyse and monitor the current scope (high-level goals) and boundaries (actors and roles involved) related to a single DBE actor
Intention	Delimit a DBE's scope and boundaries, align DBE actors' goals, analyse a DBE's resilience, and analyse a DBE's scope and boundaries related to a single actor
Dependency	Baseline: The S-map is a baseline map
	Include A-map: After commencing the S-map, it is required to perform the A-map
Related method chunk(s)	<<consists>> *I1 Delimit scope and boundaries* by goal modelling/ by interviews and negotiation/ by model review and refinement; all method chunks in A-map module; <<consists>> *I25 Align actors' goals in DBE* by DBE role-based alignment/ by modelling; <<consists>> *I33 Analyse DBE's resilience* by resilience indicator analysis; <<consists>> *I5 Analyse DBE's scope and boundaries from single actor's viewpoint* by Driver-centred/ by single actor-centred
Existing method(s) potential application	BMM, 4EM, ArchiMate, TOGAF – Business Architecture
Interface	<(situation – problem statement), define scope and boundaries, structure goal alignment, analyse resilience, and analyse scope and boundaries related to single actor >

Process (for the product part see the meta-model on Fig. 2)

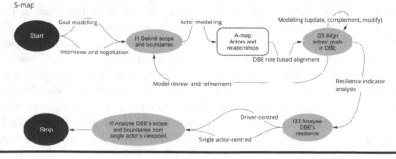

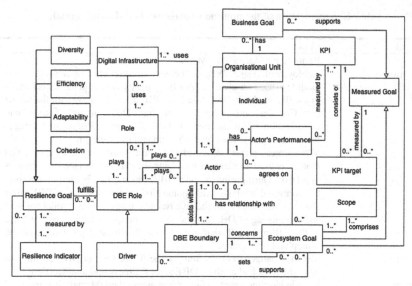

Fig. 2. Meta-model supporting the scope and boundaries (S-map) module

The objective of the runtime management (RM-map) module (Table 4) is to support DBE designers, analysts, managers, individual companies participating in DBEs, consultants to pinpoint the external and internal changes in a DBE and gain insight concerning a DBE's state during and after changes and DBE actors' fitness (the matching between assets provided by actors and assets needed in a DBE) and qualification (the assessment of the quality of assets provided by actors as compared to the required quality of corresponding assets in a DBE).

Table 4 reads in the same way as described above for Table 2. All the related method chunks of the S-map, A-map, C-map, R-map, D-map, and KIP-map modules are considered as constituents of this module due to the two include dependencies of the RM-map module. The approach and activities in TOGAF's Architecture Change Management [12] can, in some extent, be adapted to support this module – specifically, for the intentions of identifying changes and analysing the future state. The CDD method [14] can be applied to the use of this module when elaboration on capability for achieving the intentions is need.

The connection among the runtime management module, its process, and its product part concerns the module itself as well as the included modules (based on the dependencies). The classes Asset and its two sets of specialisations, Actor and its specialisations, Role, Ecosystem Goal, and Business Goal in the meta-model (Fig. 3) illustrate, for the RM-map, a general structure of the product part which is used for the intentions of identifying changes and analysing the future state during and after changes. Note that these intentions lead to the use of the five baseline maps where the connections between their processes and product parts exist in more detail. For the intention of analysing DBE actors' fitness and qualification, the reflection can be observed in the meta-model classes Asset and its two sets of specialisations, Actor and its specialisations, Measured Goal and its specialisations, Fitness Score, Qualification Score, KPI, KPI Target, and

Table 4. Specification of the runtime management (RM-map) module

Module	Content
Name	Runtime management (RM-map)
Situation	Deployment phase: When changes are suspected or observed, this module is used for clearly identifying the external and internal changes in a DBE; analysing the state of a DBE after changes (with the use of the five baseline maps); analysing DBE actors' fitness and qualification (with the use of the KIP-map; KIP-map may trigger feedback dependencies of the S-map and the A-map).
	Management phase: When changes are suspected or observed, this module is used for clearly identifying the external and internal changes in a DBE. During runtime of a DBE, this module is used at any time for continual analysis and monitoring of the state of a DBE after changes (with the use of the five baseline maps) and continual analysis and monitoring of DBE actors' fitness and qualification (with the use of the KIP-map; KIP-map may trigger feedback dependencies of the S-map and the A-map).
Intention	Identify changes in DBE, analyse the future state of DBE during and after changes, and analyse DBE actors' fitness and qualification
Dependency	Include baseline maps: After commencing the RM-map, it is required to perform the five baseline maps (if they have not been performed yet during or after any known or noticeable changes in a DBE)
	Include KIP-map: If analysing actors' fitness and qualification, it is required to perform KIP-map.
Related method chunk(s)	<<consists>> *I19 Identify possible changes occurring in and to DBE* by external context data/ by internal data; <<consists>> *I20 Analyse DBE's future state when changes occur* by new actor discovery/ by actor elimination; all method chunks in S-map, A-map, C-map, R-map, and D-map modules; <<consists>> *I32 Analyse actors' fitness and qualification in DBE based on properties (and performance)* by single actor-centred/ by DBE integrated goal-based; all method chunks in KIP-map module
Existing method(s) potential application	TOGAF -Architecture Change Management, CDD
Interface	<(situation – problem statement), discover changes, analyse DBE's future state, and analyse actor's fitness and qualification >

Process (for the product part see the meta-mode on Fig. 3)

KPI Value. As this intention lead to the use of the KIP-map, a more detailed connection between the processes and product parts related to key performance indicators and actor performance is found in the KIP-map module.

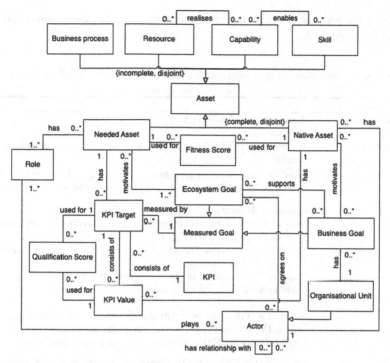

Fig. 3. Meta-model supporting the runtime management (RM-map) module

3.2 Low-Level Modularity

The objective of the method chunk *I2 Identify actors* by modelling strategy (Table 5) is to support DBE designers, analysts, managers, individual companies participating in DBEs, consultants to create model(s) of the actors, their roles and responsibilities in a DBE from viewpoint of the DBE.

As shown in Table 5, the module describes the name of a module of which a method chunk belongs to as constituent. The intention and strategy together specify a method chunk – in this case, the method chunk *I2 Identify actors* by modelling being described in this table. The input denotes artefacts or materials needed for executing activities of a method chunk. For this method chunk, the input can be either lists of the involving actors, their DBE roles and responsibilities or existing models belonging to actors. The activity describes what needs to be executed while performing a method chunk. There are two scenarios (a. and b.) for this method chunk depending on if there are existing actor models as input or not. The output denotes artefacts or materials produced by executing activities of a method chunk – in this case, DBE actor model(s) containing actors, roles, their DBE roles and responsibilities. The related method chunk(s) specifies other method chunks which have relations with a method chunk – in this case, the method chunk *I2 Identify actors* by modelling being described in this table requires (shown as <<requires>>) either of the three method chunks listed. The existing method(s) potential application, interface, and process read in the same way as described for Table 2. Since the method chunk is a constituent of the A-map module, the connection between this method chunk (as a part of the process in the A-map) and the meta-model as the product part is as described for Table 2.

Table 5. Specification of the method chunk *I2 Identify actors* by modelling strategy

Method chunk	Content
Module	Actors and relationships (A-map)
Intention	*I2 Identify actors*
Strategy	Modelling – DBE roles and responsibilities (update, complement, modify)
Input	Lists of the involving actors, roles, their DBE roles and responsibilities; existing actor models belonging to actors
Activity	Scenario a. If there are existing actor models –
	Step 1. Check if the actor models comply with the meta-model defining the product part (Fig. 1) –
	Step 2a. If yes, choose "reuse existing actor model strategy" instead for achieving this intention
	Step 2b. If no, update, complement, and modify the existing actor models according to the meta-model.
	Scenario b. If there are no existing actor models (only lists as input) –
	Step 1. Document, illustrate, and model the actors, roles, their DBE roles and responsibilities based on the meta-model (product part).
Output	DBE actor model(s) of the involving actors, roles, their DBE roles and responsibilities
Related method chunk(s)	<<requires>> Identify actors by Driver-first DBE role-based discovery OR <<requires>> Identify actors by new actor discovery OR <<requires>> Identify actors by reuse existing actor model
Existing method(s) potential application	4EM (actor resource), ArchiMate, TOGAF -Architecture Vision – Stakeholder map
Interface	<(actor list OR existing actor model), Identify actors with Modelling – DBE roles and responsibilities (update, complement, modify) strategy>

Process (for the product part see the meta-model on Fig. 1)

The objective of the method chunk *I6 Identify relationships between actors* by Driver-centred strategy (Table 6) is to support DBE designers, analysts, managers, individual companies participating in DBEs, consultants to establish a relationship network between the DBE Driver(s) and the DBE actors who have a relationship with the Driver(s).

Table 6 reads in the same way as Table 5. There is only a single scenario consisting of two steps as the activity for this method chunk.

Table 6. Specification of the method chunk *I6 Identify relationships between actors* by Driver-centred strategy

Method chunk	Content
Module	Actors and relationships (A-map)
Intention	*I6 Identify relationships between actors*
Strategy	Driver-centred
Input	DBE actor model(s) of the involving actors, their roles and responsibilities
Activity	Step 1. Check the number of drivers in the DBE
	Step 2. For each Driver, associate and link the related DBE actors with the DBE Driver in a relationship network.
Output	Driver-centred relationship network of the DBE
Related method chunk(s)	<<requires>> Identify actors by modelling – DBE roles and responsibilities OR <<requires>> Identify actors by reuse existing actor model
Existing method(s) potential application	4EM (actor resource), ArchiMate, TOGAF -Architecture Vision – Stakeholder map
Interface	<(actor model), Identify relationships between actors with Driver-centred strategy>

Process (for the product part see the meta-model on Fig. 1)

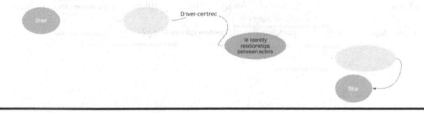

The objective of the method chunk *I33 Analyse DBE's resilience* by resilience indicator analysis strategy (Table 7) is to support DBE designers, analysts, managers, individual companies participating in DBEs, consultants to gain insight on a DBE's resilience through analysing the goal alignment among DBE's actors using resilience indicators [15].

Table 7 reads in the same way as Table 5. Since the method chunk is a constituent of the S-map module, the connection between this method chunk (as a part of the process in the S-map) and the meta-model as the product part is as described for Table 3.

Table 7. Specification of the method chunk *I33 Analyse DBE's resilience* by resilience indicator analysis strategy

Method chunk	Content
Module	Scope and boundaries (S-map)
Intention	*I33 Analyse DBE's resilience*
Strategy	Resilience indicator analysis
Input	DBE actors' goal alignment model(s) structured by using the product part defined in meta-model (i.e., resilience goals, ecosystem goals, and business goals)
Activity	Scenario a. If the goal alignment models do **not** comply with the meta-model defining the product part (Fig. 2) – Step 1. Repeat "I25 Align actors' goals in DBE by modelling" and then proceed with the following steps Scenario b. If the goal alignment models do comply with the meta-model – Step 1. Analyse the model by calculating the resilience goal support indicator for each resilience goal (i.e., Diversity, Efficiency, Adaptability, and Cohesion) Step 2. Analyse the model by calculating the resilience goal – DBE role supporting relationship indicator for each resilience goal and DBE role
Output	Measurements (and radar charts) of the resilience indicators
Related chunk(s)	<<requires>> Align actors' goals in DBE by modelling
Existing method(s) potential application	[15]
Interface	<(goal model), Analyse DBE's resilience with resilience indicator analysis strategy>

Process map (for the product part see the meta-model on Fig. 2)

4   Application Discussion

The DBE method and its high-level modules, the 11 maps, provide general application guidance by the definition of the baseline maps and the dependencies among the maps. Depending on needs of individual projects, the modules, each focusing on a design/ structural concern of a DBE, can be used in different order or simultaneously in various situations. The low-level modules as method chunks (strategies and intentions) support the detailed activities of how to perform parts of the maps (i.e., high-level modules).

Three DBE cases are used as examples to illustrate the concerns faced by and situations occurring in DBEs and how the DBE method can be used as lenses to address these concerns. The Digital Vaccine (DV) case is an operating platform-oriented DBE aiming to provide tailored preventive care for citizens based on personal needs and reduce the financial burden on the public healthcare system. The Winter Road Maintenance (WRM) case is a Latvian project bringing together multiple actors, such as citizens, public transportation, and emergency services, and supporting up-to-date information on road conditions and maintenance work on the regional level in a functioning DBE. The Higher Education (HE) case is an alliance of over ten higher education institutions with the vision of enabling deeper interactions and co-creation of knowledge and skills among citizens, schools, business companies and enterprises, and social and cultural associations in its DBE.

Since all three DBEs are operating (in the management/runtime phase), a common concern is to manage the joining and exiting of actors occurring due to external or internal changes and how to make decisions related to DBE actors' onboarding and offboarding. As shown in Table 4, the runtime management (RM-map) module can be used in situation during management phase when changes in a DBE are observed and "continual analysis and monitoring of the state of a DBE and DBE actors' fitness and qualification" are needed. By performing the RM-map, the related method chunks as constituents describing detailed activities shall be performed. The performance of the five baseline maps and the KIP-map and their related method chunks as constituents are also triggered and required.

The various combination usage of the modules of the DBE method support design and analysis of the various aspects of DBEs, those which emerged evolutionarily as well as those which are designed from scratch. These modules can be seen as analogical to polarised lenses, made for highlighting and working specific aspects or parts of the reality, in this case, the DBE. For example, the lenses focusing on runtime management facilitate the identification of changes and the understanding of the baseline structure in terms of the scope, actors, capabilities, resources, and digital infrastructures of a DBE during or after the changes. Then, depending on the situation of actors onboarding or elimination, fitness and qualification of actors can be analyses based on the measured goals, actors' assets, and corresponding KPIs, which, in turn, support decision-making concerning adding or removing actors in the DBE.

5 Conclusions

In this study, we have presented a modular model-based method for design of DBE involving diverse actors, roles, goals, and responsibilities in a complex socio-digital setting. The presented method uses Situational Method Engineering as the underlying methodology and its Map approach to facilitate modular DBE design by the means of method chunks that resolve the development of individual ecosystem's components, each having a work intention, being applicable in a situation, as well as in relation and dependencies with some other components. To support model-orientation, the method maps rely on underlying meta-models that define concepts and relationships valid for the map. We have also illustrated some applications of existing enterprise architecture and enterprise modelling approaches for realisation of the maps' activities.

The motivation for the study is the need to provide business organisations with a modularised methodological aid to facilitate the complexity of DBE design. The presented method is intended for the used by both scientists and practitioners when analysing and improving DBEs emerged evolutionarily (such as the HE case) and designing innovative multi-actor business constellations craving new characteristics for responsibilities and relations compared to traditional, dominantly bilateral business networks with low autonomy, cohesion and diversity.

References

1. Tsai, C.H., Zdravkovic, J., Stirna, J.: A meta-model for digital business ecosystem design. In: Nurcan, S., Opdahl, A.L., Mouratidis, H., Tsohou, A. (eds.) RCIS 2023. LNBIP, vol. 476, pp. 559–567. Springer, Cham (2023). https://doi.org/10.1007/978-3-031-33080-3_38
2. Hellmanzik, B., Sandkuhl, K.: A data value matrix: linking FAIR data with business models. In: Nurcan, S., Opdahl, A.L., Mouratidis, H., Tsohou, A. (eds.) RCIS 2023. LNBIP, vol. 476, pp. 585–592. Springer Cham (2023). https://doi.org/10.1007/978-3-031-33080-3_41
3. Torres, I.D.S., Fantinato, M., Branco, G.M., Gordijn, J.: Guidelines to derive an e3value business model from a BPMN process model: an experiment on real-world scenarios. Softw. Syst. Model. **22**, 599–618 (2023)
4. Tsai, C.H., Zdravkovic, J., Stirna, J.: Modeling digital business ecosystems: a systematic literature review. CSIMQ 1–30 (2022)
5. Hevner, A.R., March, S.T., Park, J., Ram, S.: Design science in information systems research. MIS Q. **28**, 75–105 (2004)
6. Tsai, C.H., Zdravkovic, J., Stirna, J.: Requirements for a digital business ecosystem modelling method: an interview study with experts and practitioners. In: Buchmann, R.A., Polini, A., Johansson, B., Karagiannis, D. (eds.) BIR 2021. LNBIP, vol. 430, pp. 236–252. Springer, Cham (2021). https://doi.org/10.1007/978-3-030-87205-2_16
7. Tsai, C.H., Zdravkovic, J., Söder, F.: A method for digital business ecosystem design: situational method engineering in an action research project. Softw. Syst. Model. **22**, 573–598 (2023)
8. Henderson-Sellers, B., Ralyté, J., Ågerfalk, P.J., Rossi, M.: Situational Method Engineering. Springer, Heidelberg (2014). https://doi.org/10.1007/978-3-642-41467-1
9. Rolland, C., Prakash, N., Benjamen, A.: A multi-model view of process modelling. Requirements Eng. **4**, 169–187 (1999)
10. Sandkuhl, K., Stirna, J., Persson, A., Wißotzki, M.: Enterprise Modeling Tackling Business Challenges with the 4EM Method. Springer, Heidelberg (2014). https://doi.org/10.1007/978-3-662-43725-4
11. The Open Group: ArchiMate® 3.1 Specification, a Standard of The Open Group. The Open Group (2019)
12. The Open Group: TOGAF® Standard, 10th Edition. The Open Group (2022)
13. Object Management Group: Business Motivation Model Version 1.3. Object Management Group®, OMG® (2015)
14. Grabis, J., Zdravkovic, J., Stirna, J.: Overview of capability-driven development methodology. In: Sandkuhl, K., Stirna, J. (eds.) Capability Management in Digital Enterprises, pp. 59–84. Springer, Cham (2018). https://doi.org/10.1007/978-3-319-90424-5_4
15. Grabis, J., Tsai, C.H., Zdravkovic, J., Stirna, J.: Endurant ecosystems: model-based assessment of resilience of digital business ecosystems. In: Nazaruka, Ē., Sandkuhl, K., Seigerroth, U. (eds.) BIR 2022. LNBIP, vol. 462, pp. 53–68. Springer, Cham (2022). https://doi.org/10.1007/978-3-031-16947-2_4

A Model-Based Approach to Decision Support for Designing Inclusive Services

Helena Zhemchugova[1]([✉])(iD), Paul Johannesson[1](iD),
and Gunnlaugur Mangnússon[2,3](iD)

[1] Stockholm University, Borgarfjordsgatan 12, 164 07 Kista, Sweden
{helena.zhemchugova,pajo}@dsv.su.se
[2] Uppsala University, Blåsenhus, von Kraemers Allé 1, 750 02 Uppsala, Sweden
gunnlaugur.magnusson@edu.uu.se
[3] University of Oslo, Helga Engs hus, Sem Sælands vei 7, 0371 Oslo, Norway

Abstract. An inclusive service is usable regardless of the functional abilities of its users. Increasing the inclusiveness of critical services such as higher education contributes to reducing disparities and can be viewed as an institutional value proposition for society as a whole. However, the notion of inclusion is becoming more multifaceted and context-dependent. Addressing it at scale often takes the "watering can" approach, which is resource-intensive and may not be effective. As a basis for better service design decisions as well as planning and allocation of resources, we introduce an approach to representing, analysing and communicating the structure of public institutional service environments. In an ontological model of inclusion in a service, we demonstrate that inclusion problems result from a mismatch between environmental factors and user characteristics. Further, using higher education as a case of application, we analyse the mismatch by creating a risk-aware goal model of a service - a university course. The viability of the approach has been validated by a group of practitioners with expertise in the design of university programmes and the power of organisational decision-making. The approach we propose enables service designers to identify and systematically address inclusion problems in their respective service environments.

Keywords: Conceptual Modelling · Public Institutional Service Design · Inclusive Education · Qualitative Risk Analysis

1 Introduction

What makes a service inclusive? In the most general view, an inclusive service is designed and delivered to meet the needs, preferences, and functional limitations of a diverse range of users [1,2]. No service, however, can be fully inclusive of any and all users across the complete spectrum of human diversity with respect to their biological, cultural, social, cognitive, and psychological characteristics. We delimit the discussion of inclusion in a service to the value proposition of the

K. Hinkelmann et al. (Eds.): BIR 2023, LNBIP 493, pp. 229–243, 2023.
https://doi.org/10.1007/978-3-031-43126-5_17

service in a particular context which then determines its inclusion problematics and constrains the search for inclusion solutions. This paper is concerned with *functional inclusion* in higher education as a public institutional service that is provided by universities as institutional establishments. University education can be regarded as a critical service given its significant role in personal development, social mobility, economic growth, and overall societal progress. It is intended to be accessible by all citizens, regardless of their functional ability [3]. Ensuring functional inclusion in university education can be seen as a value proposition to society as a whole.

Knowledge regarding how public institutional service systems, relationships, and interactions should be designed to serve diverse users is often fragmented. Service development projects often adopt a "watering can" approach to cover as much ground as possible, yet they tend to fail to serve all but the "average" user [4]. Developing inclusive services at scale, also known as "universal service design" [5,6], requires appropriate approaches for systematising the knowledge about problems that arise for non-average users at the service touch-points of (un)fair access, treatment, and exit. The main strategies for inclusion in a service have focused on modifying: the user whose characteristics are not directly compatible with the system (cf [7]) and the system environment that creates barriers for the user (cf [8]). The former is resolved by equipping users with artefacts that increase the compatibility while the latter is addressed by restructuring the environment to remove the barriers. Iterative co-creation approaches such as design thinking are useful for learning about problems experienced by users and designing solutions they welcome, and have been successful in both the private and public sectors [9]. However, such approaches may not be fully practicable in highly regulated institutional environments that are financially constrained. Institutional service designers require new analytical tools to embrace the "diverse" user systematically and within their means.

This conceptual paper proposes a model-based approach to detecting hidden inclusion problems pertaining to users' functional limitations and analysing their impact on service goals and value in public institutional services. The approach constitutes a new way of thinking about inclusion in a service and does not introduce a new modelling method or a domain-specific modelling language. The aim of the approach is to expand the understanding of inclusion problematics in the design of public institutional services and to support decisions on their revision while using modelling tools that exist. The outcome of applying this approach to public university education in this study is a qualitative risk analysis of functional inclusion in a university course.

2   Inclusive Services in Literature

2.1   Inclusive Institutional Services

Creating inclusive institutions is one of the sustainable development goals on the Agenda 2030 [10]. Services can be seen as systems where inclusion can take place at the interface between institutions and the public. [11] proposes an agenda for creating inclusive service systems by 2050, emphasising the need to understand service context, relationships, and interactions. A service is a value proposition [12] from a service provider to users and other stakeholders in the form of activities to solve their problems and meet their needs. Designing a service involves a structured and iterative process of understanding user needs, and often includes modelling and analysing their divergent values. Services can have a "good" or a "bad" fit between their projected value and the value their users are able to extract. Institutional services are intended to support the social, economic, and political well-being of society as a whole. [4] defines inclusion as a measure of service quality since being usable by everyone equally means that its projected value can extend past the "average" user. Thus, service inclusion creates equitable opportunities for diverse citizen groups as users, making institutions societally sustainable [11]. Unlike those in the private sector, public institutional services are funded by taxes or other public resources and must adhere to stringent budgets. Furthermore, they are regulated by government laws and policies, which may constrain or facilitate resource allocation and prioritisation. The interpretation of inclusion by institutional service designers determines its implementation [13].

2.2   Inclusive Education

The notion of inclusion in education has a complicated relationship with ideas of educational democracy and student diversity [14]. In the early 1990's, policy initiatives targeted facilitating access to education for all students regardless of their characteristics [15], further specialising the term "inclusive education" to students with disabilities [16]. The notion of *social inclusion* is strong in the history of education in Sweden [17] where inclusion is understood as legislative protection against discrimination on the grounds of social differences[1] [18]. Within higher education, social inclusion has been connected to the goal of broadened recruitment [19, §5] as a point of fair access. However, social inclusion or fair treatment of those who have been admitted to studies has not been sufficiently operationalised although policy instruments exist (cf [20]). Decisions about service design in education have focused on identifying non-average users and their characteristics as well as determining the "limits to inclusion" [21], how they should be drawn, and by whom [22] to support the planning of resources. Due to resource constraints, public universities have been favouring inclusion issues that are easier to identify and preferring solutions that modify the user by means of artefacts. For example, offering headphones that block out overwhelming noise and sensory stimuli are a common solution for students with non-apparent disabilities such as ADHD and autism. While useful and necessary, such solutions do not guarantee social inclusion which is critical for this group of service users. Social inclusion can support students in coping with their less apparent functional challenges and equalise their chances of living up to

---

[1] Specifically, protected categories regard discrimination on the basis of gender, gender identity or expression, sexual orientation, religion, ethnicity, disability, and age.

their academic potential. Hence, actually securing accessibility and equal participation in an institutional service demands a critical analysis and a thorough restructuring of the organisation [23] including reconsideration of service design.

2.3 Inclusive Services in Business Informatics

In business informatics, the term "inclusive design" is most frequently found in the literature on human-computer interaction [24] and design thinking [5] as well as in mixed-method studies. These approaches employ user research to identify the needs and capabilities of diverse user groups to a nuanced degree, which then supports the development of accessible and responsive services. Design thinking has been growing in the public sector [25] and can handle complexity [26]. However, due to unclear boundaries between the notions of "inclusive design" and "service design" [27], the framework lacks structural integrity for representing complex contexts [28]. A broadened design agenda that emphasises the need for inclusion of diverse users has led to toolkits that embrace business modelling and "increasingly have less and less to do with design per se" [28, p. 50]. Business modelling has been used to create sustainable value propositions [29], facilitate and enhance value co-creation [30], and align value propositions with societal needs [31]. However, business models may not properly represent service institutionality and social contexts [32]. Aware of this caveat, we propose that business modelling can provide the vocabulary and architectural scaffolding needed to locate and concretise the inclusion problematics in the structure of institutional services and thus be a potent tool for supporting their design.

3   Our Modelling Strategy

To identify and analyse the inclusion problematics in the structure of a service, we represent them in two conceptual models informed by two philosophical perspectives - ontological and phenomenological. We employ them as complementary lenses to support the representation with a more comprehensive analysis of reality [33]. The ontological perspective is concerned with the objective nature of things; it seeks to identify, group, and relate entities that exist or can be said to exist. We express it in an ontological model that locates inclusion problematics in a basic service structure, connects them to a decision-making layer in a public institutional context, and lays the foundation for thinking about them in general terms. The phenomenological perspective is concerned with exploring and describing subjective human experience. It expands the generic view of inclusion in a service with user-centric considerations and shows the dependency between the service value extracted by the users affected by inclusion issues and whether and how those issues are addressed. This perspective is instantiated in the risk-aware goal model of a university course that connects the basic service structure to the inclusion problematics specific to its environment and users.

3.1   Ontological Perspective

In information systems, ontological models are used for defining the structure, rules, and semantics of a system (cf [34]). Web Ontology Language (OWL) and Unified Foundational Ontology (UFO) are technical notations tailored to the task. Our ontological model takes the form of a UML class diagram, a notation that was not intended for this purpose. However, we view the conceptual clarity it gives to the model as an advantage when demonstrating and discussing the model with educational experts who may be unfamiliar with conceptual modelling and may find its more elaborate forms difficult to understand. We model inclusion problematics in a generic service (presented in Sect. 4) as an entity that exists for a particular purpose and follows a particular design that can change upon revision. The model is presented at a high level of abstraction and is domain-independent. It is based on existing research on service design and value proposition (cf [4,11,12]) as well as on our diverse perspectives and experiences as educators in public universities in the Nordics.

3.2   Phenomenological Perspective

Qualitative, narrative-based phenomenological analysis rarely uses models. It dominates the field of user experience (UX) research, where meeting user needs is seen as creating business value (cf [35]). Focusing on the subjective experience is also recommended for designing institutional services that are inclusive of people with disabilities [36]. A phenomenological perspective is useful for analysing the mismatch between environmental factors and user characteristics inherent in a particular service. It takes the form of a goal model of the service that instantiates relevant classes of the generic ontological model to specialise the ontological perspective to the domain of application. The goal model is then expanded with a qualitative risk analysis of how the mismatch may affect user experience, service goals, and service's projected and extracted value. The risk analysis makes use of the RAMN notation [37] created for visualising risk in holistic business models. The inclusion problematics are specialised to functional inclusion in a university course, referring to a certain type of environmental barriers that may be experienced by students possessing characteristics of limited function.

Case. The university course under analysis teaches research methodology to master's students in computer and systems sciences at Stockholm University, Sweden, at the conclusion of their studies. It was developed in 2020 and has been taught by two of the paper's authors for the past three years. Our experience as course developers and teachers informs the goal model and its risk-aware extension. Particularly, the extension is based on continuous feedback on the study experience from new cohorts of about 100 students each year. In addition to formal course evaluations conducted at the end of each year, feedback is gathered through informal interactions. As a result of the teaching staff's dedication to course development, student feedback shows a favourable opinion of the solutions we implement. However, despite these efforts, complaints regarding functional inclusion problematics continue to surface. These concern (a) functional barriers as *environmental factors* or (b) functional limitations as *user characteristics*. They manifest when students engage in course activities: (a) *"Course activities provide some students with unreasonable demands"*, and (b) *"Some students are not able to carry out course activities without unreasonable strain"*.

In the disability discourse, a "functional barrier" refers to the environmental factors that negatively influence a person with a functional impairment. We take a broader perspective and focus on barriers to functional inclusion for those individuals who may not have a disability but may experience suboptimal levels of function, whether permanent or temporary, due to other conditions and states (e.g., chronic pain or grief) that are not considered disabilities and do not confer the right to functional support and accommodations. We refer to this phenomenon as "functional variation" to differentiate it from the "average function" of the "average student". The ontological specification of the inclusion problematics in a service is as follows: (a) *"Service environment presents functional barriers for some service users"*, and (b) *"All service users possess a characteristic of functional variation"*. This inclusion problem relates to the goal of broadened recruitment [19] and occurs after admission to studies.

4   An Ontological Model of Inclusion in a Service

The model consists of four consecutive parts: existing design, inclusion problematics, design revision, and new design (see Fig. 1). The numbers on the connectors between classes show how many objects within these classes can be connected by association, e.g., "0..*" means "zero to many".

Existing Design. A *service* is offered to a *user* by a *provider* and has a tangible *desired outcome* that is connected to an abstract *value proposition*. The value proposition is aligned with the purpose of the public institutional establishment, e.g., universities work towards closing skill and knowledge gaps. It can be specialised into *projected value* - something the provider intends to deliver to the users and society at large - and the *value the user is able to extract* from the service in practise. The latter can be undermined by an *inclusion problem* which may cause the purpose of the establishment to not be reaching some user groups. It can also be supported by an *inclusion solution*. A *use plan* enables the user to engage with the service and includes *activities* to be carried out in a specific sequence, including by making use of various resources. Finally, a service is delivered in a certain *environment* which can be physical, digital, or social.

Inclusion Problematics. *Inclusion problems* may arise when users experience challenges when carrying out an *activity* as part of the *use plan*. These challenges may actualise through *user characteristics* that undermine their function and lie outside their control, e.g., having a permanent physical disability or feeling temporarily anxious. A user of a motorised wheelchair (*user characteristic*) can physically move from one place to another quicker than an average person (*strength*). However, having to take several flights of stairs to get to a lecture hall (*environmental factor*) to attend a lecture (*activity*) would highlight a *limitation* of not being able to do so (*barrier*), thus triggering an *inclusion problem*. However, for a student who enjoys good health and likes to be physically active (*user characteristic*), taking the stairs can be viewed as a *facilitator* to exercising a *strength*, and thus, no inclusion problem would occur.

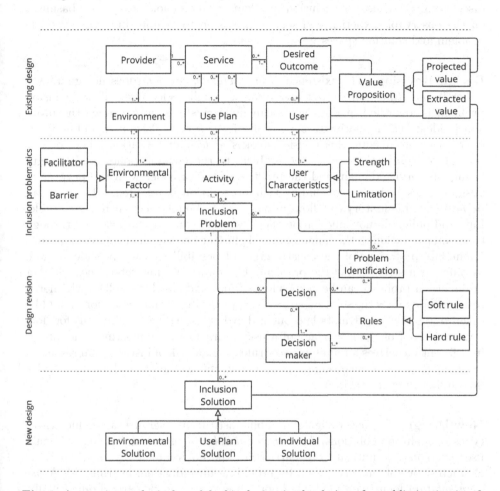

Fig. 1. A generic ontological model of inclusion in the design of a public institutional service.

This example shows that inclusion problems are not solely inherent in either the user or the environment and instead relate one or several environmental factors to one or several user characteristics. It is the mismatch between the factors and the characteristics that turns the former into barriers rather than facilitators and the latter into limitations rather than strengths, effectively hindering some users from extracting the service's full value. The number of factors and characteristics that may come into conflict with each other is presumably enormous given the diversity of environments and users, as well as the differences in how the environments are configured and users are born and developed as humans. Consequently, it may not be feasible or practically useful to identify all possible combinations resulting in a mismatch and preempt them with a solution. Instead, we suggest specialising the analysis to a particular service context and discovering the causes of inclusion problems phenomenologically, i.e., basing it on the observable experience of service provision to delimit and concretise the problem and solution spaces.

Design Revision. The existence of an *inclusion problem* does not guarantee either its *identification* or that a *solution* is sought. Vice versa, if no inclusion problem is identified, it does not mean none exists. However, once the problem is identified, it motivates a revision of the service design. In public institutional environments, this revision evokes a *decision* situation where one or several *decision-makers* relate the problem to the law and policy (*rules*) regulating the service domain and the practise of the provider with the purpose of designing a solution or concluding that no solution is required. The rules can be *hard*, i.e., mandatory to follow, or *soft*, i.e., to be followed whenever possible. Law and policy do not function on their own and can only be actuated through their interpretation in the human mind. Different decision-makers may have different interpretations of the constraints and possibilities they provide, as well as different assessments of the problem. The interpretation determines whether an inclusion problem can be acknowledged and addressed, as well as whether it restricts or enables the solution space. It can be decided that no action should be taken due to the constraints laid out in hard rules, e.g., a requirement for documented proof of the legitimacy of a user characteristic impacting function, or insufficient incentives for applying soft rules, e.g., a lack of institutional resources available for use. An *inclusion solution* follows the decision to include it in service design following the revision.

New Design. The new design of a public institutional service can include three types of inclusion solutions. An *individual solution* is about helping a certain user overcome or mitigate the barriers in the environment by modifying the characteristics of that user, e.g., by providing an individual hearing aid. A *use plan solution* focuses on modifying how an activity can be carried out. Finally, an *environmental solution* involves changing the service environment universally to reduce the number of barriers that can be experienced by some or all users. Environmental solutions can only be promoted by actors at a higher level of the organisational hierarchy, such as decision-makers and policymakers. After the new design is implemented, it reverts to the "existing design", and the problem analysis iterates in a new cycle.

5   A Risk-Aware Model of Inclusion Problematics

Goal Model. For the generic ontological model to fit the domain of public university education, we specialise its classes as follows: *service* to Course, *provider* to University, and *user* to Student. Then, the class *desired outcome* is instantiated into Goals and Means which are determined by the service provider centrally. The Means are further specialised into Strategies to represent *activities* or their modes; and into Policies and Rules to indicate what governs and constrains the Means as well as supports and compromises the Goals. Providing Quality Education is set to be the top Goal and a specialisation of the class *projected value* in the generic model. It includes Learning Outcomes of the course and Pedagogical Alignment. The classes *use plan* and *activity* are instantiated through the Means of Creating Activities such as attending a lecture, reading course literature, participating in seminars, and taking exams - according to the course plan. The dimension of functional inclusion is represented through the Goal of Functional Support as part of the Goal of Support in Learning under the higher-level Goal of Pedagogical Alignment. There are two strategies for providing Functional Support: By Request, i.e., "do nothing unless the student states a request" and By Design, i.e., "consider the functional variation in course design". Thereby, the key components of the *existing design* part of the generic model have been adapted to the target domain.

Qualitative Risk Analysis. The inclusion problematics in this course are modelled through *environmental factors* and *user characteristics* as Influencers. The following categories of Influencers were included based on data about the course: Student Characteristics, Teacher Assumptions, Teaching Culture, Teaching Resources, Course Management Prerogative, Regulation, and Compliance. Further, the goal model is expanded with their Assessment which constitutes the risk analysis[2]. Figure 2 presents a fragment of the analysis where the Influencer "Student Characteristic" (*user characteristic* in the generic ontological model) is assessed against the Strategy of "Providing functional accommodations by request" (*individual inclusion solution* in the generic ontological model). Constrained by Policy, the Strategy can only be implemented if students can provide documented proof of eligibility. The red triangle with an exclamation mark is a risk indicator, showing the mismatch between the environment and the users. The following students are at risk of functional exclusion: those who choose not to disclose their disabilities, have a condition that impacts their function but is not considered a disability, or do not have any such conditions but experience temporary functional limitations. The knowledge the complete course analysis enables us to see is intended to support course designers and other decision-makers in prioritising solutions for functional support in course development.

---

[2] A complete digital version of the model with searchable content can be downloaded at https://shorturl.at/belqZ.

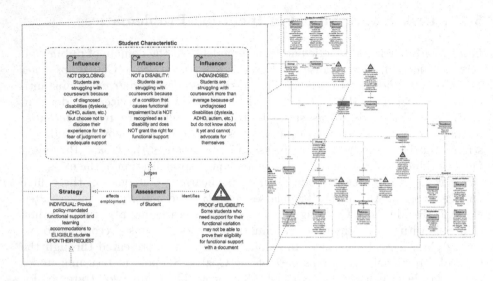

Fig. 2. A fragment of the risk-aware extension of the goal model.

6 Evaluation of the Outcome of the Approach

The outcome of the approach and the viability of the instantiated model were evaluated by expert opinion [38]. Homogeneous purposive sampling [39] was employed to engage a small group of intended users of the model and the knowledge it provides - service designers with the power of organisational decision-making. The sample consisted of four Directors of Study with expertise in managing study programmes on the doctoral, master's, and bachelor's levels at Uppsala University and Stockholm University in Sweden. Among them were three experts in special education (SE) and one in regular education (RE), representing the Department where the modelled course was offered - to validate if the model identified the correct inclusion issues. The small sample size was motivated by the need to achieve data saturation rather than statistical power [40]. The data was gathered using unstructured interview sessions [41] to discover the experts' unique perspectives while limiting the researcher bias. It was captured by note-taking after receiving the respondents' consent. The data comprised a preliminary state of knowledge and was not meant to create generalisations over the entire population of experts in similar professional roles. Rather, it provided an appropriate focus and an overview of the real-life concerns of this particular group of practitioners. We asked: *Can the knowledge this risk-aware goal model produces be used for decision support about the design of your courses and programmes with the purpose of making them more functionally inclusive for students? If yes, then how? And if not, then why not?*

6.1   Summary of Findings

A clear difference in perspectives could be seen between the service designers in SE and in RE. The former group saw the modelling approach as a well-structured form of qualitative risk analysis. All service designers in SE expressed that the model lifted and clarified the systemic inclusion issues that are important to address in their line of work but difficult to articulate otherwise. Possibly, this view can be attributed to the fact that educators in SE may have a more nuanced view of the inclusion problematics, and therefore appreciate their being made explicit. The service designer in RE, on the other hand, perceived the model as "too complicated and overwhelming for something that is so obvious". While this assessment meant that the model did not provide new knowledge, it confirmed the model's internal validity.

Correctness of Service Representation. All respondents assessed the level of representation in the model - that of a university course - as inappropriate. It was suggested that the model could instead be drawn at the level of a university programme or a higher systemic level, engaging policymakers and enabling solutions for all universities nation-wide, which was motivated by the universal character of the issues that were brought up in the analysis. Service designers in SE could see that a similar model could be created to analyse other types of inclusion problems such as language, age, and mobility. Some respondents expressed concerns about the model's reliability given that it was based on multiple sources of empirical data rather than established scientific knowledge. Others stated that the modelling approach would not fit with their work routines because of their preference for working with tacit knowledge. The service designer in RE expressed a preference for a process view that would align better with the established routine of using process checklists when processing students' requests for functional support.

Usability of the Approach. Service designers in SE deemed the approach usable as a tool for structuring delicate discussions about non-apparent inclusion issues and facilitating communication around them during institutional meetings. It was suggested that the approach could de-dramatise and de-personalise addressing the inclusion problematics by making discussions more constructive. The approach was also deemed to be time-consuming, both in terms of the time required to create a risk-aware model and to learn how to interpret it. All respondents agreed that the reasonable timeframe for using the approach for risk analysis was once per term or once per year. Feasible usage scenarios included creating a risk-aware goal model during a planning meeting to discuss resource trajectories and during a workshop session facilitated by a modelling consultant to revise the existing programmes. The service designer in RE did not see a particular usage scenario for the approach in their line of work.

Understandability of the Diagram. While the model was generally seen as having a clear structure, all respondents expressed the wish that it were made simpler, while the repeating elements were perceived as overwhelming.

This problem could be attributed to the constraints of the modelling environment ADOxx [42] that does not hide supporting elements. In the RAMN library, Assessments of Influencers for impacts on other elements are visualised as one-to-one relationships. In a thorough risk analysis, Assessments become omnipresent. Although necessary for traceability, this feature provides information noise and complicates the understanding of the model by practitioners not familiar with conceptual modelling. One respondent suggested that a graphical element could be added to indicate that the list of Influencers is not exhaustive and can be expanded, while another mistook the dependencies between the risk indicators and the course elements for causal relationships. These observations may indicate the need to introduce service designers to the modelling notation prior to their participation in the analysis facilitated by the approach. Finally, it was suggested to add indicators of responsibility for mitigating the risk - to delineate the expectations imposed on the service designers (e.g., provide solutions) from the expectations imposed on students (e.g., be proactive with disclosing the need for functional support).

Policy Compliance: Enabling and Constraining. All respondents assessed the approach as relevant to their line of work with reference to the requirement of broadened recruitment and participation of students [19, §5]. Even though the issues the model depicts were known to the service designer in RE, creating solutions in practise was either challenging or impossible because of the constraints imposed by the university policies centrally. One of such requirements obliges students to provide documented proof of eligibility to receive disability support. This requirement does not leave much room for accommodating those students who need other forms of functional support while not being disabled and not being able to provide such proof. In the existing design, this problem is addressed by making exceptions on a case-by-case basis, though such interventions are unsystematic and subject to resource availability. This finding indicates a gap between the policy guidelines and the practical possibilities for their implementation.

7   Discussion and Conclusions

The model-based approach we have proposed and evaluated provides a new way of thinking about inclusion in public institutional services. It restructures the abstract and complex issue of inclusion into a sizable practical problem that can be observed and analysed in the context of a particular service. Our findings from applying the approach to the domain of public university education indicate that it responds to the needs of service designers in special education. However, it has not found the support of service designers in regular education who view functional inclusion in a less nuanced way and whose actions are more constrained by the regulations. Given that higher education is not compulsory and access is based on merit, consideration of "special needs" is a relatively recent phenomenon. It is still more common to consider the needs of the "average" student and build services around that persona rather than ask, *Who are the individuals struggling?* and *What can we do for them?* The goal of broadening the recruitment of students challenges this tradition and urges educators to look for new ways of thinking to accommodate diverse students past the point of acceptance into studies.

The generic ontological model of inclusion in a service lays the conceptual foundation for structuring inclusive institutional services. It provides a stable analytical point of departure when addressing systemic issues concerning the subjective experiences of service users. The RAMN notation facilitates concretising the idea that environmental factors may not be intrinsically good or bad, but they can have different impacts on users with different characteristics. The diagrammatic depiction of the risk analysis shows the mismatch between the two and opens the door for reflection on the impact it can have on the quality of service and the extraction of service value by some user groups.

While the approach does not offer solutions - something our respondents wished it did - it has the potential to ensure that non-apparent but pressing inclusion problems do not get overlooked. Evaluation sessions determined that the inclusion problematics we revealed in the analysis of a course may not be course-specific but rather manifest at scale in study programmes encompassing a number of courses. For further validation of the approach, it should be tested in application to other public institutional services that are deemed critical, such as, for example, healthcare.

Internal university policies interpret national regulations in a way that can help or restrict inclusion in public institutional services. That which is stated explicitly may be followed through, while that which is neither mandated nor prohibited may remain out of focus. Swedish institutional practise shows that a broader interpretation of functional inclusion in services happens unsystematically through the efforts of individual universities. However, such efforts are difficult to propagate at scale as universities set individual priorities and work against individual budgets. Universal design is argued to hold the key to inclusive services; however, the work may need to be explicitly supported by explicit policy guidelines. Therefore, another important direction for future research is to investigate whether a similar model-based approach could support such guidelines.

References

1. Rodrigues, V.E.: Designing for Resilience: Navigating Change in Service Systems (2020)
2. Vink, J.: IN/VISIBLE (2019)
3. Logan, T.M., Guikema, S.D.: Reframing resilience: equitable access to essential services. Risk Anal. **40**, 1538–1553 (2020). https://doi.org/10.1111/risa.13492
4. Downe, L.: Good Services: How to Design Services That Work. BIS Publishers, Amsterdam (2020)
5. Begnum, M.E.N., Bue, O.L.: Advancing inclusive service design: defining, evaluating and creating universally designed services. In: Rauterberg, M. (ed.) HCII

2021. LNCS, vol. 12795, pp. 17–35. Springer, Cham (2021). https://doi.org/10.1007/978-3-030-77431-8_2

6. Clarkson, J. P., Coleman, R., Keates, S., Lebbon, C.: Inclusive Design: Design for the Whole Population. Springer London (2003). https://doi.org/10.1007/978-1-4471-0001-0

7. Weber, D.L., Brereton, M., Kanstrup, A.M.: Developing visual tangible artefacts as an inclusive method for exploring digital activities with young people with learning disabilities. Br. J. Learn. Disabil. (2022). https://doi.org/10.1111/bld.12505

8. United Nations: Accessibility and development: Mainstreaming disability in the post-2015 development agenda. Economic & Social Affairs (a)

9. Bicheno, J.: Die Service System Toolbox: Lean Thinking, Systems Thinking und Design Thinking. BoD – Books on Demand (2019)

10. United Nations: Goal 16: Promote peaceful and inclusive societies for sustainable development, provide access to justice for all and build effective, accountable and inclusive institutions at all levels. https://sdgs.un.org/goals/goal16. Accessed 14 May 2023 (b)

11. Fisk, R.P., et al.: Design for service inclusion: creating inclusive service systems by 2050. J. Serv. Manage. **29**, 834–858 (2018). https://doi.org/10.1108/JOSM-05-2018-0121

12. Osterwalder, A., Pigneur, Y., Bernarda, G., Smith, A.: Value Proposition Design: How to Create Products and Services Customers Want. Wiley (2015)

13. Eggers, W.D., Singh, S.K.: The Public Innovator's Playbook: Nurturing Bold Ideas in Government. Ash Institute, Harvard Kennedy School (2009)

14. Young, I.M.: Inclusion and Democracy. Oxford University Press, Oxford (2000)

15. Kiuppis, F.: Why (not) associate the principle of inclusion with disability? Tracing connections from the start of the "Salamanca Process.". Int. J. Incl. Educ. **18**, 746–761 (2014). https://doi.org/10.1080/13603116.2013.826289

16. The Salamanca Statement and Framework for Action on Special Needs Education. UNESCO, Ministry of Education and Science, Spain (1994)

17. Magnússon, G., Pettersson, D.: Imaginaries of Inclusion in Swedish Education. Oxford Research Encyclopedia of Education. https://doi.org/10.1093/acrefore/9780190264093.013.1682

18. Diskrimineringslag (2008:567) (E: Discrimination Act) (2008)

19. Högskolelag (1992:1434) (E: Higher Education Act) (1992)

20. Regeringen, Socialdepartementet: Strategi för systematisk uppföljning av funktionshinderspolitiken under 2021–2031 (E: A strategy for a systematic follow-up on the politics of functional barriers) (2021)

21. Hansen, J.H.: Limits to inclusion. Int. J. Incl. Educ. **16**, 89–98 (2012). https://doi.org/10.1080/13603111003671632

22. Nilholm, C.: Research about inclusive education in 2020 - how can we improve our theories in order to change practice? Eur. J. Spec. Needs Educ. **36**, 358–370 (2021). https://doi.org/10.1080/08856257.2020.1754547

23. Harris, J.C., Barone, R.P., Davis, L.P.: Who Benefits?: A Critical Race Analysis of the (D)Evolving Language of Inclusion in Higher Education. Thought & Action (2015)

24. Abascal, J., Nicolle, C.: Moving towards inclusive design guidelines for socially and ethically aware HCI. Interact. Comput. **17**, 484–505 (2005). https://doi.org/10.1016/j.intcom.2005.03.002

25. McGann, M., Blomkamp, E., Lewis, J.M.: The rise of public sector innovation labs: experiments in design thinking for policy. Policy Sci. **51**(3), 249–267 (2018). https://doi.org/10.1007/s11077-018-9315-7

26. Buchanan, R.: Wicked problems in design thinking. Des. Issues **8**, 5–21 (1992). https://doi.org/10.2307/1511637
27. Busciantella-Ricci, D., Rizo-Corona, L., Aceves-Gonzalez, C.: Exploring boundaries and synergies between inclusive design and service design. In: Di Bucchianico, G., Shin, C.S., Shim, S., Fukuda, S., Montagna, G., Carvalho, C. (eds.) AHFE 2020. AISC, vol. 1202, pp. 55–61. Springer, Cham (2020). https://doi.org/10.1007/978-3-030-51194-4_8
28. Melles, G.: The design thinking umbrella for inclusive growth in India? Discussion and case study. SDMIMD **11**, 49–56 (2020). https://doi.org/10.18311/sdmimd/2020/26141
29. Baldassarre, B., Calabretta, G., Bocken, N.M.P., Jaskiewicz, T.: Bridging sustainable business model innovation and user-driven innovation: a process for sustainable value proposition design. J. Clean. Prod. **147**, 175–186 (2017). https://doi.org/10.1016/j.jclepro.2017.01.081
30. Karpen, I.O., Bove, L.L., Lukas, B.A.: Linking service-dominant logic and strategic business practice: a conceptual model of a service-dominant orientation. J. Serv. Res. **15**, 21–38 (2012). https://doi.org/10.1177/1094670511425697
31. Butler, R.W., Szromek, A.R.: Incorporating the value proposition for society with business models of health tourism enterprises. Sustain. Sci. Pract. Policy. **11**, 6711 (2019). https://doi.org/10.3390/su11236711
32. Musulin, J., Strahonja, V.: Business model enriched with user experience, as a systemic tool in service design. Croatian Econ. Surv. **23**, 67–103 (2021). https://doi.org/10.15179/ces.23.2.3
33. Smith, D.W.: "Pure" logic, ontology, and phenomenology. Rev. Int. Philos. **224**, 21–44 (2003)
34. Green, P.F., Rosemann, M.: Business Systems Analysis with Ontologies. Idea Group Inc. (IGI) (2005)
35. Luther, L., Tiberius, V., Brem, A.: User experience (UX) in business, management, and psychology: a bibliometric mapping of the current state of research. Multimodal Technol. Interact. **4**, 18 (2020). https://doi.org/10.3390/mti4020018
36. Layton, N.A., Steel, E.J.: "An environment built to include rather than exclude me": creating inclusive environments for human well-being. Int. J. Environ. Res. Public Health **12**, 11146–11162 (2015). https://doi.org/10.3390/ijerph120911146
37. Hinkelmann, K., Onufrienko, N.: Explicitly modelling relationships of risks on business architecture. In: Cunningham, P., Cunningham, M. (eds.) eChallenges e-2014 Conference Proceedings. Institute of Electrical and Electronics Engineers Inc. (2014)
38. Walton, D.: Appeal to Expert Opinion: Arguments from Authority. Penn State Press (2010)
39. Etikan, I., Musa, S.A., Alkassim, R.S.: Comparison of convenience sampling and purposive sampling. Am. J. Theor. Appl. Stat. **5**, 1 (2016). https://doi.org/10.11648/j.ajtas.20160501.11
40. Fusch, P.I., Ness, L.R.: Are we there yet? Data saturation in qualitative research. Qual. Rep. **20**, 1408–1416 (2015)
41. Zhang, Y., Wildemuth, B.M.: Unstructured interviews. Applications of social research methods to questions in information and library science, pp. 222–231 (2009)
42. ADOxx.org: Introduction to ADOxx. https://www.adoxx.org/live/introduction-to-adoxx. Accessed 21 Jun 2023

Validating Enterprise Architecture Principles Using Derivation Rules and Domain Knowledge

Devid Montecchiari[1,2]([✉]) [ID] and Knut Hinkelmann[1,3] [ID]

[1] School of Business, FHNW University of Applied Sciences and Arts Northwestern Switzerland, Olten, Switzerland
{devid.montecchiari,knut.hinkelmann}@fhnw.ch
[2] School of Science and Technology, UNICAM University of Camerino, Camerino, Italy
[3] Department of Informatics, University of Pretoria, Pretoria, South Africa

Abstract. In *Enterprise Architecture Management (EAM)*, rules, constraints, and principles guide and govern the *Enterprise Architecture (EA)*. These can be formulated and verified in ontology-based enterprise architecture models. The automatic validation of EA principles relies on the knowledge available in the EA models. However, there is knowledge implicit in models that humans may understand but machines cannot. For example, relationships between model elements may be derived using derivation rules and domain knowledge. Formalizing derivation rules in an enterprise ontology, we can infer this implicit knowledge and make it available to the machine for reasoning. This research demonstrates the feasibility of using derivation rules to extract implicit knowledge from enterprise models allowing EA principles validation and supporting EAM. The research contribution is presented using a concrete real-world use case and implementing the derivation rules for the EA modeling standard ArchiMate.

Keywords: Conceptual Modeling · Ontology-based Modeling · Enterprise Architecture Modeling · Ontology Engineering · Semantic Lifting · ArchiMate

1 Introduction

In *Enterprise Architecture Management (EAM)*, rules, constraints, and principles guide and govern the *Enterprise Architecture (EA)*. These can be formulated as executable statements and verified in enterprise models.

In our previous work, we operationalized the formalization of *EA principles* in machine-interpretable business rules to automate their validation in EA models [25,26]. The automatic validation of EA principles relies on the knowledge available in the EA models. We utilize the ontology-based meta-modeling approach [12] to automatically transform models in an enterprise ontology [11].

K. Hinkelmann et al. (Eds.): BIR 2023, LNBIP 493, pp. 244–259, 2023.
https://doi.org/10.1007/978-3-031-43126-5_18

However, a model (and, therefore, the enterprise ontology) may contain only a part of the relationships between elements. To increase readability, a modeler might focus on relevant relationships for an intended purpose and leave others implicit. For example, if in an ArchiMate model, an *Application Component* realizes an *Application Service* and the *Application Service* serves a *Business Process*, then the Application Component *serves* the Business Process. The *serve* relationship between the Application Component and the Business Process is implicit and does not need to be modeled. In this case, a *Derivation Rule* as defined by ArchiMate [37] allows for finding the serving relationship between the application component and the business process.

This example illustrates that EA models contain knowledge that machines cannot access. To address this issue, this research seeks to align the knowledge available to machines from EA models by converting derivation rules and using domain knowledge into a format that machines can interpret to infer missing relationships between elements. This supports the automatic validation of EA principles in Ea models.

The literature review (Sect. 2) identifies a research gap (Sect. 2.5) in using derivation rules and domain knowledge to support an automated validation for EA architecture principles in EA models. An analysis of the *impact of derivation rules for the validation of EA principles* is described in Sect. 4 using ArchiMate [37] for EA modeling. Then, we showcase how using domain knowledge and derivation rules - formalized in an enterprise ontology - can support the automatic validation of EA principles (Sect. 5.1). This implementation is evaluated with a concrete use case from a running project at FHNW (Sect. 6).

2   Literature Review

The section starts by providing a brief introduction - as a background - on *Enterprise Ontology* (Sect. 2.1), *Enterprise Design* (Sect. 2.2), and *EA Management and EA Principles* (Sect. 2.3). Based on these findings and looking at related works, it is shown how *EA models and principles* (Sect. 2.4) can be represented using enterprise ontologies. However, EA models' knowledge goes beyond what is modeled, and we claim that derivation rules and domain knowledge (Sect. 2.5) can be used to infer implicit knowledge from the models usable for automatic reasoning, hence supporting the validation of EA principles.

2.1   Enterprise Ontology

Ontologies help eliminate and reduce conceptual errors and terminological confusions to shape a common understanding [38]. Focusing on the formalization of the shared conceptualization, a definition of ontology is:

> *"An ontology is a formal, explicit specification of a shared conceptualization characterized by high semantic expressiveness required for increased complexity."* [6]

An *Enterprise Ontology* is a conceptual model of the enterprise that can be used to understand the essence of an enterprise in a comprehensive, coherent, consistent, and concise way. According to Dietz and Mulder [5], *Enterprise Ontology* is one of the pillars of Enterprise Engineering that can be used to achieve *intellectual manageability*. The notions of enterprise ontology as applied in [6,38] are regarded by Dietz and Mulder [5] as *world ontology*. Such world ontologies focus on defining entities of the represented "world" and their property types most clearly and extensively. Instead, a *system ontology* focuses on understanding the essence of the construction and operation of systems [5] - in this case, the Enterprise.

2.2 Enterprise Design

Organizational concinnity aims to design, engineer, and implement the enterprise coherently and consistently [5]. EA modeling describes how an enterprise operates, creating a "blueprint" of how it should operate, and roadmapping the strategic plan for achieving its future state. The Open Group Architecture Framework (TOGAF) prescribes the creation of different architectural artifacts in the various phases of the *Architecture Development Method (ADM)* [36, Sect. 31]. An enterprise model represents elements of an enterprise, including structure, processes, information resources, actors, products, etc. [7]. ArchiMate [37] is one of the widely used EA modeling languages to develop EA Models.

2.3 EA Management and EA Principles

EA governance is presented as a building block of successful EA management and the EA management organization [2]. Typically, enterprises should define their governance bodies, roles, and responsibilities. Such a governance organization structure ensures the transparency of decision-making and the propagation of EA principles [2], achieving *social devotion*. Ahlemann et al. [2, p. 20] define:

> *Enterprise Architecture Management is a management practice that establishes, maintains, and uses a coherent set of guidelines, architecture principles and governance regimes that provide direction for and practical help with the design and the development of an enterprise's architecture to achieve its vision and strategy.*

Among other definitions of EAM, this definition emphasizes establishing, maintaining, and using EA principles, guidelines, and governance regimes. Validating EA principles in EA models is a difficult procedure for EA practitioners. This is mostly because EA principles and EA models have distinct representations that are often not machine-interpretable. While principles, guidelines, and governance regimes are written in prose, EA models are depicted visually in models. EA principles are "declarative statements that can be made more specific using design instructions. The latter can take the form of architecture models in a language such as ArchiMate" [8, p. 58]. This further complicates the necessary constant monitoring procedure on EA, potentially making it error-prone and time-consuming.

An EA principle shall be *sufficiently specific* so that it can be validated for correctness and represented *formally* to allow automatic validation [8,24]. EA principles can be described formally, semi-formally, and informally [8,26]. Business rules languages like RuleSpeak can be used to formalize rules semi-formally. [31] is a set of guidelines for expressing business rules using a natural language. R. Ross [31] defines:

- a *Governing Statement* describes a law, act, statute, regulation, business policy, or similar communication or directive in prose;
- a *Practicable statement* declares in well-structured English, the governing statement for direct use by workers or other authorized parties within some operational business process(es) or decision-making task(s);
- an *Implementation Statement* is specified in a form suitable for designing or implementing some automated system(s).

Following the step-by-step procedure in [26], EA principles are considered governing statements that can be transformed into practicable and implementation statements. As a result of the procedure, EA principles can be operationalized as business rules in Structured English Notation and translated into SPARQL queries [29]. This allows the automatic validation of EA principles which use an enterprise ontology as vocabulary.

2.4 EA Models and Principles Knowledge Representation

Semantic lifting transforms a (language) metamodel into an ontology representing the concepts covered by the modeling language [15]. Enterprise modeling can represent enterprise knowledge in a human-readable (diagrammatic) and machine-readable format (as long as it is sufficiently formal and granular) [18]. Formal enablers such as metamodels, metamodelling platforms, and formal language grammars can enable machine-interpretability and automation of certain reasoning tasks [18] such as EA ontology-based analysis [3,4,32]. Ontologies (or knowledge graphs) can help explicitly represent a language's concepts and enable tasks like logical reasoning and instances classifications [17,33].

Ontology-based Metamodeling (OBM) [12] can be used to represent the content of an EA model in a machine-interpretable format. It is proposed as a variant to the Meta Object Facility (MOF) meta-modeling framework [28] (and above-mentioned related works [16,17,33]) where ontologies are used instead of UML as metamodeling language [10]. Through semantic lifting, the structure and semantics are kept divided from the notation, and a mapping is created to link the graphical representation with the respective structure and semantics [12]. OBM can transform EA models into EA ontology-based models automatically [1]. The Agile and Ontology-aided Modelling Environment (AOAME) [22] is built according to the OBM approach and uses the enterprise ontology ArchiMEO [11].

2.5   Research Gap: Derivation Rules

A derivation rule enables automated reasoning over models to detect relevant properties as inconsistencies, and redundancies and derive implicit constructs [34]. Different modeling languages provide specific constructs for defining derived types and derivation rules [27]. For example, Object Constraint Language (OCL) can express derivation rules in UML class invariants and derivation rules [9].

In ArchiMate [37], derivation rules create valid relationships without the constituents explicit (missing intermediary elements) of the derivation available in the model; in other words, these implicit elements are assumed to exist but not graphically modeled. Omitting these implicit relationships from the model may allow better readability for humans, but the machine would not capture their knowledge unless inferred.

Derivation rules can be applied to the models, creating a complete overview of the relationships. This (hyper-) model (with all the possible admitted relationships between the elements) would be significantly less legible for a human. However, generating this (hyper-) model is necessary for a machine to fully understand the model's knowledge.

When applying Ontology-based metamodelling [12] (or–more generally–semantic lifting [10]), part of the knowledge implicit in the model cannot be directly captured in the enterprise ontology. Derivation rules allow inferring relations between elements based on other relations in a model. The derivation rules' impact is further analyzed in Sect. 4.

3   Methodology

This research contributes to the work on EA principles' automatic validation from [26] by formalizing derivation rules and using domain knowledge.

We use ArchiMate modeling language as an exemplary EA modeling language and the derivation rules prescribed in the ArchiMate specification [37, Appendix B]. ArchiMate derivation rules are used to infer indirect relationships between elements. An extensive list of permitted relationships is provided in the ArchiMate specification. There are two types of derivations rules, given the different semantics of the relationships (e.g., structural and dependency relationships):

- *valid derivations* are certainly true in any model where these rules apply.
- *potential derivations* are potentially true but uncertain.

We formalize the valid derivation rules from the ArchiMate Standard using SPARQL [29] Constructs. We prove that derivation rules can be used with domain knowledge to support the automatic validation of EA principles. Accordingly, the research can be generalized and extended with additional derivation rules from other modeling languages.

4   Impact of Derivation Rules for the Validation of EA Principles

TOGAF [36] describes a sample set of Enterprise Architecture Principles. The principle "Common Use Applications" prescribes reducing duplicative applications [36, Principle 5, Chap. 20.6]:

Principle 5: Common Use Applications
Statement: Development of applications used across the enterprise is preferred over the development of similar or duplicative applications which are only provided to a particular organization.
Rationale: Duplicative capability is expensive and proliferates conflicting data.

To check this principle, two things have to be recognized:

1. if two Application Components are the same or similar
2. if an Application Component is a duplication, i.e., if the same or similar application is used in several organizations

4.1   Using Derivation Rules

An indication for the check whether two application components are similar or the same is that they realize the same services or functions. This is visualized in Fig. 1. As APP1 and APP2 realize the same service, it can be concluded that they are same or similar. Thus, this situation violated the Architecture Principle, because APP1 and APP2 are used in two business processes.

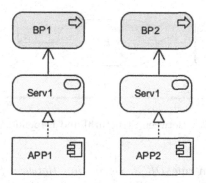

Fig. 1. Two application components realizing similar service, with same label

An automated check might look for common Application Services realized by two or more Application Components. The check must recognize that the two components APP1 and APP2 realize an Application Service called Serv1.

IF
$\{ApplicationComponents = \{APP1, APP2\} \wedge$
$ApplicationServices = \{Serv1\} \wedge$
$APP1$ realizes $Serv1 \wedge APP2$ realizes $Serv1\}$

THEN $DuplicativeApplicationComponents = \{APP1, APP2\}$

After recognizing that APP1 and APP2 are similar, one has to check whether they are used in several organizations. An indicator that there are duplicate Application Components could be that similar components are used in different Business Processes. However, in Fig. 1, there is no direct connection between the Application Components and the Business Processes. This is where we can apply derivation rules.

The notation of the derivation rules is taken from [37, Appendix B]. p(a,b):R is used to describe the relationship with name p that has concept a as source, concept b as target, and R as its relationship type. Concepts are named a, b, and c in order of appearance, relationships are named p, q, and r in order of appearance, and relationship types are named S, T, and U in order of appearance.

The *DR 3: Derivation Between Structural and Dependency Relationships* prescribes that:

"If two relationships p(a,b):S and q(b,c):T exist, with S being a structural relationship and T being a dependency relationship, then a relationship r(a,c):T can be derived" [37].

The model in Fig. 2 shows the representation of the DR3. The derived relationship *r* is added in red.

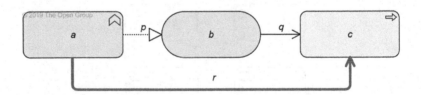

Fig. 2. DR 3: Derivation Between Structural and Dependency Relationships [37]

With the derivation rule *DR 3: Derivation Between Structural and Dependency Relationships* [37], it is possible to derive that the Application Components APP1 and APP2 serve Business Processes BP1 and BP2, respectively (Fig. 3).

With the knowledge that these Application Components are similar (see above), it can be concluded that similar Application Components are used in different Business Processes. Thus the Architecture Principle "Common Use Applications" [36, Principle 5, Chap. 20.6] is violated.

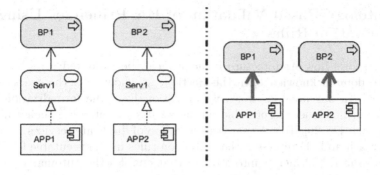

Fig. 3. Result of DR3 (in red) compared with Fig. 1

4.2   Using Derivation Rules and Domain Knowledge

In the example above, recognizing the similarity of Application Components is easy, because the two realized Application Services have the same label. In reality, the views can be created by different people who use different names for these Services, although they have the same meaning. For example, while one person might name the service for creating an invoice "Invoicing" another might call it "Billing".

Knowledge about the semantics of terms is needed to recognize this. In this case, it is just that invoicing and billing are synonyms. In real applications, similarity identification can even require more sophisticated domain knowledge.

> IF
> $\{ApplicationComponents = \{APP1, APP2\}\land$
> $ApplicationServices = \{Serv1, Serv2\}\land$
> $APP1$ realizes $Serv1 \land APP2$ realizes $Serv2\land$
> $Serv1 \sim Serv2\}$
> THEN $DiplicativeApplicationComponents = \{APP1, APP2\}$

ArchiMate models can be analyzed using the knowledge engineering space from [19] to represent the knowledge of EA models in an enterprise ontology. We distinguish between *meta-model ontology* and *application domain ontology* [26]. The *meta-model ontology* contains the knowledge about the modeling language's syntax and semantics, corresponding to the *form*. The *application domain ontology* specifies the vocabulary that can be used for the labels of the modeling elements. It can contain common-agreed terminology like Invoicing but might also contain enterprise-specific terms like product names.

The ArchiMEO enterprise ontology [11] integrates both the application domain and meta-model ontologies. It contains the ontology representation of the ArchiMate meta-model [37], and it is designed as an extendable ontology that can be specialized for different use cases [11,23,30].

5 Ontology-Based Validation of EA Principles Using Derivation Rules

Section 4 shows how Architecture Principles can be validated using derivation rules and domain knowledge. In this Section, we show, how the checks can be automated. In our previous work, we operationalized the formalization of EA principles in machine-interpretable business rules to automate their validation in EA models [25,26]. To automate the detection of duplicate services, we extend this approach and (1) represent the derivation rules in an executable format; (2) transform the EA Principle into a query that enables the automated violation check.

5.1 Creation of Ontology-Based Derivation Rules

The following section describes how each valid derivation rule can be implemented using SPARQL [29] Constructs to infer new derived relationships. A construct query can be created for each derivation rule based on the ArchiMate specifications [37, Sect. B.1]. This implementation uses the notations from the ArchiMEO enterprise ontology [11].

As described in Sect. 4.1, the DR3 (see Fig. 2) can be written in SPARQL as a Construct as shown in Listing 1.1. Based on the DR3, the query generates a new relationshipR with the source element from RelationshipP, the target element, and the relationship type of RelationshipQ.

```
CONSTRUCT {
 mod:RelationshipR a ?relationshipQType .
 mod:RelationshipR
      lo:modelingRelationHasSourceModelingElement ?conceptA .
 mod:RelationshipR
      lo:modelingRelationHasTargetModelingElement ?conceptC . }
WHERE {
 ?relationshipP
      lo:modelingRelationHasSourceModelingElement ?conceptA .
 ?relationshipP
      lo:modelingRelationHasTargetModelingElement ?conceptB .
 ?relationshipP  a ?relationshipPType .
 ?relationshipPType rdfs:subClassOf archi:StructuralRelationships .
 ?relationshipQ
      lo:modelingRelationHasSourceModelingElement ?conceptB .
 ?relationshipQ
      lo:modelingRelationHasTargetModelingElement ?conceptC .
 ?relationshipQ      a ?relationshipQType .
 ?relationshipQType rdfs:subClassOf archi:DependencyRelationships .}
```

Listing 1.1. DR3 written as SPARQL query

Based on the model in Fig. 2, the resulting inferred new Relationship r shall be a serve relationship connecting the is as follows:

```
mod:RelationshipR   a                    archi:Serve ;
  lo:modelingRelationHasSourceModelingElement
                      mod:ApplicationFunction_A ;
  lo:modelingRelationHasTargetModelingElement
                      mod:BusinessProcess_C .
```

Listing 1.2. Newly created Relationship r based on DR3

5.2 Automatic Validation of EA Principles Using Derivation Rules

The first step to validate the "Common Use Applications" EA principle (see Sect. 4) is to recognize whether two application components are similar, either by comparing the labels (see Listing 1.3) or using domain knowledge (see Listing 1.4). Both queries check whether the two application components are different but similar and, if so, infer that the applications are potentially duplicative.

```
CONSTRUCT { ?AppComp1 a eo:PotentialDuplicativeApplication . }
WHERE {
 ?AppComp1 a archi:ApplicationComponent .
 ?AppComp2 a archi:ApplicationComponent .
 ?AppComp1 rdfs:label ?label .
 ?AppComp2 rdfs:label ?label .
 FILTER (?AppComp1 != ?AppComp2 )
 }
```

Listing 1.3. Infer which elements are similar comparing the labels

5.3 Using Formalized Domain Knowledge

In contrast to Listing 1.3, Listing 1.4 checks whether two applications (?AppComp1 and ?AppComp2) have a common usage. In [21], the ArchiMEO ontology [11] was used to annotate business processes with the Process Classification Framework (PCF) from the American Productivity and Quality Center (APQC). We can express this also in EA models using (?AppUsage) and the object relationship eo:AppIsUsedFor. The following query infers that an Application Component is potentially duplicative if two different Application Components AppComp1 and AppComp2 are used for the same usage (?AppUsage), i.e. they have the same APQC process classification.

```
CONSTRUCT { ?AppComp1 a eo:PotentialDuplicativeApplication . }
WHERE {
 ?AppUsage  a apqc:AmericanProductivityAndQualityCenter .
 ?AppComp1 a archi:ApplicationComponent .
 ?AppComp2 a archi:ApplicationComponent .
 ?AppComp1 eo:AppIsUsedFor ?AppUsage .
 ?AppComp2 eo:AppIsUsedFor ?AppUsage .
 FILTER (?AppComp1 != ?AppComp2 )
 }
```

Listing 1.4. Infer which elements are similar using domain knowledge

Once the system can automatically recognize similar applications and derive the serving relationships between the Application Component and Business Process using the DR3 (see Listing 1.1), we can finally check if these applications are duplicative (see Listing 1.5).

```
SELECT ?DuplicativeApp ?rel ?BusinessProcesses WHERE {
?rel lo:modelingRelationHasSourceModelingElement
                                ?DuplicativeApplication .
?DuplicativeApp a archi:ApplicationComponent .
?DuplicativeApp a eo:PotentialDuplicativeApp .
?rel lo:modelingRelationHasTargetModelingElement
                                ?BusinessProcesses .
?BusinessProcesses a archi:BusinessProcess .}
```

Listing 1.5. Identification of business processes served by duplicative applications

6   Evaluation

FHNW University of Applied Sciences and Arts Northwestern Switzerland[1] comprises nine schools, each with various institutes. The *Update Inside FHNW* project has the goal to standardize the application stack across study programs, reducing duplicative applications, and addressing the principles "Principle 5: Common Use Applications" [36, Principle 5, Chap. 20.6].

Different study programs have independent onboarding processes supported by different applications (e.g., ONLA and a File-Based Application (FBApp) for study programs 1 and 2). This scenario can be visualized using the EA model (Fig. 4 on the left).

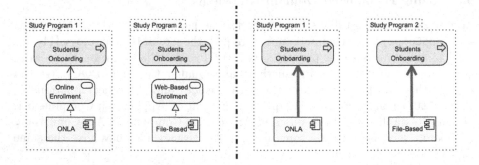

Fig. 4. Example of duplicative applications from FHNW

The model is created in the Agile Ontology Aided Modelling Environment (AOAME) to transfer the model's knowledge into ontology automatically and annotate the application components ONLA and FBApp with the APQC [14] "execute onboarding program", category 7.3.1.3 .

---

[1] https://www.fhnw.ch/en/about-fhnw/schools.

```
mod:ApplicationService_Online_Enrollment
  a          mod:ConceptualElement , archi:ApplicationService .
mod:ApplicationComponent_ONLA
  a          mod:ConceptualElement , archi:ApplicationComponent ;
eo:AppIsUsedFor apqc:7_3_1_3_Execute_onboarding_program_17050 .
mod:Realization_ONLA_Online_Enrollment
  a          mod:ConceptualElement , archi:Realization ;
  lo:modelingRelationHasSourceModelingElement
            mod:ApplicationComponent_ONLA ;
  lo:modelingRelationHasTargetModelingElement
            mod:ApplicationService_Online_Enrollment .
```

Listing 1.6. Example elements and relationships in AOAME

In this case, the services realized by the ONLA and FBApp are similar but named differently in the model. As we captured these applications' usage in the enterprise ontology, we can automatically infer their similarity using the rule (Listing 1.4).

```
mod:ApplicationComponent_ONLA
  a          eo:PotentialDuplicativeApplication .
mod:ApplicationComponent_FBApp
  a          eo:PotentialDuplicativeApplication .
```

Listing 1.7. Results on ONLA and FBApp inferred similarity

Using the DR3 (Listing 1.1), we can infer the serving relationships from ONLA and FBApp to their respective "Student Onboarding" Business Processes (see Fig. 4 on the right).

```
mod:Serve_R1 a  mod:ConceptualElement , archi:Serve ;
  lo:modelingRelationHasSourceModelingElement
                        mod:ApplicationComponent_ONLA ;
  lo:modelingRelationHasTargetModelingElement
                        mod:BusinessProcess_StOnboarding1 .
mod:Serve_R2 a  mod:ConceptualElement , archi:Serve ;
  lo:modelingRelationHasSourceModelingElement
                        mod:ApplicationComponent_FBApp ;
  lo:modelingRelationHasTargetModelingElement
                        mod:BusinessProcess_StOnboarding2 .
```

Listing 1.8. Derived serving relationships between processes and applications

Having these newly inferred relationships, we can execute the validation query (Listing 1.5) to identify the duplicative applications and the related processes. The following screenshot (Fig. 5) shows the violation of the EA principle, listing the two duplicative applications.

DuplicativeApplication	rel	BusinessProcesses
1 mod:ApplicationComponent_ONLA	mod:Serve_R1	mod:BusinessProcess_StOnboarding1
2 mod:ApplicationComponent_PLONE	mod:Serve_R2	mod:BusinessProcess_StOnboarding2

Showing 1 to 2 of 2 entries

Fig. 5. Results from the query in the Listing 1.5 executed in Apache Jena Fuseki

7 Conclusion

This research utilizes ontology-based metamodelling to transform EA models in an enterprise ontology automatically. An ontology-based enterprise architecture model can validate machine-interpretable EA principles formulated with the approach proposed in [26].

The main artifact of this research is a formalization of derivation rules from the ArchiMate Standard using SPARQL Constructs. This research confirmed and extended the previous work on EA model interpretation [26] by formalizing derivation rules to infer knowledge from models, which is implicit for the human, but absent for the machine. We prove that derivation rules can be combined with domain knowledge to support EA principles validation, but may be used more generally for reasoning over the models e.g. to aid the recognition of "enterprise smells" [33].

This has been shown with the modeling language ArchiMate [37], using the modeling environment AOAME [22] in the enterprise ontology ArchiMEO [11] for the EA principles validation, but the same formalization can be done also for other modeling languages.

Future work will investigate the generality of the approach and alternative technical implementations for the derivation rules and EA principles validation. Preliminary work has been conducted using SHACL rules[20], SHEX [35], and SWIRL [13].

References

1. Afonina, V., Hinkelmann, K., Montecchiari, D.: Enriching enterprise architecture models with healthcare domain knowledge. In: Ruiz, M., Soffer, P. (eds.) Advanced Information Systems Engineering Workshops, CAiSE 2023. LNBIP, vol. 482, pp. 17–28. Springer, Cham (2023). https://doi.org/10.1007/978-3-031-34985-0_2
2. Ahlemann, F., Stettiner, E., Messerschmidt, M., Legner, C. (eds.): Strategic Enterprise Architecture Management: Challenges, Best Practices, and Future Developments. Springer, Heidelberg (2012). https://doi.org/10.1007/978-3-642-24223-6
3. Antunes, G., Bakhshandeh, M., Mayer, R., Borbinha, J., Caetano, A.: Using ontologies for enterprise architecture integration and analysis. Complex Syst. Inform. Model. Q. 1(1), 1–23 (2014)

4. Caetano, A., et al.: Representation and analysis of enterprise models with semantic techniques: an application to ArchiMate, e3value and business model canvas. Knowl. Inf. Syst. **50**(1), 315–346 (2017)
5. Dietz, J.L., Mulder, H.B.: Enterprise Ontology. A Human-Centric Approach to Understanding the Essence of Organisation. Springer, Cham (2020). https://doi.org/10.1007/978-3-030-38854-6
6. Feilmayr, C., Wöß, W.: An analysis of ontologies and their success factors for application to business. Data Knowl. Eng. **101**, 1–23 (2016)
7. Fox, M.S., Gruninger, M.: Enterprise modeling. AI Mag. **19**(3), 109 (1998)
8. Greefhorst, D., Proper, E.: Architecture Principles: The Cornerstones of Enterprise Architecture. Springer, Heidelberg (2011). https://doi.org/10.1007/978-3-642-20279-7
9. Guerson, J., Sales, T.P., Guizzardi, G., Almeida, J.P.A.: OntoUML lightweight editor: a model-based environment to build, evaluate and implement reference ontologies. In: 2015 IEEE 19th International Enterprise Distributed Object Computing Workshop, pp. 144–147. ieeexplore.ieee.org, September 2015
10. Hinkelmann, K., Gerber, A., Karagiannis, D., Thoenssen, B., van der Merwe, A., Woitsch, R.: A new paradigm for the continuous alignment of business and it: combining enterprise architecture modelling and enterprise ontology. Comput. Ind. **79**, 77–86 (2016)
11. Hinkelmann., K., Laurenzi., E., Martin., A., Montecchiari., D., Spahic., M., Thönssen., B.: ArchiMEO: a standardized enterprise ontology based on the ArchiMate conceptual model. In: Proceedings of the 8th International Conference on Model-Driven Engineering and Software Development - Volume 1: MODELSWARD, pp. 417–424. INSTICC, SciTePress (2020). https://doi.org/10.5220/0009000204170424
12. Hinkelmann, K., Laurenzi, E., Martin, A., Thönssen, B.: Ontology-based metamodeling. In: Dornberger, R. (ed.) Business Information Systems and Technology 4.0. SSDC, vol. 141, pp. 177–194. Springer, Cham (2018). https://doi.org/10.1007/978-3-319-74322-6_12
13. Horrocks, I., Patel-Schneider, P.F., Boley, H., Tabet, S., Grosof, B., Dean, M., et al.: SWRL: a semantic web rule language combining OWL and RuleML. W3C Member Submission **21**(79), 1–31 (2004)
14. Hubert, C., Lemons, D.: APQC's levels of knowledge management maturity. APQC **2010**, 1–5 (2010)
15. Kappel, G., et al.: Lifting metamodels to ontologies: a step to the semantic integration of modeling languages. In: Nierstrasz, O., Whittle, J., Harel, D., Reggio, G. (eds.) MODELS 2006. LNCS, vol. 4199, pp. 528–542. Springer, Heidelberg (2006). https://doi.org/10.1007/11880240_37
16. Karagiannis, D., Bork, D., Utz, W.: Metamodels as a conceptual structure: some semantical and syntactical operations. In: Bergener, K., Räckers, M., Stein, A. (eds.) The Art of Structuring, pp. 75–86. Springer, Cham (2019). https://doi.org/10.1007/978-3-030-06234-7_8
17. Karagiannis, D., Buchmann, R.A.: A proposal for deploying hybrid knowledge bases: the ADOxx-to-GraphDB interoperability case. In: Hawaii International Conference on System Sciences 2018 (HICSS-51) (2018)
18. Karagiannis, D., Buchmann, R.A., Bork, D.: Managing consistency in multi-view enterprise models: an approach based on semantic queries. In: European Conference on Information Systems (2016)

19. Karagiannis, D., Woitsch, R.: Knowledge engineering in business process management. In: vom Brocke, J., Rosemann, M. (eds.) Handbook on Business Process Management 2. IHIS, pp. 623–648. Springer, Heidelberg (2015). https://doi.org/10.1007/978-3-642-45103-4_26
20. Knublauch, H., Kontokostas, D.: Shapes constraint language (SHACL). Technical report, W3C, July 2017. https://www.w3.org/TR/shacl/
21. Kritikos, K., Laurenzi, E., Hinkelmann, K.: Towards business-to-IT alignment in the cloud. In: Mann, Z.Á., Stolz, V. (eds.) ESOCC 2017. CCIS, vol. 824, pp. 35–52. Springer, Cham (2018). https://doi.org/10.1007/978-3-319-79090-9_3
22. Laurenzi, E., Hinkelmann, K., van der Merwe, A.: An agile and ontology-aided modeling environment. In: Buchmann, R.A., Karagiannis, D., Kirikova, M. (eds.) PoEM 2018. LNBIP, vol. 335, pp. 221–237. Springer, Cham (2018). https://doi.org/10.1007/978-3-030-02302-7_14
23. Laurenzi, E., Hinkelmann, K., Montecchiari, D., Goel, M.: Agile visualization in design thinking. In: Dornberger, R. (ed.) New Trends in Business Information Systems and Technology. SSDC, vol. 294, pp. 31–47. Springer, Cham (2021). https://doi.org/10.1007/978-3-030-48332-6_3
24. Marosin, D., van Zee, M., Ghanavati, S.: Formalizing and modeling enterprise architecture (EA) principles with goal-oriented requirements language (GRL). In: Nurcan, S., Soffer, P., Bajec, M., Eder, J. (eds.) CAiSE 2016. LNCS, vol. 9694, pp. 205–220. Springer, Cham (2016). https://doi.org/10.1007/978-3-319-39696-5_13
25. Montecchiari, D.: Ontology-based validation of enterprise architecture principles in enterprise models. In: BIR 2021 Workshops and Doctoral Consortium, co-located with 20th International Conference on Perspectives in Business Informatics Research, Vienna, Austria, 22–24 September 2021. http://ceur-ws.org/Vol-2991/
26. Montecchiari, D., Hinkelmann, K.: Towards ontology-based validation of EA principles. In: Barn, B.S., Sandkuhl, K. (eds.) The Practice of Enterprise Modeling, PoEM 2022. LNBIP, vol. 456, pp. 66–81. Springer, Cham (2022). https://doi.org/10.1007/978-3-031-21488-2_5
27. Olivé, A.: Derivation rules in object-oriented conceptual modeling languages. In: Eder, J., Missikoff, M. (eds.) CAiSE 2003. LNCS, vol. 2681, pp. 404–420. Springer, Heidelberg (2003). https://doi.org/10.1007/3-540-45017-3_28
28. OMG: Meta object facility (MOF) core specification, version 2.4.2. Technical report, Object Management Group (2014). https://www.omg.org/spec/MOF/2.4.2/PDF
29. Pérez, J., Arenas, M., Gutierrez, C.: Semantics and complexity of SPARQL. ACM Trans. Database Syst. (TODS) **34**(3), 1–45 (2009)
30. Peter, M., Montecchiari, D., Hinkelmann, K., Gatziu Grivas, S.: Ontology-based visualization for business model design. In: Grabis, J., Bork, D. (eds.) PoEM 2020. LNBIP, vol. 400, pp. 244–258. Springer, Cham (2020). https://doi.org/10.1007/978-3-030-63479-7_17
31. Ross: Basic RuleSpeak Guidelines. Do's and Don'ts in Expressing Natural-Language (2009)
32. Santana, A., Simon, D., Fischbach, K., de Moura, H.: Combining network measures and expert knowledge to analyze enterprise architecture at the component level. In: 2016 IEEE 20th International Enterprise Distributed Object Computing Conference (EDOC), pp. 1–10, September 2016
33. Smajevic, M., Hacks, S., Bork, D.: Using knowledge graphs to detect enterprise architecture smells. In: Serral, E., Stirna, J., Ralyté, J., Grabis, J. (eds.) PoEM 2021. LNBIP, vol. 432, pp. 48–63. Springer, Cham (2021). https://doi.org/10.1007/978-3-030-91279-6_4

34. Sportelli, F., Franconi, E.: Formalisation of ORM derivation rules and their mapping into OWL. In: Debruyne, C., et al. (eds.) OTM 2016. LNCS, vol. 10033, pp. 827–843. Springer, Cham (2016). https://doi.org/10.1007/978-3-319-48472-3_52
35. Staworko, S., Boneva, I., Gayo, J.E.L., Hym, S., Prud'Hommeaux, E.G., Solbrig, H.: Complexity and expressiveness of ShEx for RDF. In: 18th International Conference on Database Theory, ICDT 2015 (2015)
36. The Open Group: TOGAF 9 - The Open Group Architecture Framework, vol. 9 (2009)
37. The Open Group: ArchiMate 3.2 Specification (2023)
38. Uschold, M., King, M., Moralee, S., Zorgios, Y.: The enterprise ontology. Knowl. Eng. Rev. **13**, 31–89 (1998). Special Issue on Putting Ontologies to Use

Towards a Framework for Intelligent Cyber-Physical System (iCPS) Design

Sofía Abadía[1,2]([✉]) [ID], Oscar Avila[1] [ID], and Virginie Goepp[2] [ID]

[1] Universidad de Los Andes, Cra 1 N° 18A-12, Bogota, Colombia
{s.abadia,oj.avila}@uniandes.edu.co
[2] ICube INSA Strasbourg, 24 Boulevard de la Victoire, Strasbourg, France
virginie.goepp@insa-strasbourg.fr

Abstract. Cyber-Physical Systems (CPS) are considered as an important tool in Industry 4.0. They provide companies with advantages and benefits by enabling the interconnection of machines and physical devices to digital systems, allowing a real-time data-driven decision-making process. However, for the CPS to be able to support decision-making within the production process of manufacturing companies, a set of technological components need to be implemented and integrated. This paper aims to identify those components by conducting an academic literature review that also allows to understand the use of intelligent CPS in the industry. From the identification of the components, a model for an CPS architecture is proposed. The aim of the model is helping companies be prepared and informed about the layers and components that need to be considered when adopting and implementing a CPS.

Keywords: Cyber-Physical Systems (CPS) · Technological components · Architecture model · decision-making

1 Introduction

New advances on technology are leveraging the Industry 4.0, where tools like the Cyber-Physical System (CPS) play a major role [1]. The combination of physical components like sensors, actuators and controllers, and cyber components such as analysis, optimization and simulation algorithms, makes the CPS a really influential tool with the power of impacting different processes of an enterprise. The main purpose of the CPS is to integrate or "link the physical world with the virtual through flexible, cooperative, and interactive operation" [1].

The CPS is being used in different sectors like transportation, energy and manufacturing. In the manufacturing context, the CPS helps to collect data from the machines on the production line and, subsequently, to analyse it in order to identify actual or possible problems and improve the production performance. The analysis that the CPS provides can contribute to the decision-making process at workshop level.

The involvement of the CPS along the decision-making process is changing the way the interactions between humans and systems happen, as humans are delegating operational and tactical decisions to the CPS with the aim of automating and dynamically

K. Hinkelmann et al. (Eds.): BIR 2023, LNBIP 493, pp. 260–274, 2023.
https://doi.org/10.1007/978-3-031-43126-5_19

updating the production parameters or resources [2]. This opens the way for a more efficient real-time data-driven decision-making process where the interconnection between machines and logical systems enable the automation of procedures [1].

To do so, the CPS needs a certain set of physical and logical components to facilitate the analysis required for decision-making. In this context, a research question is formulated as follows "Which are the components and functionalities that enable a CPS to take part in decision-making within the production processes?". The purpose of this paper is thus to identify the technological components that are used by the CPS in order to make it intelligent and support different types of decision when designing and manufacturing products. This gives companies an advantage by helping them to make such processes more efficient.

To answer the research question, a systematic literature review is used as an analysis method with the aim of identifying the type of decisions that the CPS helps to make, the components that are currently used for a CPS and their function. To make the result clear and synthesize the findings, a model of the architecture of a CPS that support decision-making is proposed. This approach allows us additionally to identify important gaps to be addressed in further research work.

The paper is structured as follows. Section 2 presents the literature review, including the development methodology, the synthesis and the gap analysis. Section 3 describes the model proposed and presents a discussion regarding the benefits the model has for the companies that want to implement a "decision-making" CPS. Finally, Sect. 4 presents the conclusions and the future work.

2 Literature Review

2.1 Planning

In addition to identify CPS' components, functionalities and type of decisions, the literature review also seeks to determine at what organizational level it is most used and the level of automation of decision-making, i.e. whether it makes decisions on the basis of the analysis it performs or whether it provides operators with the information they need to make an informed decision.

The main selection criterion of academic articles is that their research subject is in one of the following areas: 1) implementation of a CPS, 2) use of a CPS at a specific organizational level for decision making support and 3) operation of a CPS to collect and process data and, finally, deliver recommendations. All the articles that meet the above criteria are considered as potential articles to be included into the literature review.

Once the research areas for the selection of articles are defined, an evaluation framework is developed, with which all the selected articles are evaluated and analyzed. This framework is structured in terms of three types of concepts, which are briefly described below.

1. Category: these are the main key points to be analyzed in the articles.
2. Criterion: each category has a set of criteria that help to evaluate the articles.
3. Research question: each criterion is associated with a research question, which is used to analyse the contribution of the article to the defined criteria.

Table 1 presents the evaluation framework developed for the analysis of the selected academic articles.

Table 1. Evaluation framework

Category	Criterion	Research question
Context	Size of the company	What is the size of the company studied in the article?
	Sector	Which is the sector of the company? (automotive, hardware, etc.)
	Organizational level	Which organizational level was impacted? (operational, tactical, strategic)
	Business process	Which subprocess of the production process was impacted?
CPS	Type of decision support	Does the CPS make the decision automatically, semi automatically or support it?
	Decision made	Which decisions are made/ supported/ impacted by the CPS?
	Impact	What is the impact that the support of the decision has over the organization? How is the impact measured?
	Intelligence components/functionalities	Which physical or logical components make the CPS intelligent?
		Which functionalities can the CPS perform that make it intelligent?

2.2 Realization

Having the evaluation criteria for the academic articles ready, a keyword search is started. The keywords selected describe the 3 important groups needed for the research, the first makes reference to the CPS, the second relates to the decision-making process and the third refers to the industrial sector/area. For this search, Scopus, a database that indexes academics articles published in different scientific journals, conference proceedings and book chapters, among others, is used. The query used for the research of the academic articles is presented below.

TITLE-ABS-KEY (("CPPS" OR "CPS" OR "iCPS" OR "COGNITIVE CPS" OR "CYBER PHYSICAL SYSTEMS" OR "CYBER PHYSICAL PRODUCTION SYSTEMS" OR "COGNITIVE CYBER PHYSICAL SYSTEMS") AND ("DECISION MAKING" OR "DECISION MAKING PROCESS") AND (MANUFACTORING OR PRODUCTION OR "DESIGN PRODUCT" OR INDUSTR)) AND (LIMIT-TO (SUBJAREA, "COMP")) AND (LIMIT-TO (PUBYEAR, 2023) OR LIMIT-TO (PUBYEAR, 2022) OR LIMIT-TO (*

PUBYEAR, 2021) OR LIMIT-TO (PUBYEAR, 2020) OR LIMIT-TO (PUBYEAR, 2019) OR LIMIT-TO (PUBYEAR, 2018) OR LIMIT-TO (PUBYEAR, 2017)).

As result, this query provides more than 300 records, which are downloaded to a spreadsheet with information like source, year, title and abstract. Once in the spreadsheet, a first screening of the records is performed according to the titles, verifying that the article has a relation with the research areas mentioned above; with this screening the number of articles is down to 100. Then another screening is performed by reading the article abstracts, which results in 45 articles. Finally, a third round of eliminations is conducted taking into consideration the source of the articles, selecting the articles from ranked journals and conferences, resulting in 26 articles. When reading the articles and applying the evaluation framework, it is found that certain articles are not of great relevance to the study because the analysis level they reached is too basic. At the end, the evaluation and analysis using the framework is made over 21 articles. In this case no backwards nor forward analysis is utilized.

2.3 Synthesis and Analysis

Based on the application of the review evaluation framework to the set of articles, a synthesis is presented indicating the similarities and differences between the articles and the conclusions reached.

What's the Size of the Companies Studied in the Articles?
Concerning this criterion, only in 4 out of the 21 articles the size of the company in which the study was performed is mentioned. In these cases, all of them [1-4] mention that the size of the company is small. In the other articles, no mention of the company's size is ever made so we cannot make a conclusion regarding the relevance of the company's size when implementing one of these systems. This fact could lead us to think that the size of the company has no influence on the definition of an architecture for a CPS.

Which is the Sector of the Company? (Automotive, Hardware, etc.)
Not all papers claim a specifically sector but say the CPS is implemented on a smart factory or is considered for one specific machine or workshop station within a laboratory, while others never mentioned a sector at all. Out of the 21 articles, 3 mentioned smart factories ([5-7]), 4 mentioned laboratory's workshops, machines or platforms ([2, 4, 8, 9]) and 2 did not mention any sector ([10, 11]). The other 12 articles mentioned explicitly one industry sector for the companies, but it is not possible to draw a conclusion as to the sector in which the CPS is mostly used as there is no single sector most frequently mentioned. In the articles the sectors range from mold making and resistance spot welding to beverage manufacturing and aerospace engine systems. Additionally, it is not possible to identify sector specific architecture components.

Which Business Processes Are Impacted?
The results of the literature review regarding this question are summarized in Table 2. In this analysis, we seek to determine whether the impact on each process is at a tactical or operational level. To do so, each type of impact is defined as follows: the CPS has an impact over the tactical level when it works on a process that includes a planification

activity, for instance, allocation planning, plant schedules or maintenance programming. On the other hand, it impacts the operational level when the process takes place during the production and directly affects it in real time, for example, identifying failures, controlling quality and security, etc.

The most mentioned business process is maintenance. According to the information collected from the articles, the CPS is mainly used to make decisions regarding the maintenance of machinery and the necessary reallocation of functionalities derived from this. In this case, the system can identify the machines that are not successfully completing their tasks and the reason of the malfunction. Having this information, the system creates a plan of maintenance for the machines and a plan of reallocation of resources so that the production can continue working in the best way. If the system is semi-automatic, once the CPS detects an anomaly on the machine, it is stopped, and a new scheduling and reallocation of functionalities plan is generated. This plan is then presented to an operator, who can continue with the recommended plan or make adjustments. In the case where the system just supports the decision, an alarm is generated when a machine fails, and the CPS generates the new plan and presents it to the operator. Once the operator has made her/his decision the instructions must be placed on each of the machines. The organizational level impacted in this case is the tactical level, as it requires the planification of the maintenance schedule and the plan of the resource allocation needed when a machine is in maintenance.

Other processes that are also mentioned are scheduling, resource allocation and control processes. The first 2 processes are addressed at the tactical level, while the last one (control processes) is tackled over the operational level. The scheduling and the resource allocation are considered as tactical processes for the same reason as maintenance, the CPS contributes to the processes with a generation of an action plan. In the case of the control processes, the operational level is impacted because it takes place during the production as it needs to be under constant supervision, aiming to identify a deficit on the quality production or a security problem. There is one case where the organizational level could not be identified [7] since this article mentions that different subprocesses are impacted by the CPS but fails to mention which ones.

Another finding is that there was no mention of the use of CPS at a strategic level; none of the articles mention a decision that the CPS has taken or supported at management level, all the decisions mentioned are taken at plant or shop floor level.

Table 2. Business process vs organizational level

	Tactical	Operational
Maintenance	[1, 5, 9, 10, 12–14]	
Scheduling	[1, 2, 6, 11, 12, 15]	
Control processes		[12, 16–18]

(continued)

Table 2. (*continued*)

	Tactical	Operational
Resource allocation	[3, 4, 19, 20]	
Mass individualization	[8]	
Stockpiling process		[21]
Different processes	[7]*	[7] *

Does the CPS Take the Decision Automatically or Support It?

The articles are separated based on the way the CPS makes decision. During our literature review 3 type of decision processes are identified: automatic, semi-automatic, and supported decision processes.

In the automatic process the CPS collects all the data from the sensors or wearable devices, process it, defines a plan and execute it all by itself. In this case, all the information, the plan, the implementation report and the results are reported to an operator so he/she can have knowledge of everything that was conducted. On the other hand, in the semiautomatic process, once the data is processed, the system gives a recommended plan of action to the operator for its validation; this plan is executed by a combination of human operators and machines. Lastly, in the case of supported decision-making process, the CPS can be seen as a supporting mechanism that gives the relevant information to the operator so she/he can make a plan and later send the instructions to the machine to execute the plan.

In Table 3 the articles are classified, for each type of business process concerned, according to the way the decision is made. It can be seen that in most of the articles, the CPS operates in a semi-automatic way, i.e., developing a plan that needs the operator approval before executing it on the connected machines. An example for each process is presented next.

An automatic decision-making process can be seen in [21], where the CPS is used for the stockpiling process. In this process the machines pick the product from the production belt and place it on a pile. For this the CPS identifies the form of the pile and the number of products already placed through cameras and sensors. With this info, the CPS can determine if more products need to be added to the pile or if the pile is complete and piling should be stopped. In the case where product should be added it also determines where to place it so the pile does not fall. All this process is completely automatic, as the system gives the instructions to the robotic arms for their execution.

On the other hand, [13] presents a semiautomatic model in which the physical components collect data regarding the status of the machines and products that help identify current or future failures. Here, the CPS process the data and creates a list of plans that can help solve the problem. The plans are presented to the operator for her/his validation and then the operator selects the plan to be executed. Once the operator selects the plan, the CPS passes the instructions to the machines and execute them.

Finally, in the case of the support process, [9] presents a CPS configuration for the prediction of failures of the machines. The historical data is analyzed for the identification of possible future problems. In case a possible problem is identified, the information is passed to an operator with a description of the problem so she/he can applicate a solution.

Table 3. Decision-making process vs Business process

	Automatic	Semi-automatic	Support
Maintenance	[5]	[1, 12–14]	[9, 10]
Scheduling	[2, 6]	[1]	[11, 15]
Control processes		[12, 16–18]	
Resource allocation	[3, 4]		[19, 20]
Mass individualization			[8]
Stockpiling process	[21]		
Different processes			[7]

As seen in Table 3, only in 6 articles the decision is made autonomously by the CPS. The fact that such a little number of articles studied an automatic decision-making CPS shows that the human operator still has a relevant role in the decision-making process. In most cases an operator needs to at least validate that the plan presented by the CPS is, in fact, feasible and should be executed. Even when the CPS is completely autonomous, a human - let it be an operator, a leader or a manager - needs to be informed of the decision, the plan, the execution process and the results obtained.

Which Decisions Were Made or Supported by the CPS?
Different decisions are made depending on the business process supported by the CPS. These decisions are made based on the type of data collected and the analysis made during the process. That is why Table 4 shows the result of crossing the type of analysis that the CPS performs (diagnostic, predictive, prescriptive) and the decision-making process (automatic, semiautomatic, support).

It can be seen that in most of the articles the CPS performs a diagnostic analysis, as the system collects real time data from the workstations. This is, for example, the case for the resource allocation process, where the system identifies an emerging situation and designs a plan for the distribution of resources [20]. The main decisions made by the diagnostic analysis for this case are to reallocate the resources [20], to define which machines will operate and the time of operation [3].

A predictive analysis is performed in some cases for the maintenance [9, 10, 12] and scheduling [2] processes. In this case, the system collects real time data and compares it to historical data to determine the probability of a malfunction of machine or the best schedule for the production. The decisions vary from implementing an optimized schedule based on real time and historical data [1] to perform a preventive maintenance on a machine [12].

In the case of prescriptive analysis, only one article mentions its use [13]. This article is focused on the maintenance process, where the systems uses a combination of real time and historical data to perform first a predictive analysis. Once the possibility of a malfunction is determined, the system recommends a certain maintenance operation based on passed plans for similar situations. The information is shown to an operator who decides if the recommendation should be followed.

Table 4. Type of analysis vs type of decision-making process

	Automatic	Support	Semi-automatic
Diagnostic	[3, 4, 6, 7]	[8, 11, 15, 19, 20]	[14, 16–18]
Predictive	[2, 5]	[9, 10]	[1, 12, 21]
Prescriptive			[13]

Which Physical or Logical Components Make the CPS Intelligent? Which Functionalities Can the CPS Perform that Make It Intelligent?

For this section a comparison between the 5C architecture and the identified architecture from the articles is presented. The 5C architecture is selected for the comparison analysis with the propositions made in review works as it is a commonly used framework for the implementation of CPS. Even though other models that extend it have been presented, the 5C architecture is still regularly referenced.

The 5C architecture is a framework that guides the process of implementation of a CPS [22]. This architecture has 5 levels, which are briefly described below [22].

1. Smart connection: acquire shop-floor data from the machines.
2. Data-to-information conversion: process raw data for inferring meaningful information
3. Cyber: analyse the information to obtain better insights and generate a solution.
4. Cognition: simulate the solution and present the results to the operator.
5. Configuration: self-configure the machines to execute the instructions. Generate feedback of the system.

The analysis of the articles shows that they all describe a similar architecture which can be described in terms of 4 layers, namely, data acquisition, data processing and analysis, simulation and decision-making (see Table 5).

As can be seen in Table 5, each layer has a specific functionality and includes different components (physical, logical or both) to fulfil it. The components can be of different types depending on the process the CPS is implemented for, e. g. the sensor can be a pressure sensor, a thermal imaging camera or a force sensor, among others. In the case of the Data processing and analysis layer, a great number of algorithms can be used depending on the analysis needed. For the prediction analysis, in articles [9, 10, 12, 13] some of the algorithms used are K-nearest neighbor (KNN), Dynamic Bayesian Network, Multivariable Linear Regression, Random Forest (RF) and Neural Networks. On the other hand, for the optimization analysis some of the algorithms mentioned are scheduling algorithms [1], population-based optimization algorithms [2], simulated annealing algorithms [17] and mathematical programming [21].

As for the Simulation and Decision-making layers, the same can be said, the models and methods used can vary depending on the purpose of the CPS. In addition to the

Table 5. Components and functionalities of the identified architecture

Layers	Physical components	Logical components	Functionality
Data acquisition	Sensors Wearable devices	Controllers Connectors with other systems like ERP	Collect data from shop-floor, machines and other systems
Data processing and analysis		BI components Machine learning Big data analytics Data mining	Clean and process data Generate relevant knowledge about the state of the shop-floor, machines and products Predict or optimize situations, make plans of action
Simulation		Simulation models	Simulate plans and generate results
Decision-making	Actuators	Decisional DNA Performance evaluators Decision support systems Analytical hierarchy process Controllers	Order the plans from most to least recommended based on the simulation results Inform the operator or execute the plan depending on the automation level

algorithms and methods, a CPS can also be integrated with other systems such as Digital Twins [2, 7, 9] and Multi-Agent Systems [6, 10] to interconnect the physical and digital world and facilitate the processing of information and simulations of scenarios.

Now, Table 6 presents the layers and compares them to the 5C architecture levels.

Table 6. 5C architecture vs Identified architecture

5C architecture	Identified architecture
Smart connection level	Data acquisition
Data-to-information conversion level	Data processing and analysis
Cyber level	
Cognition level	Simulation Decision-making
Configuration level	

When comparing the identified architecture of the articles with the 5C architecture it can be seen that some of the layers match. Even though they do not have the same name, the Smart connection level from 5C and the Data acquisition layer from the identified

architecture fulfil the same function, i.e., collecting raw data from the physical components present on the machines and the shop-floor. The data-to-information conversion
and the cyber level can be compared to the data processing and analysis layer. At this
point, the raw data collected is first processed in order to acquire meaningful information.
This information is then analyzed with the purpose of creating knowledge regarding the
state of the shop-floor. Lastly, in the Cognition level the functionality is the same as in
the Simulation and Decision-making layers. Based on the analysis performed on the last
layer/level, a simulation is conducted to obtain different results. These results are then
analyzed in order to select the best scenario and recommend a decision. In the case of
the Configuration level of the 5C architecture, the level does not really match with any
of the layers from the identified architecture. This point is discussed and expanded later
on.

**What is the Impact that the Support of the Decision has over the Organization?
How is the Impact Measured?**
Depending on the subprocess the CPS is implemented for, the benefits it represents
can vary, but the main one that is common in almost all the articles is optimizing the
production. For the maintenance process one of the biggest impacts is the reduction of
downtime of a machine, which in return increases productivity [13]. For scheduling is
the reduction of total lead time and break time [6]. For control and monitoring is the
reduction of materials and the mitigation of anomalies [18].

The benefits that a CPS can represent for a company at operational and tactical levels
are very important and for that reason are always mentioned by the articles. Nevertheless,
most of the articles don't present a measure for this impact, neither they present the
evaluation metrics used to determine the validity of the benefits mentioned.

2.4 Gap Analysis

Now that the articles have been analyzed in accordance with the evaluation framework,
it is time to evaluate the insights obtained from the academic review based on the basis
of the proposed research question: "Which are the components and functionalities that
enable a CPS to take part in decision-making within the production processes?".

Based on the literature review, the components of a CPS can vary depending on the
purpose of the CPS, the business process it will support, and the type of decision expected
from the system. Most of the articles explain through a graphic the architecture of the
CPS they are implementing, nonetheless there is no mention of a generic architecture
that can be exploited that indicates which components are needed for each layer of the
CPS. This is an important step and should be developed so that enterprises can clearly
understand how the CPS works and the requirements they will need to fulfil in order to
complete the process.

Now, regarding the process followed by the CPS, although some articles make the
different layers explicit, for example, in [13] the model presented has 4 layers: Data
management layer, Predictive data analytic toolbox layer, Recommended and decision
support dashboard layer and Semantic-based learning and reasoning layer, in most of
the articles the components are explained but there is no mention of structured layers
for the CPS. This shows an important gap in the review that needs to be closed, because

a structured architecture defined in terms of layers is important to determine the tools, techniques and components that should be implemented and their relationship.

Like mentioned before, the articles do not mention a specific architecture to be followed for the implementation of a CPS, but the comparison of the components and the layers of the specific architectures proposed to the 5C architecture [22] shows that some aspects of the 5C architecture are missing. Considering the type of decisions made by the CPS and the scope it has in the company, some of the CPS architectures presented in the articles reach the 3rd layer of the 5C architecture, i.e. the Cyber level, and some others reach the 4th level, Cognition level. Nevertheless, among all the articles evaluated, only one article [13] mentions the use of semantic-based reasoning to generate a feedback of the system and, even in this case, the methodology for this process is not well specified. This gap should be closed in order to allow the CPS a self-evaluation of the operation and consequently, more control over the plan and an increment of benefits.

On the other hand, like mentioned before the results obtained regarding the impact and the benefits of implementing a CPS in an enterprise are unsatisfactory. Even though in the articles the benefits are mentioned, only a little group shows a quantitative result. Most of the articles do not present metrics that help support the benefits they encounter. One of the main benefits found is the optimization of the production, which would mean more products produced in less time, but no information about this point is found in none of the articles. This is a really important point because it helps understanding if this transition is really necessary for the organization, if the costs of implementation of the CPS will actually be compensated.

3   Conceptual Model

3.1   Description of the Model

Figure 1 presents the model proposed based on the analysis of the academic literature review. This model serves as a way to synthesize all the findings of the identified architecture from the literature review. It also presents the addition of an evaluation process and learning technology that helps identify the failures in the system and learn from them. The model represents the concepts and relationships that need to be considered for the implementation of a CPS in the decision-making process through object classes. Now, the description of the meta-model is presented as follows.

A *CPS* has an *Architecture* that is composed of *Layers*: 1) Data acquisition, 2) Data processing and analysis, 3) Simulation, 4) Decision-making and 5) Configuration. Each Layer has one or multiple technologies depending on its *Functionality*. The technologies that the layers have are *Data Acquisition Technology*, *Data Processing Technology*, *Data Analysis Technology*, *Simulation Technology*, *Decision making Technology* and *Learning Technology*. *Data Acquisition Technology* is composed of *Physical Components*, namely *Sensors*, *Actuator* and/or *Wearable devices* -used by a *Human*; it also has *Logical Components* that help with the storage of data. It is used on the first layer, where all the data generated from the physical components is recollected and stored.

All of the other technologies use *Logical Components* such as *Connectors* to other systems (like ERP), *Models* and *Algorithms*. The *Logical Components* help with the processing of data to generate knowledge and use that knowledge to create plans of action. *Data Processing Technology* is used in the second layer, where the data acquired is cleaned and processed by being translated into usable information. Later, *Data Analysis Technology* is used to analyse the data and create an optimized plan for the shop-floor. Subsequently, the *Simulation Technology* is used to study the results obtained from the optimized plan. The *Decision-making Technology* is where the decision is made, it could be used by a *Human* to make the final decision or could pass the instructions to execute to a *Physical Component*.

Finally, each layer has an *Evaluation* process composed of a *Metric*, similarly, the *CPS* has an *Evaluation* too. The *Evaluation* helps identify the problems that are present on the layers and the CPS and it's passed to the *Learning Technology*, which is used on the last layer for the self-configuration of the CPS.

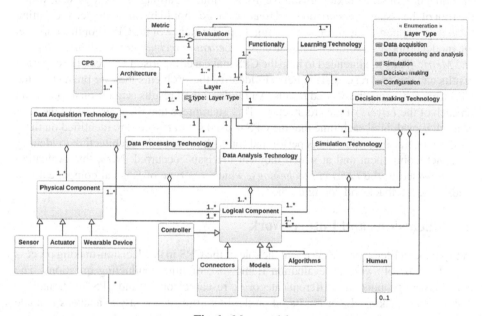

Fig. 1. Meta model

3.2 Discussion

The model can be used to identify the components, both physical and logical, that make up the architecture of a CPS that supports decision making during production processes. This is achieved by analyzing the relationships between the different technologies (data acquisition, data processing, etc.) and the types of components (physical and logical). In the model it can be seen that each one of the technologies of the CPS architecture is associated with components which can be physical or logical. Thus, for example, both the Data acquisition technology and the Decision-making technology have an association with physical component, i.e., these technologies need a physical component for their operation. Since each layer has a different functional objective, the physical components for the former is aimed for the collection of data, and the physical component of the later is for the execution of instructions. A similar analysis can be made with the other technologies to obtain the physical and logical components needed.

An important aspect in every system is the monitoring of its activity, with the purpose of verifying the obtained results and identifying issues. On this point, in the gap analysis an important discovery is that in most of the articles there is no mention about the measuring of the results obtained with the CPS. In the same way, there is no mention about how issues in the CPS are detected, except in [13]. This means that the CPS is not generating a feedback on its performance while executing its process. A feedback should be generated by the CPS in order to identify the gaps, failures and problems that take place in the execution of its process, like the incorrect operation of an algorithm or a failure in the collection of data. Taking this into consideration, a learning technology with which the root of the issues is understood and treated/solved should be implemented preventing them from happening again and enhancing the performance of the CPS. For this purpose, the model proposes a solution with the classes *Learning technology*, *Evaluation*, *Impact* and *Metric*. They are intended to help the CPS make a comparison between the expected results and the real results. This helps to identify the problems that are preventing the CPS from achieving the desired results. An *Evaluation* of results is made on the CPS and on each of the *Layers* of the architecture. This guarantees that the operation of the CPS as a full is evaluated each time that the CPS is used so that issues are identified on time. Also, an operation evaluation is performed for each layer of the architecture to identify on which component and at which moment the issue occurred. Now, this evaluation is then passed to the *Learning technology*, which is a type of Logical component that studies the feedback and configure the CPS.

4 Conclusions and Future Work

In this paper a literature review about the role of the CPS in the decision-making process is performed following an evaluation framework of nine conducting questions. The questions are grouped in 2 different categories: research context and CPS functionalities and decision making. Later on, based on the literature review, a gap analysis is made to identify the points that need to be acknowledged regarding the layers, components and functionalities of the CPS. Two of the most important findings at this point is that the papers do not exploit a commonly used framework, like the 5C architecture, for the implementation of the CPS and, when compared to the 5C architecture, the papers' CPS architectures reached only the 3rd or 4th level.

A conceptual model considering the architecture and implementation of a CPS is proposed. The purpose of the model is 1) synthesizing the literature review findings and 2) closing the gaps found previously, more specifically, the model is focused on the self-evaluation and generation of feedback necessary for the implementation of the 5th level of the 5C architecture. Finally, a discussion about the advantages of the proposed model is presented.

As future work, the conceptual model should be used on a real-life case for the implementation of a CPS in an enterprise. With this exercise, the validity and success of the model can be evaluated, and all necessary changes can be identified and resolved to get a complete guidance model.

References

1. Mourtzis, D., Vlachou, E.: A cloud-based cyber-physical system for adaptive shop-floor scheduling and condition-based maintenance. J. Manuf. Syst. **47**, 179–198 (2018). https://doi.org/10.1016/j.jmsy.2018.05.008
2. Villalonga, A., et al.: A decision-making framework for dynamic scheduling of cyber-physical production systems based on digital twins. Annu. Rev. Control **51**, 357–373 (2021). https://doi.org/10.1016/j.arcontrol.2021.04.008
3. Doltsinis, S., Ferreira, P., Mabkhot, M.M., Lohse, N.: A Decision Support System for rapid ramp-up of industry 4.0 enabled production systems. Comput. Ind. **116** (2020). https://doi.org/10.1016/j.compind.2020.103190
4. Attajer, A., Darmoul, S., Chaabane, S., Sallez, Y., Riane, F.: An analytic hierarchy process augmented with expert rules for product driven control in cyber-physical manufacturing systems. Comput. Ind. **143** (2022). https://doi.org/10.1016/j.compind.2022.103742
5. Cimini, C., Pirola, F., Pinto, R., Cavalieri, S.: A human-in-the-loop manufacturing control architecture for the next generation of production systems. J. Manuf. Syst. **54**, 258–271 (2020). https://doi.org/10.1016/j.jmsy.2020.01.002
6. Zhou, T., Tang, D., Zhu, H., Zhang, Z.: Multi-agent reinforcement learning for online scheduling in smart factories. Robot Comput. Integr. Manuf. **72** (2021). https://doi.org/10.1016/j.rcim.2021.102202
7. Waris, M.M., Sanin, C., Szczerbicki, E.: Smart innovation engineering: toward intelligent industries of the future. Cybern. Syst. **49**(5–6), 339–354 (2018). https://doi.org/10.1080/01969722.2017.1418708
8. Leng, J., Jiang, P., Liu, C., Wang, C.: Contextual self-organizing of manufacturing process for mass individualization: a cyber-physical-social system approach. Enterp. Inf. Syst. **14**(8), 1124–1149 (2020). https://doi.org/10.1080/17517575.2018.1470259
9. Pilar Lambán, M., Morella, P., Royo, J., Carlos Sánchez, J.: Using industry 4.0 to face the challenges of predictive maintenance: a key performance indicators development in a cyber physical system. Comput. Ind. Eng. **171** (2022). https://doi.org/10.1016/j.cie.2022.108400
10. Upasani, K., Bakshi, M., Pandhare, V., Lad, B.K.: Distributed maintenance planning in manufacturing industries. Comput. Ind. Eng. **108**, 1–14 (2017). https://doi.org/10.1016/j.cie.2017.03.027
11. Rossit, D.A., Tohmé, F., Frutos, M.: Production planning and scheduling in cyber-physical production systems: a review. Int. J. Comput. Integr. Manuf. **32**(4–5), 385–395 (2019). https://doi.org/10.1080/0951192X.2019.1605199
12. Kim, J., Lee, J.Y.: Server-Edge dualized closed-loop data analytics system for cyber-physical system application. Robot Comput. Integr. Manuf. **67** (2021). https://doi.org/10.1016/j.rcim.2020.102040
13. Ansari, F., Glawar, R., Nemeth, T.: PriMa: a prescriptive maintenance model for cyber-physical production systems. Int. J. Comput. Integr. Manuf. **32**(4–5), 482–503 (2019). https://doi.org/10.1080/0951192X.2019.1571236.A
14. Fantini, P., Pinzone, M., Taisch, M.: Placing the operator at the centre of Industry 4.0 design: modelling and assessing human activities within cyber-physical systems.Comput. Ind. Eng. **139** (2020). https://doi.org/10.1016/j.cie.2018.01.025
15. Nounou, A., Jaber, H., Aydin, R.: A cyber-physical system architecture based on lean principles for managing industry 4.0 setups. Int. J. Comput. Integr. Manuf. **35**(8), 890–908 (2022). https://doi.org/10.1080/0951192X.2022.2027016.C
16. Sanin, C., Haoxi, Z., Shafiq, I., Waris, M.M., Silva de Oliveira, C., Szczerbicki, E.: Experience based knowledge representation for internet of things and cyber physical systems with case studies. Futur. Gener. Comput. Syst. **92**, 604–616 (2019). https://doi.org/10.1016/j.future.2018.01.062

17. Ahmed, F., Jannat, N.E., Schmidt, D., Kim, K.Y.: Data-driven cyber-physical system frame-work for connected resistance spot welding weldability certification. Robot Comput. Integr. Manuf. **67** (2021). https://doi.org/10.1016/j.rcim.2020.102036

18. Stadnicka, D., Bonci, A., Pirani, M., Longhi, S.: Information management and decision mak-ing supported by an intelligence system in kitchen fronts control process. In: Advances in Intelligent Systems and Computing, pp. 249–259. Springer, Cham (2018). https://doi.org/10.1007/978-3-319-64465-3_25

19. Liu, M., Li, X., Li, J., Liu, Y., Zhou, B., Bao, J.: A knowledge graph-based data representation approach for IIoT-enabled cognitive manufacturing. In: Advanced Engineering Informatics, vol. 51, January 2022. https://doi.org/10.1016/j.aei.2021.101515

20. Bin Islam, S.O., Lughmani, W.A., Qureshi, W.S., Khalid, A.: A connective framework to minimize the anxiety of collaborative cyber-physical system. Int. J. Comput. Integr. Manuf. (2023). https://doi.org/10.1080/0951192X.2022.2163294

21. Yaqot, M., Franzoi, R.E., Islam, A., Menezes, B.C.: Cyber-physical system demonstration of an automated shuttle-conveyor-belt operation for inventory control of multiple stockpiles: a proof of concept. IEEE Access **10**, 127636–127653 (2022). https://doi.org/10.1109/ACCESS.2022.3226942

22. Lee, J., Bagheri, B., Kao, H.A.: A cyber-physical systems architecture for industry 4.0-based manufacturing systems. Manuf. Lett. **3**, 18–23 (2015). https://doi.org/10.1016/j.mfglet.2014.12.001

Extending Conceptual Model with Object Life Cycles

Václav Řepa[✉][iD]

Faculty of Informatics and Statistics, Prague University of Economics and Business,
W.Churchill Sqr. 4, Prague 3, Prague, Czech Republic
repa@vse.cz
http://www.vse.cz

Abstract. Conceptual modeling is traditionally regarded to be a static picture of the Real World. This opinion is also manifested in UML, where the class instance is defined as a "snapshot" of the modeled domain object. In this paper, we argue for the idea that causality, as a regular part of the modal logic should be also regarded as a part of the Real World conceptual model. In the paper, we describe the use of the life cycle model for the extension of a traditional conceptual model that allows us to enrich the traditional conceptual modeling with the Real World causality model. We also introduce the methodology for modeling business systems MMABP, which is a methodical basis for the proposed combination of Class Diagram and State Chart, and describe its principles, and rules for this combination. The importance and effects of the use of the State Chart as a complement to the Class Diagram are then illustrated by an example. By this example, the basic related problems and specifics of this way of expressing the causal Real World logic are also discussed. In the Conclusions section we then summarize the importance and position of the life cycle model in MMABP and shortly discuss its general methodical contribution to the conceptual modeling.

Keywords: conceptual modeling · object life cycle · UML Class Diagram · State Chart · MMABP

1 Introduction

The conventional perception of conceptual modeling is that it presents a static representation of the Real World. This notion is evident in UML, where a class instance is defined as a "snapshot" of the domain object being modeled. In such an approach, the conceptual model can express a basic modal logic of the given domain but it is not able to express the causality, which is nevertheless also an important part of the Real World logic.

Despite a principal insufficiency of this approach that significantly disqualifies the Class Diagram as a tool for modeling the Real World ontology, we respect the importance of the standard. Therefore, we advocate for the inclusion of

© The Author(s), under exclusive license to Springer Nature Switzerland AG 2023
K. Hinkelmann et al. (Eds.): BIR 2023, LNBIP 493, pp. 275–288, 2023.
https://doi.org/10.1007/978-3-031-43126-5_20

causality, as an important aspect of modal logic, in the conceptual model of the Real World as its integral part. For that purpose, we propose the use of a life cycle model to extend the traditional conceptual model, enabling the integration of the Real World causality model and enriching the conventional conceptual modeling approach.

The ideas presented in this paper are rooted in the Methodology for Modeling and Analysis of Business Processes (MMABP). The core principle of this methodology is the Principle of Modeling, which posits that the foundation for implementing a business system within an organization should be based on real-world facts that exist independently of the organization. Essentially, every organization, as an embodiment of a business system or idea, is a representation or model of the Real World.

MMABP recognizes two fundamental dimensions of the Real World: structure (object view) and behavior (process view). Each dimension encompasses two types of models: a global (system) view that provides an overview of the entire system, and a detailed (particular) view that focuses on individual elements within the system. The primary distinction between the global and detailed views lies in the treatment of time. The global view aims to abstract the temporal factor and emphasize the stable, time-independent aspects of the modeled system. On the other hand, the detailed model acknowledges the importance of time and places greater emphasis on it. Consequently, the global view can be characterized as object-oriented, while the detailed view leans towards a process-oriented (algorithmic) approach. The system of MMABP models and its purpose are explained by so-called MMABP Philosophical Framework [9]. The framework is built upon the following premise: The understanding of a business domain (Real World) is shaped by two fundamental phenomena: **being and behavior**, and two fundamental perspectives: **system view and particular (temporal) view** (see Fig. 1).

Being represents the Real World as it exists or may exist. It encompasses the fundamental facts about the existence and potential changes of Real World objects and their relationships. Formal descriptions of being can be achieved using modal logic. On the other hand, **behavior** represents the occurrences in the Real World resulting from the actions of Real World actors in pursuit of goals, executing plans, etc. This intentional behavior can be formally expressed through process-oriented descriptions.

The **system view** perceives the Real World as a system composed of specific elements. As the primary objective is to describe the attributes of the system, such a model must encompass the entirety of the system. This view requires abstracting individual attributes of system components, which excludes the modeling of their temporal aspects as they are always partial. Hence, the system model can be characterized as a static view.

The **particular (temporal) view** focuses on Real World events and the subsequent changes they bring. To provide precise descriptions, this model cannot cover the entire system but only a portion of it. Temporal aspects of the Real World can be formally modeled using algorithmic descriptions, which inherently exclude parallelism. Therefore, each particular model must be constructed from the perspective of a single system element, as the temporal view prevents the description of system characteristics.

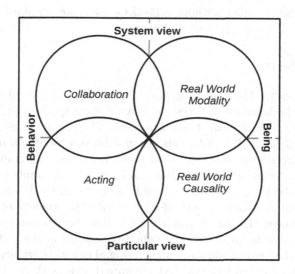

Fig. 1. MMABP Philosophical Framework [9].

By combining the above-mentioned two phenomena with the two views, four essential types of models can be derived:

- The **Modality model** of the Real World represents a static view of being, describing the system of Real World objects and their potential relationships.
- The **Causality model** of the Real World represents a temporal view of being, describing possible states in the life cycle of a specific Real World object and the potential transitions between them.
- The **Collaboration model** represents a static view of behavior, describing the system of business processes and their relationships. Given the intentional nature of behavior, process relationships always imply collaboration towards achieving defined goals.
- The **Acting model** represents a temporal view of behavior, describing sequences of actions within a particular business process intended to achieve a given process goal under possible circumstances.

Further information about MMABP Philosophical Framework can be found in [9]. The conceptual model, as an expression of the modal logic of the Real World, belongs to this framework in the **being** part. A traditional "static" conceptual model is related there to the model of the Real World modality. Since we regard the Real World causality as an integral part of the model of the being in the Real World, and at the same time we respect the importance of the standard (UML), we propose to complement the traditional conceptual model by the description of the causality in the form of so-called life cycles of those objects, during whose existence the relevant causal changes manifest themselves. For the description of the object's life cycle, we use the State Chart, another diagram from the UML. In this way, we enrich the traditional conceptual model by the description of the causality without a need to leave the standard language and consequently, to lose the effect of its integrity.

2   State Chart

State Chart (or State Machine Diagram) is originally a graphical representation used to model the behavior of a system or a software application in response to different events or changes in its environment. The origins of State Chart can be traced back to the 1940s and 1950s, when John von Neumann introduced the concept of a "finite state machine" as a theoretical model of computation [13]. The idea was to describe a system that can be in a finite number of states, and that transitions between those states based on inputs. In the 1970s, David Harel, expanded on von Neumann's work and developed the concept of State Charts [4,5] and introduced the use of graphical notations to represent the states and transitions of a system. State Charts gained popularity in the 1980s and 1990s, particularly in the field of software engineering. They were widely adopted as a modeling technique for object-oriented software design, with the Unified Modeling Language (UML) including a notation for State Charts. Today, State Charts continue to be used in a variety of fields, including software development, control engineering, and system design. They provide a visual way to represent complex behavior and help designers to reason about the behavior of a system, identify potential issues, and refine the design. Although State Chart is mainly used for the description of states and transitions in technical systems, we use it to express the causality of changes in the Real World. Such a use of the diagram is closer to the ontology modeling point of view than the engineering one. Therefore, it is critical to understand the difference between the life cycle of an object that represents causality and the behavior of the system that represents rather intentional actions. This difference is not visible from the technological (engineering) point of view, and is related to the often discussed difference between the State Chart and Petri Nets.

2.1   State Charts and Petri Nets

As follows from the MMABP Philosophical Framework, the conceptual model forms just half of the model of the Real World - the being dimension. The full model of the Real World should cover also the dimension of behaving. A clear understanding of the difference between causality (as a part of being) and behavior is crucial for understanding the essential difference between State Charts and Petri Nets. State charts and Petri Nets [1,6,7] are both modeling techniques used for modeling complex systems, but they have different origins and approaches.

State charts were developed as a tool for software engineering by David Harel in the 1980s. They are graphical representations of a system's states and the transitions between them. State charts are useful for modeling systems that have a large number of states and transitions, and for capturing the behavior of a system over time.

Petri nets, on the other hand, were developed by Carl Adam Petri in the 1960s as a mathematical model for systems that involve concurrent processes. Petri nets represent the flow of information and control in a system as a directed graph, and they are useful for modeling systems with a large number of concurrent processes and interactions.

Despite their different origins and approaches, state charts and Petri nets have some similarities in their structure and concepts. Both use graphical notations to represent the behavior of a system, and both rely on the concepts of states, transitions, and events. From the technological point of view, state charts can be seen as a special case of Petri nets, where the states and transitions are explicitly represented, and the concurrency and synchronization aspects are implicit. There are also attempts to combine state charts and Petri nets into a single modeling language, in order to take advantage of their complementary strengths. David Harel is credited with proposing such a combination. In [3] he proposed the extension of the Statecharts formalism to model the behavior of reactive systems. In the book Statecharts in the Making: Towards a User-Friendly and Comprehensive Formalism for Reactive Systems [4], the authors extend the Statecharts formalism with several features, including hierarchical state machines, concurrency, and real-time constraints. In this conception, State charts are diagrams comprised of elements that can improve visually the modeling of reactive system behaviors [5]. They extend conventional state diagrams with the notions of hierarchy, concurrency, and communication [8].

From the MMABP point of view, the natural representative of a reactive system in the Real World is a business process. Reactive systems are systems that continuously interact with their environment, sensing and responding to events and other inputs. Business processes involve a series of actions and interactions between different actors (e.g., customers, employees, systems) that respond to events or inputs in the environment (e.g., customer requests, system failures, changes in regulations). The state of a business process changes as a result of these interactions and inputs, and the process has to react to those changes to achieve its goals. In this sense, business processes can be seen as reactive systems that respond to events and inputs to achieve their objectives.

Since the business process represents achieving objectives, its description cannot be regarded as a description of causality a natural logical aspect of the Real World. Therefore, it is critically important to distinguish between the business process and the system of ontological objects, represented as concepts in the conceptual model. The use of State Chart in conceptual modeling thus can never be regarded as a description of the business process or its infrastructure (machine, IT system) but exclusively as a description of the Real World logic. This is supported in MMABP by the rules for the use of State Chart.

3   Using State Charts in MMABP

The use of an object the life cycle model in MMABP is regulated by the set of simple rules:

- **Life cycle general completeness**. Object life cycle model has to cover the whole lifetime of the object. It has to start with the event representing the creation of the object (class instance). It has to cover all possible ends of the object life, i.e. all possible kinds of demise of the instance, all possible death events.
- **Algorithmic correctness**. The life cycle model has to fulfill the following basic characteristics of an algorithm:
  - unambiguity
  - discreteness
  - and finiteness.
  In practice, it means that particular states cannot overlap in meaning as well as in time, and that any possible combination of transitions cannot lead to a deadlock.
- **General information richness**. Every internal object life cycle state has to have at least two output transitions. This rule requires every state represents some alternative reactions, which is necessary since the life cycle model represents the definition of modal logic. If there was only a single output transition, there would not be any difference between the state and the only possible following one, no "modal" information related to the state1.
- **Contextual Consistency**. The object life cycle should be consistent with its context specified in the Class Diagram. The consistency is based on the following rules:
  - Every transition between the object's states represents the change of the relationship (relationships) with another object (objects) or the transformation of the object's attribute (attributes).
  - If the class described with the life cycle is generic, and if this generalization is "dynamic" in terms of OntoUML terminology [2], the particular life cycle states should correspond to the sub-types of this generalization structure.
  - and If the class described with the life cycle is decomposed into multiple dynamic generalization structures, each of them should be defined with a standalone life cycle model.

The purpose of the above-described rules for the creation State Chart is not only to avoid possible incorrect use of the diagram but mainly to support the creation of the model as an expression of the Real World logic that is objectively given thus, it should be expressed truly and completely. For instance, the Information richness rule helps to uncover important transitions that are not implicitly visible. If there is just a single transition to the following state but the analyzer "feels" the importance of the state, it probably signalizes the need to analyze the set of relevant events in order to uncover the one that causes the missing alternative transition. The supporting power of rules is not limited only to the State Chart. For instance, the Algorithmic correctness rule can help to uncover an additional important object in the domain. The need to incorporate into the life cycle model the state that overlaps another existing state in time undoubtedly signalizes the need to take into account another object related to the object, whose role represents the given one. In other words, we uncovered that the analyzed object represents the role of another object that has multiple roles with multiple life cycles. In this way, we can even uncover the need to introduce a new generic object.

In general, every rule has the potential to force the creativity of its user.

4 Example of Object Life Cycle Model as a Complement to the Class Model

By modeling objects by means of the Class Diagram, even if extended with the OntoUML stereotypes and rules, some dynamic "(i.e. time-related) aspects of objects cannot be fully expressed. Regarding the Real World causality, we have to take into regard also the flow of time. A causal relation is a logical relationship between "prior" and "post" facts. Therefore, a time-independent description of the Real World logic like conceptual modeling, can not be sufficient for the description of the causality type of logic. The following example illustrates the limitations of traditional conceptual modeling to fully express the causal relationships together with the way, in which we can overcome this limitation by the use of the object life cycle modeling. The conceptual model in Fig. 2 describes the main object classes in the field of a traditional e-shop. The e-shop processes are based on simple essential rules:

- Every order belongs to the particular customer.
- There must be the particular e-shop employee responsible for the order.
- When the order is confirmed it is packaged in a single package that is consequently delivered to the customer.
- Payment may be made either prior or after the delivery.

  In the model, one can find the reflection of these rules in following facts:

- There are two basic kinds of *Person*: *Customer* and *Employee*.
- *Person* may be assigned to one or more *Orders*.
- There must be exactly one *Customer* (as an order owner) and one *Employee* (as a responsible employee) assigned to every Order.
- There may be no more that one *Payment* for the *Order*.
- There must be exactly one *Order* as a subject of the *Payment*.
- There are two basic kinds of *Payment*: *Prior delivery* and *After delivery*.
- *Order* may be packed in no more than one *Package*.
- *Package* contains exactly one *Order*.
- *Delivery* of the *Package* may be made but no more that once.

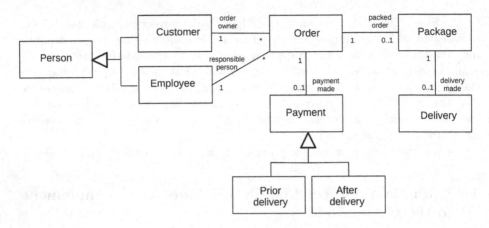

Fig. 2. Fragment of an e-shop conceptual model.

The main problem related to this model is that it admits some situations that are not correct in the Real world. For instance, the payment for the order must be always finally made. Nevertheless, there are situations, when there may be the order without a payment, especially if the payment should be made after the delivery. But if the payment should be made prior the delivery, there may not be the delivery without payment.

The problem may be partially avoided if we make a more detailed classification of the Order types in terms of the "dynamic generalization structure" according to OntoUML terminology [2]. Figure 3 shows possible improvement of the conceptual model from Fig. 2 with such classification. In dynamic generalization structure, particular sub-types correspond to the life stages of the object. Generic object class represents the common identity for all sub-type classes; they actually represent only particular periods of the object's lifetime, not different objects[1]. OntoUML marks such sub-types with the <> stereotype.

Particular sub-types of Order represent particular states (phases) of the life of the object like they can be seen in the life cycle of these objects in Fig. 5.

This improved version of the conceptual model avoids the above-mentioned problem just partially. Contrary to the previous version in Fig. 2, it expresses the fact that the responsible employee can be assigned just to the existing order after its creation, which means that the order may exist for some time even without a responsible employee. It also shows that Prior delivery and After delivery sub-types of Payment should be associated with the different parts of the order's life,

---

[1] As it is stated in [2], this interpretation contradicts the UML definition of the object instance as "an instance at a point in time (a snapshot)" [12], which requires regarding every single life phase as a standalone object with an individual identity. This inability of the language to cope with the dynamic aspects of the Real World logic causes the traditional, and still common opinion, that the conceptual model is a clearly "static" picture of the Real World.

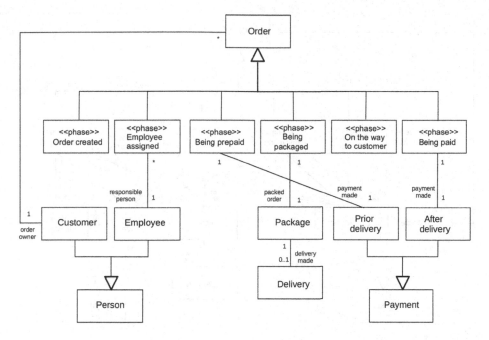

Fig. 3. Improved e-shop conceptual model.

and also the association between Order and Package takes its place later in the order life so that, it is not relevant in previous phases.

Nevertheless, this improvement does not completely cover all relevant classes associations. They can be seen in the full version of the improved model in Fig. 4. Regarding the flow of time, one has to admit that once the association with some life phase appears, if there is no event causing the disappearance of this association, it must exist in all remaining life phases until the end of the object life.

Figure 4 shows how complicated these simple facts are expressed in the Class Diagram. Moreover, even such a complex model can not describe some important logical relations of different associations as their mutual dependencies that follow from the natural exclusivity of the state transitions. For example, if the order's delivery fails, the association between Order and After delivery payment can never appear.

The certain way to overcome this limitation of the traditional conceptual model is to complement the class model with the life cycle models of those classes, whose lives contain the possible changes causing the above-mentioned logical relations of different associations (Fig. 5).

The life cycle model (see Fig. 5) enumerates the particular relevant states in the life of the object and defines possible relevant transitions between them. Every transition should be accompanied by information about the reason (usually an event) and the action that causes the transition. The relevance of the

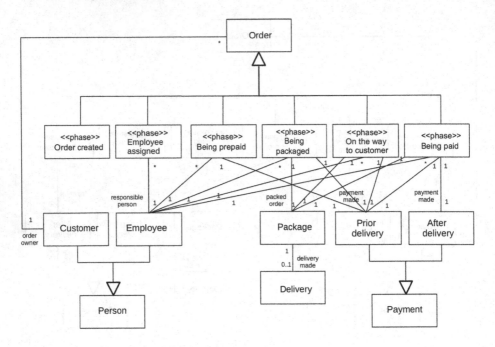

Fig. 4. Full version of the improved model.

selection of states is always given by the transitions that need to be described. In other words, we need to see such states in the life of the given object, that allow placing the events, whose logical (causal) context we need to specify, in particular transitions. The events are determined by important object relationships that are (should be) described in the conceptual model (Class Diagram). Particular events then represent important changes in relationships like the moments and circumstances of their appearance and disappearance, and of their changes (redirecting).

For example, in this model, we need to specify under which circumstances the order should be paid and how the payment differs in both its sub-types. That requires placing the event Order paid to two different transitions corresponding to both sub-types of the payment. Consequently, we need to distinguish the states Being prepaid and Being paid. Similarly, the association between the classes Order and Package requires a special state Order packaged and a second-order association between the classes Package and Delivery requires the state On the way to customer.

This model also illustrates how this description allows a detailed specification of the causal relationships of particular events, actions, and object states. For instance, one can see there that Order can be canceled in every life phase but in different contexts. In the two earliest phases, it can be canceled due to the rejection by the supplier. It the phases Being prepaid and Being paid, it can be canceled due to the payment fail. Nevertheless, both transitions differ

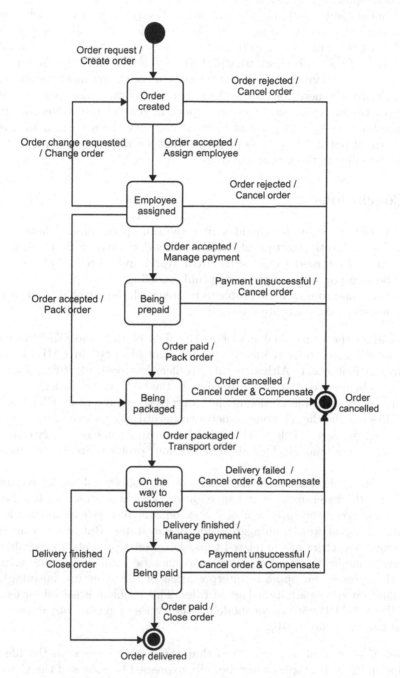

Fig. 5. Life cycle of the Order object.

in the corresponding actions. Cancellation in the phase of Being paid requires an additional compensation of already done delivery (a return), which is irrelevant in the Being prepaid phase. The Compensation actions in the transitions from the last three phases have different meanings due to the different transition reasons (fail of the expedition, transport, or payment). Transition actions actually represent relationships to the behavioral part of the business system model. They signalize the need for such actions in business processes. Also, therefore, we regard the life cycle model as an important part of the conceptual model from the business system point of view. It can serve as a tool for uncovering those parts of potential business processes that are objectively required by the natural causality in the business system.

5   Conclusions

In this paper, we argue for the idea that the conceptual model should not be regarded as a "static" picture of the Real World (a snapshot). Causality is a regular part of the modal logic of the Real World and therefore, also its model should be incorporated into the conceptual modeling.

There are also some general problems related with the use of life cycle description as a part of the conceptual model:

- Extending the conceptual model to the field of the Real World dynamics causes the need to overcome the "problem of identity" in UML mentioned above in footnote 1. Although this problem has been identified about two decades before (see [2]), it still persists in the UML meta-model.
- Consequently, the integration of the Class Diagram and State Chart in UML requires making the relationship between the object's life cycle and its context in the Class Diagram clear. That would also cause some necessary changes in the UML meta-model. This and the previous problem are also discussed in [9–11].
- Using life cycle description as a part of the conceptual model requires to combine the generalization and aggregation types of abstraction. It is because every life cycle state may represent a standalone life cycle on a lower level of detail, in other words, an aggregation of sub-states. But at the same time, the same structure in the related Class Diagram represents a generalization. Since generalization and aggregation cannot be combined in one structure (both represent an opposite interpretation of the structure meaning), this situation needs an additional set of rules. This problem is solved for example by the MMABP pattern for modeling life cycles of generic object structures that can be found in [10].

Even if we do not want to claim that the facts expressed in the life cycle description in the example cannot be fully expressed by means of the Class Diagram (especially with its OntoUML extension), the use of the life cycle model as a complement to the Class Diagram apparently simplifies the way of the description. Moreover, such a description is very close to the natural human understanding of the Real World, which is also one of the often-discussed features of the State Chart. Except for the above-mentioned semantic contradiction in the UML definition (see footnote 1), the use of the life cycle description does not require any other improvements of the language since the State Chart is a regular UML diagram. Nevertheless, other improvements are possible although not necessary. For instance, basic logical relationships between Class Diagram and State Chart can be implemented as complements in the UML meta-model. From the MMABP viewpoint, the basic logical relationships between Class Diagram and State Chart particularly are:

- The rules for creating the life cycle model of the Real World objects.
- The correspondence of the life cycle states in the State Chart and sub-type classes in the Class Diagram.
- The correspondence of transitions in the State Chart and the associations of the class to other classes.

All these rules can be implemented as complements in the UML meta-model. Nevertheless, even without such support from the language, the use of these rules can significantly improve the quality of the model. Besides this, the rules also open the space for further methodological development in the field of conceptual modeling.

Acknowledgments. The paper was supported by the Faculty of Informatics and Statistics, Prague University of Economics and Business.

References

1. Brauer, W., Reisig, W.: Carl Adam petri and "Petri Nets." In: Advances in Computer Science and Engineering: Texts, pp. 129–139. Imperial College Press (2009)
2. Guizzardi, G.: Ontological foundations for structural conceptual models. Enschede: University of Twente. Centre for telematics and information technology, Enschede; Telematics instituut (2005)
3. Modeling reactive systems with statecharts: the statemate approach. McGraw-Hill, New York (1998)
4. Harel, D.: Statecharts in the making: a personal account. In: Proceedings of the third ACM SIGPLAN Conference on History of Programming Languages. ACM, San Diego California (2007). https://doi.org/10.1145/1238844.1238849
5. Harel, D.: Statecharts: a visual formalism for complex systems. Sci. Comput. Program. **8**, 231–274 (1987). https://doi.org/10.1016/0167-6423(87)90035--9
6. Petri, C.A.: Fundamentals of a Theory of Asynchronous Information Flow. (1962)
7. Petri, C.A.: Introduction to general net theory. In: Brauer, W. (ed.) Net Theory and Applications. LNCS, vol. 84, pp. 1–19. Springer, Heidelberg (1980). https://doi.org/10.1007/3-540-10001-6_21
8. Ramos, M.A., Masiero, P.C., Penteado, R.A.D., Braga, R.T.V.: Extending state charts to model system interactions. J. Softw. Eng. Res. Dev. **3**, 12 (2015)
9. Řepa, V.: Essential challenges in business systems modeling. In: Information Systems: Research, Development, Applications, Education. Cham: Springer International Publishing AG, pp. 99–110 (2017). ISBN 978-3-319-66995-3

10. Repa, V.: Modelling life cycles of generic object classes. In: Linger, H., Fisher, J., Barnden, A., Barry, C., Lang, M., Schneider, C. (eds.) Building Sustainable Information Systems, pp. 443–454. Springer, Boston, MA (2013). https://doi.org/10.1007/978-1-4614-7540-8_34

11. Řepa, V.: Process dimension of concepts. In: Jaakkola, H., Kiyoki, Y., Tokuda, T. (eds.) Information Modelling and Knowledge Bases XIX. Amsterdam: IOS Press, pp. 322–329 (2008). ISBN 978-1-58603-812-0

12. UML superstructure specification, v2.0 document 05–07-04, Object Management Group (2004)

13. Von Neumann, J.: Theory of Self-Reproducing Automata. University of Illinois Press, Urbana, Champaign (1966)

New Trends in Data Governance

Analyzing Open Government High Value Datasets: Availability, Publishers' Contribution and Technical Specifications

Maria Ioanna Maratsi[1]([⊠]) (iD), Mohsan Ali[1] (iD), Charalampos Alexopoulos[1] (iD), Stuti Saxena[2] (iD), Nina Rizun[3] (iD), and Yannis Charalabidis[1] (iD)

[1] University of the Aegean, Mytilene, Greece
{ioanna.m,mohsan,alexop,yannisx}@aegean.gr
[2] Graphic Era University, Dehradun, India
[3] Gdańsk University of Technology, Gdańsk, Poland
ninrizun@pg.edu.pl

Abstract. Extracting value from open (government) data has been in the limelight for quite some time now, with the Open Government Data (OGD)-also referred to as the Public Sector Information (PSI)- Directive, emphasizing the need for discovery of potential related to PSI and the re-use of data. This study provides insight on high-value datasets (HVD), i.e., the OGD matching the rigorous quality standards in terms of particularly the completeness, timeliness, and machine-processability, in the European Data Portal (EDP) in order to measure various aspects of the datasets, which will help obtain further insights on the current availability status, potential interoperability possibilities, drivers and barriers. The rationale behind this approach is to identify HVD in line with the thematic categories of the PSI Directive and to put a focus on the EDP HVD across three dimensions, viz., data publishing, availability, and technical requirements which need to be met. Findings attest the need for provisioning qualitatively robust HVDs with requisite technical specifications for facilitating value derivation by the range of stakeholders. Apart from contributing towards the HVD and OGD literature, the study lends insights across the availability-value generation focus via the EDP, thereby providing policy implications and further research pointers along these lines.

Keywords: Open government data · European Data Portal · High value datasets · Technical specifications · Interoperability · Data publishers · Data availability

1 Introduction

Extracting value from open data has been in the limelight for quite some time now, with the Open Government Data (OGD)-also referred to as the Public Sector Information (PSI) Directive [1] emphasizing the need for discovery of potential related to public sector information and the re-use of data. PSI is a rich data source, which can actively assist in the transformation of a plethora of applications in society, politics, economics, legislative bodies, environment, and more. The value of publicly available information

K. Hinkelmann et al. (Eds.): BIR 2023, LNBIP 493, pp. 291–310, 2023.
https://doi.org/10.1007/978-3-031-43126-5_21

has been pursued through several Open Government Data initiatives (OGDIs), which attempt to deliver benefits and satisfy a set of defined objectives, such as enhanced transparency and accountability, innovation, improved decision-making, stimulation of data re-use, counteracting of corruption, and the provision of new services and products [2].

One of the first associations that come to mind when the term "value" is analyzed, is the one related to economic value, which can be defined as "the worth of a good or service as determined by the market" [3]. However, in the context of open data and the value creation from publicly available information, more dimensions of value are involved, one of them being the social value, which is created when resources, inputs, processes, or policies are combined to generate improvements in the lives of individuals or society as a whole [3]. To complement the aforementioned statements, shared value is based on the idea that societal needs, not only economic needs, define markets [4], so it is a parameter that needs to also be taken into consideration. In other words, public value might include the economic value in the way it was described previously, the social or cultural value which contributes to a society's well-being and prosperity, the political value which promotes public engagement and collaboration, and/or the ecological value by actively promoting sustainable development [5].

As far as high-value datasets (HVD) are concerned, a HVD, according to the revised PSI Directive [1], is defined as being listed in one of the following six thematic areas: Geospatial, Earth Observation and Environment, Meteorological, Statistical, Companies and company ownership, and Mobility. These thematic areas derive from the analysis conducted in accordance with their potential to generate and promote any of the aforementioned types of value, having significant impact on a large cross-section of society, and having the ability to be combined with other datasets under the same purpose [1].

On a parallel note, data interoperability plays an important role, in its turn, in the creation of value, since the public sector information rendered available for re-use needs to meet a number of quality criteria which potentially affect the data discoverability, availability, machine readability and accessibility. Interoperability is the key, and, in order to facilitate data re-use, it needs to be ensured through a series of requirements regarding the data format, processing, machine readability, relevant metadata and other principles [1]. Data interoperability, from a semantic, i.e., lending interpretation and sense-making to the datasets sourced from multitudinous and diverse sources [6] and technical, i.e., standardization and homogenization of the diverse technological foundations across the sources not only in terms of communication as well as the information exchanged across the communication channels [7] viewpoint, can act as a technical or operational enabler for data re-use [8]. Vis-a-vis the specific case of e-government, interoperability across the three levels, viz., technical interoperability in terms of the communication details at different levels of the government; semantic interoperability in terms of the interpretative implications of information; and, organizational interoperability in terms of the implications of information exchange for the recipient, needs to take into cognizance the infrastructures and connectedness [9–13]. Extrapolating these e-government interoperability cases to the OGD context, it falls in place to ascertain the way technical aspects of HVD are conducive for value derivation by the stakeholders, in the long-run.

With this background, this study provides insights on HVD, i.e., the OGD matching the rigorous quality standards in terms of particularly the completeness, timeliness, and machine-processability [14–16], in the European Data Portal in order to measure various aspects of the datasets, such as their availability, information about the publishers which provide the datasets, and technical specifications which will help gain further insight on potential interoperability hinders and more. The main research goal of the presented study is to identify HVD according to the thematic categories of the PSI Directive (as mentioned previously), and to retrieve the datasets from the European Data Portal to examine aspects of them linked to them, more specifically, focusing on the three dimensions of data availability, data publishers' contribution, and the technical specifications. Further insights on data interoperability, and other aspects of data quality are also indirectly targeted due to their close proximity to the topic but also emerging importance.

The remaining article is organized as follows: in the Background section, an overview of the literature regarding HVD and the proportional importance of technical specifications of data will be presented, while the Research Method section contains the description of the proposed methodological approach. The Results section consists of the data analysis and findings of the applied method, the Discussion section includes the interpretation of the findings in a meaningful context, while the Future Directions section explains the limitations of the presented study and potential ways this research could be expanded and replicated in various other implementations in the future.

2 Background

In general, value (or social welfare) is conceptualized as an aggregate measure of social and economic value [17]. The two types of value frequently discussed, as mentioned previously, are the economic (related to the worth of a product or service determined by the market) and the social value (related to the advancements and improvements in society or the individual) [17]. Benington and Moore [18] gave another dimension to the conventional definition of public value, adding to the economic and social, the cultural and political value. However, determining how OGD can contribute to the generation of those values and how this process can be quantified and measured is a task requiring a number of mechanisms to be put in place in order to achieve it [19]. In this vein, Jetzek and colleagues developed a conceptual model to demonstrate how data can produce value along the four identified mechanisms: Efficiency, Innovation, Transparency and Participation [17]. The conceptual model consists of the enabling factors for value creation, the value generating mechanisms and the impact on economic and social value, as well as the relationships among them, indicated by several analyzed hypotheses. One of the enabling factors presented, especially significant for the present study, is the technical connectivity factor, which refers to all the relevant infrastructure supporting the transfer and circulation of data among the systems of governmental agencies and more. These technologies need to be able to assist with all the tasks related to the handling, processing, visualization, and integration of data, while in parallel, support the structurization of unstructured or semi-structured data, interoperability (mainly semantic in this context), and interconnection between disparate data sources. Semantic technologies, as an integral part of the aforementioned technical connectivity, are at the heart of this construct, and, according to [17], positively affect efficiency through improved interoperability and innovation by proposing new methods and ways to analyze and transform data.

As far as the benefits of an Open Government Data Initiative (OGDI) are concerned, various studies have examined their parameters and the way they interact. In this light, the findings of a conducted study by [2] showed that the majority of benefits delivered by implemented OGDIs are of operational or technical nature, at a next phase, of economic and, lastly, of societal nature, the latter being the toughest to measure. The technical and operational benefits are closely linked to the technical connectivity mentioned previously and, among others, they include easier access to data, better data discoverability, data re-use and improved decision-making by managing to compare data from disparate sources [2]. In this light, it becomes clear that the technical dimension of available datasets in the portal is a dimension which needs to be included in any analysis aiming to bring forth conclusions regarding interoperability, technical connectivity, or the creation of value through improved technical and semantic means.

Before moving on to the specified Methodology of the presented study, it is notewor-thy to go through the existing literature on HVD and open government data in order to better understand the context of this research, as well as mentioned conducted research on interoperability and open government data, as a critical dimension which needs to be considered when talking about data and value.

2.1 Related Research on HVD with Reference to OGD

In sharp contradistinction to Big Data, HVD is not all about the volume but a juxtapo-sition of volume with quality metrics, such as, completeness, machine-processability, granularity, accessibility, timeliness, non-discriminatory and license-free [20]. Table 1 presents a snapshot of the HVD-OGDs studies, and it may be inferred that as such, specific focus on the HVD is few and far between.

2.2 Related Research on Interoperability with Reference to Open Government Data

In its crudest terms, interoperability is defined as the exchange of data and services across a network of distributed systems [32, 33]. Utility of interoperability of OGD has been underscored in a plethora of literature with specific reference to the interoperability dimensions: semantic (commonality of understanding among the data/services exchange parties to draw congruent inferences), syntactic (arriving at common schemas, sequence and arrangement of terms representing an entity), technical (covers a gamut of aspects like compatibility of technologies and systems in place as well as their open/closed nature and scope defining their formal and rigorous descriptions), operational (attaining interoperability between and among actors, the ones engaged in data sharing proto-cols) and organizational (compatibility between cross-border organizational systems in terms of processes, formats and entities) [32–35]. Whilst most of the studies hint at the theoretical value and implications of OGD interoperability [17, 36–39], as such, the research on OGD interoperability with empirical investigations is evolving. For instance, an RDF schema vocabulary is designed and validated for facilitating linkages amongst the OGD given their disparate and granular nature [40]. Likewise, in another instance, a framework of ontological interoperability of the real-time OGD was validated in the Iranian energy sector [41]. A comprehensive open-source portal for OGD interoperability is also available via the Tetherless World Constellation (TWC)'s Linking Open Government Data (LOGD) portal which is based on providing solutions to semantic interoperability [42]. In another context of Uppsala, Sweden, the empirical study on the interoperability of OGD for Green IoT (Internet of Things) is being empirically validated [39]. A sophisticated Delivering Information of Government (DIGO) platform was designed for facilitating OGD interoperability across the Swedish OGD portal and validated with mashup applications and data fusion on linked open data (LOD) cloud [43].

Another cause of concern is to produce interoperable OGD-thanks to the unique RDF (Resource Description Framework) vocabularies for creating the triplet sets alongside the relational OGD, i.e., OLAP (Online Analytical Processing) data cubes [44]- and the same is possible via ontological interoperability algorithms-case in point being the OGD portal of Iran and the ancillary data management system [45]. Similar conclusions were derived in regard to the conflicts pertaining to the structural (consequence of the different practices of modeling the structure of the OGD) and naming (the usage of different Uniform Resource Identifiers (URIs)) facets, viz. Complexities pertaining to the measurement unit; gender; temporality; parametric measurements; measures' selection; and hierarchical levels, which were empirically validated across six OGD portals covering Scotland, UK, Belgium, Japan, Italy and Ireland [46]. Similarly, drawing inferences from the case studies of Belgian air quality sensor data and the railway infrastructure data, it was shown that linked time series approach is feasible for sustainability of OGD interoperability and availability on account of data storage via improvised caching strategy which reduces the web server's CPU (Central Processing Unit) load, publishing cost and the requirement for client-server interaction [47]. Interoperability was a challenge in the US OGD given the differentials in compatibility of the portals between the legislative and executive branches of the government [48].

Having taken into consideration the extended background presented in this Section, the methodological approach for the conducted study is defined and tailored to fit the purpose of this research, which is to provide information useful regarding the 6 thematic categories of HVD in the European Data Portal, against a number of defined criteria related to their availability, interoperability and further technical details.

Table 1. Major studies identifying HVD and OGD.

Excerpt	Author/s	Inferences regarding HVD-OGDs
"High-value information is information that can be used to increase agency accountability and responsiveness; improve public knowledge of the agency and its operations; further the core mission of the agency; create economic opportunity; or respond to need and demand as identified through public consultation" (p. 2495)	[21] [22] [23] [24]	This definition was provided by Office of Management and Budget, US (OMB, 2009: pp. 7); OGD is also referred to as Public Sector Information (PSI) and the study refers to "High-value information" as being congruent to HVD
A reference to the high value datasets for statistical analysis	[25]	OGD-HVD dimension needs to be meticulously approached
High value creation potential of OGD is being referred	[26]	Value creation assessment framework does not necessarily refer to the HVD trait of OGD
There is a linkage between HVD and timely availability of the same	[27]	Given the lack of accessibility of HVD via the UK OGD portals, interoperability of lesser value OGD result in incoherent analyses
Geospatial OGD across French municipality were HVD	[28]	This calls for attention of researchers to understand why OGD-HVD is sparse and niche
"… calling attention to a set of unanswered questions about the governance issues around data release: who should decide what data is "high value" and how do they choose? How does a user know when data is fit for re-use, how does a user know what has been done to that data, and what restrictions govern its use?"	[29]	Given the authors' impetus on creating a OGD ecosystem, it is warranted that such ecosystemic approach be built on the edifice of OGD-HVD
Tracing the evolution of OGD initiative in the US, the authors mention of how the Obama government issued directives for publishing of HVDs with a caveat that it is the issuing public authority which will decide what's HVD	[30]	US OGD portal needs to be taken up in further studies to assess the provisioning of HVD-OGD after more than two decades now
There is a mismatch between the HVD and the extent to which public authority is accountable for its being HVD as far as the US is concerned	[31]	This raises the question regarding the extent to which the transparency-accountability conjunction is realized in practice in the US, thereby, providing a line of further research

3 Research Method

This section aims to describe the research method adopted in the current study. The intended outcome of this methodology is to analyze datasets retrieved from the European Data Portal (EDP) against a defined set of requirements in order to consider the following three dimensions, while in parallel, the categories of HVD as specified by the PSI Directive are kept in mind: i) the dataset's availability, ii) the dataset' publishing authorities and entities, and iii) the dataset's technical specifications. The retrieval of datasets from the EDP is conducted by applying the following filters in the Quick Search menu:

1. **Categories** (as defined by the PSI Directive):

- Geospatial
- Earth Observation and Environment
- Meteorological
- Statistical
- Companies and company ownership
- Mobility

2. **Metadata quality** (Scoring: Sufficient)
3. **Format:** All available
4. Data services: YES

   The first filter, which is about the dataset category, is specified so as to include the HVD thematic categories defined by the PSI Directive. The second filter about the metadata quality is set to "sufficient", which is the minimum, in order to allow for as many datasets as possible and to give us the opportunity to later put focus on the datasets' technical aspects when these are not considered optimal (due to metadata being one of the most important parameters to consider in this case). The same reasoning applies for the data format. The last filter, "Data services", is the filter which allows for the identification of real-time or close to real-time data. The EDP mentions that with this filter active, the datasets returned are datasets which are used in at least one data service, something that clearly implies the data is real-time or close to real-time, as the data service stream is constantly available. This filter is very important in the presented study, as it is one of the few indicators applicable to determine whether a dataset is considered high value. Real-time/close to real-time data is closely associated with high value [49, 50], however, it is an indicator which can work in conjunction with other indicators of HVD.

   Regarding the first filter in the Quick Search, it is worth noting that some high-value datasets may fit into numerous categories on the EDP, and the categories listed are not exhaustive. These categories are not mutually exclusive; some datasets may fall into multiple categories. The mapping between the 6 thematic categories of HVD and the equivalent available categories in the EU Data Portal are shown in Table 2. In line with the aforesaid, the authors aim to provide insight on the following three dimensions:

- Availability
- Publisher/s
- Technical specifications

Table 2. The mapping between the PSI Directive thematic categories for HVD and the EDP search categories.

PSI Directive HVD Thematic Categories	European Data Portal (EDP) Categories
Geospatial	Regions and cities
Earth Observation and Environment	Energy, Forestry and food, Fisheries, Agriculture
Meteorological	Environment
Statistical	Education, Culture and sport, Health, Population and society, Justice, Legal system and public safety, Science and technology, international issues, Government, and public sector
Companies and company ownership	Economy and finance
Mobility	Transport

As a metric for data availability, the number of openly available datasets per category (as defined earlier) will be considered. This will help the authors to gain some insight on the comparison for availability among the HVD categories. The second dimension, which concerns the data publisher, is considered in order to examine elements regarding the distribution of these data sources, the most active contributors of datasets and other intuitive information. The last dimension of technical specifications is an approach for data interoperability, considering that technical specifications such as available data formats, machine-readability, metadata quality, available APIs (Application Programming Interfaces), documentation, and licensing are factors which directly affect the dataset's technical and semantic interoperability. So, in this case, the analysis framework for the retrieved datasets includes the aforementioned criteria, which are applied in order to draw conclusions regarding how interoperable the HVD are, what insufficiencies exist from a technical point of view, and what could potentially be translated into more specific technical requirements for HVD, in general. The importance of the technical specifications of the available datasets and how interoperability can play a critical role for HVD is also emphasized by the conceptual model by [17], referred to as "technical connectivity" and as one of the dimensions of the conceptual model (the aspect the authors are focusing on in this study), which strengthens the inclusion of this dimension in the proposed approach.

Overall, the methodological steps to achieve the aforementioned steps are described in Fig. 1 starting with the retrieval of the high-value datasets from the EDP having first applied the Quick Search filters with a final examination of the three dimensions of availability, data publisher analysis and technical specifications. In the following Section, the results of the applied methodology and analysis framework are presented and explained in further detail.

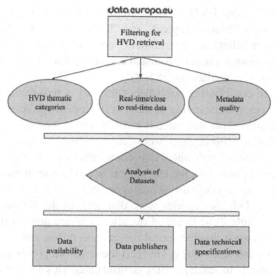

Fig. 1. A flowchart of the research methodology.

4 Results

The three-dimensional outcome of the applied methodology is described and analyzed in this Section. These three dimensions are explained first, followed by some general remarks on the analysis results and other derived information of significance within the context of this study's focus.

4.1 Availability

To begin with, the authors initiated the analysis by examining the criterion of the availability of high-value datasets (Table 3).

Table 3. The availability of HVDs and number of publishers per category.

HVD Categories	Geospatial	Earth Observation and Environment	Meteorological	Statistical	Companies and Company Ownership	Mobility
Total number of datasets	523	2	795	73	1426	92
Total number of publishers	17	1	17	15	20	9

The majority of available HVDs come from the category "Companies and company ownership", followed by "Meteorological" and "Geospatial" data. "Mobility", "Statistical" and "Earth observation and Environment" come afterwards, with the latter being the category with the fewest datasets. A visual representation of the results is presented in Fig. 2. Apart from the availability of HVDs on the EDP (denoted in blue), Fig. 2 depicts the number of contributing publishers (denoted in red) per HVD thematic category. To gain a deeper understanding of these results, descriptive statistics is applied. The descriptive statistics show that there is a difference among the 6 HVD categories. Based on the established criteria, there were 2,911 high-value datasets (HVDs) identified, and the total number of publishers that contributed data in each distinct category was 79. The number of publishers per category is not the same in number and distinct. For instance, the geospatial HVD dataset category contains 526 datasets published by 17 distinct publishers. Other categories were distinct, but the statistical datasets category is mapped (see Table 2) to Health, Education, Culture and sport, Population and society, International issues, Justice, Legal system and public safety, Government and public sector, Science and technology. Thus, all these subcategories are mentioned with a single label "Statistical" to make the EDP dataset categories and the HVDs categories match successfully. Furthermore, inferential statistics is applied to the number of HVDs and the publishers, and the output of the independent samples t-test is presented in Table 4. T-tests are used to compare the means of two groups to understand if there is any difference between them or not [51, 52] and the method has been applied in different studies veering around interoperability of datasets [53–56]. The independent samples t-test is used for the scenario when we need to compare the number of publishers for each category of the HVDs. For instance, the number of publishers for Geospatial data against the number of publishers for statistical data. Based on the results, the t-value (which is 2.082746) is less than the critical t-value of 2.228139 for a two-tailed t-test at alpha $= 0.05$. More specifically, the two-tailed p-value is 0.063903, which is greater than the significance level of 0.05. Therefore, we accept the null hypothesis that there is no significant difference between the means of the two groups. Based on these results, we can say that there is no evidence to suggest that the availability of HVDs is significantly different among the different categories.

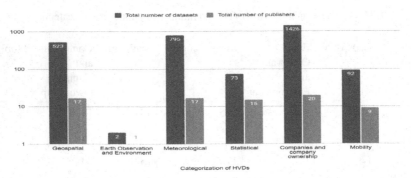

Fig. 2. Availability of HVDs on the EDP and the number of publishers per category.

Table 4. Independent samples t-test to compare the means of publishers and number of HVDs per category.

	Categorization of HVDs	Publishers
Mean	485.1667	13.16667
Variance	308101.4	48.96667
Observations	6	6
Pooled Variance	154075.2	
Hypothesized Mean Difference	0	
Df (degree of freedom)	10	
t Stat (t-value)	2.082746	
P(T < = t) one-tail	0.031951	
t Critical one-tail	1.812461	
P(T < = t) two-tail	0.063903	
t Critical two-tail	2.228139	

4.2 Data Publisher/s

The contributing data publishers in each HVDs category have been extracted from the EDP based on the criteria of search. Figure 3a captures the total number of contributing publishers for the retrieved datasets and the distribution of the publishers and HVD categories. Figure 3a shows the dataset contribution per HVD category for each data publisher. Also, Fig. 3a shows that the Joint Research Centre, for example, has only published two datasets in the Earth observations field, but has published 73 datasets in the meteorological HVD category. This provides strong evidence that publishers are more interested in publishing data in the meteorological HVD category than in the Earth observation field.

The most contributing publishers per HVD category are shown in Fig. 3b, where each HVD category is denoted, again, in a different colour. Interestingly, of all the 79 publishers-contributors, the majority of HVD has been published by the following 15 sources. Among the top data publishers for Geospatial Data are the Statistics Sweden (Statistiska Centralbyrån, SCB), the City of Dresden (Dresden Stadt), the Saxon State Office for Environment, Agriculture and Geology (Sächsisches Landesamt für Umwelt, Landwirtschaft und Geologie), and the State Office for Basic Geoinformation Saxony (GeoSN)/ Landesamt für Geobasisinformation Sachsen (GeoSN). Regarding the Earth Observation and Environment category, there were only 2 datasets available using the proposed filtering and these were offered by the Joint Research Centre. The Statistics Sweden (Statistiska Centralbyrån, SCB), the City of Dresden (Dresden Stadt), the Saxon State Office for Environment, the State Office for Basic Geoinformation Saxony (GeoSN)/ Landesamt für Geobasisinformation Sachsen (GeoSN), and the Joint Research Centre are also the top contributors for the Meteorological category but also for the Mobility category.

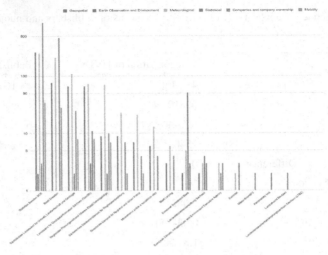

Fig. 3a. Contributing data publishers in all the HVDs categories.

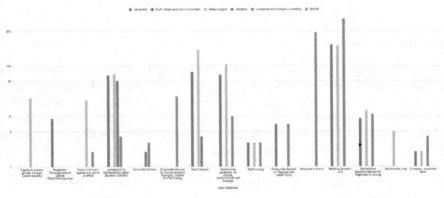

Fig. 3b. The top 15 data publishers (contributors) in all the HVD categories.

As far as the category of Companies and company ownership is concerned, the Statistics Sweden (Statistiska Centralbyrån, SCB), the Czech Ministry of Finance (Ministerstvo financí), the EU Directorate-General for Communications Networks, Content and Technology, and the Saxon State Ministry for Regional Development (Sächsisches Staatsministerium für Regionalentwicklung), while for the category of Statistical data (for which some examples of inferential statistics were applied), the top contributors are the European Medicines Agency, the Council of the European Union, and the State Office for Basic Geoinformation Saxony (GeoSN)/ Landesamt für Geobasisinformation Sachsen (GeoSN), the City of Dresden (Dresden Stadt). The latter is not so surprising considering the mapping of the HVD PSI Directive thematic categories to the EDP Search categories. The mapping is not mutually exclusive, which means that various datasets could belong to more than one data category. Interestingly, most contributors for all the HVD categories originate from three countries: Sweden, Germany and the

Czech Republic, while some European Agencies like the Joint Research Centre, the Directorate-General for Regional and Urban Policy, and other Directorate-Generals are also in the forefront in terms of HVD publishing.

4.3 Technical Specifications

Table 5 shows the "Technical Specifications" vis-a-vis the HVDs identified in the Search protocols (Fig. 1). The rationale behind the selection of those parameters derives from the mandatory technical requirements for HVD set by the European Commission with respect to what should follow the publication and re-use of the datasets [1]. These parameters are necessary to allow for the extraction of insights regarding technical aspects of the available datasets, and, potentially, pave the way towards the elicitation of new technical requirements from a portal's publisher's perspective as also from the user's perspective. As presented on Table 5, most datasets are offered in machine-readable formats, however, the distinction between machine-readable and machine-processable data needs to be referred to. In order to achieve machine-processable information, a number of intermediate steps and sophisticated techniques need to be applied, which is a demanding process, still not supported sufficiently. One would expect this could be different when it comes to HVD, however, this appears not to be the case, so the problem of non-machine-processable data remains. Most datasets are available to download by bulk download options and these datasets are accompanied by SPARQL endpoints.

The majority of the studied datasets are accompanied by appropriate documentation and a license. According to the technical requirements for HVD set by the European Commission, a Creative Commons 4.0 or equivalent license is required. The studied datasets come with their own license type, which can also be data type specific. Some of those licenses include the CC0–1.0 Universal license, data license Germany Zero 2.0, and data license Germany attribution 2.0. As far as the Extensive Metadata parameter is concerned, the EDP follows the DCAT Application Profile (AP) for data portals in Europe (DCAT-AP) [57]. This means that the metadata available needs to be compatible with the equivalent specifications as these are posed by DCAT. In this experiment, the metadata filter was set to "Sufficient", while there exist two more options of "Good", and "Excellent". The DCAT metadata requirements which are not demanded for the "Sufficient" metadata labeling, can be turned into recommendations in order for the publishers to improve the metadata quality before publishing the dataset. As mentioned previously, metadata is one of the most important enablers for the semantic interoperability and reusability of the data, so it is one of the parameters remaining in the limelight.

Table 5. The technical requirements set for high value datasets.

Technical Specifications	Smart Charts/Graphs
Machine-Readable Data	Figure 4 depicts the predominant data formats utilized within the various categories of HVDs. Each category of HVDs employs unique data formats. For instance, geospatial data is primarily distributed in JSON (Java Script Object Notation) format, which surpasses all other formats in terms of usage. Similarly, meteorological data is primarily provided in HTML (HyperText Markup Language) distributions, which exceed all other formats in terms of usage
Machine-Processable Data	Machine-readable information is not necessarily machine processable. This commonly encountered problem remains for HVD
Bulk Download API	Most of the datasets mentioned in this study are available in machine-readable formats and are accompanied by bulk download options. Additionally, these datasets can be accessed and downloaded through APIs and SPARQL endpoints
Extensive Metadata	The metadata quality was set up as "Sufficient" for searching the HVD. For EDP, this is in accordance with the equivalent DCAT (Data Catalog vocabulary) specifications
Marginal Charges Applied	Unavailable Information on the EDP
Publicly Available Documentation	Yes, most of the datasets mentioned in this study are accompanied by publicly available documentation. These datasets can also be found on federated catalogs, national data portals, and ultimately on the EDP. However, the EDP does not explicitly specify the availability of documentation. Available information/documentation may vary from portal to portal
License (CC-4.0 or equivalent license)	Most datasets have their own license type. Notably, the CC0–1.0 Universal license, data license Germany Zero 2.0, and data license Germany Attribution 2.0 are among the licenses predominantly employed

The available data formats for each HVD category (in different colours) are presented in Fig. 4. As presented in the Figure, for the Geospatial, and Companies and company ownership categories, JSON is one of the most commonly available formats, while for Meteorological datasets HTML and TIFF (Tag Image File Format) are dominant. The Statistical category is overrepresented by HTML, CSV (Comma Separated Value) and RDF XML (Resource Description Framework- Extensible Markup Language), while the Mobility Category is mostly available in ESRI (Environmental Systems Research

Institute) Shapefile (a geospatial vector data format). The very limited datasets retrieved for the Earth Observation and Environment category are available in Excel format.

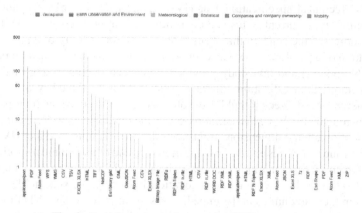

Fig. 4. Data formats used across the HVD categories.

5 Discussion

The results from the three-fold analysis are insightful according to the extant literature on HVD, availability and EDP, for that matter. Thus, vis-a-vis, the analysis at the availability pedestal, it may be inferred that Table 4 results wherein the null hypothesis of the HVDs being similar is clinched via the t-test and these results are in alignment with previous research testing for the availability-interoperability across learning management system portals [58] but not in agreement with another study seeking to understand the availability-interoperability in open source projects [53] or the availability-interoperability mismatch on account of the different standards being operative across the Industry 4.0 standards' specifications [59]. However, these disparate findings may be attributed to the specific contexts and temporality. Thus, these results are in line with our expectations given the inherent success criterion of interoperability that the more similar and congruent the datasets, i.e., HVDs in the present study, the more the propensity for them to be interoperable thereby resulting in higher value derivation and innovation opportunities. It is worth noting that higher availability and fulfilment of technical specifications for HVDs will lead to increased interoperability on the EDP, which can ultimately bring greater value to the open data ecosystem. Interoperable datasets can enable greater ease of use and integration with other datasets, thereby improving their overall value.

6 Conclusion and Future Directions

The overall purpose of the present study was to consider three dimensions (Availability, Publisher/s, Technical specifications) of HVD in the EDP, in order to gain a better understanding of the current status and elicit potential intuitive conclusions. In a way, the study addressed the concern that: "ensuring the interoperability of data catalogues, or the creation of a pan-European data catalogue, is a big challenge faced by EU policy makers" [65: pp. 32] and this study provided a nuanced understanding of the HVD-OGDs via empirical investigation. Findings show that for the three key countries, viz., Sweden, Germany and Czech Republic, the other countries need to match the pace of the HVD publishing on the EDP. Furthermore, given the differentials in terms of the HVD structural and functional dimensions right from the provisioning of select HVD across select themes and categories and down to the metadata and other technical specifications, it is important that a benchmarking framework be adopted for deriving the actual benefits of OGD-HVD via value creation and innovation by a range of stakeholders. Finally, findings from the study hinted at the impediments towards attaining HVD linkages and the same needs to be addressed in further studies with experts' opinions and academic insights.

The presented methodology and its results offer an opportunity to evaluate the availability of HVDs, their publishers, and technical specifications, and to improve the HVDs on the European data portal (EDP). In the future, the EDP could provide additional information on datasets, such as the number of downloads, views, and reuse of datasets, the number of showcases and use cases, the number of research projects and press articles, new dataset requests, marginal charges of datasets, internal statistics about portal usage, as well as the number of views and downloads of re-uses. This information would facilitate the efficient and effective discovery of HVDs through the EDP, eliminating the need for manual evaluation by publishers and across datasets.

Another possible future perspective which can be analyzed and considered would be the analysis of technical functionalities in the European Data Portal (or national data portals case studies) to identify needs of the data portal with respect to both the portals but also user perspective and, in this manner, proceed with the elicitation of requirements to be applied in this direction. This might be of great interest in alignment with the tension to shift towards more user-driven services offered by the open data portals.

Acknowledgments. The authors acknowledge the financial support from the European Union's Horizon 2020 research and innovation programme under the Marie Skłodowska-Curie grant agreement No. 955569.

References

1. Public sector information directive. 2019/0024 of the European Parliament and the Council on open data and re-use of public sector information (recast) (2009). https://eur-lex.europa.eu/eli/dir/2019/1024/oj
2. Zuiderwijk, A., Shinde, R., Janssen, M.: Investigating the attainment of open government data objectives: is there a mismatch between objectives and results? Int. Rev. Adm. Sci. **85**, 645–672 (2019)

3. REDF workshop. Types of value creation in social enterprises (2019). https://redfworkshop. org/learn/value-creation-in-social-enterprises/
4. Porter, M.E., Kramer, M.R.: Creating shared value. Harv. Bus. Rev. **89**, 62–77 (2011)
5. Benington, J.: From private choice to public value. Public value: Theor. Pract. **121**, 31–49 (2011)
6. Euzenat, J.: Towards a principled approach to semantic interoperability. In: IJCAI Workshop on Ontology and Information Sharing, Seattle, US, pp. 19–25 (2011). https://hal.inria.fr/hal-00822909/
7. Kalampokis E, Karamanou A, Tarabanis K. Towards interoperable open statistical data. In: 18th IFIP WG8.5 International Conference, San Benedetto Del Tronto, Italy, pp. 180–191 (2019). https://doi.org/10.1007/978-3-030-27325-5_14
8. Kawashita, I., Baptista, A.A., Soares, D.: Open government data use by the public sector-an overview of its benefits, barriers, drivers, and enablers. HICSS, pp. 1–10 (2022). http://hdl. handle.net/10125/79648
9. Pagano, P., Candela, L., Castelli, D.: Data interoperability (2013). https://doi.org/10.2481/ dsj.GRDI-004
10. Novakouski, M., Lewis, G.A.: Interoperability in the e-government context. Technology Note (2012). https://apps.dtic.mil/sti/citations/ADA611103
11. Sheffer Correa, A., de Assis Mota, A., Toledo Moreira Mota, L., Luiz Pizzigatti Correa, P.: A fuzzy rule-based system to assess e-government technical interoperability maturity level. Trans. Govern. People Process Policy **8**, 335–356 (2014)
12. Guijarro, L.: Semantic interoperability in egovernment initiatives. Comput. Stand. Interfaces **31**, 174–180 (2009)
13. Valle, P.H.D., Garces, L., Nakagawa, E.Y.: A typology of architectural strategies for inter-operability. In: Proceedings of the XIII British Symposium on Software Components, Architectures, and Reuse, pp. 3–12 (2019)
14. Wyns, B., et al.: Good practices for identifying high value datasets and engaging with re-users: the case of public tendering data (2013). https://www.w3.org/2013/share-psi/wiki/images/3/ 31/Share-PSI_Submission_Paper-PwC_v0.03.pdf
15. Welle Donker, F.M., van Loenen, B.: Societal costs and benefits of high-value open government data: a case study in the Netherlands. In: 21st AGILE International Conference on Geographic Information Science: Geospatial Technologies for All, Lund, Sweden, pp. 1–5 (2018). http://resolver.tudelft.nl/uuid:ff6261e6-c7a6-4d4b-be4b-888acd632afb
16. Utamachant, P., Anutariya, C.: An analysis of high-value datasets: a case study of Thailand's open government data. In: 15th International Joint Conference on Computer Science and Software Engineering (JCSSE). Nakhonpathom, Thailand, pp. 1–6 (2018). https://doi.org/ 10.1109/JCSSE.2018.8457350
17. Jetzek, T., Avital, M., Bjørn-Andersen, N.: Generating value from open government data. ICIS 2013 (2013). https://aisel.aisnet.org/icis2013/proceedings/GeneralISTopics/5/
18. Benington, J., Moore, M.H.: Public value in complex and changing times (2011). https://doi. org/10.1007/978-0-230-36431-8_1
19. Harrison, T.M., et al.: Open government and e-government: democratic challenges from a public value perspective. In: Proceedings of the 12th Annual International Conference on Digital Government Research (dg.o 2011), pp. 245–253 (2011)
20. Public resource. Open data working group (2007). https://public.resource.org/open_governm ent_meeting.html
21. Bertot, J.C., McDermott, P., Smith, T.: Measurement of open government: metrics and process. In: 45th Hawaii International Conference on System Sciences, Maui, HI, USA, pp. 2491–2499 (2012). https://doi.org/10.1109/HICSS.2012.658
22. McDermott, P.: Building open government. Gov. Inf. Q. **27**, 401–413 (2010)

23. Reggi, L., Dawes, S.: Open government data ecosystems: linking transparency for innovation with transparency for participation and accountability. In: Scholl, H., et al. Electronic Government. EGOV 2016. LNCS, vol 9820. Springer, Cham (2016). https://doi.org/10.1007/978-3-319-44421-5_6

24. Peled, A.: When transparency and collaboration collide: the USA open data program. J. Am. Soc. Inform. Sci. Technol. **62**, 2085–2094 (2011)

25. Parycek, P., Hochtl, J., Ginner, M.: Open government data implementation evaluation. J. Theor. Appl. Electron. Commer. Res. **9**, 80–99 (2014)

26. Attard, J., Orlandi, F., Auer, S.: Value creation on open government data. In: 49th Hawaii International Conference on System Sciences (HICSS), Koloa, HI, USA, pp. 2605–2614 (2016). https://doi.org/10.1109/HICSS.2016.326

27. Wang, V., Shepherd, D.: Exploring the extent of openness of open government data – a critique of open government datasets in the UK. Gov. Inf. Q. **37**, 101405 (2020)

28. Ruijer, E., Detienne, F., Baker, M., Groff, J., Meijer, A.: The politics of open government data: understanding organizational responses to pressure for more transparency. Am. Rev. Public Admin. **50**, 260–274 (2020)

29. Harrison, T.M., Pardo, T.A., Cook, M.: Creating open government ecosystems: a research and development agenda. Future Internet **4**, 900–928 (2012)

30. Linders, D., Wilson, S.C.: What is open government?: One year after the directive. In: 12th Annual International Digital Government Research Conference: Digital Government Innovation in Challenging Times, pp. 262–271 (2011). https://doi.org/10.1145/2037556.2037599

31. Unsworth, K., Townes, A.: Transparency, participation, cooperation: a case study evaluating Twitter as a social media interaction tool in the US open government initiative. In: 13th Annual International Conference on Digital Government Research, pp. 90–96 (2012). https://doi.org/10.1145/2307729.2307745

32. Charalabidis, Y., Alexopoulos, C., Loukis, E.: A taxonomy of open government data research areas and topics. J. Organ. Comput. Electron. Commer. **26**, 41–63 (2016)

33. Kubicek, H., Cimander, R., Scholl, H.J.: Layers of interoperability. In: Organizational Interoperability in E-Government, Springer, Berlin (2011). https://doi.org/10.1007/978-3-642-22502-4_7

34. Charalabidis, Y., Zuiderwijk, A., Alexopoulos, C., Janssen, M., Lampoltshammer, T., Ferro, E.: Open data interoperability. In: The World of Open Data. Public Administration and Information Technology, Springer, Cham, vol. 28, pp. 75–93 (2018). https://doi.org/10.1007/978-3-319-90850-2_5

35. Maheshwari, D., Janssen, M.: Reconceptualizing measuring, benchmarking for improving interoperability in smart ecosystems: the effect of ubiquitous data and crowdsourcing. Gov. Inf. Q. **31**, S84–S92 (2014)

36. Lodato, T., French, E., Clark, J.: Open government data in the smart city: Interoperability, urban knowledge, and linking legacy systems. J. Urban Aff. **43**, 586–600 (2021)

37. Jimenez, C.E., Solanas, A., Falcone, F.: E-government interoperability: linking open and smart government. Computer **47**, 22–24 (2014)

38. Colpaert, P., et al.: Quantifying the interoperability of open government datasets. Computer **47**, 50–56 (2014)

39. Kalampokis, E., Karamanou, A., Tarabanis, K.: Interoperability conflicts in linked open statistical data. Information **10**, 249 (2019). https://doi.org/10.3390/info10080249

40. Maali, F., Cyganiak, R., Peristeras, V.: Enabling interoperability of government data catalogues. In: Wimmer, M.A., Chappelet, J.L., Janssen, M., Scholl, H.J. (eds.) Electronic Government. EGOV 2010. LNCS, vol. 6228, pp. 339–350. Springer, Berlin (2010). https://doi.org/10.1007/978-3-642-14799-9_29

41. Masoumi, H., Farahani, B., Shams Aliee, F.: Systematic and ontology-based approach to interoperable cross-domain open government data services. Trans. Govern. People Process Policy **16**, 110–127 (2022)
42. DiFranzo, D., et al.: TWC LOGD: a portal for linking open government data (2010). https://hdl.handle.net/20.500.13015/4607
43. Machado, A.L., Parente de Oliveira JM. DIGO: an open data architecture for e-government. In: 15th International Enterprise Distributed Object Computing Conference Workshops, Helsinki, Finland, pp. 448–456 (2011). https://doi.org/10.1109/EDOCW.2011.34
44. Breitman, K., et al.: Open government data in Brazil. IEEE Intell. Syst. **27**, 45–49 (2012)
45. Masoumi, H., Farahani, B., Aliee, F.S.: An ontology-based open data interoperability approach for cross-domain government data services. In: 25th International Computer Conference, Computer Society of Iran (CSICC), Tehran, Iran, pp. 1–8 (2020). https://doi.org/10.1109/CSICC49403.2020.9050079
46. Ahlgren, B., Hidell, M., Ngai, E.C.H.: Internet of things for smart cities: interoperability and open data. IEEE Internet Comput. **20**, 52–56 (2016)
47. Buyle, R., et al.: A sustainable method for publishing interoperable open data on the data. Data **6**, 93 (2021). https://doi.org/10.3390/data6080093
48. Washington AL. The interoperability of US Federal government information: Interoperability. Big Data: Concepts, Methodologies, Tools, and Applications (2016). https://doi.org/10.4018/978-1-4666-9840-6.ch011
49. McKinsey global institute smart cities executive summary. Scribd 2018. https://www.scribd.com/document/615375365/Mgi-Smart-Cities-Executive-Summary
50. Li, W.C.Y., Nirei, M., Yamana, K.: Value of data: there's no such thing as a free lunch in the digital economy, RIETI discussion paper (2019). https://cepr.org/voxeu/columns/value-data-theres-no-such-thing-free-lunch-digital-economy
51. Dowdy, S., Wearden, S., Chilko, D.: Statistics for research. 3rd edn. Wiley-Interscience (2004)
52. Field, A.: Discovering statistics using SPSS. 3rd edn. Sage (2009)
53. Shamsi, F.A., Bamatraf, S., Rahwan, T., Aung, Z., Svetinovic, D.: Correlation analysis of popularity and interoperability in open source projects. In: International Conference on Innovations in Information Technology (IIT), Al Ain, United Arab Emirates, pp. 181–186 (2018). https://doi.org/10.1109/INNOVATIONS.2018.8605970
54. King, H.H., et al.: Preliminary protocol for interoperable telesurgery. In: International Conference on Advanced Robotics, pp. 1–6 (2009). https://ieeexplore.ieee.org/abstract/document/5174711
55. Bamoriya, P., Singh, P.: Beyond the obvious: standardization and interoperability issues in mobile banking in India. Acta Universitatis Danubius **6**, 14–27 (2013). https://www.ceeol.com/search/article-detail?id=564459
56. Perumal, T., Ramli, A.R., Leong, C.Y., Samsudin K., Mansor, S.: Interoperability among heterogeneous systems in smart home environment. In: Web-Based Information Technologies and Distributed Systems. Atlantis Ambient and Pervasive Intelligence, Atlantis Press, vol. 2 (2010). https://doi.org/10.2991/978-94-91216-32-9_7
57. DCAT. About DCAT application profile for data portals in Europe. https://joinup.ec.europa.eu/collection/semantic-interoperability-community-semic/solution/dcat-application-profile-data-portals-europe/about
58. Conde, M.A., Garcia-Penalvo, F.J., Piguillem, J., Casany, M.J., Alier, M.: Interoperability in eLearning contexts: Interaction between LMS and PLE. In: Proceedings of 1st Symposium on Languages, Applications and Technologies, Braga, pp. 205–223 (2012). https://doi.org/10.4230/OASIsc.SLATE.2012.205
59. Melluso, N., Grangel-Gonzalez, I., Fantoni, G.: Enhancing Industry 4.0 standards interoperability via knowledge graphs with natural language processing. Comput. Ind. **140**, 103676 (2022)

60. Kirstein, F., Dittwald, B., Dutkowski, S., Glikman, Y., Schimmler, S., Hauswirth, M.: Linked data in the European data portal: a comprehensive platform for applying DCAT-AP. In: Lindgren, I., et al. Electronic Government. EGOV 2019. LNCS, vol. 11685, pp. 192–204. Springer, Cham (2019). https://doi.org/10.1007/978-3-030-27325-5_15

61. Andrade, M.C., Cunha, R.O., Figueiredo, J., Baptista, A.A.: Do the European data portal datasets in the categories government and public sector, transport and education, culture and sport meet the data on the web best practices? Data **6**, 94 (2021)

62. van der Waal, S., Węcel, K., Ermilov, I., Janev, V., Milošević, U., Wainwright, M.: Lifting open data portals to the data web. In: Auer, S., Bryl, V., Tramp, S. (eds.) Linked Open Data-Creating Knowledge Out of Interlinked Data. LNCS, vol. 8661, pp. 175–195. Springer, Cham (2014). https://doi.org/10.1007/978-3-319-09846-3_9

63. Schauppenlehner, T., Muhar, A.: Theoretical availability versus practical accessibility: the critical role of metadata management in open data portals. Sustainability **10**, 545 (2018)

64. Perego, A., Cetl, V., Friis-Christensen, A., Lutz, M.: GeoDCAT-AP: representing geographic metadata by using the "DCAT application profile for data portals in Europe (2017). https://unece.org/fileadmin/DAM/stats/documents/ece/ces/ge.58/2017/mtg3/2017-UNECE-topic-i-EC-GeoDCAT-ap-paper.pdf

65. Ubaldi, B.: Open government data: towards empirical analysis of open government data initiatives. OECD 2013, vol. 22 (2013). https://doi.org/10.1787/5k46bj4f03s7-en

Open Government Data in Educational Programs Curriculum: Current State and Prospects

Georgios Papageorgiou[1]([✉]), Euripidis Loukis[1], Georgios Pappas[1], Nina Rizun[2], Stuti Saxena[3], Yannis Charalabidis[1], and Charalampos Alexopoulos[1]

[1] Department of Information and Communications Systems Engineering, University of the Aegean, Mytilene, Greece
{gpapag,eloukis,eloukis,yannisx,alexop}@aegean.gr
[2] Department of Informatics in Management, Faculty of Management and Economics, Gdańsk University of Technology, Gdańsk, Poland
Nina.rizun@pg.edu.pl
[3] Graphic Era Deemed to Be University, Graphic Era University, Dehradun, India

Abstract. Extant research on Open Government Data (OGD) has remained confined to the grappling of issues linked with its conceptual, theoretical and empirical dimensions, however focusing on the supply of OGD physical capital (ODG portals, datasets, etc.), and to a lesser degree on the demand for it (e.g., needs of potential users), but not dealing with relevant OGD human capital (human knowledge and skills concerning OGD). Furthermore, research on meta-analysis or literature reviews has not expanded its scope to unravel the formation of OGD human capital, and especially how the OGD theme is being showcased across universities' curriculum. The present research aims to contribute to filling this research gap, through an analysis of the OGD-related programs and courses offered at the graduate and post-graduate levels across the top-notch universities identified as per the indicators of the QS World University rankings, 2023. Our theoretical foundation is the widely recognized 'Human Capital Theory' from the economic science, which gives prominence to the importance of the human capital (human knowledge and skills) as an important complement of the classical physical capital (e.g., production equipment, ICT capital, etc.). Our findings indicate that there are only small number of courses concerning OGD in these top-notch universities; furthermore, a very small share of them have OGD an main topic, while most of them include only a part concerning OGD. Most of them focus on the exploitation of OGD of a specific thematic domain (mainly urban studies and health), and only a few deal with OGD in general. Furthermore, there is a prevalence of postgraduate courses, offered as part of MSC programs, followed by undergraduate courses, offered as part of BSC study programs, and to a much lesser degree short courses. Also, with respect to the objective of these OGD-related programs and courses, most of them aim at the generation of scientific value from OGD, while a smaller number aim at the generation of social-political value, and only a much smaller number at the development of economic value. Therefore, it can be concluded that the formation of OGD human capital by the examined universities is limited.

K. Hinkelmann et al. (Eds.): BIR 2023, LNBIP 493, pp. 311–326, 2023.
https://doi.org/10.1007/978-3-031-43126-5_22

Keywords: Open Government Data (OGD) · Human Capital · Universities · Curriculum · MOOCs

1 Introduction

Open Government Data (OGD) pertains to the availability of datasets concerning government operations and functioning via license-free [1, 7], which are linked with different themes contingent upon the area of administration, such as health, education, climate, tourism, environment, infrastructure, etc. [44]. The OGD can be used by scientific, social-political as well as economic actors and enable the generation of considerable scientific, social-political and economic value respectively, and in general can become a significant contribution of government to the development of the digital economy and society [7]. Due to the great potential of OGD, governments of most countries have designed and implemented OGD initiatives, and at the same time international assessments/comparisons of them are regularly conducted, leading to the calculation for each country of various standard indices like the ODIN [31], OKFN [32], Open Data Barometer [30], etc. [25, 26]. Considerable research has been conducted about the quality of OGD portals and datasets from the supply perspective (i.e. the governments' efforts at maintaining the quality of datasets) as well as the demand perspective (i.e. the perceptions of users regarding the quality of datasets) side [10, 13, 19, 22, 24, 27, 33, 38, 39, 42, 46, 49–51, 56].

However, economic science research has revealed that though the physical capital (i.e. production equipment, ICT capital (including hardware and software), etc.) and the labour are traditionally regarded as the main factors for the production of goods and services (and value in general), it is of critical importance for the efficient and effective exploitation of the former to develop appropriate 'human capital' as well; it is meant as relevant knowledge and skills of humans, and its importance increases with the complexity and sophistication of the physical capital, and this has given rise to the development of 'Human Capital Theory' [12, 28, 41] in the economic science: it gives prominence to the importance of the human capital (knowledge and skills of humans) as an important complement of the classical physical capital for the efficient exploitation of the latter. So, as mentioned above there has been considerable research concerning the OGD physical capital that has been developed by many countries (mainly the OGD portals they have developed as well as the datasets they provide), but there is a lack of research concerning the formation of relevant OGD human capital, which is quite important for the generation of value (scientific, political-social, economic) from the existing OGD physical capital. As OGD can become a significant contribution of government to the development of the digital economy and society, and governments make large investments in OGD physical capital (OGD servers, portals, datasets), it is important to develop the required 'soft complement' of it: the required OGD human capital: humans' knowledge and skills about OGD as well as its exploitation and the generation of value (scientific, social-political, economic) from them. Therefore, further research is required in the OGD domain concerning the OGD human capital formation. Given the magnitude of academic research interest in OGD - especially in the last 10 years

- it remains to be assessed as to how far has the domain progressed in the academic environments with respect to teaching; surprisingly, no research has been conducted to elucidate the infusion in academic education of this very significant domain - that is relatable to the extent to which the governments are forwarding their claims regarding the furtherance of transparent and corruption-free administration apart from bolstering citizen participation, collaboration and trust [15, 18] besides serving as a means for value creation and innovation by a range of stakeholders [20, 21]. Research pertaining to meta-analysis and reviews of the OGD-focused studies already published in academic publication outlets is well-acknowledged [3, 23, 35, 47, 48], and in order to carry forward the baton of OGD research, the present study seeks to extend its directions towards OGD human capital, by examining how OGD theme fairs across university curricula across the globe. So, it focuses on the most important mechanisms of human capital formation in general for the economy, and the universities, aiming to investigate its educational activity towards the formation of ODG human capital.

Specifically, the research questions for the present study shall pertain to the specific tributary of thought: *How has the OGD theme traversed across universities' curricula across the globe?* Specifically, the nature and scope of OGD-focused curriculum in the selected top 40 universities (based on the QS World University Rankings, 2023) were investigated using both qualitative and quantitative approaches. Thus, the present study seeks to address the need to further "communication and interaction among researchers (through the "common language" it introduces)" [6] by unravelling the maze through which such dialogue and discussion have progressed over the years in the mainstream university classroom settings. As mentioned above, the theoretical foundation of our study is the widely recognised 'Human Capital Theory' from the economic science.

The structure of the research paper is as follows: following a review of the related literature on OGD, the research design has been spelt out in detail; thereafter, the results of our research are presented and discussed, followed by some concluding remarks towards the close of the study, and also limitations, future research pointers and practitioner implications.

2 Related Research

Given the fact that OGD is an emerging domain, academic interest is also at an emerging stage [47, 48, 55]. OGD has been conceptualised as "a very heterogenous field of research" [48] involving researchers from economics, public administration, political science, etc. and initially most of the empirical investigation on OGD between 2008 and 2013 has remained confined towards aspects like transparency, participation, collaboration, technology, regulation/law, acceptance/trust in government, G2C/G2B relationship, public/citizens value and accountability. In their follow-up study focusing on a longer timespan between 2002 and 2019, Wirtz et al. (2022) [47] underlined that considerable qualitative and quantitative research has been conducted to appreciate the OGD policies/regulation/law, drivers/barriers, success/performance/value, acceptance/satisfaction, use/adoption/implementation and actors/relationships. Three areas of OGD-focused studies have been found in the meta-analysis of the research publications across 2011 and 2015: transparency, participation and collaboration [9]. Saxena

[36] identified three strands in OGD-focused research as far as the period between 2009 and 2017 is concerned: OGD-focused research with theoretical and conceptual underpinnings, applied (contextual) research and user-focused research. Finally, Saxena and Alexopoulos (2022) [37] have identified the four strands in OGD-focused research wherein the timespan extended from 2011 until 2022: research on conceptualisation and review of OGD studies; research on the benefits and challenges of OGD implementation; research on the quality of OGD portals and research on the adoption and usage of OGD.

From the foregoing, the reviews on academic publications on OGD indicate that the extant research on OGD has focused on OGD physical capital, both from a supply perspective (e.g., ODG portals, datasets, etc.), and to a lesser degree from the demand perspective (e.g., needs/satisfaction of potential users). However, it has not dealt with the formation of relevant OGD human capital (human skills concerning OGD), despite its high importance for the efficient and effective exploitation of the physical OGD capital, and the generation of scientific, political-social and economic value from it; this is imperative due to the large investments that governments have made for the development of the existing OGD capital, and the high operating costs of it (especially for selecting, processing, anonymizing and publishing new datasets). So, there is a need to widen the ambit of OGD research to appreciate how OGD themes are being discussed and deliberated in other formats - university curriculum, for instance, and this constitutes the raison d'etre for the present research.

3   Methodology

The methodology of this research includes two steps. First, we examined and assessed the most prominent rankings for evaluating academic institutions, and thereafter, we selected the most appropriate one to proceed with our research. In the second step, we used this list to identify the top universities in order to collect data on the OGD-related courses and programs they conduct, which we then analysed across their academic levels, course type, content delivery method, teaching language, thematic domains, value generation, OGD content.

3.1   Universities Ranking List Selection

At this first stage we had to evaluate the Global University rankings and decide which was more suitable for our research objectives, in order to identifying the top 40 universities. Although there is a plethora of University ranking indices that cover different qualitative aspects of higher education, the main three [17] and more influential rankings are: a) Times Higher Education World University Rankings [52], b) Quacquarelli Symonds [34], and c) Academic Ranking of World Universities [40], which are always present in several academic comparisons of global university rankings [2, 45, 53]; therefore, we concluded that we could proceed with a detailed evaluation of these three major ones.

World University Rankings Times Higher Education (THE): The THE ranking was initially part of the QS rating system, but it became independent in 2009, and thereafter, the two systems had diverged their methodologies. This system uses thirteen performance indicators grouped into five categories: teaching, citations, research, international outlook and industry income.

Quacquarelli Symonds (QS): The QS rating system was first published in 2004, and its methodology is comprised of six indicators designed to cover the educational process in its entirety. The indicators used are: the university's academic reputation, the employee's reputation, the faculty-student ratio, the number of citations per faculty, the international faculty ratio and finally, the international student ratio.

Academic Ranking of World Universities (ARWU): The ARWU ranking was developed by the Shanghai Jiao Tong University, and it was announced for the first time in 2003. Its methodology is comprised of six indicators mainly focused on research impact. The indicators are: the university alumni that have acquired a Nobel prize or a Field medal, the staff of the institution with the same distinctions, the highly cited researchers, the publications in Nature and Science, the number of publications that are part of the Science Citation Index (SCI) - Expanded and the Social Sciences Citation Index (SSCI), and, finally, the per capita academic performance of the institution.

For the purpose of the current study, ARWU was rejected since its indicators are focused mainly on research and reputation. Therefore, it does not provide an overall approach to the educational process. The QS and THE were split into two distinct indexes in 2009, and although their methodologies are diverging, they still contain significant similarities [2]. The main difference is that QS focus more on the international aspect of academic education, measuring international students and faculty members. Therefore, it is considered to provide a more well-rounded evaluation of educational institutions, and it was chosen to determine the top Universities in this research.

3.2 Data Collection and Analysis

For the data collection, initially, we identified some important fields/indicators, which are necessary for analysing the OGD-related university courses/programs. Our research plan was to analyse all the selected fields of the collected data to uncover their qualitative and quantitative aspects and to culminate in thorough results and conclusions. These important fields/indicators are:

- Program name
- The program is part of a degree/seminar/course
- Name of the institution
- Academic level
- Country of institution
- Program objectives and/or learning objectives
- Program Area of Specialization
- Program Overview
- Type of institution
- Program type
- Credits
- Entry requirements
- Content delivery
- Program cost
- Duration
- Language

- Comment
- URL

In the following paragraphs, we discuss the most important of them:

The program is part of a degree/seminar/course: This. Indicator was essential to identify whether the OGD-related teaching was provided independently or considered an aspect of a wider educational program (part of a master's or bachelor's).

Academic level:. The academic level was selected to identify in what tier of the educational process this teaching is conducted: undergraduate or graduate.

Country of institution:. The institution's country can provide essential information about the development of OGD in specific countries; however, the conclusions we can draw from this field/indicator are indicative, since we have collected data for the top 40 universities from a global ranking, and therefore we cannot make accurate comparisons between counties.

Program objectives and/or learning objectives, Program Area of Specialization and Program Overview: All these fields/indicators were used to understand the kind of educational content of the course, the type of the OGD targeted or used, or are part of the educational program and to identify their thematic categories.

Credits: Another metric we plan to examine is the credits of each course. However, this is indicative, since the universities from different countries have different systems/types of credits.

Content delivery: We distinguished two content delivery methods: in-person and online. After the identification of the main fields/indicators we need for each course/program, we proceeded to the discovery of the latter. Initially, the most widespread and popular method was used, the Google search engine. Harnessing search engines like Google (or Yahoo) for search optimisation with the help of keywords or strings is widely used in academic research, especially in webometric analyses [5, 8, 43, 54]. Furthermore, search engines, including Google Scholar, PubMed or Web of Science, are useful in conducting "(Boolean) searches with regards to precision, recall, and reproducibility" [16], which help in customised user-driven search [4]. Therefore, a query was constructed that contained three keywords, the university name, the term "open data", and the term "course"; the query was structured as "university name" AND "open data" AND course. However, the outcomes of this initial approach were not satisfactory, as it returned limited relevant results. The same query was also used in the search engines available on the university websites. Unfortunately, most universities did have their website search engine linked to Google, so we ended up with the same results. After this unfruitful attempt, we reconstructed our query by enhancing the second and third terms and the query was structured as "university name" AND ("open data" OR opendata OR open-data) AND (Bachelor OR "Executive Masters" OR Graduate OR "Higher Education" OR Masters OR MSc OR PhD OR Program OR Specialisation OR Training OR Undergraduate OR "Joint Master"). However, even with this enhanced query, the returned results, though there was some improvement, were not absolutely satisfactory, and therefore, we turned to new technologies, specifically the ChatGPT (Generative Pre-trained Transformer) application - a chatbot that OpenAI released in November 2022 - on account of the fact that ChatGPT is being increasingly used in academic research and practice which facilitates in easy access to information apart from providing tailor-made real-time answers to the queries [14]. The query we used in ChatGPT included the university's name and a question to return the courses related to OGD. Unfortunately, ChatGPT could not provide direct results; still, it provided us with scientific fields where the university offered courses related to OGD. These results helped our research endeavours as we manually examined the courses and programs offered by the faculties associated with the specific scientific fields. This process was followed for each of the top 40 Universities.

4 Results

Following the first step of the above methodology (described in 3.1), we found 36 entries (courses or programs) in total in the above top universities. The most interesting finding is that open data was mentioned directly in the title of only 4 courses, and in the description or the curriculum of the remaining 32 (30 and 2 respectively). Therefore, there are only 4 courses in these 40 top universities having open data as their main topic:

- 'Astrophysics and Cosmology with Open Data', an undergraduate course, part of the Physics BSc of the California Institute of Technology (Caltech).
- 'Unlocking the Value of Open Data', a short course (1 day seminar) of the University of Hong Kong.
- 'Unleashing Open Data with Python', a postgraduate course, part of an MSc of the Johns Hopkins University.
- 'Challenges and Opportunities of Open Data', an undergraduate course, part of a BSc of the Faculty of Informatics of the University of Toronto.

All the other entries we found are courses, short courses or seminars, and also one MSc program, which include parts that concerning open data. Therefore, we can conclude that open data still have a very limited presence in the curricula of the examined top universities, which currently have quite limited educational activities towards the development of the required OGD human capital (knowledge and skills about OGD as well as its exploitation and the generation of value from them), despite their huge potential and possible contribution the development of the digital economy and society.

4.1 Quantitative Analysis

First, we investigated the academic level of the OGD-related educational courses/programs: how many of them are available at the undergraduate academic level, how many at the postgraduate or doctoral level, and how many at both (as they can be attended by both undergraduate and postgraduate student); also, we have summer schools and seminars that are not part of any academic level and therefore we identified them as non-applicable to this metric. The results are shown in Fig. 1 below. We can see that most (52,8%) courses/programs are postgraduate, but there is a considerable share (25%) of undergraduate ones.

The research then focused on the type of courses/programs offered, where we identified six distinct types.

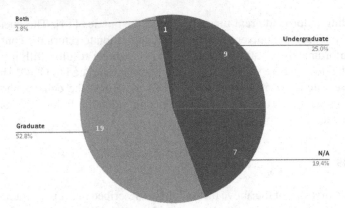

Fig. 1. Academic Levels

- Educational Module (Course) independent of any undergraduate postgraduate program
- Course Part of BSc
- Course Part of MSc
- Master's Program where most modules of the program are related to some form of open data. Summer schools
- Short Course: distance learning (online) without participation requirements
- Seminar for students or professionals
- Summer School for professionals

In Fig. 2 we can see the results: the most predominant type were courses that are part of MSc programs (44%), followed by courses that are parts of BSc programs (25%); furthermore, there also some short courses about OGD (14%).

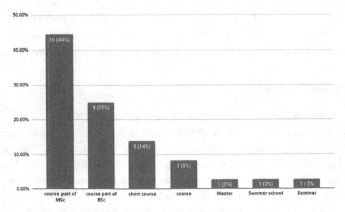

Fig. 2. Course/program Types

Next, we examined the Content Delivery methods of these OGD-related educational courses/programs, and the results are shown in Fig. 3: most of them (83%) are conducted with physical presence (In Person), while much less (17%) – mainly short courses - are conducted through ICT-supported distance learning (Online).

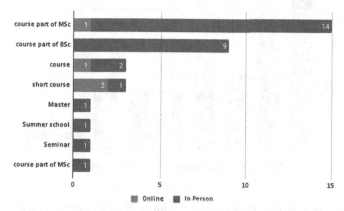

Fig. 3. Content Delivery methods per Type of Course/Program

Furthermore, with respect to the language used in these courses/programs, we have found that the overwhelming majority of them are in English language (94.4%), followed by Korean and French (2.8% each).

4.2 Qualitative Analysis

The qualitative analysis was based on the texts of the descriptions of the OGD-related courses/programs. Initially, we examined for each of them whether it concerned OGD of a specific thematic domain, or OGD in general, and the results are shown in Fig. 4. We can see that most of them concern a specific thematic domain (73%), mainly urban studies (27%), health (11%) and geospatial data (11%), while much less are generic (27%); this indicates that there is a lack of generic OGD courses, which can provide a complete and comprehensive in-depth view concerning the main OGD concepts, capabilities, frameworks as well as exploitation and value generation approaches (as courses concerning a specific thematic domain provide more limited views, focusing on the exploitation of OGD of this specific thematic domain).

It is worth mentioning these thematic OGD-related courses concern thematic domains in which large quantities of OGD are available, so it is necessary to develop knowledge and skills for exploiting them:

- **Urban:** data related to cities and urban areas, such as population, demographics, housing distribution, infrastructure, services, businesses, as well as traffic and transportation data.
- **Geospatial:** data related to location, geographic area, maps, etc.
- **Health:** data on epidemiology, diseases, public health services and healthcare (especially for COVID there is a wide availability of OGD).
- **Cultural:** cultural, historical and archaeological data
- **Physics:** data used as part of research in the physics domain, like astrophysical data.

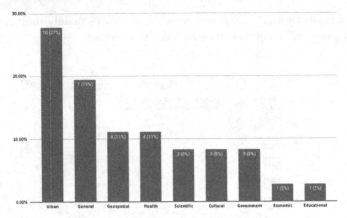

Fig. 4. Courses/programs thematic domains

- **Economic:** data on the economy, employment, business environment, growth and industry.
- **Chemistry:** chemistry-related data like molecular data.
- **Educational:** data about education, schools, students and teachers.

Next, we examined for each of these OGD-related courses/programs its main orientation with respect to the type of value (scientific, social-political, economic) generation it mainly targets. For this purpose, the classification of courses and programs was done using an open coding approach based on three fields of the collected data: the Program Objectives, the Program Area of Specialization and the Program Overview; additionally, in some cases, the curriculum of the program was also examined through the corresponding university web page. Our findings are presented in Fig. 5. We can see that most of the courses are targeting the generation a specific type of value, mainly scientific (41.7%), followed by the social–political (33.3%), and to a lesser extent (only 11,1%) economic value; the remaining (13.9%) are generic (i.e., do not focus on a specific type of value generation from OGD). Therefore, we can conclude most of the existing OGD-related courses/programs of these top Universities are oriented towards the scientific-academic exploitation of OGD (mainly for research); on the contrary, only a small share of them are oriented towards the generation of economic value from OGD (e.g., through the development of value added electronic services by combining several OGD datasets, provided by several different government agencies, and possibly private datasets as well), despite the emphasis that relevant literature (e.g. Charalabidis et al., 2018) [7] has placed on the huge potential of OGD use towards the creation of new economic activity and innovation.

Finally, we examined the content of these courses/programs, and we identified two main clusters: the smallest of them (38.9%) are dealing on the conceptual aspects of OGD (OGD concepts, capabilities, frameworks as well as exploitation and value generation approaches), while the largest (61.1%) focus on technical (mainly statistical and machine learning) methods and tools for processing OGD.

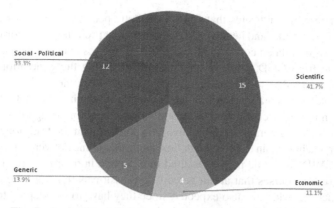

Fig. 5. Analysis based on the type of value generation from OGD

5 Conclusions

While previous OGD research has focused on the 'hard' aspects of OGD, dealing mainly with the massive OGD physical capital that has been developed by the governments of many countries, there has been limited research attention about the 'soft' aspects of OGD, and especially the OGD human capital (knowledge and skills about OGD), despite the importance of the later for the efficient and effective exploitation of the former. This study contributes to filling this important research gap, by analyzing the OGD-related programs and courses offered at the graduate and post-graduate levels across the 40 top universities of the world according to the QS World University rankings, 2023. Its theoretical foundation is the 'human capital' theory from economic sciences.

The main finding of our study is that there are only small number of courses concerning OGD (only 36) in these top 40 universities; therefore, these top educational institutions seem to make a quite limited contribution to the development of the required OGD human capital and have quite limited educational activities in this direction. Furthermore, a very small share of the identified OGD courses have OGD an main topic (only 4 out of 36), while most of them include only a part concerning OGD. This indicates that OGD is not regarded by the examined universities as a separate individual topic for teaching (though it is regarded as a separate individual topic of research); it is regarded (from a teaching perspective) rather as a part/aspect of other topics, or as a resource for researching them. Another interesting finding is that most of the identified OGD courses are thematic: they focus on the exploitation of OGD of a specific thematic domain (mainly urban studies and health); only a few deal with OGD in general. So, there is a lack of generic OGD courses, which can provide a complete and comprehensive in-depth view and knowledge concerning the main OGD concepts, capabilities, frameworks as well as exploitation and value generation approaches.

Furthermore, our study provided some interesting insights concerning the OGD-related courses and programs of the examined top universities. Firstly, there is a notable prevalence of postgraduate courses, offered mainly as part of MSc programs, and to a lesser extent courses offered as part of MSc study programs. Additionally, seminars and short courses for professionals are also present, albeit to a much lesser extent.

Secondly, our research indicates that from a thematic perspective courses concerning urban, general, geospatial and health OGD were the most prominent categories. Thirdly, most of these OGD-related courses and programs objectives concern the generation of scientific value from OGD, while a smaller number aim at the generation of social-political value, and only a much smaller number at the development of economic value. So, dominant is the orientation towards the academic-research use of OGD, but much less orientation towards economic activity and value generation using OGD.

Furthermore, the in-person lecture delivery is predominant the traditional academic levels (master, bachelor), an expected outcome since the online delivery of most courses during the COVID pandemic period resulted in a decline in their quality [11]. Finally, the majority of the courses that are targeted to professionals (e.g., short courses, etc.) use online teaching, which is also expected since they have to be adapted to the needs of the working individuals that are attending them.

The research presented in this paper has interesting implications for research and practice. With respect to research, it enriches the existing body of knowledge about OGD with useful new knowledge about the OGD human capital, and especially for the relevant educational activities for this purpose of the universities; furthermore, our research opens up new directions of research in the OGD domain concerning the existing OGD human capital as well its main formation mechanisms. With respect to practice, our findings can be very useful for the universities for the restructuring and the improvements of their curricula with respect to OGD, as they have a huge potential for the generation of not only scientific research value, but also: a) social-political value (by providing a sound basis for more substantial political debates concerning the main needs and problems of our societies), and b) economic value (by enabling the development of value added electronic services by combining several OGD datasets, provided by several different government agencies, and possibly private datasets as well). The universities have to devise means of generating interest of the students in OGD, perceiving OGD as a stratagem for furthering their employability prospects. Furthermore, our findings have implications for government agencies that are responsible for the design and implementation of policies concerning the opening/publishing government data; these policies have to include actions concerning not only the development of OGD physical capital (e.g., new servers, portals, datasets, etc.) but also OGD human capital as well, as the later is critical importance for efficient and effective exploitation of the former, and the generation of value from it (if the required OGD human capital is not developed they will run the risk of underutilization of the costly OGD infrastructures they have developed). Since the universities (at least the examined top ones) currently do not contribute considerably to the formation of the required OGD human capital, government should: i) on one hand facilitate the development of more OGD-related courses (both generic and thematically oriented) ay undergraduate and postgraduate level, though various incentives and OGD courses development financing programs; and ii) on the other hands develop other mechanisms of OGD human capital formation (e.g., OGD courses provision by national academies of public administration, free on-line some OGD-related courses, etc.)

Our study has limitations that need to be addressed by future research; beyond the basic one of having examined only 40 top universities, additional limitations are: (1)

During our data collection, we encountered several obstacles, but the most important one that has to be mentioned is the knowledge-based limit of ChatGPT, which is limited until September 2021, and most importantly, the language barrier as some universities, particularly in China, did not provide information in English about their degree programs and that resulted in their exclusion from the study; (2) Another impediment was the use of different credit types from universities, making the comparison a challenging undertaking. (3) Finally, the present research was limited in terms of the fact that stakeholders' perspectives were not factored into account, which would have been a significant contribution towards achieving a triangulation of the study findings.

Acknowledgements. We acknowledge the financial support from the European Union's Horizon 2020 research and innovation programme under the Marie Skłodowska-Curie grant agreement No. 955569. The research was partially funded by TODO project that has received funding from the European Union's Horizon 2020 research and innovation programme under grant agreement No 857592.

References

1. Afful-Dadzie, E., Afful-Dadzie, A.: Liberation of public data: exploring central themes in open government data and freedom of information research. Int. J. Inf. Manage. **37**(6), 664–672 (2017)
2. Anowar, F., Helal, M.A., Afroj, S., Sultana, S., Sarker, F., Mamun, K.A.: A critical review on world university ranking in terms of top four ranking systems. In: Elleithy, K., Sobh, T. (eds.), New Trends in Networking, Computing, E-Learning, Systems Sciences, and Engineering, LNEE. Springer, Cham, pp. 559–566 (2015). https://doi.org/10.1007/978-3-319-06764-3_72
3. Attard, J., Orlandi, F., Scerri, S., Auer, S.: A systematic review of open government data initiatives. Gov. Inf. Q. **32**(4), 399–418 (2015)
4. Bar-Ilan, J., Keenoy, K., Yaari, E., Levene, M.: User rankings of search engine results. J. Am. Soc. Inf. Sci. **58**(9), 1254–1266 (2007). https://doi.org/10.1002/asi.20608
5. Brickley, D., Burgess, M., Noy, N.: Google dataset search: building a search engine for datasets in an open web ecosystem. In: The World Wide Web Conference, 1365-1375 (2019). https://doi.org/10.1145/3308558.3313685
6. Charalabidis, Y., Alexopoulos, C., Loukis, E.: A taxonomy of open government data research areas and topics. J. Organ. Comput. Electron. Commer. **26**(1–2), 41–63 (2016)
7. Charalabidis, Y., Zuiderwijk, A., Alexopoulos, C., Janssen, M., Lampoltshammer, T., Ferro, E.: The world of open data - concepts, methods, tools and experiences. Springer International Publishing AG, Switzerland (2018)
8. Chakravarty, R., Wasan, S.: Webometric analysis of library websites of higher educational institutes (HEIs) of India: a study through google search engine. DESIDOC J. Libr. Inf. Technol. **35**(5), 325–329 (2015). https://doi.org/10.14429/djlit.35.5.8788
9. Criado, J.I., Ruvalcaba-Gomez, E.A., Valenzuela-Mendoza, R.: Revisiting the open government phenomenon. A meta-analysis of the international literature. J. eDemocracy (JeDEM) **10**(1), 50–81 (2018)
10. Crusoe, J., Simonofski, A., Clarinval, A., Gebka, E.: The impact of impediments on open government data use: Insights from users. In: 13th International Conference on Research Challenges in Information Science (RCIS), pp. (–12 (2019). https://doi.org/10.1109/RCIS.2019.8877055

11. Cavanaugh, J., Jacquemin, S.J., Junker, C.R.: Variation in student perceptions of higher education course quality and difficulty as a result of widespread implementation of online education during the COVID-19 pandemic. Technol. Knowl. Learn (2022). https://doi.org/10.1007/s10758-022-09596-9

12. Deming, D.: Four facts about human capital. J. Econ. Perspect. **36**(3), 75–102 (2022)

13. de Souza, A.A.C., d'Angelo, N.J., Filho, R.N.L.: Effects of predictors of citizens' attitudes and intention to use open government data and government 2.0. Gover. Inf. Q. **39**(2), 101663 (2022). https://doi.org/10.1016/j.giq.2021.101663

14. Farrokhnia, M., Banihashem, S.K., Noroozi, O., Wals, A.: A SWOT analysis of ChatGPT: Implications for educational practice and research (2023). (in press). https://doi.org/10.1080/14703297.2023.2195846

15. Gil-Garcia, J.R., Gasco-Hernandez, M., Pardo, T.A.: Beyond transparency, participation, and collaboration? A reflection on the dimensions of open government. Public Perform. Manage. Rev. **43**(3), 483–502 (2020)

16. Gusenbauer, M., Haddaway, N.R.: Which academic search systems are suitable for systematic reviews or meta-analyses? Evaluating retrieval qualities of Google Scholar, PubMed, and 26 other resources. Res. Synth. Methods **11**(2), 181–217 (2022). https://doi.org/10.1002/jrsm.1378

17. Hazelkorn, E.: Reflections on a decade of global rankings: what we've learned and outstanding issues. Eur. J. Educ. **49**, 12–28 (2014). https://doi.org/10.1111/ejed.12059

18. Hellberg, A.S., Hedstrom, K.: The story of the sixth myth of open data and open government. Trans. Govern. People Process Policy **9**(1), 35–51 (2015)

19. Islam, M.T., Talukder, M.S., Khayer, A., Islam, A.K.M.N.: Exploring continuance usage intention toward open government data technologies: an integrated approach. VINE J. Inf. Knowl. Manage. Syst. (2021). (In press). https://doi.org/10.1108/VJIKMS-10-2020-0195

20. Jetzek, T., Avital, M., Bjørn-Andersen, N.: The value of open government data: a strategic analysis framework. In: Paper presented at 2012 Pre-ICIS Workshop, Orlando, Florida, United States (2012)

21. Jetzek, T., Avital, M., Bjorn-Andersen, N.: Data-driven innovation through open government data. J. Theor. Appl. Electron. Commer. Res. **9**(2), 100–120 (2014)

22. Kaasenbrood, M., Zuiderwijk, A., Janssen, M., de Jong, M., Bharosa, N.: Exploring the factors influencing the adoption of open government data by private organizations. Int. J. Public Admin. Digital Age **2**(2), 75–92 (2015)

23. Kalampokis, E., Tambouris, E., Tarabanis, K.: A classification scheme for open government data: towards linking decentralised data. Int. J. Web Eng. Technol. **6**(3), 266–285 (2011)

24. Khurshid, M.M., Zakaria, N.H., Arfeen, M.I., Rashid, A., Nasir, S.U., Shehzad, H.M.F.: Factors influencing citizens' intention to use open government data-a case study of Pakistan. Big Data Cogn. Comput. **6**(1), 31 (2022). https://doi.org/10.3390/bdcc6010031

25. Lnenicka, M., Luterek, M., Nikiforova, A.: Benchmarking open data efforts through indices and rankings: assessing development and contexts of use. Telematics Inf. **66**, 101745 (2022)

26. Lnenicka, M., Nikiforova, A.: Transparency-by-design: What is the role of open data portals? Telematics Inf. **61**, 101605 (2021)

27. Lnenicka, M., Nikiforova, A., Saxena, S., Singh, P.: Investigation into the adoption of open government data among students: the behavioral intention-based comparative analysis of three countries. Aslib J. Inf. Manag. **74**(3), 549–567 (2022)

28. Mincer, J.: Human capital and economic growth. Econ. Educ. Rev. **3**(3), 195–205 (1984)

29. OpenAI. Introducing ChatGPT (2023). https://openai.com/blog/chatgpt

30. Open Data Barometer. (2022). Open Data Barometer. https://opendatabarometer.org/?_year=2017&indicator=ODB Accessed 17th Aug 2022

31. ODIN. Open Data Inventory (2022). https://odin.opendatawatch.com/. Accessed 17th Aug 2022

32. OKFN. Open knowledge foundation (2022). https://index.okfn.org/. Accessed 17th Aug 2022
33. Purwanto, A., Zuiderwijk, A., Janssen, M.: Citizens' trust in open government data: a quantitative study about the effects of data quality, system quality and service quality. In: The 21st Annual International Conference on Digital Government Research, pp. 310–318. ACM (2020)
34. QS world university rankings, Events & Careers Advice at TopUniversities.com https://www.topuniversities.com/ Accessed 18 May 23
35. Safarov, I., Meijer, A., Grimmelikhuijsen, S.: Utilization of open government data: a systematic literature review of types, conditions, effects and users. Inf. Polity 22(1), 1–24 (2017)
36. Saxena, S.: Summarizing the decadal literature in open government data (OGD) research: a systematic review. Foresight 20(6), 648–664 (2018)
37. Saxena, S., Alexopoulos, C.: Open Government Data (OGD) research: retrospection and forethoughts. J. Govern. Secur. Dev. 3(1), 1–19 (2022). https://doi.org/10.52823/IDWS4806
38. Saxena, S., Janssen, M.: Examining open government data (OGD) usage in India through UTAUT framework. Foresight 19(4), 421–436 (2017)
39. Shehata, A., Elgllab, M.: Saudi scholars' perceptions and use of open government data portals at Shaqra university, Saudi Arabia. Int. Fed. Libr. Assoc. Inst. (IFLA J.) 47(4), 493–504 (2021)
40. Shanghai Ranking at URL https://www.shanghairanking.com/. Accessed 18 May 23
41. Sweetland, S.R.: Human capital theory: foundations of a field of inquiry. Rev. Educ. Res. 66(3), 341–359 (1996)
42. Talukder, M.S., Shen, L., Talukder, M.F.H., Bao, Y.: Determinants of user acceptance and use of open government data (OGD): an empirical investigation in Bangladesh. Technol. Soc. 56, 147–156 (2019)
43. Thelwall, M.: Quantitative comparisons of search engine results. J. Am. Soc. Inform. Sci. Technol. 59(11), 1702–1710 (2008). https://doi.org/10.1002/asi.20834
44. Ubaldi, B.: Open government data: towards empirical analysis of open government data initiatives. In: OECD Working Papers on Public Governance, 22. OECD Publishing Press (2013). https://doi.org/10.1787/5k46bj4f03s7-en. Accessed 17th July 2022
45. Vernon, M.M., Balas, E.A., Momani, S.: Are university rankings useful to improve research? A systematic review. PLOS ONE 13, e0193762 (2018). https://doi.org/10.1371/journal.pone.0193762
46. Weerakkody, V., Irani, Z., Kapoor, K., Sivarajah, U., Dwivedi, Y.K.: Open data and its usability: an empirical view from the citizen's perspective. Inf. Syst. Front. 19, 285–300 (2017)
47. Wirtz, B.W., Becker, M., Weyerer, J.C.: Open government: development, concept, and future research directions. Int. J. Public Admin. (2022). https://doi.org/10.1080/01900692.2021.2019273. Accessed 12th July 2022
48. Wirtz, B.W., Birkmeyer, S.: Open government: origin, development, and conceptual perspectives. Int. J. Public Adm. 38(5), 381–396 (2015)
49. Wirtz, B.W., Piehler, R., Thomas, M.J., Daiser, P.: Resistance of public personnel to open government: a cognitive theory view of implementation barriers towards open government data. Public Manag. Rev. 18(9), 1335–1364 (2016)
50. Wirtz, B.W., Weyerer, J.C., Rosch, M.: Citizen and open government: an empirical analysis of antecedents of open government data. Int. J. Public Adm. 41(4), 308–320 (2018)
51. Wirtz, B.W., Weyerer, J.C., Rosch, M.: Open government and citizen participation: an empirical analysis of citizen expectancy towards open government data. Int. Rev. Adm. Sci. 85(3), 566–586 (2019)
52. World university rankings at https://www.timeshighereducation.com/world-university-rankings. Accessed 18 May 23

53. Ya-Wen Hou, W.J.J.: What contributes more to the ranking of higher education institutions? A comparison of three world university rankings. Int. Educ. J. Comp. Perspect. **16**, 29–46 (2017)
54. Liu, X., et al.: Identifying worldwide interests in organic foods by google search engine data. IEEE Access **7**, 147771–147781 (2019). https://doi.org/10.1109/ACCESS.2019.2945105
55. Zuiderwijk, A., Helbig, N., Gil-Garcia, J.R., Janssen, M.: Special issue on innovation through open data- A review of the state-of-the-art and an emerging research agenda. J. Theor. Appl. Electron. Commer. Res. **9**(2), 1–13 (2014)
56. Zuiderwijk, A., Janssen, M., Dwivedi, Y.K.: Acceptance and use predictors of open data technologies: drawing upon the unified theory of acceptance and use of technology. Gov. Inf. Q. **32**(4), 429–440 (2015)

Value Creation from Data Science Applications - A Literature Review

Matthias Pohl[✉][iD], Christian Haertel[iD], and Klaus Turowski[iD]

Magdeburg Research and Competence Cluster VLBA, Faculty of Computer Science,
Otto von Guericke University, Magdeburg, Germany
{matthias.pohl,christian.haertel,klaus.turowski}@ovgu.de

Abstract. In the paper at hand, a structured literature review was conducted to provide an overview of the components of value creation from Data Science applications. For this purpose, the value net as a concept of value creation was used as a framework. The value net for Data Science applications is intended to provide a helpful starting point for identifying the business value of Data Science applications in enterprises. In the future, the proposed value net is used for the classification of various projects and applications in the context of a case study. Further development as a tool for detecting value-adding potentials of Data Science in a business context is a future objective of this research.

Keywords: Data Science · Data Analytics · value creation · value creation network · literature review

1 Introduction

In today's digital age, companies that can effectively leverage Data Science have a significant advantage over their competitors. By using Data Science, businesses can gain insights into their operations and consumer behavior, allowing them to make informed decisions and stay ahead of the curve [1,2]. Further, by analyzing data, companies can identify emerging trends and technologies, enabling them to innovate and develop new products and services [3]. Data Science projects are often very complex and require careful planning, preparation, and implementation. It can be difficult to perform all the necessary steps to successfully complete a project, as underlined by the high failure rate in these undertakings [4]. There are several reasons why Data Science projects can fail or are difficult to implement, e.g., lack of relevant data, lack of qualified Data Science experts, lack of collaboration and communication between different departments, and lack of integration into existing business processes [5]. In particular, uncertain business objectives are one of the main challenges in Data Science projects according to [5]. Hence, it can be difficult to select the right data and methods to successfully complete the project. Consequently, if it is complicated to define clear goals for a Data Science project, it can be hard to identify the benefits of the results. Value creation is the process of generating benefits for stakeholders in a business or

K. Hinkelmann et al. (Eds.): BIR 2023, LNBIP 493, pp. 327–338, 2023.
https://doi.org/10.1007/978-3-031-43126-5_23

organization [6]. Hence, the question arises, how Data Science applications are involved in the value creation of companies. Various authors have investigated the impact of Data Science or Data Analytics on firm performance and endeavored to examine involved enterprise resources [7–9]. Since these works do not take into account the concrete value creation or neglect the connection between diverse stakeholders, this paper aims at an analysis of value creation mechanisms in the context of a value creation network [10] based on the scientific literature. In fact, the following research question (RQ) should be answered:

How to frame Data Science application in the context of value creation with regards to the scientific literature?

To address the research question, a structured literature review is conducted and elements are identified to characterize value creation from Data Science applications. The results are presented in a rough level of detail within the value net approach.

2   Methodology

The article employs a structured literature review (SLR) to answer the above-mentioned research question. Therefore, the framework for literature reviews by [11] is adopted. The initial step comprises defining the research scope, which is the involvement of Data Science for value creation in organizations. In the second phase, the conceptualization of the topic is conducted. Here, significant terminology is discussed and an overview of key issues to a subject is provided [12]. In the context of this paper, this step is performed in the next section to further gain input for the design of relevant search terms [11]. Afterwards, in the fourth section, the literature search process is documented, which constitutes the third step of the SLR framework. This includes the presentation of the used search query, the inclusion criteria, and the description of the filtering stages. Then, the fourth activity involves the analysis and synthesis of the considered literature items. For this purpose, in the fifth section, the publications are mapped to the value network analysis framework of [10] to appropriately classify and understand the current state-of-the-art with regards to value creation models in Data Science. In the end, these insights lead to a research agenda that enables us to derive objectives and further questions for upcoming research in the field [11] and answer the RQ.

3   Conceptualization of Topic

This second phase of the adopted SLR methodology serves the purpose of discussing significant terminology to the research topic to help with the design of the search terms [11]. Hence, in this section, the conceptual similarities and delimitations between Data Science and the relevant related areas are discussed. Furthermore, an introduction to value creation is provided.

3.1   Data Science

Data Science is generally described as "the methodology for the synthesis of useful knowledge directly from data" [13] by application of a sequence of discovery or hypothesis formulation. Since the literature features approaches that find interdisciplinary use (e.g., process models) and the terms are partially employed as synonyms, it is initially necessary to provide clarity regarding the conceptual interrelationships and delimitations. In the relatively old field of data analytics, which was originally dominated by statistics, the experiment design precisely defined the required input data to address a hypothesis [13]. For this purpose, the data analytics life cycle describes the processes to "transform raw data into actionable knowledge" [13]. This includes the steps of data collection, preparation, analytics, visualization, and access. In the 19901990ss, data mining and knowledge discovery in databases (KDD) emerged as new disciplines. In comparison to data analytics, these concepts encompass a broader set of problems as domain knowledge is involved in addition to math and statistics [13,14]. While KDD involves the "overall process of discovering useful knowledge from data" [13] and therefore comprises the complete data analytics lifecycle, data mining specifically focuses on the algorithms that are used to derive patterns from data. In summary, the analytics task of KDD can also be referred to as data mining [14]. As a further methodical framework, the Cross-Industry Standard Process for Data Mining (CRISP-DM) has been developed from industry-oriented studies [15]. In the meantime, this approach has become widespread and is used in most companies. In addition to 5 data and analysis-oriented phases, the CRISP-DM contains a process phase for the development of business objectives from data analysis projects. The phase names "Business Understanding" is to clarify besides, to which intent of business value the results could lead. Based on the business goals and the business-oriented motivation of a data analysis project, the data analysis problem and the type of project can be derived. Overall, three groups of objectives, either descriptive, predictive or prescriptive can be distinguished [16]. Descriptive analytical objectives look at the past and try to depict it or to recognize patterns and structures in it. These include, for example, mathematical statistics and clustering algorithms. The predictive objectives deal with approaches to predict and estimate future data series. Simple methods are e.g. linear regression models or classification models like a decision tree. The third group of objectives addresses the exploration of environments based on the descriptive and predictive findings. Among these are mainly simulations and optimization issues.

The National Institute of Standards and Technology (NIST) views Data Science as a super-set of statistics and data mining, since it can be interpreted as all activities in an analytics pipeline to generate insights from data [13]. The term Data Science was first mentioned in the context of large, complex, and rapidly changing datasets that called for new scalable architectures to allow their efficient storage, manipulation, and analysis. Consequently, Data Science is closely connected to the big data concept [13] and also referred to as "Big Data Science". Hence, due to the processing of big data, Data Science constitutes a complex discipline that leverages computer science skills as well to be able to "deploy large volume datasets across multiple data nodes, and how to alter query and analytics techniques" [13]. The discussion of the terms highlighted that the most obvious similarity persists in the goal, which is the extraction of insights from data. Differences can be detected in the context and scope of the respective disciplines. However, since the main portion of the literature concentrates on the analytics step, which constitutes a common activity due to the shared goal of these fields, a clear limitation of the applicability of the respective methods and techniques between these disciplines is not always directly visible.

In the course of this work, we consider Data Science as a value-creating or value-promoting activity in the context of a company and want to analyze it in terms of corporate value creation. A Data Science application represents a reusable application as a result of a Data Science project. In addition to the term Data Science, Data Mining or Data Analytics may be considered equivalent [17–19].

3.2 Value Creation

There are a variety of concepts and models of value creation discussed in the literature [6,10,20–22]. The concept of the value chain [6] is a widely used concept in the management field. It divides value-adding activities into primary activities (such as procurement, production, sales, and customer service) and supporting activities (such as human resources, technology, and facility management). The focus is on transforming inputs into outputs to achieve value for the customer. A value shop is a company that focuses on providing high-quality and customized services [20,22]. Unlike a production company that is following a value chain concept, a value shop usually works on the basis of customer requests and offers customized solutions.

An alternative concept, which considers the intra- and inter-organizational connections, is the value network model [10,20–22]. Value creation nets foster collaboration among multiple stakeholders in the enterprise context and can enable synergistic effects between these, leading to enhanced value creation. Further, value creation nets are more flexible and adaptable compared to rigid value chains or value shops. In a value chain, activities are sequentially linked, and any disruption in the chain can have significant negative consequences. In contrast, value creation nets can be reconfigured and adapt to changes in the environment or market conditions more effectively. By involving diverse actors in value creation, value creation nets encourage innovation and creativity. Different participants bring unique perspectives and ideas, fostering a collaborative environment for generating new products, services, and processes. In general, value creation nets allow an efficient utilization of resources across an enterprise. By sharing resources, knowledge, and capabilities, participants can reduce redundancies, avoid duplication of efforts, and optimize resource allocation. Besides tangible and intangible assets, a value net focuses on the value creation mechanisms and how the exchange of value between different partners is performed. The so-called Roles can be external contractual partners or internal departments or workplaces

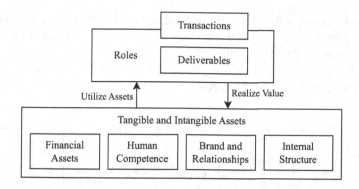

Fig. 1. An entity of a value net and its characteristics according to [10]

(see Fig. 1). A value is created by utilizing the assets, while the value is adopted by a counterparty for realizing it. Valuable physical or non-physical assets as results of the utilization are called deliverables. Here, transactions define the transfer of deliverables between parties.

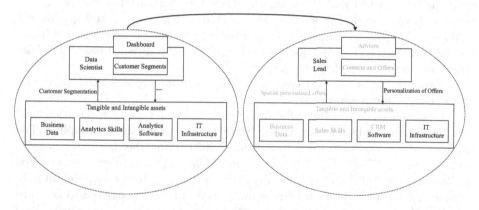

Fig. 2. An exemplary value net inclusion Data Science applications, adapted from [10]

An example of the integration of data science applications into an enterprise's value network is shown in Fig. 2. The section of this value net shows the entities of a so-called "Data Science" department and a "Sales" department. The "Data Science" department uses the available assets (e.g. Business Data, Analytics Skills, Analytics Software, and IT infrastructure) to provide Customer Segments (Deliverables) via a Dashboard Visualization (Transactions). These customer segments are converted into personalized offers (Value Realization) by the Sales Lead (Role) in the "Sales" team. These offers can then be transferred to specific commands for employees in the sales team. Thus, a network of value partners can be described.

The model of the value net will be used in the following as a framework to classify the results from the literature and to identify investigated elements of value creation according to a value net.

4   Literature Search Process

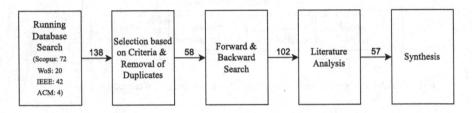

Fig. 3. Stages of the literature search and filtering process

To answer how Data Science can be applied to create value, a SLR is conducted to examine the current scientific body of knowledge for this field. In alignment with the third activity of the adopted literature reviewing framework of [11], the search and filtering process is documented in this section and graphically summarized in Fig. 3. As a result of the conceptualization of value creation in the last paragraph, the following query was designed for the keyword-based database search to capture the relevant topics [23]:

("data science" OR "data analytics" OR "data mining") AND ("value creation" OR "value generation")

The search term is specifically designed to account for the application field of value creation, which in this case is Data Science or a related discipline. The keyword search was performed in February 2023, using the databases Scopus, Web of Science (WoS), IEEE Explore, and ACM Digital Library, and resulted in 138 articles in total. To purposefully limit the findings to the meaningful publications for the research focus, the search was exclusively restricted to keyword matches. Consequently, we filtered the articles according to the stages prescribed by [11]. Only German and English peer-reviewed publications that specifically discuss value creation in data-focused disciplines (e.g., Big Data Analytics, Data Mining, Data Science) were kept in the pool. Accordingly, after the removal of duplicates, title assessment, abstract evaluation, and full examination of the papers, 58 items were left. Afterwards, a forward and backward search was executed on the remaining articles to achieve a more "complete census of relevant literature" [24]. During this step, 44 additional publications were added for the analysis.

5   Literature Analysis

For the synthesis, the 102 included articles were analyzed in the context of the value creation network of [10]. This step was applicable for 57 of the publications.

The identified elements of Data Science applications were classified according to the framework by Tangible & Intangible Assets, Asset Utilization, Value Realization, Deliverables and Transactions.

Table 1. Tangible & Intangible Assets from SLR

Tangible Assets	Intangible Assets
Infrastructure	Management Capabilities
Technology	Analytics Capabilities
Applications	Technological Capabilities
Data	Contextual Factors

Main Publications: [7, 8, 25–34]

Various studies examine the influence of Data Analytics on firm performance and are guided by the resource-based view [35]. The distinction made therein between tangible and intangible assets can also be placed in this framework with little effort [7, 36–39]. In addition to physical assets such as IT infrastructure, software applications, and data [7, 8, 25, 28, 29, 31, 33, 40–45], appropriate skills for analysis, technical handling, and management are required [7, 8, 25, 27–29, 33, 36, 37, 42, 45, 46]. There are also accompanying organizational prerequisites, such as a corresponding data-oriented corporate culture [26, 33, 37].

Table 2. Asset Utilization & Value Realization from SLR

Asset Utilization	Value Realization
Transparency & Access	Informational value
Discovery & Experimentation	Transactional value
Prediction & Optimization	Transformational value
Customization & Targeting	Strategic value
Monitoring	Infrastructural value

Main Publications: [7, 8, 25, 33, 36, 38, 47, 48]

Asset Utilization assembles the categorical methods with which value can be generated from data. The categories are mainly characterized by [8, 27, 48] and are supported by various use cases in other works [29, 37, 47, 48]. The category "Transparency & Access" includes simple methods of data management and data visualization that provide an overview of information and can be embedded in business processes. Methods of clustering and pattern identification as part of descriptive analytics can be found in the category "Discovery & Experimentation". Predictive and prescriptive analytics methods belong to the category "Prediction & Optimization". The extent to which a further subdivision may be useful to separate these two types of analytics should be discussed. For instance, forecasting methods differ significantly from simulation concepts. Furthermore, a partial overlap of data analytics methods for the purpose of individualization in the area of "Customization & Targeting" can also be expected. Recommendation systems and association analyses are to be assigned in a complementary manner. Methods for the temporal monitoring of performance indicators can be found in the "Monitoring" area.

The value from the Data Science applications is realized from the delivered results by the departments or business partners as described in Sect. 3. It is distinguished in the literature in five categories [36,48], which are listed in Table 2. Informational value includes decision support or knowledge discovery. Transactional value primarily comprises business value objectives such as cost savings, revenue growth, or productivity gain. General organizational benefits are declared as transformational value. Development of employee skills, customer loyalty, or market positioning are considered as strategic value. Finally, infrastructural targets can be summarized in one category. In most of the work, these value categories are manifested with concrete scenarios, e.g., in health [27,38] or marketing [43].

Table 3. Deliverables & Transactions from SLR

Deliverables	Transactions
Analytical Model	Data
Model Parameter	Scalable Service
Insights	Product
Enablers & Solutions	Money
Main Publications: [8,27,37,42,49,50]	

The deliverables are related to the output of the asset utilization. A clear separation between deliverables and a transaction form is complicated and is not made in any form in the literature. Following the definition [10], one could distinguish between an intangible output as a deliverable from asset utilization as well as a tangible transferable asset. On the one hand, models, parameter sets, decision insights, and other proposed solutions can be considered as deliverables, while on the other hand, products, services, physical media, or monetary exchanges can be defined as transactions.

While in most works Data Scientists, Data Engineers, or business users are mentioned very superficially as known Roles, in [29], the Roles are considered more specifically. In addition to Data Analyst and Analytics Expert, Roles such as Data Owner, Data Steward, Data Architect, Developer, and System Engineer are also considered. Overall, these activities can be separated into groups of data, IT, and business roles. The extent to which the different distribution of Roles leads to specific value exchanges must be investigated further, thus the rough division of roles is sufficient in the first instance.

6 Conclusion and Outlook

In the paper at hand, an SLR was conducted to provide an overview of the components of value creation from Data Science applications. For this purpose, the value net as a concept of value creation was used as a framework [10] for the literature analysis. Within the scope, the results of the analyzed works could be classified in the framework of the value net. The literature synthesis could be illustrated in a high level of detail in the presentation (see Tables 1, 2 and 3).

The individual characteristics of these high-level categories could not be fully deduced from the literature. Individual methods for asset utilization can be identified [29,47,51,52], while, in addition, the concepts for value realization cannot be listed completely due to the wide range of applications. The value net for Data Science applications is intended to provide a helpful starting point for identifying the business value of Data Science applications in enterprises. In the future, a classification of various projects and applications in the value net will be presented in the context of a case study. In addition, a sophisticated generalized value net for Data Science applications will help to identify their business value [2]. Further development as a tool for detecting value-adding potentials of Data Science in a business context is a future objective of this research.

References

1. Martinez, L.S.: Data science. In: Schintler, L., McNeely, C. (eds.) Encyclopedia of Big Data, pp. 1–4. Springer, Cham (2017). https://doi.org/10.1007/978-3-319-32001-4_60-1
2. Chen, H., Chiang, R.H.L., Storey, V.C.: Business intelligence and analytics: from big data to big impact. MIS Q. **36**(4), 1165–1188 (2012)
3. Cao, L.: Data science: a comprehensive overview. ACM Comput. Surv. **50**(3), 1–42 (2018)
4. VentureBeat: Why do 87% of data science projects never make it into production? (2019). https://venturebeat.com/2019/07/19/why-do-87-of-data-science-projects-never-make-it-into-production/
5. Martinez, I., Viles, E., Olaizola, I.G.: Data science methodologies: current challenges and future approaches. Big Data Res. **24**, 100183 (2021)
6. Porter, M.: Competitive Advantage: Creating and Sustaining Superior Performance. Simon and Schuster (1998)
7. Wamba, S.F., Gunasekaran, A., Akter, S., Ren, S.J.F., Dubey, R., Childe, S.J.: Big data analytics and firm performance: effects of dynamic capabilities. J. Bus. Res. **70**, 356–365 (2017)
8. Grover, V., Chiang, R.H., Liang, T.P., Zhang, D.: Creating strategic business value from big data analytics: a research framework. J. Manag. Inf. Syst. **35**(2), 388–423 (2018)
9. Pohl, M., Staegemann, D.G., Turowski, K.: The performance benefit of data analytics applications. Procedia Comput. Sci. **201**, 679–683 (2022)
10. Allee, V.: Value network analysis and value conversion of tangible and intangible assets. J. Intellect. Cap. **9**(1), 5–24 (2008)

11. vom Brocke, J., Simons, A., Niehaves, B., Reimer, K., Plattfaut, R., Cleven, A.: Reconstructing the giant: on the importance of rigour in documenting the literature search process. In: ECIS 2009 Proceedings (2009)
12. Baker, M.J.: Writing a literature review. Mark. Rev. 1(2), 219–247 (2000)
13. National Institute of Standards and Technology: NIST big data interoperability framework: Volume 1, definitions. Technical report, NISTIR 8103, National Institute of Standards and Technology (2015). https://doi.org/10.6028/NIST.IR.8103
14. Fayyad, U.M., Piatetsky-Shapiro, G., Smyth, P.: From data mining to knowledge discovery in databases. AI Mag. 17, 37–54 (1996). https://www.aaai.org/ojs/index.php/aimagazine/article/view/1230
15. Shearer, C.: The CRISP-DM model: the new blueprint for data mining. J. Data Warehous. 5(4), 13–22 (2000). https://dl.acm.org/doi/10.5555/772920.772926
16. Nalchigar, S., Yu, E.: Designing business analytics solutions: a model-driven approach. Bus. Inf. Syst. Eng. 62, 61–75 (2020)
17. Pohl, M., Bosse, S., Turowski, K.: A data-science-as-a-service model. In: Proceedings of the 8th International Conference on Cloud Computing and Services Science, Funchal, Madeira, Portugal, pp. 432–439. SCITEPRESS - Science and Technology Publications (2018)
18. Haertel, C., Pohl, M., Nahhas, A., Staegemann, D., Turowski, K.: Toward a lifecycle for data science: a literature review of data science process models. In: Proceedings of the Pacific Asia Conference on Information Systems (PACIS). AIS (2022)
19. Pohl, M., Haertel, C., Staegemann, D., Turowski, K.: Data science methodology. In: Wang, J. (ed.) Encyclopedia of Data Science and Machine Learning, pp. 1201–1214. IGI Global (2022)
20. Stabell, C.B., Fjeldstad, O.D.: Configuring value for competitive advantage: on chains, shops, and networks. Strateg. Manag. J. 19(5), 413–437 (1998)
21. Biem, A., Caswell, N.: A value network model for strategic analysis (2008)
22. Thompson, J.: Organizations in Action: Social Science Bases of Administrative Theory. McGraw-Hill, New York (1967)
23. Rowley, J., Slack, F.: Conducting a literature review. Manag. Res. News 27(6), 31–39 (2004)
24. Webster, J., Watson, R.T.: Analyzing the past to prepare for the future: writing a literature review. MIS Q. 26(2), 13–23 (2002)
25. Marjanovic, O.: A novel mechanism for business analytics value creation: improvement of knowledge-intensive business processes. J. Knowl. Manag. 26(1), 17–44 (2022)
26. Mikalef, P., Pappas, I.O., Krogstie, J., Giannakos, M.: Big data analytics capabilities: a systematic literature review and research agenda. IseB 16(3), 547–578 (2018)
27. Brossard, P.Y., Minvielle, E., Sicotte, C.: The path from big data analytics capabilities to value in hospitals: a scoping review. BMC Health Serv. Res. 22(1), 134 (2022)
28. Elia, G., Raguseo, E., Solazzo, G., Pigni, F.: Strategic business value from big data analytics: an empirical analysis of the mediating effects of value creation mechanisms. Inf. Manag. 59(8), 103701 (2022)
29. Fadler, M., Legner, C.: Building business intelligence & analytics capabilities - a work system perspective. In: International Conference on Information Systems, ICIS 2020 - Making Digital Inclusive: Blending the Local and the Global. Association for Information Systems (2020)
30. Falahat, M., Cheah, P., Jayabalan, J., Lee, C., Kai, S.: Big data analytics capability ecosystem model for SMEs. Sustainability 15(1), 360 (2023)

31. Ylijoki, O., Porras, J.: A recipe for big data value creation. Bus. Process. Manag. J. **25**(5), 1085–1100 (2019)
32. Chen, D.Q., Preston, D.S., Swink, M.: How the use of big data analytics affects value creation in supply chain management. J. Manag. Inf. Syst. **32**(4), 4–39 (2015)
33. Mirarab, A., Mirtaheri, S., Asghari, S.: A model to create organizational value with big data analytics. Comput. Syst. Sci. Eng. **35**(2), 69–79 (2020)
34. Klee, S., Janson, A., Leimeister, J.: How data analytics competencies can foster business value- a systematic review and way forward. Inf. Syst. Manag. **38**(3), 200–217 (2021)
35. Barney, J.: Firm resources and sustained competitive advantage. J. Manag. **17**(1), 99–120 (1991)
36. Edu, S., Agoyi, M., Agozie, D.: Integrating digital innovation capabilities towards value creation: a conceptual view. Int. J. Intell. Inf. Technol. **16**(4), 37–50 (2020)
37. Fay, M., Kazantsev, N.: When smart gets smarter: how big data analytics creates business value in smart manufacturing. In: International Conference on Information Systems 2018, ICIS 2018. Association for Information Systems (2018)
38. Galetsi, P., Katsaliaki, K., Kumar, S.: Big data analytics in health sector: theoretical framework, techniques and prospects. Int. J. Inf. Manage. **50**, 206–216 (2020)
39. Ghasemaghaei, M.: Are firms ready to use big data analytics to create value? The role of structural and psychological readiness. Enterp. Inf. Syst. **13**(5), 650–674 (2019)
40. Miller, H.G., Mork, P.: From data to decisions: a value chain for big data. IT Prof. **15**(1), 57–59 (2013)
41. Verhoef, P.C., Kooge, E., Walk, N.: Creating Value with Big Data Analytics. Routledge (2016)
42. Hanafizadeh, P., Harati Nik, M.: Configuration of data monetization: a review of literature with thematic analysis. Glob. J. Flex. Syst. Manag. **21**(1), 17–34 (2020)
43. Meierhofer, J., Meier, K.: From data science to value creation. In: Za, S., Drăgoicea, M., Cavallari, M. (eds.) IESS 2017. LNBIP, vol. 279, pp. 173–181. Springer, Cham (2017). https://doi.org/10.1007/978-3-319-56925-3_14
44. Neifer, T., Lawo, D., Esau, M.: Data science canvas: evaluation of a tool to manage data science projects. In: Bui, T.X. (ed.) Proceedings of the Annual Hawaii International Conference on System Sciences, vol. 2020-January, pp. 5399–5408. IEEE Computer Society (2021)
45. Popovič, A., Hackney, R., Tassabehji, R., Castelli, M.: The impact of big data analytics on firms' high value business performance. Inf. Syst. Front. **20**(2), 209–222 (2018)
46. Côrte-Real, N., Ruivo, P., Oliveira, T.: Leveraging internet of things and big data analytics initiatives in European and American firms: is data quality a way to extract business value? Inf. Manag. **57**(1), 103141 (2020)
47. Ferro-Díez, L.E., Villegas, N.M., Díaz-cely, J.: Location data analytics in the business value chain: a systematic literature review. IEEE Access **8**, 204639–204659 (2020)
48. Elia, G., Polimeno, G., Solazzo, G., Passiante, G.: A multi-dimension framework for value creation through big data. Ind. Mark. Manage. **90**, 617–632 (2020)
49. Kaufmann, M.: Big data management canvas: a reference model for value creation from data. Big Data Cogn. Comput. **3**(1), 19 (2019)

50. Dupada, S., Gedela, R.K., Aryasri, R.C., Acharya, R.: Building value chain through actionbale benchmarking for sustainability and excellence. In: 2013 2nd International Conference on Information Management in the Knowledge Economy, pp. 24–30 (2013)
51. Bose, R.: Advanced analytics: opportunities and challenges. Ind. Manag. Data Syst. **109**(2), 155–172 (2009)
52. Hajiheydari, N., Talafidaryani, M., Khabiri, S.: IoT big data value map: how to generate value from IoT data. In: ACM International Conference Proceeding Series, pp. 98–103. Association for Computing Machinery (2019)

Knowledge Visualization Towards Digital Literacy Development: Critical Success Factors

Janina Kotze and Hanlie Smuts[✉] [iD]

University of Pretoria, Pretoria, South Africa
hanlie.smuts@up.ac.za

Abstract. Industry 4.0 brought digital technology changes at a rate unparalleled to the past. Consequential to such change, the importance of a digitally literate society is emphasized. Digital literacy is, however, vast and subject to the fast-paced changes of Industry 4.0. The challenge then lies in learning and developing digital literacy. Knowledge visualization (KV) is considered a means to address this challenge, through its use of visual mechanisms to transfer complex insights. The purpose of the study was to identify factors of KV that, if addressed, can facilitate successful knowledge creation and transfer in a digital literacy learning and development process. We employed a systematic review of existing literature to reveal several critical success factors (CSFs) of KV towards digital literacy learning and development. The KV CSFs were presented in an online questionnaire to respondents to rank and possibly expose additional CSFs. The study produced 20 kV CSFs toward digital literacy learning and development, that can serve as a guide for KV in future digital literacy learning and development endeavors.

Keywords: Knowledge visualization · learning and development · digital literacy · critical success factors · connectivism learning theory

1 Introduction

Industry 4.0 is characterized by an unprecedented rate of advancements in digital technology, which enable global digital connection, data creation and sharing, and discoveries spanning the physical, digital and biological arenas [1]. The unique challenge lies in this scale of diffusion of digital technology–and the demand on humans to improve, and expand, their digital literacy at an equal pace to embrace the world of opportunity on offer [2]. Knowledge of digital technology is a prerequisite for a digital citizen to effectively, safely and securely operate as a consumer and producer in the digital economy [1]. Digital literacy is a mentality and understanding of digital technology, starting from a functional competency level of using digital technologies, to eventually participating as a responsible digital citizen who grasps the human and social impact of digital actions [3, 4]. The learning to progress along the levels described by Gallardo-Echenique et al. [3] requires learning in digital multimodal environments. Such learning is supported by the concept of multimodality where visualization of knowledge through various modes are integral to learning and knowledge transfer [3, 5].

K. Hinkelmann et al. (Eds.): BIR 2023, LNBIP 493, pp. 339–350, 2023.
https://doi.org/10.1007/978-3-031-43126-5_24

KV, in the context of digital literacy, brings these two concepts together to understand how KV can enable digital literacy learning and development. In the pursuit of this understanding, the research paper explores critical success factors, which (in the information science (IS) domain) have been used to define factors that would determine success and result in value-add [6]. This research, therefore, asks, *"What are the knowledge visualization critical success factors towards the development of digital literacy?"*. The research findings enable the identification of key pillars for successful KV design, toward digital literacy learning and development.

Section 2 presents the background of the study followed by Sect. 3, the methodology. Sections 4 and 5 detail the data analysis and discussion of these CSFs, and the conclusion in Sect. 6 completes the research paper.

2 Background

Industry 4.0 created a world that includes digital domains alongside offline reality where people and organizations can alternate between these domains and reality with connected technology [7, 8]. This alternation is necessary not only to support working organizational processes but also to effectively operate as an individual in this digital world. This revolution is also characterized by an unprecedented rate of advancements in digital technology, which enable global digital connection, data creation and sharing, and discoveries spanning the physical, digital and biological arenas [1]. The unique challenge lies in this scale of diffusion of digital technology, and the demand on humans to improve, and expand, their digital literacy at an equal pace to embrace the world of opportunity on offer [2]. Digital literacy reaches beyond the ability to use software applications and digital technologies; it encompasses the softer skills to operate effectively and efficiently in digital environments [3].

2.1 Digital Literacy

Digital transformation will require digital competencies and skills by individuals to navigate information sources and orientate themselves (navigate and make meaning) to connect, participate and create an identity [9]. Information overload presents a significant barrier to the acquisition of digital competencies and skills, and require processes, technology and abilities to filter out the necessary information from the masses [10]. Additional barriers, as a side effect of Industry 4.0 and digital exclusion, include accessibility and efficient use of technology, and limited participation in a digital culture society due to age, income, location, education, etc. [10]. In whichever way people are involved–their ability to effectively, efficiently and responsibly create, implement, maintain, consume or produce, is dependent on access to digital technology and appropriate digital literacy, within the specific context of the application [11].

Martin [4: p.167] suggested digital literacy to be, an "awareness, attitude and ability of individuals to appropriately use digital tools and facilities" in the context of specific life situations, in order to enable constructive social action [12]. Extending the concept of literacies to digital literacies several researchers have provided an account for what is required to be 'digitally literate', in terms of skills or competencies (both from a 'technical' and an 'ethos' standpoint) [9, 13–16]. This research study adopted digital literacy as the requirement to practice of the necessary skills to effectively use digital technologies, in a process to navigate, make meaning, express and communicate. It is practiced within digital knowledge spaces (bound by context), cultural settings and through social interactions, at levels of maturity directed by socio-cultural impacts.

2.2 The Concept of Knowledge Visualization

Knowledge visualization (KV) (as a mechanism in the knowledge creation and transfer processes) involves passing on insights, experiences, attitudes, values, expectations, perspectives, opinions and predictions between at least two people [17]. Although closely related, information visualization and KV are not interchangeable concepts. Information visualization is aimed at visually representing data, in such a way that it creates order within and among the data. It enhances information and data recovery, promotes access and is able to present large data sets. Conversely, KV's main objective is strengthening collaboration and communication to create and transfer knowledge, through rich visualizations that make explaining complex concepts easier [17–20].

The use of visualization makes it possible to manage larger volumes, more complex knowledge in the creation and transfer of knowledge [21]. It is an effective strategy to address information overload, symptomatic of Industry 4.0 [17]. KV presents different perspectives to be understood when defining KV, which include the type of knowledge to visualize (what), why is knowledge visualized (why), and how will KV be executed (how) [17].

2.3 Knowledge Visualization in the Context of Digital Literacy Learning and Development

The socio-cultural aspects of digital literacy incorporate social learning based on observation, imitation and modelling other behaviour [22]. However, social learning with the emphasis on direct involvement as researched by Reed et al. [23] discusses learning through sharing knowledge in social units, e.g. person-to-person over a network of person-to-person connections [22]. The term 'social learning' focuses on human networks that may be enabled by technology and not on the explicit participation of digital technology as part of the network. The connectivist learning theory goes a bit further by adding digital technology to the equation for deep learning. It is centralized around deep learning that occurs as a result of learner-learner and learning-technology interactions [24]. Connectivism addresses two aspects relating to digital technology networks, not addressed by traditional learning theories [25]. Firstly, learning that is achieved and kept outside of individuals (within technology, networks or organization). Secondly, learning in a digitally charged environment involves masses of information and knowledge (with a shortening lifespan). In this instance discernment of what to learn is a critical part of the continual learning process [25].

3 Methodology

The aim of this study was to identify the knowledge visualization critical success factors towards the development of digital literacy. In order to address this aim, the study was executed in a two-step process. Firstly, we executed a systematic review of the literature with the objective to identify KV CSFs related to the research question [26, 27]. In this SLR we follow the instructions and recommendations suggested by Rouhani, Mahrin, Nikpay, Ahmad and Nikfard [27], consisting of 3 consecutive steps: (1) planning provides the preparation of how the SLR will be executed, (2) execution implements the plan derived in step 1, and (3) analysis and presentation of the results. In terms of planning the systematic review, the search string "knowledge visualisation" or "knowledge visualization" and ('model' or 'framework' or 'factor' or 'element') was applied to search in four digital libraries, namely, ACM Digital Library, ABI/INFORM Collection (ProQuest), EBSCOhost and Emerald Insight. In using EBSCOhost, the list of databases included were Academic Search Complete, Business Source Complete and Library & Information Science.

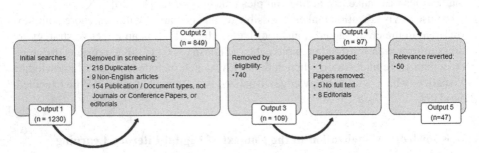

Fig. 1. Systematic process to create corpus for analysis.

The initial literature search yielded 1 230 results and was limited to articles posted from 2010 onward. These results were screened to remove duplicates, non-English papers, editorials and other non-peer reviewed publications shown in Fig. 1. The screening resulted in 849 papers to be analyzed for eligibility consisting of a review of the abstracts to ensure the research papers align to the research objective. The eligibility review resulted in 109 papers to be included in the analysis and synthesis, plus an additional paper by Wang, Chen and Anderson [24], identified through backward reference searching, totaling 110 papers as input for analysis. We excluded 8 editorials and 5 papers where we were unable to retrieve the full-text paper. The analysis of the papers also revealed 50 papers that were removed (relevance reverted) because the full text indicated misalignment with the purposes of this paper. The remaining 47 research articles were analyzed, and themes identified, which became the KV CSFs towards digital literacy learning and development.

The KV CSFs extracted from the systematic review of literature are listed in Table 1, including the number of times the KV CSFs appeared in the research articles and references thereof. The KV CSFs are numbered (first column) and KV CSF Keywords as a short identifier is displayed in the second column. Broader descriptions and explanation of each KV CSF is contained in the third column. The KV CSFs were categorized under the 3 different perspectives, indicated in column four. The perspectives of KV (described in Table 3) are knowledge type ('what'), visualization goal ('why') and visualization format ('how') [17] .

The second step of the research study included data collection via an online questionnaire that consisted of two parts. Respondents ranked the KV CSFs by indicating the level to which they agree with each of the stated KV CSFs using a Likert scale from strongly disagree to strongly agree. In addition, respondents were requested to answer open-ended questions, aimed at understanding the respondents' level of understanding and engagement with KV and digital literacy. We applied volunteer sampling, with the snowball sampling technique [26], posted the research questionnaire on LinkedIn to a network of professional connections and 53 respondents participated.

4   Data Analysis and Findings

The KV CSFs extracted from the systematic review of literature are listed in Table 1, including the number of times the KV CSFs appeared in the research articles and references thereof. The KV CSFs are numbered (first column) and KV CSF Keywords as a short identifier is displayed in the second column. Broader descriptions and explanation of each KV CSF is contained in the third column. The KV CSFs were categorized under the 3 different perspectives, indicated in column four. The perspectives of KV are knowledge type ('what'), visualization goal ('why') and visualization format ('how') [17]. The findings depicted in Table 1 (accessible here https://www.researchgate.net/publication/372477657_Table_1pdf) were used to design the on-line questionnaire. Data obtained from the Likert scale rankings in the questionnaire were analyzed to determine the central tendency. Central tendency is statistically measured by mean, mode and median–indicating the average value, the most common value and the middle value of a dataset [28]. The mean was used to rank the 13 kV CSFs as shown in Table 2 where the first column indicates the rank assigned to each KV CSF. A short label for each KV CSF is indicated (KV CSF Keywords), accompanied by a KV CSF heading and the assigned KV perspectives. Further quantitative data analysis was performed on the distribution of the mean values of the 13 kV CSF. The analysis was aimed at identifying ranking levels within the dataset. The 13 mean values of the KV CSF were considered as the dataset, and statistical analysis revealed a confidence level of 0.219, using a confidence level percentage of 95% [29–31]. Applying the confidence level 0.219 to the mean (4.23) of the dataset (13 mean values of the KV CSF), resulted in an upper and lower bound of 4.45 and 4.01 respectively. Open-ended question analysis revealed additional CSFs for knowledge visualization (KV) as a mechanism to create and transfer digital literacy knowledge depicted in Table 3. These were ranked separately based on frequency count.

Table 2. Ranked KV CSFs

Rank	KV CSF Keywords	KV CSF Heading	Perspective	Mean	Median	Mode
1	Balanced visuals	A balanced approach to simplicity, aesthetics, clarity, consistency, and text supplements	How	5,18	5	5
2	Visuals within context	Visualisations should align to context	How	4,60	5	5
3	Beyond ICT skills	Digital literacy as opposed to digital competence	What	4,37	4	4
4	Wayfinding and sensemaking	Enables 'wayfinding' and 'sensemaking'	How	4,33	4	5
5	Digital literacy baseline	Consideration of audiences' existing levels of digital literacy and competency	What	4,29	4	5
6	Defined purpose	Purpose has been defined	Why	4,27	4	4
7	Drives deep learning	Drives deep learning	Why	4,15	4	4
8	Fluid content	A balanced approach to structured and unstructured content and information	How	4,13	4	4
9	Outcomes & content aligned to Purpose	Outcomes & content aligned to purpose	What	4,12	4	4
10	Network interaction	Enables and promotes network interactions	How	4,04	4	4
11	Technology-based	Based within digital technology platforms	How	3,96	4	4

(continued)

Table 2. (*continued*)

Rank	KV CSF Keywords	KV CSF Heading	Perspective	Mean	Median	Mode
12	Actively created visuals	Requires participants' active involvement and creation	How	3,87	4	4
13	Clear scope	The scope of the digital literacy content is clearly defined	What	3,75	4	4

Table 3. Resulting additional KV CSFs based on open-ended question analysis

Rank	CSF #	Added KV CSF Keywords	Added KV CSF Heading	Perspective	N
1	14	Fit for purpose	Technical features of the selected KV tool is fit for purpose, considering the type of knowledge and audience in the knowledge creation and transfer process	How	6
2	15	Digital technology access	Ensure knowledge receivers have access to the digital technology relevant to the scope of the KV	How	5
3	16	User friendly	Technical features of the selected KV tool is fit for purpose, considering the type of knowledge and audience in the knowledge creation and transfer process	How	4
4	17	User guideline	Clear guidelines on how the platform works to assist effective use	How	2
4	18	Leadership buy-in	Participation and buy-in of top management and executives, to participate in knowledge visualisation processes towards creating and transferring knowledge	How	2

(*continued*)

Table 3. (*continued*)

Rank	CSF #	Added KV CSF Keywords	Added KV CSF Heading	Perspective	N
4	19	Monitoring	A function to monitor and validate use, knowledge transfer and improvement of digital literacy to adjust and improve the knowledge visualisation	How	2
4	20	Portable, easily accessible	Access to a tool/platform for Knowledge Visualisation needs to be easy. The solution should be portable/mobile–to easily integrate continuous learning and sharing in day-to-day processes and culture	How	2

5 Discussion and Contribution

This research paper undertook to identify and rank CSFs of KV towards the learning and development of digital literacy. A theoretical framework (collated from existing literature) was used as the backdrop to report the research findings considering 5 elements, namely, digital literacy, knowledge visualization, connectivism, digitally charged environment and socio-cultural environment (refer Sect. 2.3 and Fig. 2).

Learning and development (making sense and gaining insight) are enabled by KV in the creation and transfer of knowledge through sharing, communication and collaboration. A systematic review of existing literature (SLR) was conducted to identify KV CSFs towards the learning and development of digital literacy and produced 13 kV CSFs that were ranked through the research questionnaire. The analysis of the open-ended questions revealed an additional seven KV CSFs, that were ranked based on frequency in responses resulting in a final list of 20 kV CSFs. Each of the KV CSFs was categorized under one of the three KV perspectives (Knowledge Type (what), Visualization Motive (why), Visualization Format (how)). The KV perspective is used in the process of associating a theoretical framework element with the KV CSFs. The KV perspective for each KV CSF determined an initial association with an element.

The initial association was reviewed for each KV CSF individually, referring to the literature from which the KV CSF was identified as well as the literature from which the specific element was defined. Figure 2 also depicts a distribution of the highest to lowest ranked KV CSFs. The rank for each KV CSF is indicated with green, amber and red frames. Four initial KV CSFs from existing literature, are allocated in the 'Digital literacy' row, and in the 'what' KV perspective column. These KV CSFs relate to what digital literacy is, and its role as the type of knowledge ('what' KV perspective) for the KV process. The KV CSFs 'Beyond ICT skill', 'Digital literacy baseline' and 'Aligned to Purpose' are within rank level 2. The remaining KV CSF ('Clear scope') falls within rank level 3. The 'Digital literacy' element has no KV CSFs categorized under the visualization motive (why), or visualization format (how) KV perspectives. Seven KV CSFs are allocated to the 'Knowledge visualization' row. Two of the seven are initial KV CSFs from existing literature, falling within rank level 1, allocated to the 'how' KV perspective column. This two KV CSFs, 'Balanced visuals', and 'Visuals within context', describe criteria associated with the KV process and mechanisms.

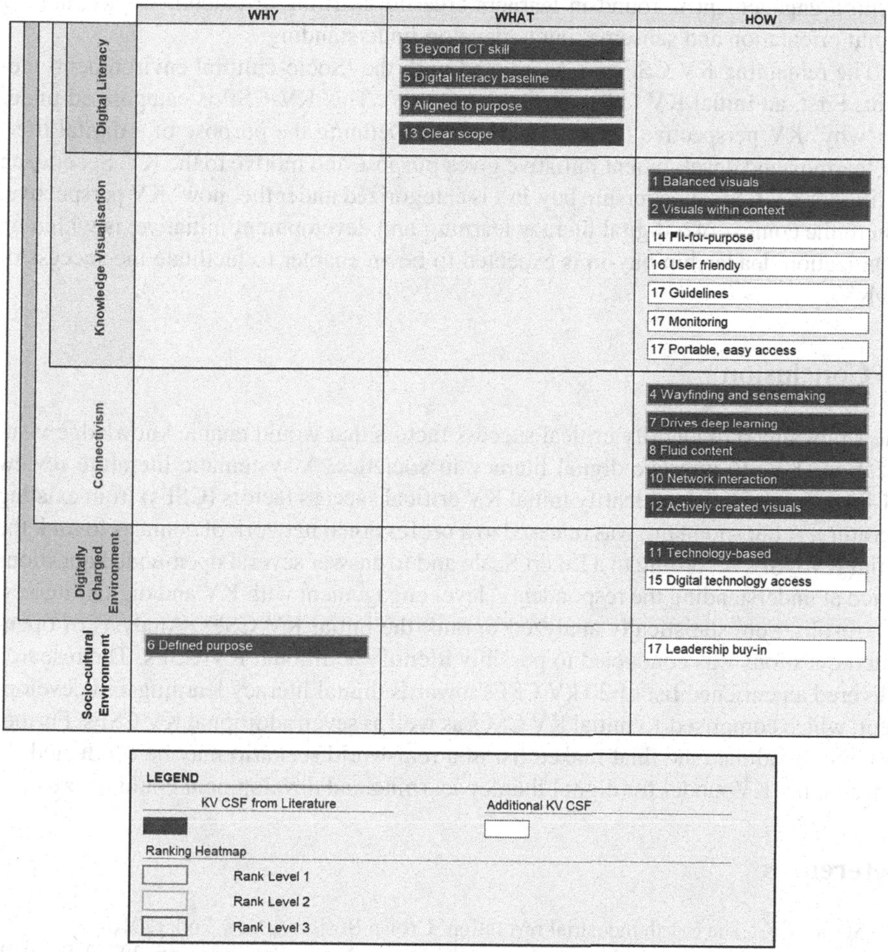

		WHY	WHAT	HOW
	Digital Literacy		3 Beyond ICT skill	
			5 Digital literacy baseline	
			9 Aligned to purpose	
			13 Clear scope	
	Knowledge Visualisation			1 Balanced visuals
				2 Visuals within context
				14 Fit-for-purpose
				16 User friendly
				17 Guidelines
				17 Monitoring
				17 Portable, easy access
	Connectivism			4 Wayfinding and sensemaking
				7 Drives deep learning
				8 Fluid content
				10 Network interaction
				12 Actively created visuals
	Digitally Charged Environment			11 Technology-based
				15 Digital technology access
	Socio-cultural Environment	6 Defined purpose		17 Leadership buy-in

LEGEND	
KV CSF from Literature	Additional KV CSF
Ranking Heatmap	
Rank Level 1	
Rank Level 2	
Rank Level 3	

Fig. 2. Ranked knowledge visualization CSFs grid towards digital literacy development.

The remaining five are additional KV CSFs, also allocated to the 'how' KV perspective column. These additional KV CSFs convey the research respondents' overwhelming focus on success factors relating to knowledge visualization format ('how' KV perspective)–five of the seven additional KV CSFs are allocated here.

Five initial KV CSFs from existing literature are associated with the 'connectivism' element, four of the five KV CSFs fall within rank level 2, and the last one is in rank level

3. Connectivism guides how learning can be addressed to enable successful learning in a digital age [25], which supports all KV CSFs categorized under the 'how' perspective and none under the 'why' and 'what' KV perspectives.

The five KV CSFs ('Wayfinding and sensemaking', 'Drives deep learning', 'Fluid content', 'Network interaction' and 'Actively created visuals') align with the theory and principles of connectivism and connectivist learning [24]. The KV CSFs address connections between persons and technologies in a digital network: deep learning (deep learning engagement is found in learners creating learning artefacts); wayfinding for spatial orientation and sensemaking to develop understanding.

The remaining KV CSFs are associated with the 'Socio-cultural environment' element. First, an initial KV CSF, 'Defined purpose'. This KV CSF is categorized under the 'why' KV perspective, within rank level 2. Defining the purpose of a digital literacy learning and development initiative gives purpose and motive to the KV. Second, an additional KV CSF, 'Leadership buy-in', is categorized under the 'how' KV perspective. Where the context of a digital literacy learning and development initiative, is within an organization, leadership buy-in is expected to be an enabler to facilitate the success of the KV.

6 Conclusion

The study aimed to identify critical success factors that would enable knowledge visualization (KV) to improve digital literacy in societies. A systematic literature review (SLR) was conducted to identify initial KV critical success factors (CSFs) from existing literature. A questionnaire was released to a professional network of contacts to rank the initial KV CSFs according to a Likert Scale and to answer several open-ended questions aimed at understanding the respondents' level engagement with KV and digital literacy. The results were statistically analyzed to rank the initial KV CSFs. Analysis of open-ended questions was conducted to possibly identify additional KV CSFs. The research delivered an enriched list of 20 kV CSFs towards digital literacy learning and development, which comprised 13 initial KV CSFs as well as seven additional KV CSFs. Further research to validate the final ranked list in a real-world scenario may be conducted. In addition, the KV model for digital literacy learning and development could be created.

References

1. Schwab, K.: The fourth industrial revolution. Crown Business, New York (2016)
2. Botha, D.F.: Knowledge Management and the Digital Native Enterprise, pp. 207–239 (2019)
3. Gallardo-Echenique, E., Oliveira, J., Marqués Molías, L., Esteve, F.: Digital competence in the knowledge society. MERLOT J. Online Learn. Teach. (JOLT) 11, 1–16 (2018)
4. Martin, A.: digital literacy for the third age: sustaining identity in an uncertain world. eLearning Papers 1, 1–15 (2009)
5. Jewitt, C.: Multimodality and literacy in school classrooms. Rev. Res. Educ. 32, 241–267 (2008)
6. Patel, T., Bapat, H., Patel, D., Van der Walt, J.D.: Identification of critical success factors (CSFs) of BIM software selection: a combined approach of fcm and fuzzy DEMATEL. Buildings 11, 1–21 (2021)

7. Bulfin, S., McGraw, K.: Digital literacy in theory, policy and practice: old concerns, new opportunities. In: Henderon, M., Romeo, G. (eds.) Teaching and digital technologies: Big issues and critical questions, pp. 266–281. Cambridge University Press, Melbourne (2015)
8. Xu, M., David, J., Kim, S.: The fourth industrial revolution: opportunities and challenges. Int. J. Finan. Res. **9**, 90 (2018)
9. Martin, A.: Chapter 7 Digital literacy and the "digital society". Digital literacies: Concepts, policies and practices, vol. 30, pp. 151–176. Peter Lang Publishing, New York (2008)
10. Bawden, D., Robinson, L.: The dark side of information: overload, anxiety and other paradoxes and pathologies. J. Inf. Sci. **35**, 180–191 (2008)
11. Van Alstyne, M.W., Parker, G.G., Choudary, S.P.: Pipelines, platforms, and the new rules of strategy. Harvard Business Review, pp. 54–62 (2016)
12. Soby, M.: Chapter 6 Digital Competence — From Education Policy to Pedagogy: The Norwegian Context. Digital literacies: Concepts, policies and practices, vol. 30, pp. 119–150. Peter Lang Publishing, New York (2008)
13. Bawden, D.: Chapter 1 Origins and concepts of digital literacy. Digital literacies: Concepts, policies and practices, vol. 30, pp. 17–32. Peter Lang Publishing, New York (2008)
14. Jenkins, H.: Confronting the Challenges of Participatory Culture: Media Education for the 21st Century. The MIT Press, Cambridge (2009)
15. Reyna, J., Hanham, J., Meier, P.: The Internet explosion, digital media principles and implications to communicate effectively in the digital space. E-learn. Digital Media **15**, 36–52 (2018)
16. Ryberg, T., Georgsen, M.: Enabling digital literacy. Nordic J. Digit. Lit. **5**, 88–100 (2010)
17. Eppler, M.J., Burkhard, R.A.: Knowledge visualization: towards a new discipline and its fields of application, pp. 1–29. Research Gate, Hershey, PA (2004)
18. Van Biljon, J., Osei-Bryson, K.-M.: The communicative power of knowledge visualizations in mobilizing information and communication technology research. Inf. Technol. Dev. **26**, 637–652 (2020)
19. Eppler, M.J.: What Is an effective knowledge visualization? insights from a review of seminal concepts. In: Marchese, F.T., Banissi, E. (eds.) Knowledge visualization currents: From text to art to culture, pp. 3–12. Springer, London, London (2013)
20. Smuts, Hanlie, Scholtz, Iddo-Imri.: a conceptual knowledge visualisation framework for transfer of knowledge: an organisational context. In: Hattingh, M., Matthee, M., Smuts, H., Pappas, I., Dwivedi, Y. K., Mäntymäki, M. (eds.) I3E 2020. LNCS, vol. 12067, pp. 287–298. Springer, Cham (2020). https://doi.org/10.1007/978-3-030-45002-1_24
21. Renaud, K., Van Biljon, J.: Charting the path towards effective knowledge visualisations. In: Proceedings of the South African Institute of Computer Scientists and Information Technologists, pp. 1–10 (2017)
22. Lankshear, C., Knobel, M.: New literacies: Everyday Practices and Social Learning. Open University Press, New York (2011)
23. Reed, M.S., et al.: What is social learning? Ecol. Soc. **15**, 1–10 (2010)
24. Wang, Z., Chen, L., Anderson, T.: A framework for interaction and cognitive engagement in connectivist learning contexts. Int. Rev. Res. Open Distrib. Learn. **15**, 121–141 (2014)
25. Siemens, G.: Connectivism: a learning theory for the digital age. Int. J. Instr. Technol. Distance Learn. **2**, 3–10 (2005)
26. Saunders, M.N.K., Lewis, P., Thornhill, A.: Research Methods for Business Students. Pearson, New York (2019)
27. Rouhani, B.D., Mahrin, M.N.R., Nikpay, F., Ahmad, R.B., Nikfard, P.: A systematic literature review on Enterprise Architecture Implementation Methodologies. Inf. Softw. Technol. **62**, 1–20 (2015)
28. Oates, B.J.: Researching Information Systems and Computing. SAGE Publications, Thousand Oaks (2006)

29. Cowles, M., Davis, C.: On the origins of the .05 level of statistical significance. Am. Psychol. **37**, 553–558 (1982)
30. Fisher, R.A.: The arrangement of field experiments. J. Ministry Agric. Great Br. **1**, 503–513 (1926)
31. Fisher, R.A.: Statistical Methods for Research Workers. Oliver and Boyd, London (1950)

Correction to: Managing Variability of Large Public Administration Event Log Collections: Dealing with Concept Drift

Flavio Corradini⬛, Caterina Luciani⬛, Andrea Morichetta⬛, and Marco Piangerelli⬛

Correction to:
Chapter "Managing Variability of Large Public Administration Event Log Collections: Dealing with Concept Drift" in: K. Hinkelmann et al. (Eds.): *Perspectives in Business Informatics Research*, LNBIP 493, https://doi.org/10.1007/978-3-031-43126-5_3

The original version of Chapter 3 was published with the incomplete acknowledgements section. The chapter along with the book has been corrected.

The updated original version of this chapter can be found at
https://doi.org/10.1007/978-3-031-43126-5_3

Author Index

© The Editor(s) (if applicable) and The Author(s), under exclusive license
to Springer Nature Switzerland AG 2023
K. Hinkelmann et al. (Eds.): BIR 2023, LNBIP 493, pp. 351–352, 2023.
https://doi.org/10.1007/978-3-031-43126-5

by Baker & Taylor Publisher Services

Printed in the United States
by Baker & Taylor Publisher Services